Key Lists

||||||| |||||||||| ||| ||| ||||||||||||| ||| |||
W9-BWN-720

Planning and Drafting a Paper

Revising and Editing a Paper

A Brief Guide to the Book

THE
BEACON
HANDBOOK

THE
BEACON
HANDBOOK

Robert Perrin   *Indiana State University*

Houghton Mifflin Company   Boston
Dallas   Geneva, Illinois
Lawrenceville, New Jersey   Palo Alto

Text Credits

p. 37: ©1982 by Houghton Mifflin Company. Reprinted by permission from *The American Heritage Dictionary, Second College Edition.*   p. 481: Extract reprinted from *The White House: An Historic Guide* by permission of the White House Historical Association.   p. 482: Extract reprinted from *Treasures of Tutankhamun* by permission of The Metropolitan Museum of Art.   p. 493: The lines from "The Whipping" are from *Angle of Ascent: New and Selected Poems* by Robert Hayden, and are used with the permission of Liveright Publishing Corporation. Copyright ©1975, 1972, 1970, 1966 by Robert Hayden.   Extracts in "Writing a Research Paper" reprinted from THE MISMEASURE OF MAN by Stephen Jay Gould, by permission of W. W. Norton & Company, Inc. Copyright ©1981 by Stephen Jay Gould.

Art Credits

p. 39: The name *TV Guide* and the TV Guide logo are registered trademarks of Triangle Publications, Inc.   p. 401: ©1984 by Houghton Mifflin Company. Reprinted by permission from WEBSTER's II: NEW RIVERSIDE UNIVERSITY DICTIONARY.   p. 433: *Readers' Guide to Periodical Literature* Copyright ©1986 by the H. W. Wilson Company. Material reproduced by permission of the publisher.   p. 435: *Education Index* Copyright © 1984, 1985 by the H. W. Wilson Company. Material reproduced by permission of the publisher. p. 437: Copyright ©1985 by The New York Times Company. Reprinted by permission.

Printed in the U.S.A.

Library of Congress Catalog Card Number: 86-81298

ISBN: 0-395-39067-2

DEFGHIJ-M-89

CONTENTS

3 Writing the Essay Exam   86

4 Logical Thinking   91

Contents

14 Consistency of Verb Tenses 204

15 Mood 209

16 Adjectives and Adverbs 211

SENTENCE VARIETY AND EMPHASIS   219

17 Sentence Length   220

18 Coordination   223

19 Subordination   228

Contents

33 Semicolons   344

34 Colons   350

Contents

40 Italics   374

41 Quotation Marks   378

Contents

PREFACE

In my years of teaching composition, I have used handbooks irregularly—and for good reason. The pattern went something like this. Knowing that my students needed a reference book to help them solve their writing problems, I would order a handbook. But I would discover that my students could not use the handbook effectively because the explanations were so cursory that they made sense only to someone who already understood the problem being discussed. So, for a semester or two, I would eliminate the handbook from my list of texts. Later, I would decide again that my students and I needed reference materials to work with together, and I would order another handbook. But each time I reintroduced a handbook into my list of texts, I would feel a sense of frustration. One would be too prescriptive to fit the modified process orientation of my class. Another would be so nonjudgmental, so linguistically descriptive, that it would offer no clear-cut advice to help my students with their writing problems. One would offer no explanations but would simply present rules and examples labeled *wrong* and *right*. Another would hedge on issues of grammar so cryptically—comma splices were labeled *weak,* and corrected sentences were labeled *better*—that my students could not decide what principles to apply to their work. So even though I knew handbooks should serve a practical purpose in a writing classroom, I was never satisfied with the handbooks I found; they did not strike the balance I was looking for.

As a result, I decided to write a handbook that I hoped would differ in small but important ways from those on the market. I wanted my handbook to be informed by current theories of rhetoric, placing the major issues of writing in a rhetorical context. I wanted a thorough but brief unit on composing, yet I did not want to lose sight of the fact that this was a handbook, not a rhetoric. I wanted to offer explanations that were brief, nontechnical, and lucid. I wanted to acknowledge that writing problems could be solved in alternative ways, stressing the effects that such choices have on writing; at the same time I wanted to offer clear directions on matters that are ruled by standard conventions of writing. I wanted a research unit that treated the process of research, not just the mechanics. In short, I wanted to write a handbook that was current, clear, and comprehensive. Now, after several years of concentrated work, I have completed *The Beacon Handbook.*

Notable Features

A number of features should make *The Beacon Handbook* attractive to both teachers and students.

* *Rhetorical principles* guide the handbook's organization, precepts, and explanations. *The Beacon Handbook* begins with an examination of the whole composition, stressing that early writing activities give meaning to later work with grammar, sentences, usage, diction, punctuation, and mechanics. Explanations concentrate on how writers' choices affect their writing, how grammatical and technical matters create meaning, and how errors change the impression a piece of writing makes.

- *Nontechnical explanations* clarify issues of writing whenever possible. Some shared technical terms (*subject, predicate, clause,* and so on) must be used, but when everyday language can be used, it is.

- *Student samples* illustrate the principles under discussion. Samples from professional writers are often so sophisticated and skillfully presented that they can intimidate students. To avoid the frustration that results when students attempt to model their work after writers they are not ready to imitate, student samples are used most of the time.

- *Written-in revisions and corrections* approximate the natural messiness of the revision process. Too often, perfectly typeset pairs of *incorrect/correct* or *awkward/improved* samples create confusing signals for students. To show that omissions, substitutions, and insertions are the means by which revisions and corrections are made, modifications handwritten in a contrasting color are presented.

- *Parenthetical explanations* accompany most sample sentences. Textual explanations supply clear but general principles; the parenthetical explanations offer discussions of the specific applications of the principles.

- *Checklists* allow students to evaluate their work independently or in peer editing sessions. Ranging from questions to ask when choosing a topic for a paper to questions to ask during revision, these checklists provide focused criteria for assessing written work. A guide to the most important checklists appears on the endpapers.

- *Sentence exercises* follow most major topics in the handbook, providing traditional kinds of practice. When the principles under discussion are simple ones, five numbered sentences serve as a quick review; when the concepts are difficult or multifaceted, ten or more sentences are included.

- *Answers* for the first five items in each sentence exercise group appear in the back of the book. Students who read sections independently of classroom instruction can double check their work to make sure that they have, in fact, understood and applied the principles.

- *Paragraph exercises,* which appear at the end of most major units in the handbook, help students apply newly-learned skills. Emphasizing that rhetorical and grammatical choices must often be made within a context, these paragraphs give students a sense of the complexity of the writing process. These paragraphs also function as review exercises.

- *The process of research* is emphasized in a thorough, sequentially-ordered unit that begins with selecting and evaluating potential topics for research and ends with suggestions for preparing the final copy of the paper. Throughout the unit, lists of questions guide students in their work, and exercises offer the necessary practice. One student's work on a research project (her paper is included as a sample) links the individual discussions—stressing that each aspect of research work, no matter how isolated or mechanical it seems, has a bearing on the final paper.

- *The annotated research paper,* the development of which is traced in the research unit, provides an example of serious and effective use of research materials and methods. The research paper examines the internment of Japanese Americans during World War II. The annotations address rhetorical, stylistic, and technical issues. A sample outline is also provided.

- *MLA (1984) and APA documentary forms* are explained. The primary discussions in the research unit are based on MLA's parenthetical style, but a thorough, cross-referenced guide to APA style is also given for those students who need to use an alternative form.

- *Discussions of business letter form, résumé form, and manuscript form* are included in the appendix, providing samples of these specialized writing concerns. Although these sections may not be directly applicable to classroom work, students are likely to refer to them to answer questions as they arise.

- *A guide to word processing* is included in the appendix, offering a useful introduction to the challenges and benefits of using this increasingly available technology. These materials are derived from four years of practical experience using and teaching word processing.

- *Glossaries of usage and terminology* provide brief explanations of commonly confused words and the major terms used in the handbook. Samples accompany each brief discussion so that students do not have to refer back to lengthy discussions in the handbook itself.

- *Multiple referencing guides* help students find the discussions they need. A clear table of contents; tabbed headings; distinct precept headings; a thorough index; a list of cross-referenced correction symbols, a topic list, and a list of major checklists on the endpapers; and many cross-references within the text itself—all work together to offer students multiple methods of locating material.

- *Resources for Practicing Research,* a casebook of readings and writing activities, accompanies the handbook. Rather than providing more sentence exercises in a workbook format, *Resources* provides five sets of readings: Emily Dickinson's *"Because I Could Not Stop for Death,"* Solar Energy, American Educational Standards, The Trade Deficit, and Federal Support for the Arts. These readings, drawn from many different sources, form the basis of sixteen writing activities —ranging from evaluating a source to identifying transitional devices, from preparing for an interview to producing a sample research paper. This specific and directed practice allows students to develop research and writing skills within a carefully designed framework.

- *The Instructor's Manual* includes answers to all the sentence and paragraph exercises in the handbook. It also includes sample answers to many of the activities in *Resources for Practicing Research.* In addition, the Instructor's Manual includes discussions of using the handbook in a variety of classroom situations, a sample fifteen-week syllabus, and a series of exercises for introducing students to the handbook.

- *Also available to the instructor* upon adoption are Works-in-Progress: Houghton Mifflin College Word Processing; three forms of diagnostic tests (on duplicating masters or computer disks); a reference/correction chart; and the Grade Performance Analyzer, an easy-to-use electronic grade book.

Acknowledgments

The Beacon Handbook has been thought about, planned, written, evaluated, rewritten, reevaluated, rewritten again, edited, and finally presented in its completed form. Throughout these stages of development, the staff at Houghton Mifflin has given me sound technical advice and candid criticism. They have been honest in their evaluations, which has helped make *The Beacon Handbook* a better book, and they have been patient and friendly, which has helped me remain enthusiastic throughout many months of work. In addition, they have made it possible for me to receive important evaluation and advice from a large number of teachers who served as reviewers of the manuscript:

Alma G. Bryant, University of South Florida

Therese Brychta, Truckee Meadows Community College

Edward A. Cairns, California Polytechnic State University

Barbara Carson, University of Georgia

Michael R. Cross, Tulsa Junior College

Paul Curran, State University of New York at Brockport

Hephzibah C. Roskelly, University of Massachusetts—
Harbor Campus

Haskell Springer, The University of Kansas

Richard F. Thompson, Northern Virginia Community
College

Victor J. Vitanza, University of Texas at Arlington

Melinda Wright, The Ohio State University

Showing their special commitment to *The Beacon Handbook,* my editors allowed me to ask teachers in a variety of writing classes to teach from the manuscript of the book. Through this class testing, I discovered which sections worked well with students and which needed further revision. The teachers who taught from the manuscript deserve special thanks: Peter Carino, Indiana State University; Janet Eldred, University of Illinois at Urbana-Champaign; Cynthia Lynch Frazer, Old Dominion University; and Mary Soliday, University of Illinois at Urbana-Champaign. Their day-by-day, week-by-week work with the manuscript and their subsequent evaluations proved invaluable as I prepared the final draft. My students, too, have helped me assess the materials through their writing activities. They enthusiastically served as test-subjects and frankly—sometimes it seemed too frankly—offered their views. They helped me refine a manuscript that is intended for students like them. In particular, I would like to thank Yasuko Kawamura for allowing me to use her preliminary research work and her research paper as the basis for much of the discussion in the research unit.

Finally, the members of my family—my wife Judy, my son Christopher, and my daughter Jennifer—have been remarkably patient while I have been subsumed in a project that has taken much of my time, energy, and attention. I appreciate their understanding and support.

R.P.

THE
BEACON
HANDBOOK

THE COMPOSING PROCESS

A natural extension of people's desire to share what they know, writing is a systematic way to present ideas, insights, experiences, and facts. No two people will approach the writing process in exactly the same way, for individual habits and ways of thinking lead people naturally through different methods of drafting and revising. Nevertheless, most experienced writers follow patterns that can be used as guidelines.

The following discussions—on planning and writing full-length papers, on writing paragraphs, on writing responses to essay questions on exams, and on thinking logically—will guide you through the most important stages of the writing process. Use these guidelines as points of departure, however, modifying them when necessary to meet your needs. Move through the steps in different order, or eliminate certain procedures when they seem unnecessary. Most of all, *write*—for it is by writing that you will learn the most about effectively communicating with other people.

1 Full-Length Papers*

The process of writing a full-length paper is complex but manageable. It involves narrowing a subject to discuss it thoroughly, analyzing readers to share ideas with them effectively, organizing ideas to present them clearly, and revising an original draft of a paper to present thoughts smoothly and systematically. Writers clearly cannot deal with all these matters at once. It simply is not possible.

To manage the process of writing effectively, most writers

---

* Throughout this section, the exercises will take you through the steps of writing a paper. Be sure to keep the work on your paper from each exercise to use in later ones.

work through a group of stages similar to those presented in this section. Yet the overall process seldom moves in patterned fashion from idea to final paper. Instead, most writers alter the stages to suit their needs, sometimes moving far ahead in the process when a thought suddenly emerges or backtracking to an earlier stage of the process when a change needs to be made. As you read the following discussions, remember that the process is flexible.

1a To begin, select a general subject.

There will be times when instructors assign topics for writing, and then you must make sure that you stick to the topic. Yet even with assigned topics, some leeway exists. Consider doing some related reading to decide on an interesting way to approach the topic, or consider special insights you can bring to your discussion.

When you have the option of choosing your own topic, enjoy the freedom you are given. Remember that the most effective writing comes from a writer's interest in or commitment to a subject. You will not write well, under most circumstances, if you care nothing about your subject—if you are only pushing a pencil to complete an assignment. Therefore, when you can select a subject for a paper, consider subjects that genuinely appeal to you.

How can you bring subjects into the open? How can you pull subjects "out of the air" when they do not immediately occur to you? Try the following strategies:

Consider the things you regularly do.

Think of all the activities and jobs you do. People work, listen to music, shop, watch television, plan trips, eat, exercise, read, fix cars, make clothes, and do hundreds of other things every week. Do not eliminate these topics because they are routine. Some routines can be very interesting.

Consider your areas of expertise.

Each person has special knowledge. Some people are film buffs, some are scuba experts, and some are computer whizzes. What is your specialty? The things that you know about a favorite subject can provide a wide range of topics. Be open-minded, too. Most people are informed about a wide range of subjects, not just one topic.

Consider the people you know.

All of us know a variety of people, and they can be interesting to write about. What do they look like? What do they do? How do they interact with other people? People are always fascinated by others.

Consider places where you have been.

Have you been to Spain, Montreal, the Smithsonian Institution, or some other special place? Do not think only about faraway places. What about Uncle Fred's farm, your city's police station, or the locker room at the community pool? Sometimes familiar places are interesting, too, if you consider them carefully.

Consider your unusual experiences.

If you have had experiences that others have not, you have the makings of a good paper. People are naturally curious about the unknown—if your experiences are unknown to them, share what you have learned.

Consider the problems people face.

Problems—personal, social, economic, political—demand a great deal of our attention. If the problems are meaningful ones, ones that you have thought about, they can make useful subjects for papers.

Consider changes in your life.

Life is not a simple, linear event but instead is filled with changes. Think about some changes in your life. Did you move across-country one summer? Did you get married? Did a family member die? Changes like these influence behavior and can lead to interesting writing. Think about underlying feelings and insights and why you remember these experiences.

Consider your likes and dislikes.

Think of all the things you like and dislike—make a pair of lists: spy novels, seafood, poodles, pink fingernail polish, reunions, rock music, the color orange, and so on. Not all items on the list will be worth attention, but some may stimulate enlightening discussions of attitudes.

Consider your strong opinions.

Strong opinions are more serious versions of likes and dislikes because they generally deal with important matters. Do you believe in book censorship? Do you support tax breaks for oil corporations? Do you think college prepares students for life? A double list of pros and cons might be a good way to sort out your opinions.

Consider current events.

What happens around you can be fascinating to write about, whether it is Soviet-American relations or the construction of a new motor speedway. Make sure, however, that you have been following the current event closely so that you have something specific to say.

Consider the subjects you have studied.

From courses in school you have learned a great deal. Use that information to share insights or knowledge, remembering that everyone has not learned the same things while in school. You may have something new to share.

Consider what you have learned through general reading.

Most people read fairly frequently, even though they may not think of themselves as doing "serious" reading. Use your informal reading—in popular books, magazines, newspapers —as a way to think about topics.

Consider subjects you have heard discussed on television programs.

In your regular television viewing, you have undoubtedly heard hundreds of subjects discussed. Think about issues addressed on morning talk shows, situations used in comedy programs, or ideas discussed on informative television programs.

EXERCISE □ *General Subjects*

Using the thirteen strategies above, list at least twenty-six potential subjects for a paper, at least two for each strategy. Identifying more will offer more choices.

1b Develop ideas through prewriting.

Most writers have discovered that they cannot move directly from selecting a topic to planning and writing a paper. Such a quick jump from the general idea to the paper itself does not give them sufficient time or opportunity to explore the topic, decide how they honestly feel about it, or consider possibilities for developing the discussion.

To provide time and opportunities to think about a topic, writers have developed a wide range of prewriting strategies to help them explore their ideas. The following discussion covers several of the most useful strategies.

Freewriting

Freewriting is an unstructured and, in some ways, unfocused writing strategy. To freewrite, all you need to do is to think briefly about the topic and then begin writing. Freewriting is usually done in sentence form, but it has no other constraints. Write quickly. Do not worry about grammatical or mechanical matters like subject-verb agreement or spelling. Do not concern yourself with neatness, form, or other matters that are important when someone else will read your writing. Avoid the tendency to labor over sentences or to worry about logical connections among ideas—all those matters can be attended to later. Instead, write down all your thoughts on a topic; write until you can think of nothing else to write.

Although freewriting is seemingly without purpose or order—at least by traditional classroom standards—it gives writers an important chance to write down ideas that might not get written down under stricter circumstances. It also allows writers to relax and make connections among ideas that might on the surface appear slightly unusual.

Much, if not most, of what you put on paper during freewriting will not be used in your paper, but sometimes the freedom of this prewriting strategy allows writers to make startling connections, present ideas in a fresh way, or develop an example that may later prove useful.

Journal writing

Journal writing, writing thoughts and observations in a notebook or on collected sheets of paper, is essentially writing for yourself. Like freewriting, journal writing gives you a chance to record ideas that you can evaluate later; unlike freewriting, journal writing is often structured and developed.

Because journal writing gives you the freedom to comment on any subject in any form you wish, it offers you the chance to be honest. You can explore your feelings about people, actions, events, ideas, and other topics—in short, anyone or anything that concerns you. In addition, the reflective nature of journal writing encourages you to observe, think, and analyze, and those mental activities can help you greatly in other writing.

Responding to the journalistic questions

For decades, newswriters have used a familiar set of questions to focus their reports and articles: who? what? when? where? how? and why? As a writer, you can also use these questions to help you examine the facets of a subject that interests you.

Because the journalistic questions provide an established focus for analyzing a subject, they usually will not lead you to fresh insights or allow you to make provocative connections among ideas. They will, however, provide you with a specific, organized method for exploring a subject.

Brainstorming

Brainstorming is making a quick list of items related to a subject. Get pen and paper ready, think for a few seconds about the subject, and then start listing all the items you can think of. This is a free association of ideas: write down everything that comes to mind, making no attempt to analyze or sort ideas. The activity should be unstructured, and you should write until you can think of nothing else.

Gabriel, a student in an introductory writing course, had noted that he disliked the way people depend on status symbols. With that general subject in mind, he made this brainstorming list:

cars	special appliances	Cabbage Patch dolls
Porsche	dishwashers	electronic cars
Mercedes	garbage disposals	train sets
Corvette	designer clothes	bicycles
fancy apartments	jeans	radios
fancy houses	Yves St. Laurent	boats
swimming pools	Adolpho	cabins
fancy furniture	Pierre Cardin	country club
stereos	watches	

VCRs	diamond rings	travel
computers	gold necklaces	number of phones
pool tables	glasses	number of cars
posters	contacts	Angela
video games	private schools	Ronnie
snowmobiles	toys	Laura
large-screen TVs		

Notice that the list ranges freely as one idea leads to another in no particular order. The length of the brainstorming list, however, suggests that Gabriel has some strong impressions of status symbols and that he sees them in many different circumstances.

Grouping ideas

Once you have done some brainstorming to generate lots of ideas on a subject, group those ideas to identify narrow topics for discussion. These groups can take many forms. Work flexibly with your original list, remembering that this process of grouping items is intended to help you see clusters of information, not simply arrange the material. For that purpose, repeat items from the original list in several groups if you wish, and add new items whenever you think of them. One or several of the following questions may guide you when grouping ideas:

Can you classify some items from your list together? Do items from your list fit together to "define" one type of subject or one facet of a larger subject? Gabriel, for instance, made the following classifications from his original brainstorming list. Notice that he added new items as he grouped his subjects.

Cars	**Houses**	**Clothes**
Mercedes	pools	jeans

Corvette	furniture	Adolpho
Porsche	appliances	Pierre Cardin
Camaro Z28	yards	Yves St. Laurent

Accessories	**Toys**
rings	Cabbage Patch dolls
necklaces	electronic cars
glasses	trains
contacts	bicycles
watches	expensive games

Can you concentrate on people? Because discussions that describe people and their actions and interests are often livelier than general or abstract discussions of a topic, use the names of any people you mentioned on your brainstorming list to help you focus your topic. Group the names of people on your list with the items you associate with them. Gabriel, for instance, mentioned a few people in his list, so he grouped each name with other items, then added more information to some groupings.

Angela	**Ronnie**	**Laura**
designer clothes	travel	Corvette
rings	private school	stereo
necklaces	Camaro Z28	computer
telephone	bicycle	fancy home
dolls		bicycle
tree house		

Does chronology affect your subject? Depending on your general subject, you might establish a sequence of topics that is arranged chronologically by hours, days, weeks, months, or years. Such an arrangement divides a subject by what happens first, second, third, and so on. As he examined his list, Gabriel realized that he had included items related to different age groups. He then divided his list to describe status symbols ranging from those of children (the youngest group) to those of adults (the oldest group).

Children	Teenagers	Young Adults	Adults
toys	stereos	cars	homes
bicycles	telephones	apartments	cars
radios	cars	clothes	cabins
posters	clothes	stereos	travel
			appliances

Can you compare or contrast items on your list? Sometimes you will notice differences or similarities between items on your brainstorming list. If these comparisons and contrasts are interesting, you can group items accordingly, expanding your lists when that is helpful. Gabriel, for instance, saw parallel status symbols for children and for adults.

Children	Adults	General Categories
bicycles	cars	transportation
toys	appliances	nonessential items

EXERCISE □ *Prewriting*

Select one of the subjects from the first exercise and complete a brainstorming list of at least twenty-five items. (More items would be even better.) Then group items from the list, using one of the questions presented above if you wish. Remember that individual items may be used in more than one group, and remember to add more items if you think of them. (You might want to try two or three kinds of groups to see which works best.)

1c Identify a specific topic for your paper.

With some prewriting complete, consider what specific aspect of your subject interests you most or provides the best topic for a paper.

At this point, you are working toward a specific, narrowed topic, and a few questions can help you select the most promising one.

Which topic is most original? Since originality is important in writing, consider selecting the topic with the freshest outlook. Select the one that is uniquely yours.

Which topic comes closest to what you want to say about your subject? Follow your interests and approach the topic to suit your needs. Remember, however, that readers must be drawn into the discussion.

Which topic is most informative? Sometimes you will know more about one facet of your subject than another, in which case concentrate on that aspect.

Which topic is the most useful? Consider selecting one approach to a subject over another because it has clearer application to day-to-day activities. Consider the topic's usefulness to you and to your readers.

Which topic promises to be most interesting? Effective writing is interesting, so consider which approach allows you to include interesting details, facts, and descriptions.

Ultimately, the choice of a narrowed topic will be subjective. *You* will have to select the most promising topic. Make sure, however, that your topic offers something special, and then state your basic idea in a phrase or sentence.

One last time, consider whether the topic is sufficiently narrow to discuss. Does the topic include more than you can explain in your paper? Can you restrict the topic even further? If you can do so effectively, revise the topic and make another jotted list.

Gabriel, for instance, thought the comparison between children's and adults' status symbols offered the most original approach to his subject. He then clarified his topic with this phrase: "similar status symbols for children and adults." At first, Gabriel thought about comparing the childhood and adult status symbols of the three people on his list, but he realized that doing so would make for too long a paper and might seem repetitive. Then, to see if he could further narrow his topic, Gabriel reexamined his list to see if one of its parts could be effectively treated in isolation. He finally decided that discussing only one subject—bikes and cars, for instance—would not allow him to make the universal point he wanted, so he kept his original choice of comparing two subjects.

You will need to decide for yourself when your topic is sufficiently narrow. Sometimes completing two or three stages of narrowing a topic will be enough. Other times you will have to do more. You may need to complete another brainstorming list and group the items from that list. These decisions will be subjective ones and will depend on how specific you were when you began your work.

Planning and writing are ongoing, flexible, recursive, and sometimes uncertain processes. In these early stages of planning a paper—and throughout the writing stages—you should expect to evaluate your work, return to earlier stages of work, modify elements of your work (sometimes slightly and sometimes noticeably), or in some instances change the focus of your work altogether. These are all natural occurrences during the act of writing.

EXERCISE □ *A Specific Topic*

Review your topic groups and select the one that would probably produce the best paper. Describe the narrowed topic in a
phrase or sentence, consider narrowing the topic further, and
be ready to explain why you chose the narrowed topic.

1d Identify your role, readers, and purpose.

As you think about your narrowed topic and begin to develop and structure the particular ideas of the paper, consider
the context of the writing situation—your role, readers, and
purpose. Carefully thinking about these three interrelated elements will help you make choices as you write—choices of
what discussions to include in the paper, what kind of development each discussion will require, and what kind of writing
style will be most effective.

Your role

In what role are you writing? If you are writing about
horse racing, for instance, are you writing from your experience
as a spectator or as a jockey? Are you a fan? Are you an opponent of horse racing? If you are writing about city life, are you
writing as a city dweller or as a visitor to cities? These alternative kinds of roles—and there are, of course, many more possibilities—will establish not only how much you know about the
subject but also your special point of view for discussing it. Essentially, understanding your individual perspective on the
topic—whether you are writing as an authority, an unbiased
observer, or a questioning nonspecialist—is important for establishing the context of the paper.

Gabriel, for instance, saw himself as a person unaffected by status symbols, but he also saw himself as a careful observer of people who rely on status symbols. That made him a perceptive outsider, a role that would give him some distance from the subject and would allow him to be objectively critical.

Your readers

Writing is to be read, so you must carefully consider your reading audience. Are your readers specialists on the subject, or do they know little about it? For instance, if you were writing a paper on installing a sink, you would need to consider how much your readers already know about the subject. If they know basic plumbing procedures, your explanations could be brief (one knowledgeable plumber writing to other knowledgeable people). If, however, readers know nothing about plumbing except how to turn on a faucet, you would have to describe tools clearly, define terms carefully, and explain procedures thoroughly (a specialist writing to nonspecialists).

Also consider what tone will be appropriate for your readers. You should not write your papers to match your readers' ways of presenting information, but you should accommodate your work to suit their needs and expectations. Consider, for instance, whether your readers use and enjoy humor. If they do, then you have the freedom to make your papers humorous. If, on the other hand, your readers express themselves formally, you might want to present your discussions formally, too. You cannot copy the tone used by your readers in their spoken comments and written work—you are an individual with an individual way of presenting your ideas —but you should carefully consider your readers' preferences and expectations to insure that they respond well to your written work.

Evaluating your readers is especially important for establishing the context of your paper. They will bring to their reading a body of knowledge about your subject (minimal, extensive, or somewhere in between). They will also bring a set of expectations. Readers may expect certain kinds of discussions or may expect some subjects to be treated informally and others formally. Although you need not cater totally to your readers—you may want to offer them some surprises—you should realize that analyzing their knowledge and expectations will help you plan and write effectively.

Gabriel had a fairly easy time when considering his readers, for he would be writing for a general audience, and virtually everyone, he decided, is either concerned with status symbols or knows someone who is. Yet he had to be aware that many people probably had not thought about the connection between the status symbols of adults and those of children. He also decided that a somewhat informal tone was best suited to his audience, for few people become very serious when discussing subjects like status symbols.

Your purpose

In the simplest terms, your purpose in most writing will be to complete an assignment. Such a narrow view of your purpose, though, will not help you write effectively. Instead, think of your purpose more abstractly—consider why you are writing about a selected topic (to inform, to describe, or to persuade, for instance). Also consider how you are writing about it. Sometimes your purpose will seem clear, even in early stages of planning. At other times, your purpose will not be initially clear but will emerge as you write. Work flexibly and acknowledge the importance of naturally developing a purpose for a paper, rather than imposing a purpose.

The following discussions, which are necessarily general, may help you evaluate your purpose (or purposes) for writing a paper:

Informative papers share ideas, insights, experiences, and information. Because their primary purpose is to share knowledge about a subject, they require clear details, well-selected facts, and representative examples. Write such papers carefully to make sure that you have supplied complete and accurate discussions of your subject.

Descriptive papers also share experiences and information, but they record sensory impressions to enable readers to become part of the situation being described. A descriptive paper requires careful word choices and appeals to some or all of the five senses (sight, smell, sound, taste, and touch). Allow plenty of time to refine your language and details.

Persuasive papers present arguments on an issue. They require logical connections between ideas, systematic use of information, and especially careful use of examples. Although clear, logical connections are necessary in all kinds of papers, logic is especially important in persuasive papers. Carefully examine each idea to make sure that it honestly supports the thesis statement and test each idea to make sure that you have not inadvertently incorporated any logical fallacies (see Logical Thinking, **4**).

These general purposes of papers often overlap, since not many writing situations call for (or naturally develop into) a pure purpose. For instance, most persuasive papers are also informative, and informative papers are often descriptive. As you develop a paper and make choices about structure, content, and style, you will discover how natural it is to blend the purposes that a paper serves. If you work flexibly, the purpose (or purposes) of your paper will emerge as you think about your topic.

Gabriel, for instance, discovered after his prewriting that comparisons and contrasts between status symbols were potentially interesting and could help him make a persuasive point. His comparison and contrast on parallel status symbols would be informative. To that end, he would need to select representative examples, incorporate good descriptive details, and use words carefully, all to help convince readers of his point about the absurdity of status symbols.

EXERCISE □ *Role, Readers, and Purpose*

Jot a list that identifies your role, readers, and purpose for the paper you are planning. Be ready to explain how the analysis will influence your planning and writing.

Example

role	Gabriel Villachez, a person unimpressed by status symbols. I do notice people and the things that seem to impress them.
readers	Teacher and classmates. They are all aware of status symbols. They may be impressed by objects of status —and will certainly know people who are.
purpose	To write an informative and persuasive paper.

1e Write a working thesis statement.

A *thesis statement* is a sentence (or sometimes several sentences) that clearly identifies the topic of a paper and presents an opinion. Often placed near the end of the introductory paragraph, a thesis statement explains the idea in a paper and shows readers the direction the paper will take.

During the early stages of writing, thesis statements are often tentative or incomplete. Although these *working* thesis statements (tentative ones) are not in final form, they help writers focus their work from the start.

A thesis statement—either final or working—has two basic parts and an optional third part.

1. A thesis statement identifies the specific and narrow topic of the paper.

2. A thesis statement presents a clear opinion about the topic; it does not merely state a fact about it.

3. A thesis statement sometimes includes a qualification, a phrase or a clause pointing out some inconsistency or apparent contradiction. If the opinion is positive, the qualification is often negative, and vice versa.

Presenting a topic and an opinion in a thesis statement requires attention to detail and careful evaluation of the central idea. A thesis statement reflects the purpose the paper will serve, but it also contributes to the paper in other important ways. It helps to establish the tone of the paper, it acknowledges the readers' understanding of the topic, and it suggests the fairness of the discussion. When thesis statements are not carefully planned and written, they create confusion for readers and make the central idea of the paper unclear. Consider, for instance, these ineffective thesis statements:

Attics are places to store belongings. *(Although this thesis statement presents the topic, it contains no opinion. Instead, it states an acknowledged fact. What purpose could this paper possibly serve?)*

Driving a taxi one summer enabled me to comprehend that patrons in a hurry are quite typically at their least appealing. *(This thesis statement includes a narrowed topic and presents an opinion, but the tone of the thesis statement is inappropriately formal considering the topic.)*

Cats make weird pets. *(This thesis statement includes a narrowed topic and presents an opinion, yet it does not sufficiently acknowledge readers' varied perceptions. Probably half would be cat lovers. In addition, the word choice* weird *is not very accurate.)*

Liquor advertisements glamorize the drinking that leads to thousands of deaths each year. *(The topic and opinion are clear, but this thesis statement ignores the variables in this controversial situation.)*

First drafts of thesis statements are often as weak and indirect as these are. There is nothing especially wrong with that. Careful writers, however, revise weak thesis statements to improve them. Questions like these can help:

1. *Is the topic clear?* Will readers easily recognize the narrow topic? If they will not, try different words or phrases to present the topic more clearly and accurately.

2. *Is an opinion clearly presented?* Have you expressed a view that can be understood and argued so that readers will want to read the discussion to see how you reached your conclusion? If no opinion is included, state one.

3. *Is the tone of the thesis statement appropriate for the topic?* Is a serious subject presented seriously? Is a lighthearted topic presented informally? In particular, balance the topic and tone by reconsidering word choices.

4. *When appropriate, have you qualified your opinion?* If your opinion is highly controversial or potentially unpopular, have you acknowledged opposing views? Have you set limitations to make your view more acceptable? If not, add some necessary qualifications or limitations.

By considering these questions, reevaluating their thesis statements, and making some appropriate revisions, the writers of the previous thesis statements improved them substantially.

Attics are great places to store useless belongings. *(The inclusion of great adds an implied opinion, and the addition of useless further defines the opinion and establishes the humorous tone of the paper.)*

Driving a taxi one summer helped me realize that people in a hurry are people at their worst. *(The changes from enabled to helped, from comprehend to realize, from patrons to people, and from least appealing to worst all make the tone conversational and therefore better suited to the topic.)*

Cats make unusually independent pets. *(The change from weird to unusually independent makes the writer's point clear. As readers, we now know what the essay's focus will be. Weird simply did not do that. In addition, this new thesis statement shows a better understanding of readers.)*

Although some advertisements now include warnings not to drink and drive, most liquor advertisements continue to glamorize the drinking that leads to thousands of deaths each year. *(This thesis statement still takes a controversial stand on the issue, but the introductory qualification and the inclusion of most helps to make this statement more balanced than the original one.)*

Gabriel's attempts to write a working thesis statement followed a similar pattern:

First attempt

Both children and adults have status symbols. *(The topic status symbols is clear, but this sentence states a fact, not an opinion to be explained. Consequently, this is not an effective thesis statement.)*

Second attempt

Status symbols for children and adults are the same. *(The topic is still clear, and an opinion has been presented, but not precisely. The two kinds of status symbols are not the same; they are merely like one another. This is not an effective thesis statement either—but it is better.)*

Third attempt

The status symbols of adults correspond to the status symbols of children. *(The topic remains clear, the choice of the words* correspond to *more closely presents the opinion Gabriel wants to explain. This is an effective thesis statement because the topic and opinion are both clearly stated.)*

Fourth attempt

Although people expect adults to be more mature and rational, the status symbols of adults correspond to the status symbols of children. *(The qualification acknowledges the assumed distinction between adults and children. The rest of the thesis statement then stresses the similarity the paper will present.)*

Fifth attempt

Although people expect adults to be more mature and rational than children, the status symbols of adults correspond to those of the younger generation. *(This last revision clarifies the sentence structure of the otherwise clear thesis statement and, in addition, makes it more stylish.)*

EXERCISE □ *Thesis Statements*

The following sentences appeared in papers as thesis statements. Read them and decide whether each effectively presents a specific topic and opinion and whether the tone is appropriate for the topic. Also decide whether any of the thesis statements need to be qualified. If any are not satisfactory, explain why and revise them.

1. Owning your own home is a pain.

2. The 1985 Summer Olympics were held in Los Angeles.

3. Prayer is okay in public schools.

4. The United States government should quickly retaliate against terrorism.

5. Foreign students are expected to take competency tests in English.

EXERCISE □ *Qualified Thesis Statements*

All the following thesis statements present specific topics and opinions. Add qualifications that would help to make the thesis statements more complete.

1. Everyone should have a full physical exam each year.

2. Organizations should not be allowed to solicit donations in public places like airports and shopping centers.

3. Women should not always be awarded custody of children in divorce settlements.

4. Parents should be actively involved in their children's educations.

5. Drivers and passengers should be required by law to wear seat belts.

EXERCISE □ *Thesis Statements*

Construct a thesis statement based on your specific topic. Make sure that the topic and opinion are clearly presented. Also add a qualification if it will help present your idea more effectively.

1f Organize and outline your paper, adding new ideas when necessary.

The organization of your paper should develop naturally from the materials you have prepared during prewriting. A number of general patterns of organization can be effectively used or modified.

Chronological arrangement

Chronological arrangement presents paragraphs in time order, following the order of what happened first, second, third, and so on. Although chronological arrangement will not be suitable for all subjects, it can be used to present personal narratives and some general discussions. When presenting ideas chronologically, make sure that your description of the sequence of events (or topics) is accurate and clear.

Spatial arrangement

Spatial arrangement presents discussions according to the physical placement of features. Such discussions must follow a linear pattern. For instance, a person could be described by beginning with a description of the face and hair and ending with a description of the feet. A town might be discussed by "leading" readers from an area in the northern part of town to an area in the southern part. A restaurant could be described by detailing the things someone would see when walking through. Spatial arrangement can be used for only a limited number of subjects, but when physical features are important, no other arrangement works as well.

Topical arrangement

Topical arrangement is best used when your ideas on a subject can be divided into groups, each presenting an aspect of your subject or an example that supports your thesis. Topical arrangement can follow a number of specific patterns—from your most important point to your least important, for instance, or from your least important point to your most important. An effective alternative to these sequential patterns, however, is a mixed arrangement. This pattern presents your second most effective discussion (paragraph) at the beginning of the body of the paper, to draw readers into the discussion. Your most effective discussion (paragraph) is then placed at the end of the body of the paper, to close the discussion with some especially convincing evidence. Other paragraphs are sandwiched between these two, where they offer further support.

Other methods of arrangement

A number of other patterns of organizing a paper can be used, even though they are more typically used to organize information within paragraphs. Entire papers can be developed using comparison and contrast, analogy, cause and effect, process, classification, and definition. Their development follows the principles discussed for paragraph development, but each element of the discussion is expanded to make it paragraph length. (See Paragraphs, pages **65–81**.)

The most important thing, however, is to select, modify, or combine these patterns of organization to suit the materials you have developed, rather than to select a pattern of organization and manipulate a topic to fit the pattern. Once you have developed materials and discovered which pattern of organization is most suitable, you are ready to outline your main ideas.

An *outline* is a structural plan that uses headings and subdivisions to clarify the main features of a paper. Writing an outline can help you decide which ideas seem closely related and can give you a starting point for the overall structure of your paper.

Some writers create very general, informal outlines, while others prefer to create highly systematic, formal ones. If you are given the freedom to develop your own outlining strategies, use trial and error to discover the form that works best for you. Remember, however, that classroom work and some other kinds of specialized writing may require certain outlining procedures to allow instructors and supervisors to evaluate the work easily. When you are asked to follow specific procedures, follow them carefully.

Informal outlines

Informal outlines do not rely on any traditional system of labels for each part. Instead, they use lists, simple numbered headings, brackets, arrows, dots, dashes, or other markings to show levels of importance. Because they do not rely on a specific system for labeling, they are often more easily and more quickly written than formal outlines. In addition, because these arrangements do not look so complete, so final, writers sometimes feel freer to modify them. These two advantages may be important enough to help you choose informal outlining as your method to structure papers.

Gabriel, for instance, could have informally outlined his materials in one of these several patterns (or some other similar form):

Transportation		Special Purchases	
bicycles	brands	toys	dolls
	accessories		cars
cars	brands	"toys"	kitchen appliances
	accessories		other appliances

Paragraph 1: Transportation

Bicycles

brands—Schwinn, Hutch, Haro

accessories—seats, trim, tires

Cars

makes—Mercedes, Audi, Corvette

accessories—interiors, trim, wheel covers

Paragraph 2: Special Purchases

Toys

dolls—Cabbage Patch, Gerber

cars—electronic, foreign made

"Toys"

kitchen appliances

other appliances

These patterns of informal outlining—and hundreds of other forms people have created—are functional as long as *writers* can use them. When outlines must be submitted to *readers*, however, formal outlines are usually best because they depend on a system that is universally understood. In formal outlines, the following guidelines help writers distinguish among major parts of a paper.

- Roman numerals *(I, II, III)* usually indicate major topics in a paper. Think of these entries as whole paragraphs, or even blocks of two or three paragraphs.

- Capital (upper-case) letters *(A, B, C)* typically indicate large divisions of each topic. Think of these as suggesting clusters of sentences in a paragraph.

- Arabic numbers *(1, 2, 3)* normally are used for clarifications of a division. Think of these as sentences.

- Lower-case letters *(a, b, c)* frequently indicate details. Think of these as items within sentences.

In addition to these general patterns, other outlining procedures are generally understood and expected:

- Parallel forms must be used throughout. Use fragments and words throughout to produce a topic outline, or use sentences throughout to produce a sentence outline. Yet another possibility, still parallel, is a mixed outline, one that puts topic sentences at Roman numeral divisions and then has fragments for the rest of the outline.

- Each element must include only one idea. If you have more than one idea, subdivide.

- Divided topics must have at least two parts (an *A* and *B*, a *1* and *2*, and so on).

- Details must support or explain the heading under which they appear.

- Introductory and concluding material is separated from the outline.

• Headings of the same level must line up at the same margin.

Working within the general guidelines for formal outlining, Gabriel could have written two versions of his plan. The first sample, a mixed outline, uses sentences at the Roman numeral, or paragraph, level and then uses fragments for the topics to be treated within each paragraph. The second sample, a full-sentence outline, uses sentences at every level to achieve extra clarity. Notice that in the full-sentence outline some of the subdivisions—the brands of bicycles, for instance—are eliminated because they serve as brief examples and not as major points of discussion.

A Mixed Outline

INTRODUCTION

Thesis statement: Although people expect adults to be more mature and rational than children, the status symbols of adults correspond to those of the younger generation.

   I. Transportation provides major status symbols for children and adults.

      A. Children's bicycles

         1. Special brands

            a. Schwinn

            b. Hutch

            c. Haro

        2. Special accessories

          a. Seats

          b. Trim

          c. Tires

    B. Adults' cars

        1. Special makes

          a. Mercedes

          b. Audi

          c. Corvette

        2. Special accessories

          a. Interiors

          b. Trim

          c. Wheel covers

II. Special purchases also provide status symbols for

    children and adults.

    A. Children's toys

        1. Dolls

          a. Cabbage Patch

          b. Gerber

        2. Toy cars

          a. Electronic

          b. Foreign-made

B. Adults' "toys"

    1. Kitchen appliances

        a. Food processors

        b. Microwave ovens

    2. Other household appliances

        a. Water Piks

        b. Cordless telephones

CONCLUSION

A Full-Sentence Outline

INTRODUCTION

<u>Thesis statement</u>: Although people expect adults to be more mature and rational than children, the status symbols of adults correspond to those of the younger generation.

  I. Transportation provides major status symbols for both children and adults.

    A. Children want their bicycles to be exceptional.

      1. Children prefer Schwinn, Hutch, and Haro bikes because they are "big names."

      2. Children want special accessories—seats, trim, and tires—to suggest that their bikes are not ordinary.

B. Adults buy exceptional cars to show that they, too, are exceptional.

   1. Adults spend large amounts of money for special makes of cars: Mercedes, Audi, Corvette.

   2. Adults also want special accessories—leather interiors, special trim, and unusual wheel coverings—to show that they know the "best features" of cars.

II. Special purchases also provide status symbols for children and adults.

A. Children's toys often suggest status.

   1. Certain dolls like the Cabbage Patch or Gerber dolls set children apart from the crowd.

   2. Electronic or foreign-made toy cars are also status symbols.

B. Adults have "toys" that set them apart from their friends and acquaintances.

   1. Kitchen appliances—like food processors and microwave ovens—are high-tech status symbols.

   2. Other household appliances convey status as well: Water Piks and cordless telephones.

CONCLUSION

Because of the simplicity and freedom of informal outlines and the clarity and completeness of formal outlines, many writers use both strategies—but at different stages of writing. In the earliest stages of planning—when writers are deciding what should come first, second, third, and so on—informal outlines seem to work best. They help writers easily decide where large blocks of material (paragraphs) should go. It is also easier to revise an informal outline as a paper develops and reorganization seems necessary. At later stages of writing, however, writers often use formal outlining to make sure that smaller elements—parallel details, for instance—are presented systematically.

Remember one other thing as well: both informal and formal outlines are plans, not descriptions of what you *must* do. If you plan a paragraph, for instance, and then find that you cannot write it well, reexamine your scheme and change it if you need to. Sometimes plans will not work because they are flawed. In such a case, do not frustrate yourself by trying to make a bad one work. Instead, decide *why* it does not work and make appropriate changes.

EXERCISE □ *Outlining*

Structure your paper, using either an informal or formal system. Add important details as you work and evaluate the arrangement of your materials. If you are completing a formal outline, double-check it carefully against the accepted standards for outlining.

1g Plan your title and your introductory and concluding paragraphs.

The title and the beginning and ending paragraphs of a paper are important because they make the first and the final impressions on readers. As a result, they deserve special attention. When to plan and write these special parts of a paper will vary from one assignment to the next. They can be developed and written at any time during the process of composition, or they can evolve as you write.

You will want to give the *title* of a paper some serious thought. A good title is at once descriptive, letting readers know what the paper is about, and imaginative, sparking readers' interest. A straightforward title, like "Divorce in America," is clear and direct but not particularly thought provoking or interesting. On the other hand, an imaginative title, like "When Promises Fail," may create interest but leaves readers wondering what topic the paper discusses. The best kind of title combines clarity and interest, as does the title of Roberta Greene's pamphlet: " 'Til Divorce Do You Part." This title mentions the topic, divorce, but also includes a play on the wording of traditional wedding vows. Another alternative is the two-part title, the first part imaginative, the second part descriptive: "When Promises Fail: Divorce in America." (Note the use of the colon to separate the two parts of the title.)

Once you think of an effective title, type it according to standard conventions: center it on the first page of your paper and use capital letters for the first letters of important words (see Capitalization, **39b**). Also note that the titles of papers, unlike those for articles or books, require neither quotation marks nor italics (underlining).

The *introduction* serves several purposes in a paper: it eases readers into your discussion, it creates interest, and it clarifies your subject and opinion before the main part of the paper begins. Although writers have developed a number of approaches to beginning a paper, most opening paragraphs start in a general way with an introductory strategy (or sometimes several) and end specifically, presenting the thesis statement.

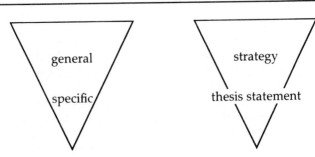

To create interest at the beginning of an introductory paragraph, writers often use one or several strategies. The following list includes twelve of the most commonly used strategies, with example paragraphs relating to the subject of television.

Allusion: Refer to a literary work, a media presentation, or a mythical, religious, or historical person or event.

Family Ties, The Cosby Show, and *Cagney and Lacey.* These shows are very different, yet they have one thing in common: they show as central characters strong, intelligent mothers who work outside the home. The women presented in these television programs are unusually impressive role models for young women, and many other television programs are following suit, presenting stronger, more independent, and more resourceful women as major characters.

Analogy: Make a comparison that is interesting, helpful, and related to the topic.

In the early 1900's, when movie houses began to open across the nation, critics predicted the decline of American education. Children, they said, would lose their ability to read, to concentrate, and to think. In the early 1950's, when televisions came into widespread use, critics again predicted a similar decline in American education. Yet the first generation to grow up watching television—the "baby boomers"—have been well educated, and subsequent generations have proved themselves as well. In fact, educational opportunities have been expanded, not hindered, by television.

Anecdote: Begin with a brief story describing an incident related to the topic.

Two Fridays ago, my friend Angie and I went shopping in the afternoon. We browsed in most of the stores at Lafayette Square and then stopped at Godfather's for our favorite sausage, mushroom, and green pepper pizza. We were casually gossiping about some of our friends when Angie suddenly sat up very straight. She quickly glanced at her watch and said in a frenzied tone, "Did you know it's almost 8:30?" She sprang from her chair, rushed to the counter, hurried back with a cardboard pizza box, slid the remaining pizza slices inside, and closed the top. As we rushed from Godfather's to her car, she growled, "Hurry. Come on. Get the lead out." What brought about this sudden change in Angie? *Dallas,* that's what. For like many Americans who under normal circumstances seem perfectly rational, Angie will radically alter her life to see the latest episode of her favorite program.

Definition: Define a term important to the discussion, but avoid defining terms already understood, unless such a definition serves a special purpose.

The American Heritage Dictionary defines *television* this way:
> The transmission of visual images of moving and stationary objects, generally with accompanying sound, as electromagnetic waves and the reconversion of received waves into visual images.

The process sounds extremely complex, and it is. But are the "visual images ... [and] accompanying sound" that American viewers see and hear worthy of the technological capabilities necessary to produce them? Not really. Idiotic situation comedies, sleazy game shows, and trashy nighttime dramas continue to break the technological promise that television made.

Description: To create interest, use a carefully worded description of something related to your topic.

You can meet them almost anywhere: at a party, at the grocery store, at church, at school, or at your child's daycare center. Who are they? They are the anti-televisionists. They smugly stand in their all-cotton clothes, or ride in their imported cars, or shop for their all-natural foods—and use every opportunity to scorn television viewing. If they have a television at all, it is a 1965 black-and-white Zenith portable that they use to watch episodes of *Masterpiece Theatre* on PBS. They would never be caught buying a copy of *TV Guide* and would never allow their children to watch cartoons on Saturday mornings. Although these anti-television types are partly correct when they scornfully dismiss "the boob tube" as a waste of time, they are missing a great deal of harmless video fun.

Epigram or proverb: Use a one-sentence statement of a general truth. Make sure it is related to the topic.

In the last three decades, the phrase "time is money" has taken on a new meaning as television advertising has emerged as one of America's big businesses. Those thirty-second and sixty-second commercials must have a substantial impact on viewers because advertisers spent $10.2 billion on commercials in 1979, according to Joel Swerdlow in his article "What Is Television Doing to Real People?" (*Wilson Quarterly,* Winter 1981). Yet advertising does more than sell products. It also, in large part, determines the fads in American society.

Facts and figures: Begin with some hard pieces of information, statistics, and the like—when they are useful or interesting.

In 1965, *I Spy* premiered on NBC, presenting a black actor in a starring role on prime-time television for the first time. In the years that followed, other black characters have captured America's interest: George Jefferson, Fred Sanford, and, most recently, Cliff Huxtable. Yet black characters, with rare exceptions, have remained secondary in most television programming, probably because of economic, rather than social, reasons.

Illustration: Use a photograph, cartoon, chart, or diagram that is related to the discussion. Be sure to comment on it in the introductory paragraph.

The logo above is well known across the United States. It appears on the cover of the most complete, most stylishly presented, and best-written guide to the world of television. Other magazines may attempt to copy its format, but *TV Guide* remains the only first-rate reference for television viewers because of its critical reviews of programs, its feature articles, and its comprehensive listings.

New discussion of an old subject: Explain why a topic that may be "old hat" is worth examining again. Consider looking at it in a new way.

Parents have grown tired of hearing that violence on television produces or at least encourages violence among children. Yes, the point has been made before. Yes, the arguments against certain kinds of programming remain the same. But the issue continues to plague us, and violence on television continues to affect children, more children each year. As parents, then, we must continue to address the problem. If we cannot control the networks' choice of programs—and the failures of lobbying groups have shown that we cannot—then we must closely monitor the television shows that our children watch.

Question: Use a question or series of questions related to the subject.

What role did Vivian Vance play on *I Love Lucy?* What role did Don Knotts play on *The Andy Griffith Show?* What role did Marla Gibbs play on *The Jeffersons?* If you know the answers to these questions, you would do well in a television trivia game. And you also know that secondary characters, especially those in situation comedies, add depth to the plots and characterizations presented. In short, "second bananas" are often a very important part of the bunch.

Quotation: Use what someone else has said or written in a poem, short story, book, article, or interview. Identify the person and the source clearly.

> Television communicates the same information to everyone simultaneously, regardless of age, sex, level of education, or life experience. Therefore, television eliminates many of the important ways that we distinguish between children and adults.
>
> The preceding comment, made by Neil Postman in an interview for *U.S. News & World Report* (19 January 1981), aptly describes the unfortunate blending of generations that is occurring in American society. Children are being presented with issues they are not ready to understand, let alone resolve. To guarantee that children have time to be children, parents must restrict the kinds of programs they allow their children to watch.

Startling statement: Use a statement with some element of surprise to get readers' attention and interest.

Fifteen thousand to twenty thousand hours. That represents the average number of hours a typical fifteen-year-old has watched television. Astonishing as it seems, this figure reflects our national dependence on the tube. To make sure that at least part of this viewing time is used productively, parents should insist that children watch some educational programs that expand their basic understanding of the world around them.

Gabriel considered several possible strategies for the introductory paragraph of his paper. By planning several beginnings, he was able to select the best one.

definitions	*status:* the position or rank of an individual in relation to others
	symbol: a material object representing something, often something abstract
anecdote	a description of an incident with Ronnie (best friend); fourth grade; new bicycle; at my house
description	a description of a Porsche 911, a $55,000 sports car —carefully commenting on its accessories

Gabriel decided that the definition did not have much promise because most people know what status symbols are, and the definition would add little clarification. The straight description might be interesting, but it would not establish a suitable tone for his paper. As a result, he chose the anecdote because it could be interesting, representative, and humorous, thus setting the tone for the paper.

A *conclusion* also serves several purposes in a paper: it eases readers out of the discussion, it reemphasizes the point of the essay one last time, and it makes a final impression on readers.

Writers also vary their concluding paragraphs considerably, but most concluding paragraphs begin with a brief but specific summary of the paper and then present a general observation about the topic by using a concluding strategy.

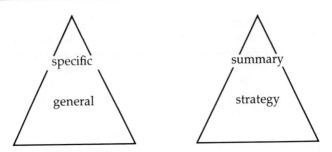

Some introductory strategies can also be used as concluding strategies: allusion, analogy, anecdote, description, epigram or proverb, illustration, and quotation. In addition to these strategies, others work especially well for conclusions. The following list includes the most common of these additional strategies, with sample paragraphs relating to the subject *television*.

Appeal for action: Ask readers to do something specific—write letters, organize committees, send donations, and so on.

> So, if you are concerned about the quality of programming on television, do something other than complaining to family, friends, and acquaintances. Call your local stations to make your feelings known. Write to the major networks to express your views. Form a group of concerned citizens and send petitions to television executives. Join the National Coalition for Better Television. If you do not act, you in a sense forfeit your right to criticize television. Become active today to guarantee better television programming tomorrow.

Issue a challenge: Ask people to change behavior or rethink an issue. This does not include taking specific action.

> The challenge for parents is this: we must find ways to engage our children in other activities besides television viewing. We may not be able to occupy all of our children's time, and we may not be able—or want—to wean them completely from television. But

we must think about what we want for our children and what we expect from them. We must take steps now to make them less dependent on a medium that encourages passivity.

Repeat the pattern of the introduction: Use the strategy in the introduction again, with some changes based on what has been learned in the paper, to frame the discussion.

Playwrights have known for centuries what few television viewers realize: secondary characters create much of the interest and action in a successful comedy. Praising the big-name stars is fine, but let's give some of that praise to the secondary performers who help to make the stars shine. After all, who can imagine Lucy without Ethel, Andy without Barney, or Louise without Florence?

Summary: Use a lengthy summary that reassesses the major points presented in the paper. This is the most predictable and least interesting strategy.

Television does, in fact, serve important educational purposes. It allows viewers to see places—faraway cities and foreign countries—that they might not otherwise see. It allows viewers to witness activities—the Olympics, presidential inaugurations, and concerts—that they might otherwise be unable to attend. It also gives viewers the chance to "get to know" famous or important people like Beverly Sills, Jack Nicklaus, Margaret Thatcher, or Bishop Desmond Tutu. Television has its faults, but its educational possibilities are staggering.

Visualize the future: Predict what a situation will be like in the near or distant future. Be realistic.

In the last fifteen years, technological advances have radically altered television viewing habits in America. Cable systems and satellite services have expanded viewers' choices of programs. High-resolution color screens have improved the quality of the images that people watch. Sales of advanced forms of television technology have been phenomenal, as people abandon their antennas and black-and-white sets to take advantage of better services and equipment. Who knows? Perhaps in another fifteen years, large-screen color televisions with stereo sound will be common in American living rooms, and 20-inch color consoles will be relegated to the basements.

Gabriel also developed three plans for his concluding strategy:

issue a challenge	"Do not fall victim to advertising's touting of status symbols. Instead, be smart and get the best value for your dollar."
repeat the pattern of the introduction	use Ronnie again in a similar situation; last week; a new Camaro Z28; my apartment.
epigram or proverb	A fool and his money are soon parted.

Gabriel decided that the challenge did not specifically match the purpose of his paper and that the proverb was slightly uninteresting. Using another parallel anecdote seemed the best strategy. You, too, will need to consider alternative strategies for conclusions to select the most effective one.

EXERCISE □ *Introductory and Concluding Paragraphs*

Develop at least two strategies for your introduction and two for your conclusion. Make sure that your strategies will create interest and are closely connected to the topic of your paper.

1h Write a rough draft of your paper.

The *rough draft* is the first written form of a paper. As such, it is usually very messy and inconsistent. It is, in a general sense, the sentence form of the outline, but you will discover that it does not develop detail by detail, sentence by sentence, paragraph by paragraph. Rather, some parts will develop smoothly and clearly the first time, while others will develop only after three or four tries. That is a typical pattern for most writers because writing a rough draft is a good deal more complicated than writing one sentence for every division of an outline.

Writing a rough draft is a shifting process that requires you to think, plan, write, rethink, rewrite, replan, and rewrite again. Somewhat ironically, if you expect writing a rough draft to be easy, it will be difficult, because changes and problems will seem out of place in an easy process. If you expect writing a rough draft to be difficult, however, and if you are prepared to make many kinds of changes, you will be flexible enough to write a rough draft effectively.

Because writing a rough draft is different for different writers—and will even vary from paper to paper for the same writer—no specific set of advice will always apply. Some general strategies, however, do seem helpful in most situations.

Gather all your materials together. Your work will be easier if all your prewriting materials and writing supplies are in one place. That way, you will not have to interrupt your work to find a needed item.

Work one paragraph at a time. Work in any order, rereading parts of the outline, and focus on distinct portions of the paper.

Do not worry about technical issues. Attention to details like spelling, punctuation, and mechanics will slow you down at this point.

Concentrate on shaping the ideas. Get the ideas working together, saving technical work until revision.

Remember your thesis statement. As you write, include no information or explanations that do not directly or indirectly support or explain your controlling idea.

Keep your readers in mind. If you decided, for instance, that readers know very little about your topic, explain terms and procedures carefully.

Remember the purpose of the paper. If your paper is descriptive, make sure that word choices and details create the appropriate effect and provide the proper insights.

Give some attention to word choices. Although it will probably not be possible in the rough draft stage to produce a paper with consistent tone, choose words carefully to reduce subsequent revision. Keep in mind, however, that you can refine your word choices later.

Rethink troublesome sections. As you write, you may discover that the plan is not working. Perhaps an example is not developing well, perhaps the descriptions are ineffective, or perhaps the order of the paragraphs no longer seems logical. If so, rethink those sections and rework the paper.

Modify the outline when necessary. An outline is a *plan*—and changing plans is a fact of life. But if you change the outline, do so carefully, looking at the outline as a whole. One major change should not disjoint the whole paper.

Skip troublesome sections on a first writing. Sometimes it pays to skip over a particularly difficult section to work on easier sections. That practice may make completing the problem sections easier.

Insert new words and phrases. Use arrows to insert words, phrases, or whole sentences between lines. Do not worry about the neatness of the rough draft. A rough draft should be *rough*—and that usually means messy as well.

Reread sections as you write. Reading what you have recently written will help you keep the tone of even the rough draft fairly consistent.

Work on alternatives for sections. When you are faced with a problematical section, write several versions. Then select the one that works best.

Periodically, give yourself a break from writing. Interrupting your writing too often will create problems with consistency. Getting away from the work for a while, however, is necessary to maintain some balance and to get some critical distance.

EXERCISE □ *A Rough Draft*

Write a rough draft of your paper. Concentrate on major ideas in paragraphs. Include both an introductory strategy and a thesis statement in the first paragraph. Make sure the paragraphs in the body of the paper contain clear topic sentences (see **2b**) and adequate support. Include a summary and a concluding strategy in the last paragraph. Finally, remember that rough drafts are seldom neat.

1i Revise your paper's content.

When you are finally satisfied with the rough draft of a paper, set it aside for as long as possible. Several days would be excellent, but if that is not possible, then stop working on the paper for at least several hours. Do the dishes, play frisbee, watch television, fold the laundry, or go bicycling. Do *anything* else. These activities will give you a needed break from the long process of writing the paper and will allow you to return to the paper fresh. Rested and relaxed, you can examine the rough draft critically before you revise it.

When you return to your paper, examine its contents and revise any faulty paragraphs or parts of paragraphs. Ask yourself questions like these:

☐ Is the introductory strategy interesting and appropriate? (See **1g.**)

☐ Does the thesis statement clearly present the topic and an opinion about it? (See **1e.**)

☐ Do the topics of the paragraphs truly support the thesis statement?

☐ Is a topic sentence clear in each paragraph? (See **2b.**)

☐ Are paragraphs effectively developed? Do the descriptions, facts, and examples clarify the thesis statement? Do the comparisons, contrasts, and analogies make sense? Are causes and effects logically connected? Are processes clearly presented? Does the system of classification work? Are definitions clear? (See Paragraphs, **2e-2h.**)

☐ Does all information in each paragraph relate to the topic sentence?

☐ Are the paragraphs arranged in the most effective order? Would another pattern work better?

☐ Does each paragraph follow logically from the one before it?

☐ Is the concluding summary logical? (See **1g.**)

☐ Does the concluding strategy end the paper effectively and restress the idea in the thesis statement? (See **1g.**)

If your content revisions have been extensive, you may need to complete a second (or third) full draft of the paper. Doing so will take time, but it will be time well spent if it makes working with the manuscript easier during later stages of revision.

As shown in Figure 1, Gabriel made two major content revisions in the rough draft of his introductory paragraph: he deleted a sentence that did not relate to his anecdote, and he shifted the position of a block of sentences to create a smoother transition from the strategy to the thesis statement.

One day when I was 10 my best friend, Ronnie, rode up to my house on a new bicycle. It was a black schwinn ten speed bicycle with crome trim. Ronnie smiled as he put down the kickstand. He asked if I wanted to see the best bicycle that Atterson Bikes had? The price tag was still hanging from the handlebars. Ronnie & his parents are like many people. They hope that if they spend enough money for the best brands their social status will be represented in their latest purchases. My bicycle which I had inherited from my older brother, was an average kind of bike, so of course I was interested in seeing and riding Ronnies newest status symbol. It was the latest indication that Ronnies parents would spend lots of $ to make sure that everyone knew there son had the best. There was little difference in Ronnies attitudes and that of his parents. You might assume that adults who work might spend it more wisely and not invest so much in status symbols. Not so. Although people expect adults to be more mature and rational than children, the status symbol of adults correspond to those of the younger generation.

Figure 1   A rough draft.

EXERCISE □ *Content Revision*

Reread your paper and respond to the ten basic questions on page **48**. Unless you can answer each question with a strong "yes," revise appropriate portions until the content is consistently good throughout.

1j Revise the style of your paper.

Content revisions should clear up any major inconsistencies with sentence logic in the paper, but beyond the matter of *what* your paper includes is the issue of *how* the content is presented.

When you have developed strong content in the paper, refine your style, using these questions as guides:

□ Are the lengths of sentences varied? (See **17**.)

□ Are enough kinds of sentence types used? (See **7** and **20**.)

□ Are descriptions vivid, interesting, and clear throughout the essay? (See **2f**.)

□ Are word choices accurate and appropriate? (See **28** and **29**.)

□ Are sentences as concise as possible? (See **27**.)

□ Are most sentences written in the active voice? (See **26**.)

□ Are transitions included to connect ideas? (See **2o**.)

When Gabriel began style revisions, his two primary concerns were choppy sentences and word choice. He combined several sentences to connect related ideas and substituted specific words for general ones. In addition, he added some transitions to make clearer connections between ideas. Figure 2 shows what he did.

One, ~~day~~ *Saturday* when I was 10 my best friend, Ronnie, rode up to my

house on a new ~~bicycle. It was a~~ black schwinn ten speed bicycle

with crome trim. Ronnie, ~~smiled~~ *beamed* as he put down the kickstand/

and ~~He~~ asked if I wanted to see the best bicycle that Atterson Bikes

had? Of course I was interested in seeing and, *maybe* riding Ronnies new-

est status symbol/, ~~It was~~ the latest indication that Ronnies parents

would spend lots of $ to make sure that everyone knew there son

had the best. , *Not by accident, the* ~~The~~ price tag was still, ~~hanging~~ *dangling* from the handle-

bars. Ronnie & his parents are like many people/ *who* ~~They~~ hope that

if they spend enough money for the best brands their social status

will be represented in their latest purchases. There was little dif-

ference in Ronnies attitudes and that of his parents/ *although one* ~~You~~ might

assume that adults who work, ~~might~~ *would* spend it *money* more wisely and not

invest so much in status symbols. Not so. Although people ex-

pect adults to be more mature and rational than children, the

status symbol of adults correspond to those of the younger gener-

ation.

Figure 2   A style revision.

EXERCISE □ *Style Revision*

Having revised the content of the paper, now turn to its style. To answer the questions in the text, make notes—on sentence lengths, kinds of sentences, or word choice, for instance.

1k Revise your paper to eliminate technical inconsistencies.

The final stage of revision should be technical revision—focusing on grammar, punctuation, mechanics, spelling, and manuscript form. Assuming that your earlier content and style revisions have eliminated major problems with structure and development, you are ready to do the technical revisions that make the presentation of the smaller details of the paper precise.

Ask yourself the following general questions and also watch for technical errors you habitually make in writing.

□ Are words spelled correctly? (When in doubt, *always* look them up.) (See **46.**)

□ Are any words omitted?

□ Are words unnecessarily repeated? (See **27a.**)

□ Are commas used properly? (See **31** and **32.**)

□ Is specialized punctuation—periods, question marks, exclamation points, commas, semicolons, colons, dashes, parentheses, brackets, and ellipsis points—accurate? (See **30** and **33–38.**)

□ Are elements of mechanics—capitalization, italics, quotation marks, apostrophes, hyphens, numbers, and abbreviations—properly used? (See **39–45.**)

□ Are all sentences complete? (See **8.**)

☐ Do elements of sentences agree in number and gender? (See **10** and **11.**)

☐ Are all antecedents clear? (See **24.**)

☐ Are all modifiers positioned logically? (See **25.**)

Gabriel's technical revisions involved spelling, mechanics, and punctuation. He used his handbook to check rules of capitalization and comma placement. He used it to check the use of quotation marks, symbols, and abbreviations. In addition, he changed the verb tense in one sentence and corrected several errors in agreement. See Figure 3 (to make it easier to pick out technical revisions, the draft has been retyped with earlier changes incorporated).

EXERCISE ☐ *Technical Revision*

Return to your paper to complete this last stage of revision. Work slowly and carefully, using this handbook to help solve special problems with grammar, mechanics, and punctuation.

1l Prepare a final copy to submit.

Preparing the final copy of a paper to submit is not only a matter of rewriting or typing; there are a number of special concerns. Your instructor will outline the appropriate patterns for preparing a final manuscript, but sample manuscript guidelines are also included in the appendix at the back of the book (see **63**).

EXERCISE ☐ *A Final Copy*

Prepare the final copy of your paper. Work carefully. Proofread the final copy and make any last-minute corrections. As a

One Saturday when I was ~~10~~ ten, my best friend, Ronnie, rode up to

my house on a new black $\overset{S}{\text{s}}$chwinn ten speed bicycle with ~~crome~~ chrome

trim. Ronnie beamed as he put down the kickstand and asked if I

wanted to see "the best bicycle that Atterson Bikes had." Of course I

was interested in seeing and maybe riding Ronnie's newest status

symbol, the latest indication that Ronnie's parents would spend

lots of ~~$~~ money to make sure that everyone knew ~~there~~ their son had the best.

Not by accident, the price tag was still dangling from the handle-

bars. Ronnie ~~&~~ and his parents are like many people who hope that if

they spend enough money for the best brands their social status

will be represented in their latest purchases. There was little dif-

ference in Ronnie's attitudes and that of his parents, although one

might assume that adults who work would spend money more

wisely and not invest so much in status symbols. Not so. Al-

though people expect adults to be more mature and rational than

children, the status symbols of adults correspond to those of the

younger generation.

Figure 3 A technical revision.

safeguard, photocopy the final manuscript before you submit the paper.

1m A sample paper

Gabriel Villachez

English 101

13 November 86

Status Symbols: The Latest, the Fanciest—the Best?

One Saturday when I was ten, my best friend Ronnie rode up to my house on a new black Schwinn ten-speed bicycle with chrome trim. Ronnie beamed as he put down the kickstand and asked if I wanted to see "the best bicycle that Atterson Bikes had." Of course I was interested in seeing and maybe riding Ronnie's newest status symbol, the latest indication that Ronnie's parents would spend lots of money to make sure that everyone knew their son had the best. Not by accident, the price tag was still dangling from the handlebars. Ronnie and his parents are like many people who hope that if they spend enough money for the best brands their social status will be represented in their latest purchases. There was little difference in Ronnie's attitude and that of his parents, although one might assume that adults who work would spend money more wisely and not invest so much in status symbols. Not so. Although people expect adults to be more mature and rational than children, the status symbols of adults correspond to those of the younger generation.

Transportation provides major status symbols for children and adults. Children like Ronnie see their bicycles as extensions of themselves. Owning an exceptional bicycle, they think, will make them exceptional children. Avoiding reliable brands that have reasonable prices, these children prefer Schwinn, Hutch, or Haro bikes, bikes with "big names" and equally big price tags. The little status seekers want special molded seats, decorative stripes, unusual bar pads, and brightly colored wheel spokes—all of which suggest that their bikes are not ordinary. Similarly, many adults buy exceptional cars to demonstrate to the world that they, too, are exceptional. They sink disproportionately large parts of their paychecks into expensive cars: Mercedes wagons, Audi sedans, and Corvette Sting-Rays. They load their cars with fancy accessories—leather seats, special trim, and decorative wheel covers—to demonstrate that they know the best when they see it. In both cases, transportation is not the primary concern. A Huffy bicycle or an Escort coupe would get them where they want to go.

Children and adults also use special purchases of nonessential items to emphasize their status. Children's toys, for instance, often suggest status. Having a sixty-dollar Cabbage Patch doll or even a twenty-five-dollar Gerber baby doll can set a seven-year-old apart from the crowd. So can a fifty-dollar remote-controlled model Porsche or a foreign-made Lamborghini model. Whether the toy is worth the price is not the issue; rather, the issue is whether a child can have a toy other children want too but cannot necessarily have. Adults also have "toys" that set them apart from their friends and acquaintances. Food processors—notably Cuisinarts —became a status symbol several years ago. People bought them and displayed them prominently on their cabinets, whether they used them or not. Microwave ovens, especially when they were first introduced, were high-tech symbols as well. Even appliances as unusual as Water Piks and technical gadgets as specialized as cordless telephones have become adult toys that convey status. Like children, adults often are not concerned with the value of a purchase but are more interested in having the latest, the fanciest, and the best.

The transportation and special purchases of children and adults often reflect the same irrational attitudes. Rather than serving dependable, functional, and practical purposes, they are used to show position or rank—to symbolize status. It is depressing to think that these pretentious attitudes, often begun in childhood, continue into adulthood. In fact, Ronnie, now twenty-four, stopped by my apartment last week to show me his latest purchase: a black, heavily accessorized Camaro Z28. Black is still his favorite color and, like many grown-up people who are still childish, Ronnie allows status symbols to remain a major part of his life.

2 Paragraphs*

The building blocks of writing, *paragraphs* present discussions of single facets of a subject. In isolation, a paragraph describes or explains one idea, but when it is part of a series of paragraphs in a paper, it develops one aspect of a paper's larger idea.

There is no magical rule for the length of paragraphs, but a few general principles seem true. Short paragraphs are useful for presenting simple ideas or for creating emphasis, but too many in a row make a paper seem choppy and underdeveloped. On the other hand, long paragraphs are useful for presenting complex ideas that require a great deal of explanation, but too many of them in a row can tire readers because they require so much concentration.

The best general rule about paragraph length, then, is to make paragraphs long enough to explain ideas fully—and no longer. But whether a paragraph is brief or long, it must be clear and unified to present ideas effectively.

2a Develop a single idea in a paragraph.

By standard convention, a paragraph should develop one idea, offering explanations of one important point. That point may be isolated—for instance, in a response to a question on a test. More often, however, one paragraph works with other paragraphs to help support the larger idea of a paper.

In planning a paragraph, present one idea, not two or three. If you try to explain too many separate ideas, the paragraph will be too long and will probably shift focus. Such a shift in focus is distracting at best and confusing at worst. To avoid problems with length and focus, develop only one idea. Look, for instance, at this poorly planned paragraph:

> The Metropolitan Museum of Art in New York City is an impressive example of nineteenth-century architecture. Made of stone

---

* Throughout this section, the exercises will take you through the steps of writing a paragraph. Be sure to keep the work on paragraphs from each exercise to use in later exercises.

with massive columns and elaborately carved scrollwork, it is institutional architecture of the sort we expect in public buildings. Across town, the Guggenheim Museum of Modern Art is built of unadorned stone. This museum has curved walls and spiraling bands of windows. Its design is rather severe, unusual, and utilitarian.

Because this paragraph briefly describes two museums without connecting them in any particular way, it is not unified. The first two sentences discuss the Metropolitan Museum's architecture, and the last three sentences confuse matters by turning to a different museum, the Guggenheim. By combining these two discussions in one paragraph without making any logical connections, the writer creates an unnecessary shift in subject. The writer could add sentences to show the relationship between the Guggenheim and the Museum of Modern Art, or the topics could be treated in two separate paragraphs like these:

The Metropolitan Museum of Art in New York City is a fine example of nineteenth-century public architecture. Made of stone —with massive columns, tall casement windows, and elaborately carved cornices—it is institutional architecture of the sort we expect in public buildings. It is reminiscent of the Louvre in Paris, the British Museum in London, and a vast number of public buildings in Washington. It is familiarly impressive, suggesting a grand purpose.

Across town, however, the Guggenheim Museum of Modern Art presents a twentieth-century view of public architecture. Built of unadorned stone, the facade is broken only by spiraling bands of simple windows. In 1937, when the museum was dedicated, the severity of its design made it seem very modern, very alien. Yet the Guggenheim Museum changed the way Americans perceived institutional architecture, and we now find similar designs in everything from public libraries to municipal parking garages.

By separating the discussions of the two museums, the writer is able to treat each one more fully. In addition, readers can concentrate their thoughts on one museum at a time, without any abrupt shifts.

Sometimes a paragraph will include ideas related to more than one topic, because during writing loosely connected ideas slip in. The process of writing often involves sorting ideas as you write—discovering which ideas work together and moving sentences from paragraph to paragraph. Poor focus is typical in early drafts, but including unrelated information takes a paragraph in more than one direction. For instance, look at this poorly organized paragraph:

> Hurricanes are cyclones that develop in the tropical waters of the Atlantic Ocean. Forming large circles or ovals, they have winds of 75 miles per hour or higher and can measure 500 miles across. Years ago, hurricanes were named after women—Irene, Sara, Becky, for example—but now they are also named after men. They usually form hundreds of miles from land and then move slowly to the northwest at about 10 miles per hour. For reasons unknown, they pick up speed rapidly when they reach the twenty-fifth parallel. That means, in very practical terms, that they reach peak speed and destructive power by the time they hit North American coastlines. Hurricanes that form in the Pacific Ocean are commonly called typhoons.

Here, all the material concerns hurricanes, but the paragraph is not unified around one topic. Most sentences describe how the storms form and move, but some sentences include interesting but indirectly related material. To improve the focus of the paragraph, the unrelated material should be omitted and perhaps used in other paragraphs.

> Hurricanes are cyclones that develop in the tropical waters of the Atlantic Ocean. Forming large circles or ovals, they have winds of 75 miles per hour or higher and can measure 500 miles across.

They usually form hundreds of miles from land and then move slowly to the northwest at about 10 miles per hour. For reasons unknown, they pick up speed rapidly when they reach the twenty-fifth parallel. That means, in very practical terms, that they reach peak speed and destructive power by the time they hit North American coastlines.

2b Use a topic sentence to identify the main idea in a paragraph.

A good *topic sentence* usually serves two purposes: it names a paragraph's topic, and it explains how the topic is treated. In a full-length paper, each topic sentence in each body paragraph describes one facet of the overall thesis statement, clearly signaling how the paper is being developed. When a topic sentence begins a paragraph, it works like a road sign, guiding readers through writing (see Deduction, **2c**). When a topic sentence ends a paragraph, it summarizes a paragraph's idea (see Induction, **2d**).

Some authors write occasional paragraphs without topic sentences, letting the paragraph imply the point they are making. They feel that including a topic sentence in every paragraph makes writing mechanical and predictable. That may be true, but omitting topic sentences is also potentially confusing, for readers may not fully understand the point being made or may misinterpret it. Therefore, using topic sentences is the surest way to keep writing clear.

Each of the revised paragraphs on art museums contains a topic sentence that clearly identifies the subject and how it will be discussed:

The Metropolitan Museum of Art in New York City is a fine example of nineteenth-century public architecture.

Across town, however, the Guggenheim Museum of Modern Art presents a twentieth-century view of public architecture.

As readers begin each paragraph, they understand which museum they will be reading about, and they know that each museum will be discussed as an example of public architecture rather than, say, a place for learning or socializing. In addition, the second paragraph's topic sentence shows that the two museums are being contrasted. The topic sentences, therefore, direct attention and focus the discussion.

EXERCISE □ *Topic Sentences*

The following paragraph was developed from a poor topic sentence that led to ineffective organization and writing. Revise the topic sentence to give it clearer focus and then strike out any unrelated material in the paragraph.

In the early days of television, children in major roles represented middle-class children who were stereotypically good-looking and clever. Timmy, the boy on *Lassie*, had well-cut blond hair, sparkling eyes, a straight-toothed smile, and even dimples. On *Ozzie and Harriet*, David and Ricky were ideal sons of perfect suburban parents. They were handsome, with dark hair, broad smiles, stylish clothes, athletic physiques, and perfect manners. Cathy, the youngest child on *Father Knows Best*, represented the ideal middle-class girl. She was small, slightly pudgy, girlish with just a touch of tomboyishness, and cute. With her hair in neatly plaited pigtails, she scampered around in clean sports outfits or dresses, using her impish smile and bright eyes to manipulate those around her. Even Theodore on *Leave It to Beaver* was good looking in an offbeat kind of way. His hair was often messed up, but it was always well cut; his face was sometimes dirty, but the dirt did not hide his smooth, freckled skin for long. His clothes were often rumpled, but they were never worn out. In addition, all these children were shrewd beyond their years, although they often made harmless mistakes and acted foolishly, especially Beaver. With these attractive stereotypes on television, it is no wonder parents of real children felt cheated.

EXERCISE □ *Topic Sentences*

Using four of the subjects below, write topic sentences. Make sure that your topic sentences specifically identify the subject and also clearly describe how you will discuss it.

Example

Subject: lawyers

Topic sentence: Sometimes, lawyers act more as interpreters than as advocates.

1. negligent landlords

2. librarians

3. news magazines

4. baseball players' salaries

5. greeting cards

6. tasteless jokes

7. the police on television

8. sneakers

9. cats

10. water conservation

2c Use deductive development for straightforward discussion.

Deductive development, a structural plan for paragraphs and papers, moves from a statement of an idea to the particular descriptions, examples, explanations, and facts that clarify it. Deductive development is the most common structural pattern for paragraphs because it offers writers the security of stating their main ideas first and then adding appropriate clarification. Readers also appreciate the clarity of deductive paragraphs because they know from the start the purpose of a paragraph. The following paragraph is written deductively:

topic sentence — **At long last, the metric system is becoming an accepted standard of measurement in the United States.** As people have grown accustomed to driving

detail 1 — and servicing foreign cars, they have grown accustomed to talking about and using metric tools. Even in Sears advertisements, the availability of metric socket wrenches and similar tools is announced with-

detail 2 — out surprise. People with headaches now take tablets

	or capsules containing 400 milligrams of aspirin.
detail 3	Typists use correction fluid that comes in 18 milliliter
	bottles and draw straight lines using rulers that list
detail 4	centimeters as well as inches. Even people planning
	parties buy Coke, Pepsi, or 7-Up in liter bottles or buy
summary	wine in 750-milliliter bottles. The metric system has
	clearly become an accepted way for Americans to
	measure the things that they buy and use.

As readers, we know from the beginning where the paragraph is headed, since the topic sentence names the subject, the metric system, and the point to be made: the system has been accepted by Americans. Then, in a series of details, the point of the topic sentence is elaborated and summarized. Readers have no surprises in store because deductive development clearly directs their thinking.

2d Use inductive development to create suspense, interest, or special effect.

Inductive development, an alternative structure for paragraphs and papers, begins with descriptions, examples, explanations, and facts and ends by stating the main idea. It inverts the pattern used in deduction, and thus, in an inductive paragraph, the topic sentence comes last. Sometimes you will want to withhold your final judgment to create interest, to build suspense, or to present a wide range of examples—leading readers along without specifying the direction in which you are taking them. This suspended approach to paragraph development is sometimes risky, but when well handled, induction can be very effective. Make sure, however, that all discussions are clearly focused and that the closing statement is, in fact, proved by the information or ideas that precede it in the paragraph.

This sample paragraph describing one feature of *Who's Afraid of Virginia Woolf?* has been arranged inductively to concentrate attention on the details of the play. Readers are presented first with a series of brief examples, building detail by detail to the topic sentence at the end of the paragraph.

<table>
<tr><td>detail 1</td><td>The scenes that begin and end Edward Albee's Who's Afraid of Virginia Woolf? include the two primary char-</td></tr>
<tr><td>detail 2</td><td>acters, George and Martha. The second scene and the next-to-the-last scene include George and Martha, plus the other couple involved in the dramatic action:</td></tr>
<tr><td>detail 3</td><td>Nick and Honey. In the middle scenes of the play, each character has a scene alone with each of the other characters. For instance, George has at least one</td></tr>
<tr><td>detail 4</td><td>separate scene with Nick, Honey, and Martha. In addition, each character has a solitary time on stage, pro-</td></tr>
<tr><td>topic sentence</td><td>viding an opportunity for isolated introspection. The amazing pattern in this network of scenes illustrates that Who's Afraid of Virginia Woolf? is an intricately structured and carefully balanced play.</td></tr>
</table>

In induction, readers are led through a discussion not knowing exactly where they are headed. One detail should build upon another, and by the time readers reach the topic sentence, they should know what the focus is. By suspending the topic sentence, a writer can emphasize details over generalizations.

EXERCISE □ *Deductive and Inductive Development*

Using two of the topic sentences you wrote earlier, write two paragraphs—one deductive and one inductive. Underline the topic sentence and number the details in the margin of the paper. Be ready to explain why you chose the pattern of development you did for each paragraph. (Use the examples on pages **65–66** and **67** as models.)

2e Allow your purpose and paragraphs to develop together.

As you begin writing, you will get a sense of how you want paragraphs to develop. You will have ideas or information to share, and certain patterns of presentation will seem natural to use: description, analogy, or classification, for instance. (See **2f–2k** for discussions of basic patterns of paragraph development.)

Although it is possible to identify a pattern of development and then select information to fit the pattern, such work is often awkward and unnatural. A better strategy is to complete some prewriting activities, decide on a general purpose for the whole paper, and then let the patterns of the paragraphs develop naturally.

For instance, a student might plan a paper on wood-burning stoves. If the general purpose were to recommend these stoves because they save on energy costs, a series of paragraphs might develop naturally. For an audience that is unfamiliar with such equipment, a student might need to define a wood-burning stove. To stress savings, the student might discuss the effects that using a wood-burning stove has on fuel bills. To explain these stoves to uninformed readers, the student might compare a wood-burning stove to a fireplace or a traditional furnace. To stress savings further, the student might use facts or examples to illustrate the main idea.

It is important for these decisions about paragraph development to be made during the process of writing. Then they will be natural extensions of the writer's larger purpose, rather than predetermined patterns into which material is forced.

2f Use descriptions to develop a topic sentence.

Sometimes a topic sentence will be developed best by descriptions, carefully worded explanations that help readers visualize examples. For readers to appreciate description, they often need clear details so that they can imagine what it would be like to be part of an event or situation. In such an instance, description will serve your purpose in writing.

topic sentence	**On the day before the wedding, all was chaos at Aunt Betty's house.** Presents, wrapped in pastel
detail 1	paper and decorated with satiny ribbons, were stacked on the television and on the stereo, were piled in chairs, and were scattered on the floor by the
detail 2	window. Paula's wedding dress and Ricky's and Bill's tuxedos were hanging in the doorway that led to
detail 3	the hall. Half-filled glasses, dried cheese, crumbled crackers, and overflowing ashtrays remained from an
detail 4	impromptu celebration the night before. Parked inside the dining room door was the vacuum cleaner, suggesting that someone had thought of cleaning up
detail 5	but clearly had not followed through. On the dining room table, thank-you cards, wrapping paper, tape,
summary	and scissors were scattered. Who would believe that from this chaos a beautiful bride and her family would emerge the next day?

2g Use an extended example to develop a topic sentence.

Sometimes a single, well-presented example will best develop a topic sentence. As general evidence, examples show readers, even if they do not agree with your final assessment, how you reached the conclusion you did. To be convincing, examples need to be representative and clear. Do not use extremely positive or negative ones, for they will seem exceptional rather than typical (see **4a**). In addition, present the example fully, answering as many of the following questions as apply: (1) Who was involved? (2) What was involved? (3) When did the event take place? (4) Where did it take place? (5) What was the sequence of events? (6) What were the important details? (7) How did people react? (8) Why did it occur? If you answer several of these questions and add any appropriate descriptions, an example will present one representative situation that will illustrate the topic sentence.

topic sentence	**I gained an early sense of responsibility because both of my parents worked.** When I was in the fifth
when?	grade, my mom returned to full-time work, and I was
who?	on my own. When I arrived home at 3:30, I had
what details?	simple chores to do. I had to change into my play clothes, feed and water the dogs, bring in the mail,
what was involved?	and put my schoolbooks in my room. Then, if my folks left a special message on the refrigerator—say, to set out some meat to thaw—I was expected to do that, too. Of course, I sometimes forgot to do some of
why?	these things, but I was very much aware that these were my chores to do before I went out to play. Had
summary	Mom and Dad been home to nag me into doing them, I doubt I would have developed the early sense of responsibility that I did.

2h Use facts to develop a topic sentence.

Sometimes a topic sentence will be developed best with supporting facts. Readers are naturally skeptical, but when factual information supports the idea in a paragraph, readers will see why you reached the conclusion you did. If you use facts that you gather yourself, no problems should arise. If, however, your facts come from other sources, document them according to accepted standards (see Logic, **4b,** and Notes, **54**).

topic sentence	**Our university has done too little to accommodate the handicapped students who go to school here.**
fact 1	Yes, all the sidewalks have ramp accesses, but during snowy weather these ramps are not cleared of snow.
fact 2 fact 3	Only one dormitory out of five is equipped with ramps, special restroom facilities, and elevators. In addition, parking lots A, B, and F—the lots used by most commuting students—have a total of only seven parking spots designated for handicapped drivers.
fact 4 summary	Two of these are located next to curbs, making movement around a car difficult. With these problems, how can we expect handicapped students to feel they are getting proper treatment?

EXERCISE □ *Descriptions, Examples, and Facts*

Write three paragraphs. Develop one using descriptions, one using examples, and one using facts. Be ready to explain why you chose the pattern of development you did. Here are some possible topic sentences.

1. Telephones often ring at awkward moments.

2. I know from personal experience that seat belts save lives.

3. _____ (name a restaurant) is efficiently operated.

4. Caring for an infant is time-consuming.

5. A crowded park is no place for a picnic.

6. Car-pooling is a good way to save money.

7. _____ (name a high-school teacher) was clearly organized.

8. _____'s (name someone) garden is a showplace.

9. Owning a horse is expensive.

10. _____ (name a magazine) offers a wide range of articles.

2i Use a paragraph of comparison and contrast to develop a topic sentence that suggests similarities or differences.

As you think about the main idea in a paragraph, you may discover similarities or differences that are useful to your discussion. To clarify those similarities or differences for your readers, present balanced explanations of your paired topics.

When writing a paragraph of comparison and contrast, choose one of two patterns of organization. One pattern is called *whole-to-whole development*, because one whole subject is discussed and then the other whole subject is discussed. This pattern, also called a *divided pattern*, stresses the two subjects rather than the qualities being compared.

topic sentence *People* **magazine and the** *National Enquirer* **differ notably in their use of photography.** *People,* for instance, uses lots of posed pictures by noted photographers like Francesco Scavullo. The photos show newsmakers at their best: made up, well dressed, prepared. *People* also uses a number of candid shots, but most seem less than candid. Instead, they look as if

People covered first

they were planned to "look candid." Because *People* is printed on high-quality paper, the photos give the magazine some class. The *Enquirer*, on the other hand, uses a limited number of posed photographs—none by any known photographers—and seems to relish surprise shots where newsmakers are "caught in the act"—whatever that is. The *Enquirer*'s candid shots look truly candid. We see stars with bags under their eyes and frazzled hair. The *Enquirer*'s photos, printed on newsprint, are grainy, often blurred, and of poor quality. Although *People* and *Enquirer* are both gossip magazines, their photographs give the two magazines very different images.

Enquirer covered second

summary

The other pattern for comparison and contrast is called *part-to-part* or *alternating pattern*. In this arrangement, the qualities being compared are most important, and the subjects are used as examples.

topic sentence

The arrangement of the periodical collection makes Monticello Public Library (MPL) an easier library to use than Southridge City Library (SCL). SCL houses a fine collection of magazines, journals, and newspapers, but they are located in small sections throughout the library. Current magazines are conveniently located on the main floor, but some periodicals are located on the second floor, and some are on a lower level. By comparison, all of MPL's periodicals are located on the first floor in one large area. At SCL the indexes to newspapers are found in the main reference room on the main floor, but the microfilm and microfiche collection and viewing equipment are located on the lower level, making the materials a problem to use. At MPL, however, newspaper indexes are in the periodical section, just a few steps away from the microfilm and microfiche collection and viewing

quality 1

quality 2

summary   equipment. Although the periodical collections at SCL and MPL are comparable, the convenient arrangement at MPL makes that collection much easier to use during research than the collection at SCL.

2j Use an extended analogy to develop a topic sentence.

A paragraph of analogy stresses similarities between two subjects, but it serves a different purpose than a comparison and contrast paragraph does. While the comparison and contrast paragraph explains similarities and differences between two subjects that are roughly equivalent, a paragraph of analogy explains similarities between two subjects that are seemingly unrelated. In addition, in paragraphs of analogy a known subject is compared with something unknown to clarify a special idea for readers.

When writing a paragraph of analogy, select your subjects carefully so that the connections you make are not too farfetched or mysterious. Use detailed descriptions and explanations to clarify the similarities you want to stress.

topic sentence **Trisha's behavior is rather like that of Goldilocks in the children's story.** She drops by, invited or not,
quality 1 and finds ingenious ways of getting inside, from locating our hidden key to telling our landlady that
quality 2 she's a cousin from Texas. She will eat anything she finds—from cake to deli meats—and offer comments like these: "This is too spicy," and "This is too salty."
quality 3 She is hard on furniture, too, having broken several spindles on a kitchen chair when she tipped it back-
quality 4 ward. In fact, she feels so much at home that during one of our late-night parties we found her "sleeping in our bed." Apparently she did not think it was too hard or too soft.

EXERCISE □ *Comparison and Contrast, and Analogy*

Write one paragraph that is developed using comparison and contrast and one using analogy. Remember that comparison and contrast can follow either whole-to-whole or part-to-part organization. Some possible topics follow.

Comparison and Contrast

1. *Sports Illustrated* and *Sport* both concentrate their attention on major spectator sports.

2. _____ and _____ (name two brands of ice cream) have comparable features.

3. "Night people" and "morning people" eat very different kinds of foods.

4. The effect of seeing a horror film on television is greatly different from that of seeing one at the theater.

5. _____ and _____ (name two people) have very different work habits.

Analogy

1. For _____ (name someone), getting ready for a date is like a religious ritual.

2. Going to see *Rocky Horror Picture Show* is like attending an initiation for a secret society.

3. Plants are like people.

4. Too much parental attention is like sleeping under three quilts.

5. Taking the SAT (or ACT) is like participating in a triathlon.

2k Use a paragraph of cause and effect to explain a sequence important to your topic sentence.

When an action results from other actions or circumstances, the most common way to explain the relationship is to present the causes in a clear series and then summarize the result. Remember that your readers may be unfamiliar with the situation you describe and will therefore need clear explanations to understand how the cause and effect relationship works. This paragraph describes a cause and effect relationship in clear chronological order:

lead sentence	In a sense, Alberto created his own problems. Several times each month, he chose to sleep late, missing his
cause 1	eight o'clock chemistry class. He seldom read assign-
cause 2	ments and took only scattered notes during lectures.
cause 3	During labs, Alberto actively participated, but he turned in few lab reports, and some of those were
cause 4	late. He did not review before exams, thinking that what he had learned in high school would be enough,
cause 5	and, when taking exams, he did not double-check his
effect: topic sentence	computations or his answers. **It came as no surprise to his classmates and friends, then, that Alberto failed Chemistry 101.**

2l Describe a process to develop a topic sentence.

A process paragraph outlines the series of steps required to complete an action. To guarantee that readers (who may be unfamiliar with the process) can follow your explanation, present the steps accurately and completely and describe any unusual procedures carefully.

topic sentence	**Balancing a checkbook is a simple but necessary process in keeping financial records.** When your
step 1	monthly statement arrives from the bank, arrange
step 2	your canceled checks in numerical order. Separate
step 3	any deposit, withdrawal, or bank-draft slips. Then work your way through your checkbook, noting
step 4	which checks have been canceled. Do the same for
step 5	deposits, withdrawals, and bank drafts. That done, use the form on the back side of the bank statement to record the numbers and amounts of checks that are still outstanding—that is, checks that have not been
step 6	cashed. After recording these, total the amount and subtract it from your current balance (listed on the
summary	front side of your statement). If your addition and subtraction have been accurate all month, your checking balance should match the result.

EXERCISE □ *Cause and Effect, and Process*

Write two paragraphs: one using cause and effect and one using process development. Here are some possible topic sentences.

Cause and Effect

1. _____ (name someone) decided not to attend college.

2. Consequently, _____ (name a store) closed.

3. It is obvious why _____ (name someone) was the best

   player on the _____ (name one) team.

4. It was no surprise, then, that _____ and _____
   (name a couple) got a divorce.

5. Clearly, _____'s (name someone) rudeness was dis-
   rupting the discussion.

Process

1. Starting a campfire is a simple procedure.

2. Completing a tax form—if you do not itemize—is not very
   difficult.

3. To prepare for a speech, proceed through orderly steps.

4. Changing the oil in a car is a fairly easy process.

5. If you are systematic, planning a vacation is easy.

2m Use a paragraph of classification to explain an important feature of a topic.

As a pattern of development, classification grows from our natural tendency to divide subjects into groups when we discuss them. These kinds of paragraphs are important for readers because they order information and distinguish among varied parts of a topic. A paragraph of classification will typically name the class to which a subject belongs and then divide that subject into its subgroups. The classification must follow the same principle for subdivision, creating roughly equivalent subgroups that do not overlap. A brief description of each subgroup is usually necessary to distinguish among them, and the descriptions must focus on the same aspects.

class under discussion

topic sentence	**There are four different kinds of nonsmokers, and their reactions to smokers are decidedly differ-**
subgroup 1	**ent.** *Laissez-faire* nonsmokers, the first group, have never smoked but have no particular feelings about people who do. They are not bothered by smoke and do not mind if people around them
subgroup 2	smoke. "It bothers me some" nonsmokers make up the second group. Their feelings about smoking are not terribly strong, but they would rather not be around people who smoke. They often stay near windows and doors, where they can comfortably
subgroup 3	breathe without creating a scene. The "I dislike smoke" nonsmokers constitute the third group. They are bothered by smoke and will firmly ask smokers to stop; they stand up for their rights but
subgroup 4	avoid showdowns. "Antismokers," the fourth kind of nonsmokers, are people sparked by a zeal to rid the world of one of its "greatest evils." Often ex-smokers with the commitment of converts, they post signs, hide ashtrays in meeting rooms, and use
summary	confrontational tactics. Although nonsmokers show different levels of enthusiasm in their opposition to smoking, a wise smoker will try not to light up in the presence of anyone who does not smoke.

2n Use a paragraph of definition to explain a key word or concept.

A paragraph of definition, somewhat like a dictionary definition, attempts to clarify the exact meaning of a word or concept that is important in understanding a paper. Such paragraphs should first place the subject in a class and then distinguish it from other items in the same class or describe its notable characteristics. Giving examples and using comparison and contrast are two common methods of explanation in these extended definitions.

topic sentence	**For the seven people in the United States who have not seen or heard of MTV (Music Television), let me explain what a music video is.** In the sim-
class	plest terms, a music video is a three-to-five minute
differ- entiation	film that interprets a song. Unlike the concert foot- age from years past, where television viewers simply watched a singer or group perform a song in concert,
charac- teristics: 1	music videos often use poetic, visual images to tell the story in a narrative song. Musicians dress in cos-
2	tumes (the more outlandish the better), travel to far- away locales (the more exotic the better), and act out
3	sequences that illustrate the meaning of a song's
4	lyrics. When possible, technical camera work and clever editing give music videos a novel look and
summary	often a frenetic pace. Music videos originated to allow those listening to songs to view performers, but now music videos have become a medium unto themselves—offering visual as well as auditory ex- citement.

EXERCISE □ *Classification and Definition*

Write one paragraph that uses classification as its method of development and one that uses definition. Some possible topic sentences follow.

Classification

1. Children in situation comedies can be divided into _____ categories.

2. There are _____ basic types of friends.

3. On the basis of dress, there are _____ kinds of college professors.

4. Baseball fans fall into _____ categories.

5. There are _____ basic kinds of calendars.

Definition

1. Stock-car racing is a specialized form of automotive competition.

2. A blind date is, of course, a date, but it is not like other dates.

3. Political cartoons are cartoons with a satiric purpose.

4. Pocket calculators are mechanical devices that do mathematical computations.

5. A household budget is a system for managing money.

2o Use transitional words and phrases to link details in paragraphs.

The information in a paragraph must fit together smoothly, no matter what pattern of development is used. Sometimes the sequence of details will be so closely linked that readers will move easily from one part of a paragraph to the next, clearly understanding the connections among ideas. Sometimes, however, readers need signals to show them how ideas are related.

The English language is rich in transitional words and phrases. Coordinating, subordinating, and correlative conjunctions are the most commonly used transitional words, but there are many others. Use them in sentences to connect ideas smoothly.

To Present Additions

also, and, besides, equally important, first, further, furthermore, in addition, moreover, next, second, too

To Present Similarities

also, in the same manner, likewise, moreover, similarly

To Present Differences

but, however, in contrast, nevertheless, on the contrary, on the other hand, still, yet

To Present Examples

for example, for instance, in fact, specifically, to illustrate

To Present Restatements or Summaries

finally, in brief, in conclusion, in other words, in short, in summary, on the whole, that is, therefore, to sum up

To Present a Result

accordingly, as a result, consequently, for this reason, so, then, therefore, thereupon, thus

To Present Chronological Relationships

after, afterward, before, during, earlier, finally, first, immediately, in the meantime, later, meanwhile, next, second, simultaneously, soon, then, third, when, while

To Present Location

above, below, beyond, close by, farther, here, in the distance, nearby, opposite, over there, there, to the left, to the right, under

Note: Many of these words and phrases are adverbial and often relate to whole sentences. When they do—especially when they begin sentences—they are normally set off by commas (see **31d** and **31f**).

The following paragraph makes use of a number of transitional words and phrases, each designated by boldface type. Notice how they emphasize the connections among ideas.

	Moving does not have to be a traumatic experience
chronology	if you plan properly. **First of all,** make arrangements with a moving company well in advance. Two to four weeks will usually be enough to re-
contrast	serve a moving date and to pack carefully, **but** you may need more time if your family is a busy one. Begin collecting boxes, cartons, and cases early, since many stores crush rather than keep boxes.
chronology	**Second,** clean the house to which you are moving
result	**so that** you will not have to move furniture and
addition	boxes in order to clean. **Besides,** who needs to be scouring sinks and tubs when pictures need to be
chronology	hung and closets arranged? **Third,** pack your belongings following some kind of logical plan. Pack
example	similar items together—**for instance,** dishes, glasses, and silverware—so that the later process of
similarity	unpacking will progress smoothly. **Similarly,** pack each individual's belongings together as much as
chronology	possible. **Fourth,** use index cards or slips of paper to identify where boxes should be deposited in the new house: front bedroom, middle bedroom,
example	dining room, kitchen, **for example.** Such labeling
result	will make unloading easier for movers and will, **as a result,** make the process quicker and less expensive than a disorganized move usually is. The four steps will not make moving trouble-free. They

contrast
summary

will, **however,** make your move less chaotic and
less traumatic. **In short,** careful planning makes
for easy moving.

2p Repeat key words, phrases, and sentence structures to link ideas in paragraphs.

To keep ideas flowing smoothly within a paragraph, consider selectively repeating some sentence elements. Although
needlessly repeating words sometimes makes writing wordy
(see Conciseness, **27**), controlled repetition gives key words
special emphasis and helps tie ideas together. Similarly, although excessive use of the same sentence structures creates
predictable, uninteresting writing (see Sentence Variety, **17–19**),
some consciously repeated structures can link similar ideas and
create balance. The key concepts here are *selective, controlled,*
and *conscious.* Remember, too, that careful repetition of sentence elements is an effective way to provide coherence and
unity within a paragraph or a paper.

Words and phrases

Words and phrases that create special meaning can be effectively repeated in paragraphs. However, consider using
variations of the key words or phrases, some synonyms (words
with the same meaning), and some pronouns to create variety
even as you repeat ideas. The following paragraph, for instance, repeats variations of words and phrases (all in boldface
type) to create emphasis:

Mirth is surely one of humanity's greatest gifts, for the ability to
laugh—to appreciate the pleasure or absurdity in daily activities
—allows people to keep problems in perspective. Children are
natural **laughers.** In situations, both appropriate and inappropri-

ate, the **giggles, snickers, chuckles,** and outright **guffaws** of children can emphasize their innocence, their joyful ignorance of the problems of the world. **Levity** among adults is, unfortunately, far less common, but **it** is equally welcome. How wonderful are the adults who can react to potentially frustrating situations—a collapsed tent, a split seam in a pair of pants, a surprise guest—and see the sheer **absurdity** of their attempts to maintain absolute control. **Laughter** expresses pleasure, eases tension, and lifts the spirit. **It** is a gift we should all share more often.

Sentence structures

Repeating sentence structures also creates unity within a paragraph by presenting similar ideas in similar ways. Again, selectivity is the key, for if you strive for variety in most sentence structures, then consciously repeated patterns will stand out. The following paragraph uses repeated sentence structures (all in boldface type) to concentrate attention on similar activities.

My family never seemed more unified, more full of purpose than we did before the flood two summers ago. Dad had heard on the radio that a dam had collapsed upstream and that flooding in our area seemed certain. He **immediately called us all together, frankly explained the situation, and quickly sent us to complete our assigned tasks.** We knew from the solemn expression on his face that the situation was threatening, so we quickly began. **Jerrid released the cows** from the barn **and herded them** into the east pasture, where they could move up the sloping hills to escape the flood waters. **Angela and Ricky removed the rabbits** from their hutches next to the shed **and carried them,** in small cages, to the loft of the barn. **Walt drove the tractor** to the crest of the hill **and parked it** where it would be safe. **Mom and I gathered together what valuables we could**—some clothes, family pictures, Mom's wedding silver, Dad's best rifle, the kids' favorite stuffed toys, the quilt my grandmother made—**and loaded them** into the car and truck. **We met** again with our most important tasks completed, **climbed** into the car and truck, **and drove** up County Road 63 to escape from the torrent that was to devastate our land and home.

EXERCISE □ *Transitions and Repeated Sentence Elements*

Using one of your paragraphs, revise it to make effective use of transitions and of repeated words, phrases, and sentence structures.

3 Writing the Essay Exam

Essay questions on exams are a standard part of educational life. Yet many students have not developed effective strategies for preparing for them and writing them. The first step in preparing to write an essay question on an exam is to study. Read or reread the course materials—books, articles, or classroom notes. Review and learn the important concepts of the course and memorize any specific information that will help you explain major topics. This work is best done over a period of days or weeks, since "cramming" for an exam does not always allow you to formulate the ideas that will be the basis of your essay.

If you have studied sufficiently, you will know the course materials well. The second step is to follow certain strategies for writing essays on exams, which will help you demonstrate just how much you know.

3a Consider the point value of each question.

To make the best use of your exam time, consider how many minutes you should devote to a question. For instance, if a question is worth ten points out of a possible one hundred, you should devote no more than 10 percent of the total exam time to your response. To give the response more time and energy than that may leave you short on other portions of the exam—and still get you no more than ten points. On the other hand, if a question is worth fifty points (of one hundred), you should give it approximately half your exam time in order to produce a detailed response.

3b Consider the number of essay questions you must respond to.

If you must respond to two or more essay questions, pacing becomes very important. Quickly decide how much time each question deserves and write quickly so that you can respond to each one. An extended response to one question (ten points) and a brief, superficial response to another one (ten points) may yield only fifteen points, whereas more balanced discussions of both questions will probably yield more points.

3c Consider your choices of questions.

Instructors will often provide a choice of questions: for instance, three questions for which you must give two responses. With such an option, you will use your writing time most efficiently if you jot down a topic outline for each choice, to see how substantial your responses can be. The few moments you spend in outlining will help you avoid questions that you cannot respond to fully. False starts on unworkable responses take up valuable minutes, so do some quick planning to avoid wasting time.

3d Read each question carefully.

Instructors often are looking for specific information in responses to essay questions, so you must supply it. Many essay questions provide the implied topic sentence (or thesis statement if the response is to be long). To write a correctly focused essay, you must develop the idea presented in the question. Open-ended essay questions allow a good deal more freedom and flexibility, but you must still read the question carefully to write about the topic properly.

3e Consider your instructor's expectations regarding style, punctuation, and mechanics.

If your instructor feels that responses to exam questions must be grammatically correct, well worded, and free from errors in punctuation and mechanics, then you must account for those expectations as you write. Either you will have to write slowly enough to make sure your writing is clear, complete, and free from errors, or you will need to allow time to make corrections and revisions after you have finished your answer. Whichever approach you choose, remember that pacing yourself is crucial to writing effective responses.

3f Remember that an answer to an essay question should be organized like any other good writing.

Once you have considered the basic questions, thought about your responses, and considered the time each question deserves, you are ready to begin writing. Remember, first of all, that an essay answer on a test is like a paper, even though it is brief. As such, it should include the basic elements of a full-length paper: introduction, body, conclusion. The amount of development each part requires depends on the point value of the question. A ten-point essay will require only minimal detail, whereas a fifty-point essay will require substantial expansion. The basic structure of both responses will be identical, however.

3g Consider these sample responses to the same essay question.

To illustrate the similar structure but dissimilar development of essay responses with different point values, look at the paired samples below.

Question: What are the four speech-making strategies and how are they different?

Ten-Point Response

introductory sentence	Four basic kinds of speech-making strategies exist. Impromptu speeches are presented "on the
strategy 1	spur of the moment," without time to organize or
strategy 2	rehearse. Extemporaneous speeches are organized in outline form but are not written word for
strategy 3	word. Manuscript speeches are written in advance and then read from a written or typed
strategy 4	copy. Memorized speeches are written well in advance and then learned word for word, to be
summary sentence	presented without a written copy. These four strategies allow speakers to suit their presentations to their speaking situations.

Fifty-Point Response

introductory sentence	Situations for speech making vary, and speakers, as a result, choose among four different speech-making strategies to present their ideas most ef-
strategy 1	fectively. Impromptu speeches are given "on the spur of the moment," without a chance to orga-

nize or rehearse. These highly informal speeches are often unfocused (because of no planning) and ineffective (because of no practice), but they are the normal kinds of speeches given at organiza-

strategy 2   tion meetings and in class discussions. Extemporaneous speeches are given from prepared outlines, but they are not completely written. Rather, speakers decide what they will discuss, what details or examples to use, and then choose words as they speak. Extemporaneous speeches have the advantage of being organized but at the same time flexible, allowing speakers to modify exactly what they say to suit the needs of their audiences. For this reason, they are often the most

strategy 3   effective speeches at informal meetings. Manuscript speeches are written in complete form and then read, much like a newscast. Because they are prepared in advance, manuscript speeches are well organized and carefully worded. If they are also well rehearsed, manuscript speeches are effective in formal speaking situations because they use an exact, well-worded version of the speaker's

strategy 4   ideas. Memorized speeches are written in complete form and then committed to memory. Because they are carefully prepared, they often present solid content, but few speakers can memorize a lengthy speech and deliver it well. In addition, memorized speeches are not flexible and seem to work only in highly formal circumstances,

summary   like awards ceremonies and formal banquets. Be-
sentence   cause of the differences among these four kinds of speech-making strategies—in organization, presentation, and flexibility—they provide speakers with a number of ways to share ideas with audiences.

3h Practice timed writing.

In the last few days before you write an essay exam, practice writing under time pressure. Using your notes from class, write some sample essay questions. Then set a timer (or alarm clock) and write a series of responses. At first you may need a longer period to respond to a question than the exam will allow, but keep trying to reduce the time by minutes until it approximates the limit you will have during the exam. This kind of practice will quicken your writing pace while helping you review materials for the exam.

4 Logical Thinking

Logic is a system of orderly and reliable reasoning. To write logical papers, you must fairly and systematically present examples and evidence to support ideas. In addition, you must avoid a number of typical errors in logical thinking. Known as *logical fallacies,* these errors most often result from inappropriate or irrelevant connections between actions or ideas.

Some writers deliberately distort their reasoning to manipulate evidence and mislead readers, but most often, illogical evidence and logical fallacies appear in writing by accident. They are the result of careless thinking. Such errors in logic are not crimes by any stretch of the imagination, but they are serious flaws in papers because they undercut what may be otherwise strong arguments.

4a Select representative examples.

When you use an example to support the idea of a paragraph, you must choose that example carefully to maintain the logic of your writing. That means you must avoid using instances that are out of the ordinary.

Extremely positive examples

An extremely positive example will not convince readers of the validity of your point because they will see—if they analyze your writing carefully—that an isolated, glowing instance will not usually apply. Consider, let us say, a paragraph suggesting that state lotteries benefit individuals (part of a whole paper on the advantages of lotteries). Citing a person who won five million dollars will not be convincing because millions of people who buy lottery tickets will end up losing money. The five-million-dollar winner is therefore a very notable exception that will not prove the general point of the paragraph.

Extremely negative examples

An extremely negative example will be equally unconvincing because such situations do not address actual prevailing circumstances. In a paper on the negative effects of television viewing on children, a striking instance would be that a boy in Arizona watched superhero cartoons on television, thought he could fly, and jumped from the roof of his house and broke his back. However, this isolated example hardly represents the average experiences of normal children. It will not be very convincing.

Specifics provide excellent support for the ideas in a paper, but the illustrations must be representative to be convincing. Rarities, either positive or negative, will seem exceptions to general rules and will not bolster the logical development of a paper (see also Paragraphs, **2e**).

4b Select information for accuracy, evaluating the dependability of your sources.

Often you will need to use facts, figures, or other technical data to support the ideas in a paper. When possible, gather such information yourself rather than depending on second-hand information. Call or talk to a few knowledgeable people and take notes to guarantee precision. Consider, as well, the expertise of your source. Is the person qualified to offer information? For instance, in supporting a paper on the rising costs of child care, you would probably want to include some specific prices. Calling several reputable child care centers would yield some useful information. Talking to some parents might also be helpful, but you would need to make sure that their figures were accurate and recent. A neighbor's guess about child-care costs ten years ago would not supply the detailed information needed to make your discussion logical and complete (see also **54**).

4c Acknowledge opposing views.

A paper (and its supporting discussions, examples, and facts) will present your opinion on a subject. Yet you must acknowledge that your view will certainly not be shared by everyone. That awareness will allow you to discuss opposing views briefly, demonstrating for readers that you have considered all sides of an issue. You need not exhaustively explain conflicting points of view, but qualifying your thesis statement in a paper (see **1e**) and using qualifying words and phrases in the body of the paper will show readers how sensibly and logically you have approached the topic.

4d Avoid logical fallacies.

Hasty generalization

Generalizing from too little evidence often produces a *hasty generalization*. This fallacy, which is similar to using extreme examples (see **4a**), suggests that a writer has reached a conclusion too quickly, without thoroughly investigating an issue.

> The Bedderman Street Housing Project cost hundreds of thousands of dollars and is now a shambles. Federally subsidized housing is a waste of taxpayers' money. *(One failed housing project is not enough evidence to suggest that the whole subsidizing system has failed. A larger sampling is necessary to justify this sweeping generalization.)*

> A DC-10 crashed as it took off from O'Hare. These planes are unsafe. *(To generalize that all DC-10's are unsafe, you would have to examine the safety records of many, not just one.)*

Be especially careful not to generalize on the basis of a single example—the most common logical error that produces a hasty generalization.

Oversimplification

An *oversimplification*, a logical fallacy similar to hasty generalization, is a conclusion based on limited evidence. Usually, an oversimplification ignores subtle variations and exceptions.

> Recent elections in our district have proved that the candidate who spends the most money wins. *(This statement ignores the complexity of the campaign process. Candidates who win may, in fact, spend the most money, but the money must be spent wisely. Spending money foolishly probably would not get someone elected.)*

> The influx of foreign cars almost destroyed the American automobile industry. *(Be fair. Imported cars caused some of the problems for*

the industry, but so did high prices, car size and design, dated technol-
ogy, poor gas mileage, and other matters.)

Carefully note all sides of an issue before reaching a conclusion and remember that if we consider them thoroughly, we
find most issues are complicated.

The *either/or* fallacy

The *either/or fallacy* suggests that only two choices exist
when, in fact, there are many more. This thinking is not only
illogical but also unfair.

You should either give me a new lawnmower to replace my defective one or refund my money. *(This statement ignores the possibility of repairing the defective lawnmower.)*

Sometimes writers unconsciously—and consciously, too—
try to manipulate readers with the *either/or* fallacy. They
present the alternative they approve of in positive terms and
then present the most extreme alternative in negative terms.

For the sake of learning, we must maintain the firmest kind of discipline, including corporal punishment, in our public schools, or
we can expect chaos, disorder, and the disintegration of education
as we know it. *(The two alternatives presented are extremes, at once
ignoring moderate methods of maintaining discipline and also implying that without firm discipline the worst will happen. This technique is highly manipulative.)*

Begging the question

Frequently used to slant an issue, *begging the question* is a
form of circular reasoning. When writers beg the question,
they include in their discussions an idea that requires proof but
offer none. Instead they present the idea as if it is an agreed-

upon belief, a foregone conclusion that needs no elaboration or explanation. In doing so, writers undercut their credibility because they imply a more absolute understanding of a subject than they demonstrate in their discussions.

Since Senator Hillard is a pawn of major corporations, we can expect him to support their interests instead of ours. *(This writer provides no evidence that Hillard is controlled by corporations. The statement misleads readers by stressing an assumed—but unproved—affiliation and then merely restating it in a different way.)*

Sometimes begging the question is much subtler, embedded in a statement through word choice.

The antiwar demonstrators of the 1970's should be remembered as the cowards that they were. *(The choice of the word* cowards *defines the group—without making any attempt to prove that protesting is cowardly.)*

Fallacies of association

Fallacies of association suggest that ideas or actions are acceptable or unacceptable depending on the people associated with them. Such a fallacy ignores that ideas or actions should be evaluated on their own merits.

The hijackers were Lebanese, so obviously the Lebanese people support terrorism. *(The sentence links all people in Lebanon with a small group of terrorists. Such reasoning ignores the fact that terrorists often act on their own and do not necessarily represent a country's people.)*

Many advertising campaigns are based on fallacies of association. Avoid such questionable strategies in your own writing.

If Pennzoil products are good enough for Arnold Palmer, they must be good enough for you. *(Palmer is paid to endorse Pennzoil products. The quality may be good, but Palmer's endorsement does not make it so.)*

Non sequiturs

A *non sequitur*, simply translated as "it does not follow," is a conclusion that is not the logical result of the statements that precede it.

Cynthia Gregory is so beautiful. She is a great ballerina. *(Gregory's greatness as a dancer is based on interpretation, skill, and execution. Her beauty is not necessarily related to her dancing ability.)*

The decor of Les Saisons is exquisite, and the food is expensive. It is a great place to eat. *(Decorations and price do not necessarily equal good food.)*

Post hoc reasoning

Post hoc reasoning is named for a Latin phrase—*post hoc ergo propter hoc*—which translates as "after this, therefore because of this." *Post hoc* reasoning establishes a cause and effect relationship between two actions when, in fact, one action simply preceded the other.

Since Charles Braddock became mayor, housing prices have risen in our town. *(Although Braddock became mayor first, and then prices rose, the statement shows no necessary connection between the events.)*

A cause *must* come before an effect, but not everything that occurs before is a cause. To insure that you do not incorporate *post hoc* reasoning in your discussions of causes and effects, make sure that the effects you note can be clearly and systematically linked to the causes you identify.

Ad hominem reasoning

Ad hominem reasoning occurs when writers attack the people involved in an issue rather than the issue itself (*ad hominem* translates as "to the man"). By shifting the focus from the idea to the people, writers fail to address the attributes of what they are arguing against.

> Universities should not grant honorary degrees. After all, Ernest Hallirun, who received a degree from Lawrence Institute, is supposed to be linked to organized crime. *(The main issue should not be Hallirun but rather honorary degrees; the mention of Hallirun inappropriately sidetracks the discussion and fails to make any case against the degrees themselves.)*

False analogies

A *false analogy* is a comparison that is not built upon relevant points of similarity. For an analogy to work, the subjects must be similar in at least a few key ways. False analogies are made without establishing sufficient similarities.

> If eighteen-year-olds are old enough to get married, vote, and serve in the military, they are old enough to drink alcohol. *(This analogy suggests that activities performed when under complete control somehow have a bearing on an activity that often results in lack of control. The comparison is based on strained similarities.)*

EXERCISE ☐ *Logical Fallacies*

Explain why the following sentences are logically fallacious.

1. Jane Fonda's exercise tapes are not useful for most people.

   After all, she opposed America's involvement in Viet Nam.

2. Lots of wealthy and famous people have an American Express card, so that must be the best credit card to have.

3. I saw a woman at the store use food stamps to buy steaks, artichokes, and hand-packed ice cream. Food stamps allow the unemployed to eat very well.

4. Marilyn's grades improved after her vacation in France.

5. You bought a new suit for your interview, so I ought to be able to buy some new dishes.

6. To make a good grade in Professor Bakerman's class, all you have to do is attend class regularly and turn papers in on time.

7. We must imprison industrial spies or expect all our technological secrets to end up in the hands of the Russians.

8. Atlanta is the home of the Braves and the Turner Broadcasting System. It is a great place to raise a family.

9. If an actor lives long enough, he is sure to win an Academy Award.

10. Since smoking marijuana is immoral, we should punish anyone caught using it.

GRAMMAR

Chess, elections, basketball, driving in traffic, pinochle, and writing have at least one thing in common: all depend on generally accepted rules. True, you can modify the rules to suit individual preferences if you wish. When you do so, however, you violate the assumptions that give meaning to such activities, and confusion, or worse, often follows. In writing, grammatical principles supply important standards: establishing principles for word use, sentence formation, and punctuation. To communicate effectively with those who know the rules, a writer must understand and apply the guidelines properly.

5 Parts of Speech

The discussions and exercises in this section of the handbook concentrate on parts of speech: nouns, pronouns, verbs, adjectives, adverbs, conjunctions, prepositions, and interjections. Being able to identify words by type is useful, but it is not an end in itself. The ultimate aim is to understand how words work together in sentences, which will help you analyze your writing, identify grammatical inconsistencies, and correct any errors.

One small but important note before beginning the discussions of parts of speech: the same words can be used in different ways in different sentence contexts, and you must identify parts of speech based on how words function in sentences. For instance, *stain* is used in three different ways in the following sentences and is, consequently, labeled differently.

noun
The oriental carpet in the foyer had a large **stain** in the center, the result of an accident long since forgotten.

verb
Grape juice will **stain** skin, fabric, wood, porous floor coverings—almost anything it touches.

Many common household products—like milk, baking soda, and
vinegar—are effective **stain** *adj.* removers.

When analyzing parts of speech, keep this principle in mind.

5a Nouns

Nouns are words that name people, places, things, ideas,
qualities, and conditions.

Almost anything that needs a name can be labeled with a
noun. Proper, common, collective, abstract, and concrete
nouns are all usefully incorporated in writing.

Proper nouns name specific people, places, and things.
They are always capitalized: *Julia Child, Stockholm, Corvette.*

Roger lost his **Minolta X700** while vacationing in **Spain.**

Common nouns name people, places, and things by general
type, rather than by specific name. They are not capitalized:
chef, city, car.

My **friend** lost his 35 millimeter **camera** while vacationing in
Spain.

Collective nouns name groups of people or things: *team,
class, group, audience.* Although each group includes a number
of members, it is still *one* set. Collective nouns, as a result, are
usually singular (see Agreement, **10e, 10f, 11d, 11e**).

The **congregation** at St. Mary's has raised four thousand dollars
for the **hungry** in Africa.

Abstract nouns name ideas, qualities, and conditions: *freedom, honesty, shyness.* This is a more specific class of common
nouns.

Concrete nouns name things that can be understood through the senses: *chair, warmth, salt, noise*. This, too, is a more specific way to classify common nouns.

5b Pronouns

Pronouns are words that substitute for nouns.

Generally, each pronoun must refer to a previously stated noun, called an *antecedent*. The following sentences use no pronouns.

> The workmen John hired dropped John's desk while moving furniture into the apartment. The workmen filed a damage report. The report required John's signature.

With so many repeated nouns, the sentences seem choppy. The style improves considerably when the pronouns *his, they,* and *that* substitute for *John's, workmen,* and *report* (the antecedents).

> The workmen John hired dropped **his** desk while moving furniture into the apartment. **They** filed a damage report **that** required **his** signature.

Pronouns come in several forms: personal, possessive, reflexive, interrogative, demonstrative, indefinite, and relative. To select the appropriate pronoun, analyze how the pronoun will function in its sentence (see also Pronoun Case, **12**).

Personal pronouns refer to people or things. Their form depends on whether they are singular or plural: *I, me, you, he, him, she, her, it* (all singular) and *we, us, you, they, them* (all plural).

> The gaucho saw the stray steers just ahead, so **he** readied the bola. (He *is the pronoun;* gaucho *is the antecedent.*)

Possessive pronouns show ownership: *my/mine, your/yours, his, her/hers, its* (all singular) and *our/ours, your/yours, their/theirs* (all plural). Use the first form of each pair with a noun, but use the second form if the pronoun stands alone.

Matt, **your** solution is too idealistic. (Your *works with the noun so-lution.*)

Sharon, **yours** is very practical. (Yours *stands alone.*)

Several possessive pronouns—*my, his, her, its, our, your, their*—also function as adjectives. Because they modify nouns, even though they are pronouns, they are often called *pronoun-adjectives* to explain this dual role. There are other pronoun-adjectives as well (see Indefinite Pronouns, **5b**).

The textbook on the desk is **mine. Your** book is on the chair next to the door. (Mine, *the pronoun, stands alone, substituting for my textbook; your, a pronoun-adjective, modifies book and refers to the unidentified owner.*)

Reflexive pronouns work with nouns or personal pronouns. They show that someone or something in the sentence is acting for itself or on itself. Reflexive pronouns may also be used to show emphasis and in such cases are sometimes called *intensive pronouns.* The singular reflexive pronouns are *myself, yourself, himself, herself,* and *itself.* The plural ones are *ourselves, yourselves,* and *themselves.*

To Show Self-Related Action

Lydia and Hans cooked **themselves** a rib roast for every wedding anniversary. (Themselves *emphasizes that Lydia and Hans cooked for their own celebration.*)

To Add Emphasis

After everyone left for the concert, poor Vic had to clean the apartment **himself.** (Himself *stresses that Vic had no help.*)

Because reflexive pronouns must refer to words within the same sentence, they should not be used as subjects or as direct objects in sentences.

John and ~~myself~~ ^I renovated the cabin. (Myself *had no antecedent in the sentence.*)

Will you give your allegiance to Teresa or ~~myself~~ ^{me}? (Myself *had no antecedent in the sentence.*)

Interrogative pronouns are used to ask questions: *who, whom, whoever, whomever, what, which, whose.*

Demonstrative pronouns identify or point out nouns and can act as subjects or objects: *this, these, that,* and *those.* When these words are used with nouns, they are demonstrative adjectives. If the antecedent for a demonstrative pronoun is unclear, consider using a demonstrative adjective and the noun (see Pronoun Reference, **24a** and **24b**).

Vonin shifted her attention and began to sing to the children. That *activity* helped her control her emotions. (*Did that refer to shifting attention or singing?*)

Indefinite pronouns have no particular antecedents. Instead, they serve as general subjects or objects in sentences and present general statements. Use them carefully, because some are singular and some are plural. In addition, choose a verb form—singular or plural—that agrees with an indefinite pronoun (see Agreement, **11c**). Here are some indefinite pronouns:

all	anyone	everybody	many
another	both	everyone	neither
any	each	everything	nobody
anybody	either	few	none

106

| no one | several | somebody |
| one | some | someone |

When used alone, these words are clearly pronouns, but some of them usually modify nouns, and others may be used in possessive form to modify nouns. When they modify nouns, they clearly serve as *pronoun-adjectives* (see Possessive pronouns, page 105).

> **Any** time is the right time. *(pronoun used as an adjective to modify* time)
>
> **Somebody's** key has broken off in the mailroom door. *(pronoun used as adjective to modify* key)

Relative pronouns, substituting for a noun already mentioned in the sentence, introduce adjective or noun clauses (see Clauses, **6e,** pages 154–155). Relative pronouns allow writers to place closely related ideas within a sentence and to emphasize connections between ideas. Sometimes the relative pronoun *that* may be left out (understood) in a sentence where the noun-clause relationship is clear without it. The relative pronouns are *that, what, which, who, whom, whoever, whomever,* and *whose.* As a general rule, use *that* to introduce essential information. Use *which* when the information is nonessential (see Commas, **31h**).

Who, whom, whoever, whomever, and *whose* refer to people. *What* and *which* refer to things. *That* and *whose* can refer to people or things, but *that* most often refers to things, and *whose* most often refers to people.

> Novelists **who** achieve quick notoriety often lose favor quickly too.
>
> Anger **that** is not expressed is often the most damaging.
>
> People **whose** children attend private schools pay for education twice—through taxes and through tuition.

EXERCISE □ *Nouns and Pronouns*

Locate the nouns and pronouns in the following sentences and identify what kind each is. When they appear, also circle antecedents.

1. The Economics Department, located in Clemson Hall, is installing computers for students, so everyone in the supply-side course will have to go through some training.

2. The two boys in the courtyard fought viciously over the wallet. The taller boy growled that it was his, but the smaller boy clutched it firmly.

3. The Democrats and the Republicans blame each other for the budget deficit. Whom are we to believe?

4. Possessed by his vengefulness, Ahab treated his crew with contempt.

5. Chinese is a difficult language to learn because it is based on inflection as well as word form.

6. Bitterness dominates the work of Jonathan Swift.

EXERCISE □ *Nouns and Pronouns*

The following paragraph contains a wide variety of nouns and pronouns. Underline all nouns and pronouns.

It is all too clear that Jason is an elitist when it comes to the food he buys for himself. He would shudder if a generic product accidentally found its way into his shopping cart, and I think he'd rather starve than buy off-brands. If Jason wants canned green beans, he buys Del Monte, the blue lake variety. Or he might buy Green Giant frozen vegetables. But no one will ever find him buying Flavo-rite, Kroger, or IGA beans, let alone those that come in a can with a white and black label that reads simply "BEANS." Even with snacks, Jason's selectivity is clear. Lay's is his only brand of potato chip. No Snack-o chips, even those for dip, will ever reach his cabinets or snack bowls. Those off-brands simply do not have the consistent quality Jason demands. His preference for major brands is a source of amusement for his friends, and they often mockingly ask, "Who does he think he is, the Prince of Wales?" Jason serenely replies, paraphrasing the L'Oréal ad, "Name brands cost a little more, but I'm worth it."

5c Verbs

Verbs are words that express action (*squeeze* or *sing*) or state of being (*seem* or *was*).

Careful verb choices are critical for good writing because verbs establish the action or motivation expressed by a group of words. In addition, grammatically complete sentences must contain at least one verb (see Parts of Sentences, **6b,** and Fragments, **8b**).

Types of verbs

Verbs are classified by three basic types: action, linking, and auxiliary.

Action verbs express both physical and mental action.

> *action*
> *verb*
> Angela **parked** her car on a designated snow route. A wrecker
> *action*
> *verb*
> **towed** it away during the night.

> *action*
> *verb*
> Angela **expected** the snow to stop.

Action verbs are further classified as intransitive or transitive, depending on whether they require direct objects. A direct object is a person or thing that receives the action of the verb (has something done to it). Direct objects answer the question *what?* or *whom?*

Intransitive verbs do not require direct objects to complete their meaning.

> *subj.* *intrans.*
> *verb*
> The negative ad **campaign backfired.** *(Without a direct object, the sentence is still clear.)*

> *subj* *intrans.*
> *verb*
> After two attempts to jump the hurdle, **Enrico succeeded.**

110

Transitive verbs require direct objects to complete their meaning.

trans.
subj. verb d.o.
At last, **I earned** his **respect.** (*Without the direct object* respect, *the meaning would be unclear.*)

trans.
subj. verb d. o.
Leonardo da Vinci painted his **murals** on wet plastered walls. (*Without the direct object* murals, *the meaning would be unclear.*)

Linking verbs express either a state of being or a condition. *To be* verbs (*am, are, is, was,* and *were,* to name a few) are the most commonly used linking verbs. (*To be* verbs also act as auxiliary verbs, discussed next.) A small group of additional verbs can also function as linking verbs: *appear, become, feel, grow, look, make, seem, smell, sound, taste,* and some others. Linking verbs join the subject of the sentence or clause with a complement (either a predicate noun or a predicate adjective; see **6c,** page 141). Often a linking verb creates the equivalent of an equals sign.

With Predicate Nouns

linking
verb
Rachel **is** the best player on the volleyball team. (Rachel [*subject*] = player. *The predicate noun further identifies Rachel.*)

Note: In many cases, the subject and the predicate noun match so exactly that the sentence elements can be reversed without altering the sentence's meaning.

The best player on the volleyball team is Rachel.

With Predicate Adjectives

linking
verb
Woodrow Wilson **was** enthusiastic about the League of Nations.

(Woodrow Wilson [*subject*] = enthusiastic [person]. *The predicate adjective describes Wilson.*)

Auxiliary verbs, also known as *helping verbs,* are used with main verbs to form *verb phrases.* (*Verb phrases* are groups of words that together express an action or state of being). We commonly use verb phrases to clarify time references, to explain states of being, or to establish patterns for questions.

Some of the most commonly used auxiliary verbs are forms of *to be: am, is, are, was, were, been, being.* Other common auxiliary verbs include *will, do, did, may, might, must, could, should,* and *would.*

verb phrase
aux. verb
Ophelia **will enter** from stage right.

verb phrase
aux verb
Carla's pigs **have uprooted** every plant in the garden.

Verb phrases can be separated by modifiers or can be restructured to form questions. Auxiliary verbs, however, always appear before main verbs.

┌ verb phrase ┐
aux.   v.
Ophelia **will** probably **enter** from stage right.

┌ verb phrase ┐
aux.   v.
Have Carla's pigs **uprooted** every vegetable in the garden?

EXERCISE □ *Verbs*

Insert verbs in the blanks in the following sentences. Identify all your verbs as action, linking, or auxiliary.

Example
aux.

___Does___   Richard honestly expect to receive a scholarship?

1. The Kennedy Center program, "Honors for Lifetime Achievement," _____ over thirty performers.

2. *The Maltese Falcon* _____ a first-rate film.

3. Lea _____ been a first-rate pianist, but she broke two fingers on her left hand.

4. The EPA _____ long neglected chemical dumps.

5. Has blindness _____ the music of Ray Charles or Stevie Wonder?

Forms of verbs

Verbs have four principal forms: infinitives, present participles, past-tense forms, and past participles. *Infinitives* are a verb's primary form. (They often appear with *to*.) Present participles are formed by adding *-ing* to the infinitive. Changes in the past forms of verbs are complicated by the existence of *regular verbs* and *irregular verbs*.

Regular verbs are verbs that form the past tense and past participles consistently. *Past-tense forms* of regular verbs are made by adding *-d* or *-ed* to the infinitive. *Past participles* of regular verbs, in most instances, are the same as the past form. Most verbs in English are regular verbs.

Infinitive	Present Participle	Past Form	Past Participle
select	selecting	selected	selected
inform	informing	informed	informed
cook	cooking	cooked	cooked

Irregular verbs are verbs that form the past tense and past participles in a variety of ways. Because they follow so many

patterns of transformation, irregular verbs are sometimes difficult to use in their past forms. The best approach is to become
familiar with the following irregular verbs:

Infinitive	Past Form	Past Participle
arise	arose	arisen
awake	awoke, awakened	awakened, awoken
be	was/were	been
beat	beat	beaten, beat
begin	began	begun
bend	bent	bent
bite	bit	bitten
blow	blew	blown
break	broke	broken
bring	brought	brought
build	built	built
burst	burst	burst
catch	caught	caught
choose	chose	chosen
come	came	come
cost	cost	cost
creep	crept	crept
deal	dealt	dealt
dig	dug	dug
dive	dived, dove	dived
do	did	done
drag	dragged	dragged
draw	drew	drawn
dream	dreamed, dreamt	dreamed, dreamt
drink	drank	drunk
drive	drove	driven
drown	drowned	drowned
eat	ate	eaten

Infinitive	Past Form	Past Participle
fall	fell	fallen
fight	fought	fought
find	found	found
fly	flew	flown
forbid	forbade, forbad	forbidden
forget	forgot	forgotten, forgot
freeze	froze	frozen
get	got	got, gotten
give	gave	given
go	went	gone
grow	grew	grown
hang	hung	hung
hang (execute)	hanged	hanged
have	had	had
hear	heard	heard
hurt	hurt	hurt
keep	kept	kept
know	knew	known
lay (put)	laid	laid
lead	led	led
lend	lent	lent
let	let	let
lie (recline)	lay	lain
lie (tell untruth)	lied	lied
lose	lost	lost
make	made	made
read	read	read
ride	rode	ridden
ring	rang	rung
rise	rose	risen
run	ran	run
say	said	said

Infinitive	Past Form	Past Participle
see	saw	seen
send	sent	sent
set (put)	set	set
shake	shook	shaken
shine	shone, shined	shone, shined
shoot	shot	shot
shrink	shrank, shrunk	shrunk, shrunken
sing	sang	sung
sink	sank	sunk
sit (take a seat)	sat	sat
slay	slew	slain
sleep	slept	slept
speak	spoke	spoken
spin	spun	spun
spring	sprang	sprung
stand	stood	stood
steal	stole	stolen
sting	stung	stung
strike	struck	struck, stricken
swear	swore	sworn
swim	swam	swum
swing	swung	swung
take	took	taken
teach	taught	taught
tear	tore	torn
throw	threw	thrown
wake (to be awake)	woke, waked	waked, woken
waken (to rouse)	wakened	wakened
wear	wore	worn
wring	wrung	wrung
write	wrote	written

Verb tenses

Verb tenses place the situation described in a time frame, with the moment of writing (or speaking) as the present, and with events occurring at some point in the past, at the time of writing, or at some point in the future. English has six basic tenses: present, past, future, present perfect, past perfect, and future perfect.

Present tense indicates that something is occurring at the present time or that the subject habitually performs an action.

The plums **are** ripe.

Marla **plays** the viola.

Past tense indicates that something has already occurred and is now past. The past tense of regular verbs is formed by adding *-d* or *-ed*.

The plums **were** ripe.

Last year, Marla **played** the viola at a city-wide recital.

Future tense indicates that something has not yet happened but will happen in the future. Future tense is formed by adding the auxiliary *will* to the infinitive. *(Shall,* an alternative auxiliary that is used to indicate first-person singular and plural or, in second and third persons, determination, is rarely used in current writing.)

The plums **will be** ripe soon.

Next April, Marla **will play** the viola at her sister's wedding.

Present perfect tense indicates that something began in the past and continues to the present time or that it occurred in the past at an unspecified time. Present perfect verbs are formed by using the auxiliary *has* or *have,* plus the past participle of the verb. For regular verbs, the past participle is the same as the past-tense form of the verb (for variations, see the list of irregular verbs, pages **114–116**).

The plums **have been** ripe since the rain stopped.

Marla **has played** the viola since sixth grade.

Past perfect tense indicates that an action began in the past, continued for a while, and ended before another event in the past. Form the past perfect by adding the auxiliary *had* to the past participle.

Before we picked them, the plums **had been** ripe for several days.

Marla **had played** the viola at two weddings before she graduated from high school.

Future perfect tense indicates that an action will be completed in the future but before a certain time. The future perfect is formed by adding the auxiliaries *will have* to the past participle.

By Saturday, the plums **will have been** ripe for several days.

As of September, Marla **will have played** the viola for eight years.

Progressive tenses indicate continuing actions. Progressive tenses are made with a form of the verb *be (is, was, will be, have been, had been,* or *will have been)* and the present participle *(-ing)* form of the verb. For every basic tense, an equivalent progressive tense exists.

present progressive: *is playing*

past progressive: *was playing*

future progressive: *will be playing*

present perfect progressive: *has been playing*

past perfect progressive: *had been playing*

future perfect progressive: *will have been playing*

Although verb tenses are sometimes difficult to distinguish and label, it is important to understand the time distinctions they make possible. Because writing explains relationships among events and ideas, using appropriate verb tenses will guarantee clear descriptions (see also Consistency, **14**).

EXERCISE □ *Verb Tenses*

In the following sentences, first identify the verbs and then label the tense of each one. Then revise each sentence to change its verb tense. Make other appropriate changes as well.

Example

past

Jeremy left the laundry on his way to work.

future

Jeremy will leave the laundry on his way to work.

1. This April, my wife and I will have been married sixteen years.

2. Plato's, the off-campus bookstore, carries works by some little-known poets.

3. Chris has interrupted my work frequently during the past week.

4. Margaret had spoken often about her family, so we had known she was homesick.

5. Will you drive me to the train station Thursday evening and say good-by?

EXERCISE □ *Verbs*

The following paragraph contains a variety of verbs. Locate them and identify their tenses.

Collecting door-to-door for charity is a satisfying way to help the needy. First, I do not mind walking, and I feel fairly comfortable asking for donations when the cause is a good one. Last January, for instance, I collected for the March of Dimes, surely a good cause. Although I had anticipated some problems, most people treated me well and gave what they could. One man said that he gave at work, but he still donated a dollar. Another man told me he had stopped giving money to charities because the money helped the organization but not the needy. He offered me a Coke, however. One woman said she lost her purse while shopping and as a result could not write a check, but she raided her change jar and gave me a small donation. An old couple explained that they had trouble paying bills, yet even they gave a small amount. With these kinds of responses, I always promise myself that I will continue to collect money, knowing that by the spring of each year I will have helped the needy.

5d Adjectives

Adjectives are words that modify or limit a noun or pronoun. Adjectives come in three forms: positive, comparative, and superlative.

A *positive adjective* directly modifies a noun or pronoun.

These are **clear** instructions.

A *comparative adjective* compares two people, places, things, ideas, qualities, conditions, or actions.

These are **clearer** instructions than we had last time.

A *superlative adjective* compares three or more items.

These are the **clearest** instructions I've ever seen.

(See also Adjectives and Adverbs, **16e-i**.)

All adjectives answer one of these questions about the words they modify: *what kind? which one? how many?* or *whose?*

red hair (*what kind?*)

the **fourth** stall (*which one?*)

sixteen advertisements (*how many?*)

Jeffrey's toolbox (*whose?*)

Adjectives are often positioned immediately before the nouns or pronouns they modify, but they can also follow the verb.

Regular adjectives precede the words they modify. They often appear in clusters.

adj. adj. n.   *adj.   adj. n.*
The **red velvet jacket** is hanging in **Shirley's hall closet.**

Note: When a series of adjectives functions as one modifier —when each word cannot sensibly be used alone to modify the noun or pronoun—hyphenate the series of words (see Hyphens, **43c**).

In 1982, American car manufacturers reintroduced **two-tone** cars. *(Not two cars or tone cars but two-tone cars. American manufacturers or car manufacturers, on the other hand, makes sense.)*

Predicate adjectives follow a linking verb but modify the subject of the sentence or clause (see Linking Verbs, pages **111– 112**). *pred. adj.*

The sleeping child was obviously **content.**

Note: If a series of modifiers works as a unit but is in the predicate adjective position, the adjectives are not hyphenated.

Off-the-cuff comments can lead to misunderstandings.

But: Toni's comments were **off the cuff,** but they were sensible.

In addition to traditionally defined adjectives, some other words also work as adjectives. The articles *a, an,* and *the* work like adjectives, and *this, that, these,* and *those* can function as demonstrative adjectives.

Owning **a** player piano can be enjoyable.

Only **the** good die young.

These bananas are too green to eat.

5e Adverbs

Adverbs are words that modify verbs, adjectives, other adverbs, or groups of words. Adverbs come in three forms: positive, comparative, and superlative.

A *positive adverb* directly modifies a verb, adjective, other adverb, or group of words.

Erica runs **fast.**

A *comparative adverb* compares two people, things, or actions.

Erica runs **faster** than I do.

A *superlative adverb* compares three or more people, things, or actions.

Of all the members of the relay team, Erica runs **fastest.**

(See also Adjectives and Adverbs, **16e–i**.)

All adverbs typically answer one of these questions: *how? when? where? how often? to what extent?* or *why?*

The old astronomer **cautiously** approached the telescope. (How *did the astronomer approach?*)

Anton **first** laughed out loud. (When *did he laugh?*)

Celia dropped hints **everywhere.** (Where *did she drop hints?*)

By answering these questions about various types of words, adverbs add detail and emphasis to sentences.

Modifying Verbs

That cabbie drives **carefully.**

Modifying Adjectives

That cabbie is an **unusually** good driver.

Modifying Other Adverbs

That cabbie drives **very** cautiously.

Modifying Entire Sentences

Unfortunately, the cabbie did not drive carefully enough.

123

Adverbs frequently end in *-ly*, although many words ending in *-ly* are not adverbs, and many adverbs do not end in *-ly*.

> Desdemona's **lovely** costume had been **well** designed. (Lovely *is an adjective;* well *is an adverb.*)

Use the *-ly* ending as a tentative guide, but identify adverbs by how they are used in sentences, not by a two-letter ending.

Because it is so commonly used, one adverb deserves a specific mention—*not*. This adverb modifies a verb in a highly specialized way, negating the idea presented by the verb itself. *Not* is positioned after a single verb or between an auxiliary and a main verb.

> The farmhouse was **not** occupied when it burned.

EXERCISE □ *Adjectives and Adverbs*

Identify the adjectives and adverbs in the following sentences. Label the adjectives as regular adjectives (r.a.), predicate adjectives (p.a.), pronoun-adjectives (pro.-a.), articles (art.), or demonstrative adjectives (d.a.). Draw arrows to show what word or group of words each adjective and adverb modifies.

Example

That old female elephant paced slowly and rhythmically around the enclosure.

1. Stepping forward, the security guard gruffly said, "Let me see your staff identification card now."

2. For a second-year student, Tarita plays the French horn rather well.

3. Campers who plan to stay in the Rockies should remember that mountain nights can be extremely cold.

4. Luckily, our flight from Pittsburgh to Chicago was as late as our originating flight. We made our connection, and our trip was not completely disastrous.

5. Pediatric dentists must be friendly, gentle, and patient. These qualities are important when one is working with small children.

6. Yoshiko selected a gold quartz watch with a luminous dial and a mesh band.

EXERCISE □ *Adjectives and Adverbs*

The following paragraph contains a variety of adjectives: regular adjectives, predicate adjectives, articles, and demonstrative adjectives. It also contains adverbs that modify verbs, adjectives, other adverbs, and entire sentences. Identify the adjectives and adverbs in the sentences and label them by type.

My favorite spot at Aunt Ruth and Uncle Dan's house is the small secluded patio just outside their bedroom. Every time I quietly open the sliding doors and step outside, I know I will feel more peaceful. The 8-by-8-foot patio is brick, meticulously set in a herringbone design. A comfortable, well-padded lounge chair provides a place to sit, and a small redwood table is a convenient spot to place my usual drink, a tall glass of Aunt Ruth's lightly spiced tea. Once comfortably seated, I always enjoy the various flowers, my favorite feature. Close to the front edge of the patio are pink, plum, red, and yellow moss roses, gently trailing their waxy green stems onto the dull red bricks. Slightly back, radiating away from the patio, are miniature yellow and orange marigolds, with their dense, round flowers set against dark green, sharp-edged leaves. Close behind those are Aunt Ruth and Uncle Dan's prize roses —white, pink, red, and yellow tea roses that are carefully pruned. The small buds, usually a darker color, contrast noticeably with the large open blossoms, which always remind me of fine damask. I always love to escape from the cheerful but noisy family activities to this secluded spot where the flowers are so beautiful. Inevitably, a visit to this floral oasis makes me feel more tranquil than before.

5f Conjunctions

Conjunctions are words that join words, phrases, or clauses. They link similar items, explain alternatives, show contrast, clarify chronological relationships, and explain causes and effects. Conjunctions are classified by three types: coordinating, subordinating, and correlative.

Coordinating conjunctions link roughly equivalent sentence parts. *And, but, for, nor, or, so,* and *yet*—these coordinating conjunctions are the most commonly used of all conjunctions.

> In a desk drawer in his office, Todd always keeps a needle **and** thread. *(joining words)*

> Struggling for modernity **but** ruling in the old style, Peter the Great imposed a tax on beards. *(joining phrases)*

Subordinating conjunctions introduce subordinate clauses and link them to independent clauses. A subordinate clause cannot stand alone as a sentence. An independent clause can, but when it is joined with a subordinate clause, the two form a complex sentence (see Kinds of Sentences, **7c, 7d**). Some common examples of subordinating conjunctions are *after, although, as if, as long as, because, before, even if, if, so that, that, unless, until, when, wherever,* and *while.*

> ⌐―――――― *subordinate clause* ――――――¬
> **While** Gilbert has been stationed in the Philippines, he has returned home only once.

> ⌐― *subordinate clause* ―
> Interest rates will continue to rise **as long as** the national debt grows!

Correlative conjunctions always work in pairs and give sentences additional emphasis. There are four pairs of correlative conjunctions: *both . . . and, either . . . or, neither . . . nor,* and *not only . . . but also.* The pairs of words, phrases, or clauses joined by these correlative conjunctions must be in parallel form (see Parallelism, **22b**).

> **Both** Mobil **and** Atlantic Richfield underwrite programs for the Public Broadcasting Service. *(Two parallel nouns are effectively joined by the correlative conjunctions.)*

A successful gardener **not only** must select plants carefully **but also** must attend to them painstakingly. *(The verb phrases joined by the correlative conjunctions contain parallel verbs—*must select *and* must attend to*—and parallel sentence structures: verb + direct object + adverb.)*

Conjunctive adverbs make logical connections between ideas, but they do not link sentences in a traditional grammatical way. Because conjunctive adverbs must be part of independent clauses, sentences using them must be punctuated carefully (see Commas, **31l**, and Semicolons, **33b**). The following list includes the most commonly used conjunctive adverbs:

accordingly	however	nonetheless
also	incidentally	otherwise
anyway	indeed	similarly
besides	instead	still
consequently	likewise	then
finally	meanwhile	therefore
further	moreover	thus
furthermore	nevertheless	
hence	next	

Note: A simple strategy for distinguishing between short conjunctive adverbs and other short conjunctions is to count the letters in the word. All conjunctive adverbs contain at least four letters, while coordinating conjunctions contain either two or three letters.

Like ordinary adverbs, conjunctive adverbs can appear in any position in a sentence.

Nedal originally planned to travel home to Beirut. **However,** the prospects for peace appeared dim.

Nedal originally planned to travel home to Beirut. The prospects for peace, **however,** appeared dim.

Nedal originally planned to travel home to Beirut. The prospects for peace appeared dim, **however.**

Because conjunctions and conjunctive adverbs often have parallel meanings, they offer alternative ways to present the same idea. The coordinating conjunctions *but* and *yet,* for example, signal a contrast between the ideas in the clauses, while stressing their equal importance. The subordinating conjunctions *although, even though,* and *though* also signal contrast but emphasize one clause over another. The conjunctive adverb *however* also signals contrast but keeps the ideas separate. Consider these alternatives as you write.

Coordinating Conjunction

Children learn to use computers with ease, **but** most adults learn with some difficulty.

Subordinating Conjunction

Although children learn to use computers with ease, most adults learn with some difficulty.

Conjunctive Adverb

Children learn to use computers with ease. Most adults, **however,** learn with some difficulty.

EXERCISE □ *Conjunctions*

Add conjunctions to the following sentences. In each case, label the conjunctions as coordinating or subordinating.

1. _____ *Sports Illustrated* and *Sport* are remarkably similar magazines, I do not understand why Murray subscribes to both.

2. Agatha Christie novels line my shelves, _____ I have never really enjoyed films based on her works.

3. Mortgage rates were 14 percent _____ we bought our house, _____ our monthly payments were less than rent on a similar house.

4. _____ Julia and Alexei were adopted when they were quite young, their parents waited a number of years to explain the situation to them.

5. Alison D'Elia, _____ she worked as an independent landscape architect, completed an internship at Blumfield Nurseries.

5g Prepositions

Prepositions establish relationships between words.

A preposition introduces a group of words, a *prepositional phrase*. These phrases contain a preposition and a noun or pronoun: the *object of the preposition*. In addition, prepositional phrases often contain modifiers (see Prepositional Phrases, **6d**, pages **143–144**).

I left Newport **after vacation.** (*preposition with its object*)

I left Newport **after** my summer **vacation.** (*preposition with its object and modifiers*)

Prepositional phrases modify specific words or phrases. They sometimes work like adverbs (answering a question like when?

where? or how often?) and sometimes like adjectives (answering a question like what kind? or whose?).

Aunt Leona takes a brisk walk *prep.* **after** every *obj.* **meal.** *(How often does she take walks?)*

The curtains made *prep.* **of** *obj.* **gingham** were our favorites. *(What kind of curtains?)*

That theory *prep.* **of** *obj.* **Newton's** displaced one that dated to Aristotle's time. *(Whose theory was it?)*

Most of the commonly used prepositions are single words, but some are made up of two or more words.

One-Word Prepositions

about	beyond	off
above	but	on
across	by	onto
after	concerning	out
against	despite	outside
along	down	over
among	during	past
around	except	since
at	for	through
before	from	throughout
behind	in	till
below	inside	to
beneath	into	toward
beside	like	under
besides	near	underneath
between	of	until

up	with	without
upon	within	

A Sampling of Multi-Word Prepositions

according to	in addition to	inside of
ahead of	in case of	in spite of
as well as	in front of	instead of
because of	in place of	rather than

EXERCISE □ *Prepositions*

The following paragraph contains a number of prepositional phrases. Find them, mark them with parentheses, and label the prepositions and objects. Watch especially for prepositions of more than one word.

Over the years, I have accumulated and framed a large collection of art reproductions, some of them small and interesting and some of them large and impressive. To avoid the cost of professional framing, I now make frames from easy-to-get and affordable materials. I go to my local lumberyard and buy decorative molding, the kind normally used for woodwork in houses. To make my frames, I glue and nail the narrow strips of molding onto wider strips, making sure I have a notch on the underside to secure the glass. Then, after twenty-four hours of drying time, I measure the size of a picture and cut the pieces accordingly. I always use a miter box and backsaw so my corners are precise. With glue, as well as corner braces, I secure the sides of the frame together. After this process, I need only finish the frame, using stain or paint, have glass cut, insert the picture, and secure it in place with a piece of heavy cardboard. In spite of the time required for my do-it-yourself framing, I have framed many pictures at a cost well below that charged at a frame shop. That leaves me more money to spend on other pictures for my collection.

5h Interjections

Interjections are words that express surprise, show emotion, or provide conversational transitions in sentences.

Okay, I'll try the steamed oysters if you insist.

Oh no! You didn't use aluminum foil in the microwave oven!

Well, I suppose we will have to change the tire ourselves.

Strong interjections may be used alone, followed by a period or exclamation point, while milder interjections are usually joined to a sentence with a comma (see **30d** and **31n**). Because interjections are conversational and do not function grammatically as part of a sentence, use them sparingly in formal writing.

REVIEW EXERCISE □ *Parts of Speech*

The following paragraph includes samples of all the parts of speech: nouns, pronouns, verbs, adjectives, adverbs, conjunctions, prepositions, and interjections. Label all the words.

Do you have a tendency to misplace your keys? Well, I do. I can misplace them at any time and in any place. By the time I was ten, I had lost at least eight house keys—even though my parents had tried putting them in "secret" places and had gotten me a chain to hang them on around my neck. Okay, I was careless. When I was sixteen and got my driver's license and keys to the family car, my folks hoped I had finally learned my lesson. Unfortunately, I had not. I frequently lost my car keys while I was on dates, so I often double-dated to avoid embarrassment. I sometimes lost my keys at work—either in the parking lot or in the shop—and had to call home for a ride. The inconvenience and embarrassment were terrible. Now, everywhere I go, people take my keys away from me for safekeeping. I used to be very self-conscious about all this attention, but it only bothers me a little now. At least I know that when I am ready to leave, someone will hand me my car keys, and I can drive home.

6 Parts of Sentences

Sentences are independent groups of words with a subject and verb. Because they express complete thoughts, sentences do not depend on other groups of words to make their meanings clear. As such, they are the basic units of written communication. This section will help you recognize the parts that make up sentences and how these parts work together to form coherent statements.

6a Subjects

Subjects identify the people, places, things, ideas, or conditions on which sentences focus.

A subject consists of one or more nouns or pronouns, together with any related modifiers. Although subjects usually appear near the beginning of sentences, they are sometimes located near the end.

Note that subjects can *never* come from a prepositional phrase. The nouns and pronouns in such phrases serve as objects of the preposition and cannot also be subjects.

Subjects fall into three categories: simple, complete, and compound.

Simple subjects are single words that act, have something done to them, or are described in a sentence.

Machiavelli changed the way rulers thought about government. (Machiavelli *performed the action,* change.)

Did **she** share her ideas with Leon? (She *did or did not* share.)

Newspapers are delivered early in the morning in our area. (Newspapers *have something done to them. They are* delivered.)

Note: Sometimes the subject *you* is unstated but understood in an imperative sentence (a request or command).

[You] Open the door this minute!

Complete subjects contain the *simple subject* plus all related modifiers: adjectives, adverbs, and prepositional phrases. To

identify the simple subject within the complete subject, eliminate prepositional phrases and modifiers and look for the word
(or words) upon which the idea of the sentence focuses.

complete subject
simple subj.

The art **supplies** for a course in basic design should not be very
elaborate.

complete subject
simple subj.

My very best **friend,** Rhonda, currently plans to be a veterinarian.

complete subject
simple subj.

Housing **costs** in California could make a pup tent look attractive.

Compound subjects are two or more simple subjects joined
with a conjunction.

compound subj.
simple subj.   *simple subj.*

Philip and his **brother** had different views on religion.

compound subj.
simple subj.   *simple subj.*

Honesty and **trust** are important parts of friendship.

compound subject
simple subj.   *simple subj.*

My grandparents' wedding **picture** and a family **portrait** hang in
our front hall.

EXERCISE □ *Subjects*

In the following sentences, underline the complete subjects and
label the simple subjects. Put a check mark by any sentence
that has a compound subject.

1. Atlanta and Nashville exemplify urban growth in the South.

2. Will you ask the librarian to include *Ironweed* on his requisition?

3. Please leave the room quietly.

4. All the offices at the city hall were closed on Martin Luther King Day.

5. Seals, whales, and some types of otters are endangered species.

6b Predicates

Predicates express the action or state of being in sentences.

A predicate consists of one or more verbs, together with any modifiers or complements. (Complements are discussed next.) Like subjects, predicates are identified as *simple, complete,* or *compound.* When a sentence is also a question, the parts of the predicate are usually separated by the subject.

Simple predicates contain single verbs and their auxiliaries, if any. The simple predicate states what the subject of the sentence does, what it is, or what has been done to it.

Machiavelli **changed** the way rulers thought about government.
Did she **share** her ideas with Leon?
Newspapers **are delivered** early in the morning in our area.

137

Complete predicates are made up of the simple predicate plus all related modifiers—adjectives, adverbs, and prepositional phrases—and any complements.

[handwritten: complete / simple / pred.]

The art supplies for a course in basic design **should** not **be** very
[handwritten: predicate]
elaborate.

[handwritten: complete predicate / simple / pred.]

My best friend, Rhonda, currently **plans** to be a veterinarian.

[handwritten: complete predicate / simple / pred.]

Housing costs in California **could make** a pup tent look attractive.

Compound predicates are two or more simple predicates joined with a conjunction. Often, they share the same subject.

[handwritten: compound predicate / simple pred. / simple pred.]

Philip **reconsidered** and **refined** his interpretation of the film.

[handwritten: compound predicate / simple pred. / simple pred.]

True friends **are** sensitive to each other's needs and **offer** help
when asked.

[handwritten: simple pred. / compound predicate / simple pred.]

We **found** my grandparents' wedding picture in the attic, **framed**

[handwritten: simple pred.]

it, and **hung** it in the front hall.

EXERCISE □ *Predicates*

In the following sentences, underline the complete predicates and label the simple predicates. Put a check mark by any sentence that has a compound predicate.

1. We anxiously awaited the release of *A Passage to India* and were thrilled with it.

2. Soccer is growing more popular in the United States.

3. Have you ever thought about the history of your family?

4. The package containing the music box arrived three weeks after Nedah's birthday.

5. In Kentucky, many people buy and recondition used cars.

EXERCISE □ *Subjects*

The following paragraph contains eleven sentences. Identify the simple subjects and simple predicates in each sentence, watching carefully for compound subjects and predicates.

The alley that runs behind the houses in our neighborhood gives curious hints of the lifestyles of the people nearby. Mrs. Luchetti's garage door is almost always left open. She is making another quick trip to the store. Empty Pampers boxes are stacked next to the Joneses' trash can. Carol and Carl, the twins, are still babies. A small pile of smashed cigarette butts and scattered matches lie near the Fernandezes' back gate. Jim's attempt to quit smoking is only an attempt. And the toppled garbage can by the Leisters' garage identifies the food and paper strewn nearby. The Leisters are still eating well and still have not learned to dog-proof their trash. Walking down an alley may not always be pleasant. It can usually be illuminating, however.

6c Complements

Complements are words or groups of words that complete the meaning of a sentence by explaining the action or state of being described.

Complements sometimes explain who or what is needed to complete the idea in a sentence, identifying for whom or for what something was done. They may also restate or describe the subject of the sentence. When a sentence has a complement, the complement will follow the verb and will be part of the complete predicate. Four kinds of complements exist: *direct objects, indirect objects, predicate nouns,* and *predicate adjectives.* Each can appear in a compound form.

Direct objects complete the action presented by a transitive verb, answering the question *what?* or *whom?*

Senator Packhard supported the doomed **Equal Rights Amendment.** (What *did she support?*)

Time magazine chose **Peter Ueberroth** as its "1984 Man of the Year." (Whom *did* Time *choose?*)

Indirect objects indicate *to whom* or *for whom* the action of a sentence is intended. When indirect objects are used, they will follow transitive verbs but will always precede direct objects.

The librarian handed **Michael** the bibliography. (To whom *did he hand the bibliography?*)

Before talking to reporters, the winning cyclist tossed the **coach** her water bottle and hat. (To whom *did she toss the bottle and hat?*)

To determine whether a noun or a pronoun is an indirect object, place it in a prepositional phrase using *to* or *for*. Almost all sentences with indirect objects can be sensibly rewritten this way. But note that when the word *to* or *for* is used, the word is no longer an indirect object but is the object of a preposition (see Prepositional Phrases, **6d,** pages 143–145).

The librarian handed the bibliography **to Michael.**

Before talking to reporters, the winning cyclist tossed her water bottle and hat **to the coach.**

Predicate nouns follow linking verbs and restate or identify the subject of a sentence. When a linking verb is used, the correlation of the subject and the predicate noun is so close that the sentence usually suggests an equation of sorts (see Linking Verbs, **5c,** pages 111–112).

Cliff was the only **man** who attended the children's concert. *(Cliff = man; man defines or restates who Cliff was; concert, on the other hand, is a direct object, explaining what he attended.)*

The new album was a critical **success** and a commercial **failure.** *(album = success; album = failure)*

Note: Because the relationship between the subject and the predicate noun is so close, such sentences can often be reordered without altering the meaning.

The only **man** who attended the children's concert was **Cliff.**

Predicate adjectives follow linking verbs and directly modify the subject of a sentence. They, too, create equationlike descriptions.

Dr. Nuñez is always **cautious** when prescribing drugs. *(Dr. Nuñez = cautious [person])*

Angie was **depressed** and **angry** because she forgot the audition. *(Angie = depressed [person]; Angie = angry [person])*

EXERCISE □ *Complements*

Underline the complements in the following sentences and label them as direct objects (d.o.), indirect objects (i.o.), predicate nouns (p.n.), or predicate adjectives (p.a.). Remember that compound complements are possible.

Example
i.o.   *d.o.*
Gabriel gave **Ron** only brief **instructions**, knowing that the young
p.n.
scholar was an experienced **researcher.**

1. The doctor gave the runner a shot of cortisone.

2. Michelangelo was not only a gifted sculptor but also a great painter and architect.

3. The standard-sized *Oxford English Dictionary* is too expensive and too bulky for most small libraries.

4. Marilyn reluctantly left her canary at her brother's home.

5. The troubled counselor skimmed the pebble across the water.

EXERCISE □ *Complements*

The following paragraph contains a number of complements: direct objects, indirect objects, predicate nouns, and predicate adjectives. The complements occur in both independent and subordinate clauses. Underline and label each complement.

Launching my family's boat has become a routine process now that we have all discovered what duties we perform best.

Dad backs the trailer down the ramp until it just reaches the edge of the water. Then I dash to the trailer and dislodge the safety clips that hold the boat securely in place. That done, Dad backs the trailer and boat into the shallow water. I give the boat a nudge, and it floats from the trailer, becoming a "free spirit" that always tries to head downstream. Dad, who always seems a bit muddled by the procedure, has to be reminded to drive away and park the car and trailer. When he gets back, I start the boat's engine. At this point, my brother, Shawn, gets up from where he has been sitting, picks up his book, and saunters over to the boat. You see, Shawn's approach to helping is to stay out of the way.

6d Phrases

Phrases are groups of words that cannot function independently as complete sentences because they do not include either subjects or predicates; they must be part of a sentence.

Whole phrases often function as nouns, adjectives, or adverbs. Three kinds of phrases are most commonly used: *prepositional phrases, verbal phrases,* and *appositive phrases.*

Prepositional phrases

A *prepositional phrase* consists of a preposition, its object (a noun or pronoun), and any modifiers. Prepositional phrases function most often as adjectives or adverbs and infrequently as nouns (see Prepositions, **5g**).

The dog limped **across the yard to the lighted doorway.** *(Both phrases work as adverbs, answering the question "Where did the dog limp?")*

My anxiety **about the dental work** was intense. *(The phrase works as an adjective, answering the question "Which anxiety?")*

EXERCISE □ *Prepositional Phrases*

The following sentences contain a variety of prepositional phrases. First place the phrases in parentheses, and then circle the word or words each phrase modifies.

Example

Drinking sparkling (water)(from France and Italy) has become a (sign)(of distinction)(among young professionals).

1. In recent decades, doctors of all specialties have stressed the importance of a good diet and daily exercise.

2. Cindy waded into the water that was rushing down the flooded street.

3. When the value of the dollar rises in world money markets, the price of imports from foreign countries goes down in the United States.

4. After talking to her older sister for a short while, Maria felt better about pledging a sorority.

5. At every camping site, Mr. Grebowski found a rock or stone for the rock garden in his backyard.

Verbals and verbal phrases

Verbals are verb forms that are used as other parts of speech.

Verbals come in three forms: gerunds, participles, and infinitives.

Gerunds are *-ing* forms of verbs that work as nouns.

Reading is my favorite winter sport.

Participles are *-ing*, *-ed*, *-d*, *-n*, and *-t* forms of verbs that function as adjectives. The *-ing* forms are present participles, which describe something happening now. The other forms (*-ed*, *-d*, *-n*, and *-t*) are past participles, which describe something that has happened already. (For a listing of unusual past participles, see Irregular Verbs, pages **113–116**.)

Scowling, the tax assessor repeated the question. (Scowling *is a present participle modifying tax assessor.*)

Exhausted, the spaniel collapsed next to the bag of decoys. (Exhausted *is a past participle modifying* spaniel.)

Infinitives combine the word *to* with a verb and are used as nouns, adjectives, or adverbs.

To win is their only goal. (To win *works as a noun—the subject of the sentence.*)

The office secretary is an important person **to know.** (To know *works as an adjective, modifying* person.)

Lance was too excited **to sleep.** (To sleep *works as an adverb, modifying* excited.)

Verbal phrases are formed when verbals are used with complements or modifiers. Such groups of words are identified as *gerund phrases, participial phrases,* or *infinitive phrases.*

Gerund phrases combine a gerund and its complements and modifiers; the entire phrase works as a noun.

Climbing Mount Everest was their lifelong ambition. *(The gerund phrase is the subject of the sentence.)*

I really enjoy **playing** chamber music. *(The gerund phrase is the direct object of* enjoy.)

Harrison reread the instructions for **assembling** the bicycle. *(The gerund phrase is the object of the preposition* for.)

EXERCISE □ *Gerund Phrases*

In the following sentences, underline the gerund phrases, identifying the gerunds and their objects and modifiers (when they have them). Then identify whether each phrase is used as a subject, direct object, predicate noun, or object of a preposition.

Example

Arriving late at a dinner party is impolite. (The gerund phrase is

the subject of the sentence.)

1. Roger surprised his roommate by bringing home a pet boa

   constrictor.

2. Eating and getting warm were the tired ranger's main con-

   cerns.

3. Upton Sinclair outraged America by revealing the truth about the meat-processing industry.

4. Martina's summer activities are sleeping, eating, and sleeping some more.

5. When I visit new cities, I go searching for buildings with unusual architectural styles.

Participial phrases combine a participle and its modifiers; these phrases are used as adjectives. Like other adjectives, participial phrases must be placed near the nouns they modify (see Dangling Modifiers, **25e**).

Standing on the wooden bridge, Nathan watched small leaves float by, **swirling** in the current. *(The first participial phrase modifies Nathan; the second modifies leaves.)*

Recently **seated** at a table by the door, Carlos had not noticed his friends nearby. *(The participial phrase modifies Carlos.)*

EXERCISE □ *Participial Phrases*

In the following sentences, underline the participial phrases and label the participles. Then circle the word each phrase modifies.

Example

Poised at the edge of the diving platform, Robert looked apprehensive.

147

1. The jeweler marveled at the emerald brooch, glistening against the dark velvet background.

2. Hurt by the overly critical comments, Marlene swore never to write a play again.

3. Pleased that she had been elected president of the NOW chapter, Ms. Abernathy thanked the members, promising to lead them well.

4. His most recent sculpture, carved of smoky gray marble, clearly resembled a wing.

5. Excited by the prospect of a new job, Nicole began making plans to move to San Diego.

Infinitive phrases combine an infinitive and its complements and modifiers; these phrases function as nouns, adjectives, or adverbs. When infinitive phrases are used as adjectives, they must be placed near the nouns they modify (see Dangling Modifiers, **25e**). When they work as adverbs, however, they can frequently be moved to various places in the sentence, as other adverbs can be.

To be responsible, we must act without prejudice. *(The infinitive phrase, working as an adjective, modifies* we.)

The experiment was too dangerous **to contemplate** seriously. *(The infinitive phrase, working as an adverb, modifies the predicate adjective* dangerous.*)*

┌──── *phrase* ────┐
  inf.   ┌── *inf.*
Rachel must learn **to control** her temper if she wants **to get** along
┌─ *phrase* ─┐
in this office. *(Both the infinitive phrases work as nouns. Both are direct objects, describing* what *she must learn and* what *she wants.)*

EXERCISE □ *Infinitive Phrases*

In the following sentences, underline the complete infinitive phrases and identify the infinitives. Then explain whether the phrases are used as nouns, adjectives, or adverbs.

Example

If we consider hit shows over the past decade, we find that it is

infinitive
impossible to underestimate the tastes of the American television

audience. *(The phrase works as an adverb, modifying* impossible.*)*

1. To prepare for her trip to Europe, Judy reviewed her French and German.

2. To escape from the exploding water balloons was impossible.

3. More than anything else, we want to be happy in our work.

4. To illustrate how simply one could live, Thoreau dwelled for a year in the woods near Walden Pond.

5. To be a fine dancer requires extraordinary ability and unwavering self-discipline.

Appositives

Appositives are words or groups of words that explain, describe, define, identify, or in some way restate a noun already included in a sentence.

If an appositive provides necessary explanation, no commas should be used. If the appositive merely provides additional but nonessential information, however, separate the appositive from the rest of the sentence with commas (see Commas, **31h, 31i**).

> Mitchel, **a friend of mine,** was audited by the IRS and fined one thousand dollars. (*Because the appositive provides nonessential information, the commas are needed.*)
>
> The painting *American Gothic* has been laughably used in advertising. (*Because* American Gothic, *the appositive, is necessary to the meaning of the sentence, no commas should be used.*)

EXERCISE ☐ *Appositives*

Combine the following pairs of sentences to form single sentences with appositives. Place commas carefully.

> Example
>
> Riverside Mall, has 120 shops. ~~Riverside Mall is~~ ☞
>
> (the largest mall in the area.)

1. The quilt was done in a star pattern. The quilt was Harriet's project for her crafts class.

2. The arrangement of yellow roses and bronze chrysanthemums made a lovely centerpiece. The flowers were a gift from Cindy's grandmother.

3. The deadline for National Merit Scholarship applications has already passed. Applications were due on July 15.

4. My favorite golf course is closed for reconditioning. It is called the Oakland Park Eighteen.

5. Mattie places absolute trust in Nathan. Nathan is her oldest son.

Absolute phrases

Absolute phrases modify whole sentences rather than individual words.

These specialized verbal phrases consist of nouns and participles, usually with modifiers. They can be positioned anywhere in a sentence but must be separated from the rest of the sentence by commas (see **31g**).

The car having broken down yesterday, we took the truck.

We took the truck, the car having broken down yesterday.

EXERCISE □ *Phrases of All Kinds*

In the following sentences, underline and label the prepositional, gerund, participial, infinitive, appositive, and absolute phrases.

Example

participial phrase   *prep. phrase*

Opening the door slowly, Rick saw a light in the kitchen.

1. Giving blood, the gift of life, is an almost painless way to help people in need.

2. Finding time to practice is one of the most difficult aspects of playing a musical instrument.

3. Suffering from severe headaches, Marge, always a cautious person, decided to limit her social activities during the winter.

4. Maintaining dignity even in defeat, Robert E. Lee joined Ulysses S. Grant at Appomattox to sign the surrender agreement.

5. Her brow knitted in frustration, the judge asked the lawyers to approach the bench.

EXERCISE □ *Phrases*

In the following paragraph, first mark the prepositional, appositive, and absolute phrases by placing them in parentheses. Then underline the gerund, participial, and infinitive phrases and label each one by type.

When I was twelve, my friend Shannon and I used to visit the people at Willowbrook Nursing Home regularly. At first, we went out of curiosity. Our grandparents having died some time before, we wondered what older people were like. The first time we went, uncertain and uncomfortable, we were not sure how to behave. However, stopping to see "the folks" was soon more fun. Hearing Mrs. Whitcolm's stories about Model T's always made us laugh. Playing checkers or sometimes poker with Mr. Dermitakis, Mrs. Murzcek, and Mr. Thomas was a challenge: they had more inclination to practice than we did. Helping Mr. Jurardo with crossword puzzles tested our skills. We even enjoyed the lectures against rock'n'roll music from Mrs. Aberly, a former choir director, but we were rather worried when she tried to get us to listen to some Perry Como albums. We learned a great deal from our older friends, their collective wisdom having been amassed over several lifetimes. We learned about their families and about them as people. Mostly, we learned that the elderly have a lot to offer children: stories, skills, and insights. Knowing now what I would have missed, I am glad Shannon and I stopped at Willowbrook. Besides, who but Mrs. Murzcek, that sly old card shark, would have taught twelve-year-olds how to cheat at poker?

6e Clauses

A word group that contains a subject and predicate is a **clause.** A clause is either independent or subordinate.

Independent clauses (sometimes called *main clauses)* are grammatically complete and can be used alone as sentences.

Although they can be used independently (and are then simple sentences), these clauses are often combined with other clauses to form more complicated sentences.

> *subj.* *pred.*
> **Rachel approached** the door tentatively.

> *subj.* *pred.*
> The fan **belt was** not in stock.

> *subj.* *pred.*   *subj.* *pred.*
> The Joad **family lost** their farm, and then **they left** for California.
> *(Two independent clauses join here to form a compound sentence.)*

A *subordinate clause* (sometimes called a *dependent clause*) also contains a subject and predicate but is *grammatically incomplete*. *Subordinate* means "of secondary importance," and in grammatical terms that means that a subordinate clause must be joined to an independent clause for a complete idea to emerge. Subordinating conjunctions (see **5f**, page 127) and relative pronouns (see **5b**, page 107) signal this dependent relationship.

> *conj.* *subj.* *pred.*
> **because she was** unsure of her appointment time

> *pron.* *subj.* *pred.*
> **that Kevin needed** for his car

Clearly, these subordinate clauses are not complete sentences. To make them grammatical, join them to independent clauses to form complex or compound-complex sentences (see **7c, 7d**). You can also eliminate the subordinating conjunction or relative pronoun to form a simple sentence. These alternative structures create different kinds of emphasis. Complex or compound-complex sentences stress the interrelationships of ideas, while distinct simple sentences leave ideas separate. The choice depends on your intended meaning.

> Rachel approached the door tentatively **because she was unsure of her appointment time.** *(complex sentence)*

Or: Rachel approached the door tentatively. She was unsure of her appointment time. *(two simple sentences)*

The fan belt **that Kevin needed for his car** was not in stock. *(complex sentence)*

Or: Kevin needed a fan belt for his car. It was not in stock. *(two simple sentences)*

Subordinate clauses function in sentences as nouns, adjectives, or adverbs, depending on what information they provide or how they incorporate subordinating conjunctions and relative pronouns. Noun clauses can function as any other noun can—and therefore can be used as subjects, objects, or complements. Notice, however, that sentences incorporating noun clauses do not have to be complex. Sentences using adjective or adverb clauses, on the other hand, will be complex sentences.

As Nouns

Whoever wrote this paper should pursue further study. *(used as the subject of the sentence)*

Even Congress knows **that military spending is out of control.** *(used as the direct object of knows)*

Sell the land to **whoever agrees not to develop it.** *(used as the object of the preposition to)*

As Adjectives

The armor **that Mordred wore** was rusty and dented. *(modifies armor)*

Select a name **that can be easily spelled.** *(modifies name)*

As Adverbs

clause
subj. pred.
Whenever I want your advice, I will ask for it. *(modifies* ask*)*

clause
subj.   pred.
Jessica paints more carefully **than I usually do.** *(modifies* carefully*)*

EXERCISE □ *Clauses*

Underline the subordinate clauses in the following sentences and indicate whether they are used as nouns, adjectives, or adverbs.

1. Wherever I hang my hat is home.

2. The lawyer thinks that we should reschedule our court date.

3. Because he is very tall, Nguyen has trouble finding jeans that are long enough.

4. The desperate action that you propose is unwarranted.

5. That the church window needed repairing was obvious to the congregation.

EXERCISE □ *Clauses*

The following paragraph contains a number of subordinate clauses. Underline them and identify how they are used: as nouns, adjectives, or adverbs.

When the credits run at the end of a film, few audience members pay much attention. They do not seem to know that the people whose names are listed are sometimes as important to the movie as the actors are. For instance, producers control and organize the entire production, finding people who will finance the film and hiring creative people who will actually make it. That directors are in charge of the cinematography is well known, but many people fail to realize that they also choose and coach actors and find locations and technicians. When the camera work is finally completed, editors begin their task. They take thousands of feet of film, select the best shots, and piece together the version of the picture that we eventually see. Besides the producers, directors, and editors, hundreds of other people are involved in the making of a film. Learning who they are and what they do can make you a more appreciative audience member.

7 Kinds of Sentences

For most purposes, *sentences* are classified by their structure, by how many and what kinds of clauses they contain. Four basic sentence types exist—*simple, compound, complex,* and *com-*

pound-complex—and being able to distinguish among them will help you to revise more effectively.

7a Simple sentences

A *simple sentence* contains one independent clause and presents a clear relationship between the subject and predicate.

Simple sentences are sometimes complicated, however, because they often contain compound subjects, compound predicates, and any number of modifiers and phrases.

    subj.   *pred.*
Governor O'Brian attended. *(simple subject; simple predicate)*
    subj.   *pred.*   *d.o.*
Governor O'Brian attended the meeting. *(A direct object has been added.)*
   subj.   *subj.* *pred.*   *d.o.*
Governor O'Brian and his **assistant attended** the meeting. *(The sentence now has a compound subject to go with the simple predicate and its direct object.)*
   subj.   *pred.*   *d.o.*   *pred.*
Governor O'Brian attended the meeting and **made** the opening
  d.o.
speech. *(A compound predicate; each predicate has its own direct object.)*

7b Compound sentences

Compound sentences contain two or more independent clauses. The clauses are joined by a coordinating conjunction (see **5f,** page 127).

Compound sentences express balanced relationships between separate sets of subjects and predicates (see Coordination, **18a**). Notice that commas are normally placed before the coordinating conjunctions in compound sentences. An alternative is to form a compound sentence by using a semicolon to join the independent clauses, with no coordinating conjunction. Compound sentences with semicolons stress the extremely close connection between ideas.

subj.   pred.   conj.   subj.   pred.   pred.
Bluebirds are getting scarcer, **but ornithologists do** not **know** why.

subj.   pred.   subj.   pred.   pred.
Or: **Bluebirds are** getting scarcer; **ornithologists do** not **know** why.

subj.   pred.   conj.
Dickens assailed the workhouses in *Oliver Twist,* **and** in *Bleak*
subj.   pred.
House **he took on** the courts of chancery.

subj.   pred.
Or: **Dickens assailed** the workhouses in *Oliver Twist;* in *Bleak*
subj.   pred.
House **he took on** the courts of chancery.

7c Complex sentences

Complex sentences contain at least two clauses: one independent clause and one or more subordinate clauses. The clauses are joined by either subordinating conjunctions (see **5f,** page 127) or relative pronouns (see **5b,** page 107).

Subordinate clauses may be put at the beginning, middle, or end of sentences, each position shifting the emphasis (see Subordination, **19a**). Generally, place the most important information at the beginning of the sentence. Also note that comma usage varies depending on the placement of subordinate clauses (see Commas, **31c**).

┌──────── *sub. clause* ────────┐ ┌── *ind. clause* ──
conj.   subj. pred.   *subj.   pred.*
Because they are not always the wisest, the **bravest** often **suffer**
defeat.

ind. clause · *sub. clause*
subj. pred. conj. subj. pred.

The **bravest** often **suffer** defeat **because they are** not always the wisest.

ind. clause
sub. clause
subj. conj. subj. pred. pred.

The **bravest, because they are** not always the wisest, often **suffer** defeat.

7d Compound-complex sentences

Compound-complex sentences contain three or more clauses—at least two independent clauses and one subordinate clause. This kind of sentence can include several more clauses as well.

sub. clause *ind. clause*
conj. subj. pred. subj. pred.

Because the **museum was** closed on Monday, **we visited** the

ind. clause
conj. subj. pred.

United Nations instead, **and** then **we went** to the museum on Tuesday.

ind. clause *sub. clause*
subj. pred. pron. pred.

Monica opened a checking account **that gave** her access to the

ind. clause
conj. subj. pred.

autoteller, **and** then **she** never **used** the machine.

EXERCISE □ *Sentences*

Combine the following groups of simple sentences to form compound, complex, or compound-complex sentences. Try to create at least one sentence of each type.

Example

although the

~~The~~ script for *A Night to Remember* is emotionally manipulative;

t

~~T~~he acting demands respect. *(complex)*

1. Religion is the opiate of the masses. Marx said so. He was just looking for a scapegoat.

2. The opening game was over. The team members' enthusiasm continued to build.

3. We ordered the books. The books did not arrive until late in October. The carton was mashed. They were still a welcome sight.

4. It rained most of spring break. Then classes started again. It was beautiful.

5. George C. Scott declined the Academy Award for *Patton.* Afterward, he refused to talk to reporters.

7e Classifying sentences by purpose

In addition to classifying sentences by their grammatical structures, writers can classify sentences by their purposes.

A *declarative sentence* presents a statement.

God does not play dice.
—Albert Einstein

An *exclamatory sentence* presents an emphatic statement.

Give me liberty, or give me death!
> —Patrick Henry

An *imperative sentence* presents a command.

Ask not what your country can do for you—ask what you can do
for your country.
> —John F. Kennedy

An *interrogative sentence* presents a question.

What *is* the answer? . . . In that case, what is the question?
> —Gertrude Stein

EXERCISE ☐ *Sentences*

The following paragraph contains thirteen sentences. Label
each as simple, compound, complex, or compound-complex.

Somebody must have sold my name to a mailing service,
for I get at least one mail-order catalog a week. Some come in
mailing wrappers, but most come unwrapped, with wrinkled
covers and turned corners. Many people complain bitterly
when they receive these unrequested catalogs. I do not. I love
to look through them when they first arrive, and sometimes I
surprise myself by ordering some of what they offer. I bought a
cotton sweater from an order house in Connecticut because I
liked the color. I purchased a three-legged stool and a pair of
candleholders from a place that claimed to make "authentic co-

lonial reproductions." I was not sure if the designs were authentic, but I liked them anyway. From an import house, I ordered a set of refrigerator magnets that looked like brass letters for typesetting. I even ordered a "Neurotic State University" T-shirt from a sleazy novelty catalog. I suppose that I am one of those curious consumers who keep mail-order houses in business. I enjoy my surprise mail and look forward to my "wish books" from Yankee Clearing House, Orient Express Imports, Novelty Products, and the others. Keep them coming.

BASIC ERRORS IN WRITING

Errors of any kind keep writing from being completely effective, but some errors are more serious than others. Mistakes in typing or spelling are often simple oversights and are easy to correct. Larger sentence errors, however, are more critical. Whatever their origin, they reflect an incomplete grasp of basic sentence structures, and they confuse and frustrate readers. Such distractions obscure important ideas and make reading a chore. For the sake of your meaning and your readers, learn to recognize the major errors taken up in this unit. Carefully check for them and correct them.

8 Fragments

Fragments are groups of words that improperly take the form of sentences, with capital letters at the beginning and terminal punctuation at the end.

People often think fragmented thoughts and use fragments in notes or rough drafts. Although these notations may be clear to the writer, readers prefer complete, grammatical sentences that state ideas fully.

Fragments may look like sentences and be punctuated as such, but remember that a complete sentence must contain a subject and a verb and that a subordinate clause is not a complete sentence (see Sentences, **6a, 6b,** and **6e**). Correct sentence fragments by using one of four strategies, depending on the kind of fragment.

8a Add a subject when a fragment does not contain one.

Fragment

Brian is addicted to Indiana Jones. **Saw *Raiders of the Lost Ark* eleven times.**

166

Complete

Brian is addicted to Indiana Jones. **He** saw *Raiders of the Lost Ark* eleven times.

8b Add a verb or join the words to another sentence.

Fragment

Rachel, an avid collector of china figurines. She paid eighty-five dollars for extra insurance coverage.

Complete

Rachel **was** an avid collector of china figurines. She paid eighty-five dollars for extra insurance coverage.

Rachel, an avid collector of china figurines, **paid** eighty-five dollars for extra insurance coverage.

8c If a fragment is a subordinate clause, either drop the subordinating conjunction or connect the fragment to an independent clause.

Watch carefully for subordinating conjunctions that begin sentences. If the sentence does not include an independent clause, you have written a fragment, which needs to be corrected. Often, the presence of a subordinate-clause fragment means that you need to complete a complex or compound-complex sentence (see **7c** and **7d**).

Fragment

Some students have to postpone starting college. **Because the cost of attending has risen.**

Complete

Some students have to postpone starting college. The cost of attending has risen. *(The subordinate conjunction has been dropped.)*

167

Because the cost of attending college has risen, **some students have to postpone starting.** *(Here the subordinate clause becomes part of a complex sentence.)*

8d If the fragment is an unattached phrase, connect it to a related sentence.

Fragment

Stavros had designed the sets for many plays. **Seven while in high school.**

Complete

Stavros had designed the sets for many plays, seven while still in high school. *(The phrase is simply connected to the preceding sentence, where it modifies* designed.*)*

8e Use fragments sparingly for special effect.

Sometimes, even in a final draft, you will want to emphasize a key word or perhaps a phrase by isolating it. Then it is acceptable to use a fragment. However, use this strategy only to achieve an intended effect—for instance, supplying an answer to a question.

G, PG, R, and *X.* These symbols are used in classifying films and are intended to restrict the audiences that see American films. The coding system is itself an admirable idea, but does it work? No. Too many parents disregard the implied advice of the rating system, and too few theater owners adhere to its guidelines when selling tickets.

EXERCISE ☐ *Fragments*

Revise these fragments. Add subjects or verbs when needed, or use an independent clause to complete the idea in a dependent clause or phrase.

Example

Apartheid, a social system that separates blacks from whites, *has existed in South Africa for decades.*

1. The local exercise gym, with the newest, most technically advanced equipment.

2. As the skier quickly approached the jump.

3. *Abbey Road,* one of the Beatles' best albums.

4. Three days before her surgery.

5. Itzhak Perlman, a world-renowned violinist.

6. Just outside the entrance to the cave.

7. Because we thought the trail was too narrow and too steep.

8. For Barbara to enter law school.

9. Located on Wall Street, next to the Stock Exchange.

10. Unless Marco can explain the problem to the company representative.

EXERCISE □ *Fragments*

The following paragraph includes a number of fragments, some of which are clearly grammatical errors and others intended for special emphasis. Correct the unintentional fragments by adding subjects or verbs, by dropping the subordinating conjunctions, by forming a complex sentence, or by attaching phrases to appropriate sentences. If you let a fragment stand, be ready to explain what purpose it serves.

New York. St. Louis. Knoxville. New Orleans. Los Angeles. These cities have all hosted those pretentious, glorious, overly expensive, and enjoyable activities known as World's Fairs. Filled with exhibits, amusements, and restaurants. World's Fairs offer people a chance to learn about the world while enjoying themselves. At these large fairs, nations from around the world build pavilions to showcase their national achievements. Often sending examples of their best technology, art, and historical treasures. Dancers, singers, and musicians. Enjoy seeing native costumes and folk dances that illustrate the diversity of the world's cultures. Sometimes, even specialties of individual fairs have become common later on. St. Louis, the city where the ice-cream cone was invented. It has since become a standard treat worldwide. World's Fairs, originally planned to "bring the world closer together," have outlived their purpose. Because people now travel by airplane and can see the countries of the world. They see much more than can be seen in national exhibits at World's Fairs.

9 Comma Splices and Fused Sentences

Comma splices and *fused sentences* contain two or more independent clauses that are not properly separated (see **6e**).

In a comma splice, the independent clauses are inaccurately joined with a comma, which is not a firm enough separation. A comma splice incorrectly suggests that one clause is subordinate to the other. In a fused sentence (also called a *run-on sentence)*, independent clauses are simply placed one after the other, with no punctuation at all.

During writing, thoughts may run together in a way that causes comma splices and fused sentences to go unrecognized. For readers, however, they are usually glaring errors that cause significant confusion and irritation. Correct comma splices and fused sentences using one of four methods.

9a Separate incorrectly joined independent clauses to form two sentences; use a period.

Chin was extremely fashion conscious, he viewed his clothes as a form of self-expression.

9b If the independent clauses are very closely related, separate them with a semicolon.

Nick and Sheri decided their relationship was no good, when their children reached college age, they got a divorce.

9c Use independent clauses to form a compound sentence if the independent clauses are closely related; use a comma and a coordinating conjunction.

The experienced sky diver hurtled toward the ground, she felt no fear.

Luisa was a talented pianist, she didn't practice to maintain her skills.

9d Make one clause dependent to form a complex sentence; use a subordinating conjunction and, if necessary, a comma.

because

Sonia reread the sonnet ^she was still not satisfied with her interpretation of the imagery.

although

^Darryl began carpentry as a hobby, he now works for a local home-improvements business.

9e Do not mistake conjunctive adverbs (*besides, furthermore, however, nevertheless, still, then, therefore,* and others) for coordinating or subordinating conjunctions.

Conjunctive adverbs logically connect ideas, but they do not link independent clauses in the traditional grammatical ways coordinating conjunctions do. Use a period or a semicolon to separate the independent clauses (see **5f,** pages 128–129).

Comma splice

Corporate mergers are often like marriages, however, some unfriendly ones are like abductions.

Correct

Corporate mergers are often like marriages. However, some unfriendly ones are like abductions.

Corporate mergers are often like marriages; however, some unfriendly ones are like abductions.

EXERCISE □ *Comma Splices and Fused Sentences*

Correct these faulty sentences by altering their punctuation, by adding a comma and a coordinating conjunction, or by adding a subordinating conjunction (and a comma if necessary).

Example

Because

t

∧ The quality of American musicals was poor in 1985, no Tony
Awards were given for best actor or actress in a musical.

1. Wilfred was terribly bored by the article on economies-of-
   scale, he read it until he fell asleep.

2. Sally Ride was the first woman astronaut she appeared on
   the covers of six major magazines.

3. The stoplight on Fourth Street and Davis Avenue should be
   synchronized with other lights on Fourth Street drivers are
   slowed down unnecessarily.

4. Jack wore size thirteen shoes, he always had to place special orders to get current styles.

5. The U.S. women's volleyball team won the silver medal at
   the 1984 Olympics, it was the first U.S. team to make the
   finals in that sport.

EXERCISE □ *Comma Splices and Fused Sentences*

The following paragraph contains a number of comma splices
and fused sentences. Correct them by using periods or semicolons between the independent clauses or by rewriting the sentences to form compound, complex, or compound-complex
sentences.

Book censorship in American high schools has become a standard practice these days, individuals and groups have applied pressure to school boards everywhere. The books that have been censored range widely in subject they range widely in literary quality as well. No book seems to be beyond the reach of book censors. Books treating sexual situations, like *A Farewell to Arms*, have been banned, books that contain questionable language, like *The Catcher in the Rye*, have been banned, too. *The Grapes of Wrath* has been censored in some communities because of its presentation of socialist ideology, *Lord of the Flies* has been removed from libraries because of its violence. Even a book like *Huckleberry Finn* is now being questioned it has racially unflattering dialect. The American Library Association has come to the defense of these books, however that has not kept them on bookshelves and reading lists in many American high schools.

10 Subject-Verb Agreement

Subject-verb agreement requires that singular verbs be used with singular subjects (one person, place, thing, or idea). Singular verbs in the present tense usually end in s. Plural subjects (more than one—usually indicated for nouns with an s, as in *lamps*) must be used with plural verbs. (See pages **592–594** for clarification of verb endings.)

10a Use a verb that agrees with the subject
of the sentence, not with words that come
between the subject and verb.

Modifiers that separate subjects and verbs sometimes
present problems. Writers are most often confused by prepositional phrases, especially by nouns serving as objects of prepositions. The nouns in these phrases should not influence your
choice of verbs.

> The **swallows** of Capistrano **are** becoming less predictable. *(Do
> not let Capistrano, a singular noun in a prepositional phrase, lead
> you astray.)*

> This **father** of four sons **was** normally a patient person. (Sons, *al-
> though plural, is part of a prepositional phrase.)*

Subjects in sentences and clauses, however, are not always this
simply presented, so additional guidelines are helpful.

10b Use a plural verb with a compound
subject, a subject with two or more items,
joined by *and.*

┌compound subj┐ *plural verb*
The **princess** and the **frog kiss** at the end of the story.

┌compound subj┐ *plural verb*
The basketball **coach** and his best **player are** both excitable people.

Note: Compound subjects that are normally seen as one
unit are singular and require a singular verb.

> **Scotch and soda,** like most drinks made with hard liquor, **is** less
> popular now than it was ten years ago. *(The two liquids are mixed
> in a single drink, so the singular verb is correct.)*

10c Use a verb that agrees with the nearest
part of a compound subject joined by *or*
or *nor*.

This statement also applies to subjects joined by *either . . .
or* or *neither . . . nor.* All of these conjunctions ask readers to
consider alternatives, so match the verb to the number of the
closer subject.

Singular Subjects

Walking or running is a great way to get exercise. *(Walking* is;
running is.)

Plural Subjects

Albums or books are ideal for gifts that have to be mailed.
(Albums are; *books* are.)

When part of a compound subject is plural and part is singular, the verb can only agree with one part. In such cases,
match the verb to the closer subject.

Singular and Plural Subjects

Neither the turntable nor the **speakers work.**

Neither the speakers nor the **turntable works.**

Note: The second sentence pattern, although grammatically correct, sometimes seems awkward. If it seems too awkward, revise the sentence.

Either the **turntable is** not **working,** or the **speakers are** at fault.

10d Generally, use singular verbs with
indefinite pronouns.

Indefinite pronouns—*anyone, each, either, everybody, none,
someone,* and others—have no particular antecedents. Most of

them are singular, but some are plural. Use the verb form that agrees with the number of the pronoun. Be especially careful using pronouns like *everyone* or *everybody,* for they require singular verbs even though the pronoun sounds plural. Use *one* or *body* to guide you. (See Indefinite Pronouns, **5b,** pages 106–107.)

Somebody needs to get my mail while I am gone.

Both of the papers **were** assigned during the first week of class.

10e Use a singular verb with a collective noun that emphasizes the unity of a group.

The **troupe** of mimes **performs** every Tuesday at two o'clock. *(The troupe performs as a whole unit, so a singular verb is appropriate.)*

The **herd** of cattle **was** worth over one million dollars. *(A herd is one large group of animals; consequently, a singular verb is needed.)*

10f Use a plural pronoun if a collective noun stresses the several group members as a collection of individuals.

The **troupe** of mimes **perform** their individual skits after the main program. *(Since all the members will perform separately, the plural form is correct.)*

10g With expletive constructions—*here is, here are, there is,* and *there are*—choose the verb according to whether the noun following the verb is singular or plural.

Here and *there* are neither singular nor plural, so the verb must agree with the noun that follows. A singular noun requires *is;* a plural noun requires *are.*

Here **is** the **chapter** of my forthcoming novel.

There **are** too many unimaginative **programs** on television.

10h **In a clause introduced by a relative pronoun—*who, which,* or *that*—use a verb that matches the number of the pronoun's antecedent.**

Flooding in the spring is a **threat** that **requires** our attention. (That *refers to* threat, *a singular predicate noun. Consequently, the verb in the clause must be singular.*)

Alan gave Gina the two **sweaters,** which **were** made of Shetland wool. (Which *refers to* sweaters, *a plural direct object. The verb, as a result, must also be plural.*)

10i **Use a verb that agrees with the subject, not with a predicate noun following a linking verb.**

A subject and predicate noun often agree in number, but when they do not, match the verb to the subject of the sentence.

A major **expense** for operating a school **is** salaries for administrators, teachers, and custodians. (*Although the word* salaries *is plural, the subject of the sentence is* expense, *a singular noun. Therefore, the verb must also be singular.*)

10j **Use a singular verb with *every* or *each,* even when the subject is compound.**

Every man, woman, and child **was** evacuated before sunset. (Every *emphasizes the people individually, so a singular verb is appropriate.*)

Each actor and musician **was** asked to stand to be acknowledged. (Each *also emphasizes individual people, making the singular verb necessary.*)

10k Generally, use singular verbs with plural nouns that have singular meanings (for instance, *news, politics, bionics,* and *mumps.*)

Politics makes strange bedfellows. (Politics—*as a single, inclusive activity—needs a singular verb.*)

Geriatrics is the study and care of elderly people. (Geriatrics *is a single discipline, so a singular verb is necessary.*)

Exceptions: Several common exceptions to this principle are *pants, scissors, socks,* and *trousers.* These are all considered plural even though they come in units. When these words are used with *a pair of,* however, *pair* dominates and the verb is singular.

Scissors are necessary for sewing. (*The logic is that scissors have two functional parts, making the plural verb appropriate.*)

A **pair** of scissors **is** in the top drawer. (*The word* pair *emphasizes that the parts act as a single unit, making the singular verb necessary.*)

10l Use singular verbs when fractions, measurements, money, time, weight, and volume are considered as one unit.

Four days is such a short vacation. (*The days are considered as one block of time, so a singular verb is correct.*)

Six hundred dollars seems to be a great price. (*The dollar amount is interpreted as one price, so the singular verb is needed.*)

10m Use singular verbs with titles of single works, even when words in the title are plural.

Types of Drama **is** the required text for English 102. *(Because* Types of Drama *names one book, the singular verb is required.)*

Grownups **is** a funny, poignant play by Jules Feiffer. (Grownups *names one play, so a singular verb is necessary.)*

10n When words are used as words, use a singular verb, even when the words are plural.

Media **is** often misused when people should use *medium* instead. (Media *is the single word discussed as a word. A singular verb is correct even though the word is plural.)*

In news broadcasts, *persons* **has become** a standard but annoying substitute for the word *people*. *(Because* persons *is one word, a singular verb must be used.)*

EXERCISE □ *Subject-Verb Agreement*

In the following sentences, select the verb that is needed to maintain subject-verb agreement.

1. Two hundred dollars a month (is/are) much less than Amanda (expects/expect) to pay for rent.

2. The football team (has found/have found) that aerobics (is/are) quite a challenging form of exercise.

3. *Sitcoms,* the word most writers (uses/use) when discussing one type of television program, (is/are) the abbreviated form of *situation comedies.*

4. We (suspects/suspect) that our economy (is going/are going) to suffer.

5. Elliot, our bird dog, (become/becomes) as still as a statue when he (discovers/discover) where a bevy of quail (is located/are located).

6. *Of Mice and Men* (present/presents) a literary example of social bonding among misfits.

7. Their commercials make it (seem/seems) as if Sunkist and Mountain Dew (produces/produce) great times for young people who (drink/drinks) them.

8. No one in the organization (seems/seem) aware that both primary officers (is planning/are planning) to resign.

9. Either Brad or his roommates (is/are) responsible for weeding and watering the alumni garden.

10. Each unauthorized student and faculty member who (is caught/are caught) on the trampoline will be barred from the gym for a month.

11. The price (includes/include) airfare, room, board, taxes, and tips.

12. A list of rowing crew members (is/are) posted outside the

locker room, and members (is/are) expected to attend the first practice on Tuesday.

13. The class (submits/submit) essays every Monday.

14. *The Sounds of Silence* (was/were) Simon and Garfunkel's first best-selling album.

15. Neither Willy nor his sons (seems/seem) mature enough to deal with misfortune.

EXERCISE □ *Subject-Verb Agreement*

The following paragraph includes many errors in subject-verb agreement. Correct the misused verbs and draw an arrow to the subject with which your corrected verb agrees.

There is more and more adults attending college at a later age. Either to change careers or to get the education they missed are their motive. Anyone walking on a college campus is likely to see students in their thirties, forties, fifties, and even sixties carrying books and talking with friends. Almost every class and laboratory now include at least one of these "nontraditional" students. Because their difficulties and their situation are often so different from those of eighteen- and twenty-one-year-olds, these students face problems that seems unusual to a younger student. Some of these adults organizes their schooling around full-time jobs. Others care for families, as well as attends class. Nobody says that going to college and getting a degree is easy for anyone, but an adult student with adult responsibilities have extra problems to cope with. As this situation becomes more common, everyone are learning to adjust more easily, for the beginnings of recognition appears to have already taken place. Even the media has begun to recognize this trend in American education. With humor and sympathy, *Kate and Allie* provide insights into the problems adults face when attending college. Who knows? Given a chance today, maybe even Lucy Ricardo or John Walton might enroll in a class or two.

11 Pronoun-Antecedent Agreement

Pronoun-antecedent agreement requires that a singular pronoun be used with a singular antecedent (the word to which the pronoun refers) and that a plural pronoun be used with a plural antecedent. In short, antecedents and pronouns must agree in number.

sing.
antecedent   *sing.*
                                 pron.
Abigail raced up the stairs to **her** apartment.

*plural
antecedent*   *plural
                      pron.*

Children often look to **their** parents for encouragement and guidance.

In addition, pronouns must agree with the gender of their antecedents. Plural pronouns do not have gender, but singular pronouns involve four choices:

he	him	his	himself
she	her	hers	herself
it	it	its	itself

It used to be acceptable to use *he* and its variations as general pronouns when referring to nonspecific antecedents. Today, the general use of *he* is seldom acceptable because such usage fails to acknowledge women suitably—and also reinforces stereotypes.

To alleviate this problem, use plurals when possible for general sentences or rephrase the sentence entirely. However, do not try to skirt this issue by using a plural pronoun like *their* with a singular antecedent. Doing that only introduces another grammatical problem. Another way to solve this problem is to use paired words: *he or she, his or hers,* and so on. Use paired pronouns carefully, however, or your sentences may develop a distracting rhythm.

Sexist

A good **surgeon** carefully explains procedures to **his** patients.

Nonsexist

Good **surgeons** carefully explain procedures to **their** patients. *(Here a plural noun is used with a plural pronoun.)*

A good **surgeon** carefully explains procedures to **his or her** patients.

Nonsexist but Incorrect

A good **surgeon** carefully explains procedures to **their** patients. *(The plural* their *does not agree with the singular* surgeon.)

Nonsexist

Good **surgeons** carefully explain procedures to patients. *(Here, the possessive pronoun is omitted completely without substantial loss of meaning.)*

In those instances when your generalizations are based on personal experiences, use a specific antecedent instead of a general noun. It, in turn, will dictate a specific pronoun choice, which will help you avoid sexist language.

Dr. Knepper carefully explains procedures to **his** patients.

Dr. Shukiel also explains procedures thoroughly to **her** patients.

Beyond these concerns about gender, a variety of special circumstances determine pronoun-antecedent agreement.

11a Use plural pronouns to refer to compound antecedents joined by *and.*

compound antecedent *plural pron,*
Curt and Steve devoured **their** burgers.

compound antecedent *plural pron.*
Female **whales and dolphins** fiercely protect **their** young.

11b Use a pronoun that agrees with the nearer antecedent when compound antecedents are joined by *or* or *nor.*

The same is true for antecedents joined by *either . . . or* or *neither . . . nor.* Such compound subjects present alternatives, so the pronoun refers to each subject individually.

Singular Antecedents

Neither Enrique nor Milt completed **his** lab work. *(Enrique/his; Milt/his)*

Plural Antecedents

The **teachers or** the board **members** should clarify **their** position. *(Teachers/their; members/their)*

When part of a compound antecedent is singular and part is plural, the pronoun can agree with only one part. Therefore, match the pronoun to the nearer antecedent.

Singular and Plural Antecedents

The ambassador or the **Sandinistas** must modify **their** terms. *(Sandinistas/their)*

Note, however, that if the singular comes last in the construction, the sentence sounds awkward. Thus, always place the singular noun first or consider rewriting the sentence to make it smoother.

Awkward

The Sandinistas or the **ambassador** must modify **his** terms. *(ambassador/his)*

Smoother

If the **ambassador** will not change **his** stance, the **Sandinistas** will have to modify **their** terms. *(ambassador/his; Sandinistas/their)*

11c Generally, use a singular pronoun when an indefinite pronoun is the antecedent.

Indefinite pronouns—*anyone, each, either, everybody, none, some,* and others—are usually singular in meaning, but some are plural. Let the number of the indefinite pronoun guide you. Test the use of pronouns with troublesome antecedents, especially *everybody* and *everyone*, by double-checking the verb. With a plural verb, use a plural pronoun.

> **Everyone** who swims at McKinley Quarry risks **his or her** life. (Everyone *refers to people one at a time, as does the pronoun cluster* his or her. *In addition, the singular verb helps keep this usage clear. You would not say* everyone who swim.)

> **All** signed the petition, and then **their** regional representative sent it to the national headquarters. (All *refers to the several signers, so the plural* their *is correct.*)

11d Use a singular pronoun with a collective noun to stress the unity of the group.

> The **audience** showed **its** approval through applause. *(The audience is perceived as a single unit, creating a unified response.)*

> The **flock** returned to **its** roost. *(The flock acts as a large group.)*

11e Use a plural pronoun with a collective noun to stress the several group members as a collection of individuals.

> The **audience** raised **their** voices in song. *(This sentence stresses the many voices of the audience members.)*

> The **flock** sprang from **their** perches. *(Although a flock is one group of birds, this sentence stresses that a number of birds left a number of perches. Also consider rephrasing the sentence.)*

11f Choose relative pronouns according to their antecedents.

A *relative pronoun* must match the type of word to which it refers. *Who, whoever, whom, whomever,* and *whose* refer to people. *Whatever, which,* and *whichever* refer to animals and things. *That* refers to people or things, but usually to things (see Relative Pronouns, **5b,** pages 107–108). Additionally, *that* introduces information essential to the meaning of a sentence, while *which* may introduce nonessential information (see also Commas, **31h** and **32g**).

> Hardy created **Tess, whom** fate would undo. *(Tess is a fictional character, so a pronoun for people is required.)*
>
> The **handgun that** was found in the elevator had never been fired. *(A handgun is an object, requiring a pronoun that refers to things.* That *is the preferred pronoun since the clause distinguishes this gun from other guns.)*
>
> The geology professor displayed the quartz **crystal that** I found. *(A crystal is a thing, so either* that *or* which *would be correct.* That *is more effective here, however, because the clause is essential.)*

EXERCISE □ *Pronoun-Antecedent Agreement*

In the following sentences, most pronouns have been omitted. Insert appropriate pronouns and be ready to explain how they maintain pronoun-antecedent agreement. Sometimes there will be a choice of correct pronouns.

Example

Speed skaters ___*who*___ do not maintain proper form will add unwanted seconds to ___*their*___ skating times.

1. Scott and Monica Padewski sold _____ produce at a roadside stand.

2. After Sonia or the other secretaries complete _____

day-to-day work, _____ should begin training on the computer.

3. _____ of the bridge players were experienced, so _____ played seriously and well.

4. Neither Rick nor Bill could cook _____ own meals, so each of the boys ate most of _____ meals at a neighborhood restaurant.

5. The copy editors and the reviewers agreed that _____ original assessment of the manuscript had been correct, so _____ returned _____ to the author.

6. A flight attendant _____ is friendly and efficient will succeed in _____ work.

7. When a salmon or trout is leaping that way, _____ will rarely strike a lure.

8. I prefer to write with pencils _____ have hard leads. Doing that, I can also use _____ for my drafting projects.

9. After the tournament, the debate team celebrated _____ victory by going dancing.

10. The old limbs _____ supported the abandoned tree house shook violently in the storm.

EXERCISE □ *Pronoun-Antecedent Agreement*

Most pronouns in the following paragraph have been omitted. Insert the appropriate pronouns, making sure to maintain pronoun-antecedent agreement.

Everyone seems to carry photographs of _____ family members and friends in a wallet or billfold. Pictures of people _____ we feel close to, as a result, make our wallets and billfolds bulge. Trisha, a woman _____ I work with, has a billfold _____ must contain fifty pictures of _____ friends and family. _____ especially likes informal snapshots _____ show people as _____ really are rather than as _____ appear in pictures taken at a studio. Gary, another person at work, keeps only a few pictures in _____ wallet. _____ are studio photographs of _____ wife and children, usually with big smiles on _____ faces. On the other hand, I carry a wider assortment of pictures. I like those formal pictures _____ show _____ friends at _____ best. But I also carry candid pictures _____ I have taken. Thank goodness for _____ easy-to-use Kodak Disc. During off-hours at work, or when sharing stories with new acquaintances, these pictures offer glimpses of the people _____ we hold dear.

12 Pronoun Case

Pronoun case describes the three forms that pronouns assume when they are used in different ways in sentences.

Subjective case describes pronouns used as subjects (see **6a**) or predicate nouns (see **6c,** page 141).

Objective case describes pronouns used as direct objects or indirect objects (see **6c**) or as objects of prepositions (see **6d**).

Possessive case describes pronouns used to show ownership.

Most pronouns—and all nouns as well—appear in the subjective case *(someone, Alicia)* and the possessive case (usually formed by adding *'s: someone's, Alicia's).* Personal pronouns and pronouns produced with variations of *who,* however, appear in all three cases. Of special note are a small number of pronouns that do not use an apostrophe to form the possessive case: *his, her, hers, its, ours, yours, theirs,* and *whose.* These are possessive pronouns, and adding an apostrophe to them would be incorrect. Do not confuse these pronouns with certain words that sound the same. *It's* is a contraction for *it is,* and *who's* is a contraction for *who is.* Give special attention to the ways in which possessive pronouns and words that sound the same are used.

Personal pronouns are modified in the following ways to form the cases:

		Subjective	Objective	Possessive
Singular	1st person	I	me	my, mine
	2nd person	you	you	your, yours
	3rd person	he, she	him, her	his, hers
		it	it	its
Plural	1st person	we	us	our, ours

2nd person	you	you	your, yours
3rd person	they	them	their, theirs

Pronouns formed with variations of *who* change in these ways to form the cases:

Subjective	Objective	Possessive
who	whom	whose
whoever	whomever	

Use the following guidelines to select the proper pronoun cases.

12a Use the subjective case when the pronoun works as a subject or a predicate noun.

Although most writers have little trouble using personal pronouns in the subjective case, two kinds of problems can arise. When a sentence has a compound subject, writers are often unsure of what case to use. To decide, isolate each part of the subject and then choose the appropriate pronoun.

Just after sunrise, Kendal and **she** waded into the stream to fish. (Kendal *waded;* she *waded; consequently,* Kendal and she *waded.)*

When a pronoun in the subjective case is used as a predicate noun, restating or identifying the subject, it often sounds extremely formal. Do not avoid that seeming formality by misusing pronoun case. Instead, invert the subject and predicate noun if you find that usage more natural.

We discovered that "the mad scribbler" was **he.** *(The predicate noun, signaled by the linking verb, must be in the subjective case; if that seems too formal, invert the subject and predicate noun:* He was "the mad scribbler.")

12b Use the objective case when a pronoun works as a direct object, indirect object, or object of a preposition.

Writers sometimes have problems choosing a pronoun for a compound object. To solve the problem, isolate each part of the object, and then the objective case will sound natural.

> The tax form had to be signed by both **him** and Eileen. *(By* him; *by* Eileen. *Do not write* he and Eileen.)

A direct object answers the question who? or what? and thereby completes the idea in a sentence. An indirect object answers the question to whom? or for whom? and provides other useful information. A pronoun that answers these questions—because they are objects—should be in the objective case.

> The sportswriters voted **him** the tournament's outstanding player. *(As the direct object of* voted, *answering the question* whom?, *the pronoun must be in the objective case.)*

> Please give **me** your completed questionnaires. *(As an indirect object, answering the question* to whom?, *the pronoun must be in the objective case. To test such usage, create a phrase with the preposition* to: *you would not say* to I.)

12c Use the objective case for subjects of infinitives.

Although all other pronouns that serve as subjects are in the subjective case, a pronoun used as the subject of an infinitive must be in the objective case—making it a clear exception.

> We found **him** to be an enjoyable guest. *(Imagine the sentence with* he *to see why this usage will not cause you many problems.)*

12d When a pronoun functions as an appositive, use the case required for its antecedent.

Because an appositive simply restates a noun, its position can always be switched with that of the noun. If a pronoun in an appositive restates a subject of a clause, use the subjective case. Conversely, if a pronoun in an appositive restates an object, use the objective case.

> The two boys, Gerald and **he,** were responsible for opening the shop on Saturdays. *(Because* Gerald and he *restates the subject of the sentence, the pronoun must be in the subjective case.)*

> Certificates of merit were given to the runners-up, Abigail and **her.** (Abigail and her *restates the object of the preposition,* runners-up, *so the pronoun must be in the objective case.)*

12e When using *we* (the subjective case) or *us* (the objective case) with a noun, choose the case that would be correct if the noun were omitted.

> I think that **we** bicyclists ought to demand special cycling lanes. *(Without* bicyclists, *the clause reads* we ought, *a correct use of the subjective case.)*

> Organizational policy prohibits **us** committee members from meeting informally. (Members *is a direct object, so the adjoining pronoun must be in the objective case. Few would write* policy prohibits we from meeting.)

12f In constructions where words are omitted or understood, use the appropriate case as if all the words were included.

These shortened forms, called elliptical constructions, sometimes sound awkward. If using the correct pronoun sounds excessively formal, add the omitted words.

The Piersons arrived twenty minutes later than **we.** *(The complete thought is that they arrived twenty minutes later than we did. Few would say than us did.)*

We expected the Goldbergs to arrive before we expected **her.** *(The complete thought is that we expected them to arrive before we expected her to arrive.)*

12g Use pronoun-adjectives (the possessive pronouns *my, your, his, her, its, our, your,* and *their*) when a possessive construction also includes a noun.

Although **my** scores and Wilma's were better than **her** exam scores, **her** presentations were clearly the best. *(These pronouns in the possessive case serve as pronoun-adjectives.)*

12h Use independent possessive pronouns *(mine, yours, his, hers, its, ours, yours,* and *theirs)* to substitute for a possessive-and-noun construction.

Although these pronouns are technically in the possessive case, they can serve as subjects, predicate nouns, direct objects, indirect objects, and objects of prepositions.

The blue car outside is **mine;** the red one is **his.** *(In both instances the pronouns are in the possessive case but work as predicate nouns.)*

12i Use pronouns in the possessive case *(my, your, his, her, its, our, your,* and *their)* to modify a gerund.

When a gerund (an *-ing* verb that functions as a noun) is used in a sentence, an accompanying pronoun must be in the possessive case (see Gerunds, **6d,** pages 145–146).

I was annoyed by **his** leaving the party early. *(The annoyance resulted from the person's leaving, not the person himself.)*

The director commented that **their** dancing was the best part of the musical number. *(The choice of pronoun reflects what was the best part. Them dancing would have stressed the people; their dancing stresses the dancing.)*

Note: Do not allow an *-ing* form to completely determine use of case. Instead, interpret the sentence carefully. Sometimes the present participle functions as an adjective modifying a direct object-pronoun.

We watched **them** dancing in the gazebo. *(Here them serves as a direct object and must be in the objective case. Dancing in the gazebo modifies them.)*

To double-check your use, try changing the *-ing* form to a simple verb.

We watched **them** dance in the gazebo. *(The sentence is still sensible.)*

EXERCISE □ *Pronoun Case*

The following sentences contain errors in pronoun case. Cross out the incorrect pronouns and replace them with appropriate ones. Be ready to explain your substitutions. If using the correct pronoun case makes a sentence sound awkward, revise the sentence.

1. Although Mr. Simmons disapproved of them going to the video arcade, Teresa and Irene went anyway.

2. Her and Cheng promised to clean up the lab after we completed the experiment.

3. When the settlement was finally reached, five thousand dollars was awarded to she and her sister.

4. The two lawyers, Tarita Dowell and him, placed several brief advertisements in the local newspaper.

5. Us workers at the Ford plant have made too many wage concessions already.

6. Although a number of reporters gathered useful information, the interpreter of the facts was clearly him.

7. The general public is unaware of the duties expected of we nurses.

8. We found she to be a skilled seamstress as well as a creative designer.

9. Because we organized our time, we expect to finish our work before them.

10. The realtors—Jordan, Elise, and her—quickly surveyed the property, writing down facts that could be included on the multiple-listing form.

12j Use *who* or *whoever* (subjective case) as subjects in subordinate clauses; use *whom* or *whomever* (objective case) as complements.

This usage is problematical. To determine which case is appropriate, restate the idea of the clause to determine how the relative pronoun functions. A simple strategy is to use *he* (subjective) or *him* (objective) in the restatement, matching the *m* in *him* with the *m* in *whom* when the objective case is required.

> Luke Walters is a dental student **who** has a bright future. *(The restatement, "He has a bright future," shows correct use of the subjective case.)*
>
> Luke was a student **whom** I met during my second year of study. *(The restatement, "I met him," shows why the objective case is correct.)*
>
> We plan to offer the scholarship to **whoever** writes the most creative essay. *(The restatement, "He writes the most creative essay," illustrates the correct use of the subjective case. Although the preposition to might suggest that the objective case is required, the whole clause forms the preposition's object. Do not be misled.)*
>
> The board will approve the appointment of **whomever** we select. *(The restatement, "We select him," clarifies the need for the objective case.)*

12k Use *who* (subjective case) when the pronoun serves as the subject of a question; use *whom* (objective case) when the pronoun works as the object in a question.

These interrogative pronouns, too, can pose problems. However, developing a hypothetical response helps determine which case to use. Once again, use *he* and *him* as guides, matching the *m* in *him* with the *m* in *whom*.

> **Whom** should I call in case of an emergency? *(Call him.)*
>
> **Who** left the heap of dirty clothes on the washer? *(He did.)*

EXERCISE ☐ *Pronoun Case*

In the following sentences, place *who, whom, whoever,* or *whomever* in the blanks. Be ready to explain why your choices present the proper use of pronoun case.

1. _____ do you think was a better boxer, Ali or Spinks?

2. I would recommend Isaac Asimov's books to anyone _____ loves science fiction.

3. Although Richard Burton never won an Academy Award, he was an actor _____ I greatly admired.

4. If we need some assistance in planning the tournament, _____ should we ask for help?

5. Adam and Miguel will drive to Florida with _____ responds to their notice on the bulletin board.

EXERCISE ☐ *Pronoun Case*

In the following paragraph, select the proper pronouns. Be ready to explain your choices.

I thought working as a lifeguard at the community pool would give me a chance to earn some money while getting some sun over summer break. It sounded great, but I had forgotten that most of the people (who/whom) visited the pool were children (who/whom) were dropped off by their parents.

Generally, I like kids, but in smaller groups. I found (they/them) to be unusually rowdy, obnoxious, and undisciplined. Whenever I cornered a few boys and girls (who/whom) were causing trouble, they blamed (whoever/whomever) was out of favor that day. When I got tired of (them/their) fighting in the water, I would make the ringleaders sit by my chair. That was effective for about ten minutes. Several times I caught the same kids sneaking candy bars into the pool area in their swimming suits. I thought no one had more patience than (I/me), but the fourth occurrence, as the saying goes, "did me in." I went to Mr. Gerrardo and Ms. Parsons, the pool managers, to get some support. I wanted the kids thrown out of the pool for the day, but Mr. Gerrardo and (she/her) told me to threaten the kids some more. I did. It did not help. After a few weeks of such nonsense, I asked myself, "(Who/whom) needs this kind of irritation?" I know now that (we/us) college students trying to earn some easy money over summer break have it rough.

13 Using Verb Tenses

Tenses are changes in verbs to indicate when things happened or existed in relation to when you write about them (see Verbs,

5c, pages 117–119). These changes in time are shown through helping verbs or different verb endings. *Regular verbs* follow a set pattern for forming tenses. (For an example of a full conjugation of the verb *to teach,* see the Glossary of Terms, pages **592–594.**)

Present tense:	complete(s)
Past tense:	complete**d**
Future tense:	**will** complete
Present perfect tense:	**have (has)** complete**d**
Past perfect tense:	**had** complete**d**
Future perfect tense:	**will have** complete**d**

Progressive Tenses

Present progressive:	am (are) planning
Past progressive:	was (were) planning
Future progressive:	will be planning
Present perfect progressive:	have (has) been planning
Past perfect progressive:	had been planning
Future perfect progressive:	will have been planning

Irregular verbs change tenses through modifications in spelling or word form and follow a different pattern from regular verbs (see Irregular Verbs, pages **113–116**).

In writing, use appropriate verb tenses to clarify when actions or conditions occur. To do so, carefully think about the situation and about when the events or conditions occurred in relation to one another.

13a Use the present tense to express repeated or habitual action.

The present tense can be effectively used to describe actions that occur at the time of writing or to describe a standard procedure. If an action or series of actions is often repeated, you can effectively describe it by using the present tense.

Eleanor **works** on her poetry every day. (*Writing poetry is an ongoing project of Eleanor's.*)

Deposit a coin into the slot, **wait** for the dial tone, and then **dial** the appropriate number. (*Since the procedure is common, the present tense is useful for describing it.*)

13b Use the present tense to express general truths and scientific principles.

Because truths and principles do not change, they are always accurate in the present.

The force of gravity **determines** the flow of water in rivers and steams. (*It always has and always will.*)

13c Use the present tense to describe artistic and literary works.

Because these works continue to exist in the same form, describe them in the present tense.

Picasso's painting *Guernica* **contains** images of chaos and terror. (*Contains is in the present tense because the painting still depicts these images.*)

13d Use the past tense to describe completed actions or conditions that existed in the past.

In writing, the past tense is often the most appropriate tense because much of what we write about has already taken place.

My great-grandfather **emigrated** from Rumania in the late nine-teenth century. *(His trip is long since past.)*

13e Use the future tense to describe actions that will occur or conditions that will exist in the future.

Future tense is frequently used to describe expected actions or conditions.

The Olympic Committee **will hold** its next meeting in Geneva, Switzerland. *(They have not convened yet but plan to.)*

13f Use the progressive tense to express present, past, or future actions or conditions.

I **am writing** this now.

Mary **is reading** over my shoulder.

I **was writing** yesterday as well.

Mary and Sasha **were writing,** too.

I **will be writing** in most of my courses.

13g Use the present perfect tense to describe actions that occurred or conditions that existed at an unspecified time in the past or that began in the past and continue to the present.

Beethoven's piano concertos **have been** favorites of mine since I **took** a music appreciation class. (Took *is in the past tense because the class is over;* have been *is in the present perfect because the pref-erence began in the past and continues to the present time.)*

13h Use the past perfect tense to describe actions that began or conditions that existed in the past but were completed before some other past event.

Ned **had expected** the package to arrive by Saturday. (Had expected *implies that it is Sunday or later. According to this sentence, the sequence follows this order: package expected, Saturday, the present.*)

13i Use the future perfect tense to describe actions that will be completed in the future but before a certain time.

Margaret **will have finished** the quilt well before Mother's Day. (*Mother's Day is in the future. Finishing the quilt will also be in the future, but before Mother's Day.*)

14 Consistency of Verb Tenses

Verb tense signals chronology, placing events and actions in relationship to the time when a writer is describing them. These are important signals. Of additional importance is consistency of verb tenses. Readers expect a uniform presentation of tenses that allows them to understand clearly the relationships among ideas.

Consistently using past tense to describe past actions or using present tense for present actions causes few problems for writers. When you need to express different chronological relationships, a few general guidelines will help you maintain consistency with other, more complicated series of verb tenses.

14a Use infinitives to match the tense of the main verb.

Infinitives (to swim, to subscribe, to record) automatically match the tense of the main verb. Using infinitives causes few problems for writers.

Ryan **wants to be** an aerospace engineer. (Wants *suggests a present desire, and the infinitive automatically coordinates with the present tense.*)

The patient **was to arrive** well before his nine o'clock appointment. (Was *presents a past arrangement, and the infinitive automatically coordinates with the past tense.*)

14b Use present participles to express action that coincides with that of the main verb.

The present participle, like the infinitive, is chameleonlike and automatically matches the tense of the main verb.

Hearing of their engagement, Joyce immediately congratulated her two friends. (*The hearing and congratulating occur at approximately the same time in the past.*)

Running down the stairs, Steve remembered that he had left the coffee pot plugged in. (*Running and remembering are simultaneous in this sentence, both occurring in the past.*)

14c Use past participles and perfect participles to express action or to describe conditions that occurred before that of the main verb.

Past participles (*hurried, welcomed, driven*) and perfect participles (*having hurried, having welcomed, having driven*) establish a chronological sequence: the action or condition presented by these participles occurred first, followed by that of the main verb.

Reassured by the revised weather forecast, Bette packed to go to the beach. *(Bette was first reassured, and then she packed.)*

Having walked these hills all her life, the injured hiker knew exactly where she was. *(She had been in the hills before her injury. Because of that fact, she knew where she was.)*

14d Generally, use past tense or past perfect tense in a subordinate clause when the verb in the independent clause is in the past or past perfect tense.

Vance **had** to draw the model three times before he **got** the effect he **wanted.** *(The use of* had *in the independent clause establishes that this series of actions took place in the past. Logic requires that the other verbs,* got *and* wanted, *also be in the past.)*

Before the plumber **arrived,** the sink **had overflowed** onto the bathroom floor. *(The use of* had overflowed *establishes that the mess occurred before some other past action.* Arrived *must consequently be used to place the plumber's rescue also in the past.)*

14e Use any tense in the subordinate clause when the verb in the independent clause is in the present, future, present perfect, or future perfect tense.

These tenses express so many chronological possibilities that any number of options are available, so long as the meaning of the sentence is clear.

Some scientists currently **think** that exercise **will prolong** life. *(Current thoughts are followed by future projections.)*

The band **will begin playing** one hour after the reception **has begun.** *(The start of the reception precedes the band's playing.)*

EXERCISE □ *Tenses*

In the following sentences, select the verbs that are appropriate to the meanings of the sentences. Avoid inconsistent shifts in tense.

1. Although Melissa (is/was) a meticulous housekeeper, her children have not yet learned to help her.

2. Armando smoked cigarettes for nine years, and then he (quits/quit).

3. Although I (want/wanted) (to see/to have seen) *La Cage aux Folles* on Broadway, I could not get tickets.

4. Candy, because she (needs/needed) (to take/to have taken) her medication, momentarily left the meeting.

5. In our part of the country, the planting season (begins/began) each year in May.

6. (Rushing/Having rushed) (to catch/to have caught) the taxi, John stumbled on the steps of the office building.

7. When everything (goes/went) well, Jamaal was pleasant (to be/to have been) with.

8. In *Cabaret,* the film by Bob Fosse, Sally Bowles (is/was) a singer at the Kit Kat Klub in Berlin.

9. (Reading/Having read) *Great Expectations* once before, Kate was not interested in (reading/having read) it again.

10. Jesse was (to register/to have registered) for the class before noon on Friday.

11. Because of the partial success of implanting artificial hearts at the Humana Medical Center, more of these devices (are going to be/were going to be) implanted in the future.

12. In his autobiography, *A Time to Heal,* Gerald Ford (explains/explained) why he pardoned Richard Nixon.

13. The rough surface texture of Van Gogh's *Starry Night* (is/was) not discernible in reproductions.

14. Clearly, Walter Cronkite (has not expected/had not expected) his mother to speak at the 1985 awards ceremony.

15. Galileo was imprisoned by the Catholic Church for declaring that the earth (revolves/revolved) around the sun.

EXERCISE □ *Tenses*

Select the appropriate verbs in the following paragraph. Make sure that there are no unnecessary tense shifts.

Stray animals (seem/seemed) (to know/to have known) that our household (is/was) an easy mark. We (cannot prove/could not prove) it, but we (think/thought) that the animal grapevine (tells/told) seasonal "basket cases" (to come/to have come) to our house. Last spring, for instance, a small tabby cat (shows/showed) up with whiskers gone, a skinned leg, and ribs showing. Although my husband briefly (complains/complained), he (sees/saw) that the cat (needs/needed) our kind of help. (Grumbling/Having grumbled) a little, my husband (arranges/arranged) a box in our garage for the cat (to sleep/to have slept) in. We (name/named) the cat right away—Scrappy. He eventually (recovers/recovered) and (moves/moved) into the house. We (have known/had known) for a long time that someday we must stop our adoptions. But for right now, we (plan/planned) (to help/to have helped) animals that (need/needed) a good home.

15 Mood

Mood, indicated by verb form, refers to the way writers present their ideas and information. Sometimes writers want to stress the factuality of information *(indicative mood)*. Sometimes they want to give commands *(imperative mood)*. Sometimes they want to stress that information is conditional or contrary to fact *(subjunctive mood)*. The three moods of verbs allow writers to make these distinctions clearly.

15a Use the indicative mood to present a fact, offer an opinion, or ask a question.

The indicative mood is the most commonly used mood, since much writing is based on fact or opinion. Using verbs in this normal pattern causes few problems.

> Ron **got** his pilot's license when he **was** nineteen.
>
> When **did** Ron **get** his twin-engine rating? *(Notice the separation of the two-part verb by the subject when the sentence is a question.)*

15b Use the imperative mood to present commands or directions.

The imperative mood is especially common in papers telling how to complete a process. The subject of an imperative sentence is usually omitted but understood.

> **Get** letters of reference from the companies you have flown for. *(You is the understood subject; get is in the imperative mood, explaining what actions to take; have flown is in the indicative mood.)*
>
> **Buckle** your seatbelts and **observe** the no-smoking signs. *(You, again, is the understood subject.)*

15c Use the subjunctive mood to describe a situation that is conditional or contrary to fact, or to express a wish.

The subjunctive mood is quite common as well, but it frequently causes problems for writers. Watch especially for the subordinating conjunctions *if* and *even if*, for they are the most common signals that the subjunctive mood—*were* instead of *was*—must be used to express a conditional statement.

> If Ron **were** to work for Britt, he would have to move to Chicago. *(Working for Britt is not a fact; it is a possibility. Consequently, the subjunctive is required.)*
>
> I wish Ron **were married,** but his flying schedule would make a normal homelife impossible. *(Ron is not married, so this statement of a wish must be in the subjunctive mood.)*

EXERCISE □ *Mood*

Where appropriate, revise the verbs in the following sentences to demonstrate correct use of the subjunctive mood.

1. If the weather was better, we would go sailing instead of going to the museum.

2. The chef insisted on eggplants that are a deep purple with no traces of discoloration.

3. Anita would live in the country if she was given her choice.

4. Ben Kingsley could not have played the part better if he was Gandhi himself.

5. Jonathan has many good qualities and would make a good supervisor—if he was not so demanding.

16 Adjectives and Adverbs

In most instances, writers use adjectives and adverbs easily, naturally, and correctly. Confusion does occur sometimes. In part, it results because writers do not completely think through the process of modification. In part, it also results because adjectives and adverbs have similar word forms. The following guidelines should help solve the most basic errors in adjective and adverb usage.

16a Use adjectives to modify nouns and pronouns.

Make sure that the word modifying a noun or pronoun is an adjective. To check this usage, isolate the word and its modifier, placing the modifier first, to see if the pair sounds appropriate. When uncertain, consult a dictionary to find the correct adjective form.

> The Frazers made **careful** plans before they planted the garden. (Careful *clearly modifies* plans. *Even in isolation, they make sense together:* careful plans.)

> The Frazers were **careful** as they tilled the soil. (Careful, *following a linking verb, still modifies* Frazers. *In isolation, the word pair is still sensible: the* careful Frazers.)

16b Use adverbs to modify verbs.

Make sure the word modifying a verb is an adverb. Isolate the pair of words to see if they sound appropriate. The adverb should make sense before or after the verb. Again, when uncertain of a word's adverb form, consult a dictionary.

> The Frazers **carefully** removed the plants from the trays. (Carefully *explains how they removed the plants. In isolation, the modifier and verb work logically together:* carefully removed *or* removed carefully.)

16c Use adverbs to modify adjectives or other adverbs.

Adverbs that modify adjectives and other adverbs are called intensifiers because they stress the modifications the other words make clear. The most common intensifier is *very*; in addition, *especially, really, seriously, terribly, truly,* and others can modify adjectives and adverbs.

> The Frazers made **especially** careful plans before they planted their garden. (Especially *intensifies the meaning of the adjective* careful.)

> The Frazers **very** carefully removed the plants from the trays. (Very *intensifies the meaning of the adverb* carefully.)

16d Distinguish between troublesome adjective and adverb pairs.

Some pairs of modifiers are commonly confused in speech and writing, and you should learn their proper use. Two of the most commonly confused pairs of words are described here. Others are treated in the Glossary of Usage at the back of the text (see **65**).

> **Bad/Badly:** Use *bad,* the adjective form, to modify nouns and pronouns, even with sensory verbs *(appear, feel, look, smell, taste,* and *sound).* Use *badly* only to modify a verb.

> That was a **bad** rendition of *Rhapsody in Blue.*

> After sitting in the sun for two hours, Monica felt **bad.**

> Even after dozens of art classes, Anita painted **badly.**

> **Good/Well:** Use *good* only to modify a noun or pronoun. Use *well* as an adverb to mean *satisfactory;* use *well* as an adjective to mean *healthy.*

> Marco was a very **good** pianist.

The rehearsal went **well** last night.

Although Anton had a slight fever, he said he felt **well** enough to play.

16e Use positive adjectives and adverbs to make direct modifications of nouns or pronouns.

Positive adjectives and adverbs imply no comparisons. They provide direct modification and appear in their simplest word form: *recent, soon, clearly, fortunate.*

adj.
The **eerie** set for *The Passion of Dracula* was **exceptional.** *adj.*

adv.
The scene changes were made **quickly.**

16f Use comparative adjectives and adverbs to compare two people, places, things, ideas, qualities, conditions, or actions.

Emphasizing some kind of distinction, comparative adjectives and adverbs are used to establish differences between two similar items. They are formed in two ways, depending on the number of syllables in the original word. If an adjective or adverb has only one syllable, form the comparative by adding the suffix *-er.* If an adjective or adverb has two or more syllables, form the comparative by adding a helping word, either *less* or *more,* before it: *more recent, sooner, more clearly, less fortunate.*

A number of two- and three-syllable adjectives—*funny* and *unhappy,* for example—will use the *-er* form. Consult a dictionary to learn which pattern to follow.

adj.   *comp. adj.*
The **eerie** set for *The Passion of Dracula* was **more detailed** and *comp. adj.*
larger than anyone expected.

comp.
adv.

The scene changes for this production were made **more quickly** than they were for *Hedda Gabler*.

16g Use superlative adjectives and adverbs to compare three or more people, places, things, ideas, qualities, conditions, or actions.

Superlative adjectives and adverbs emphasize the exceptional by comparing an item or action with a number of similar items—making these superlatives more emphatic than either positive or comparative adjectives and adverbs. Like the comparative form, they are made in two ways. If an adjective or adverb has only one syllable, form the superlative by adding the suffix *-est*. If an adjective or adverb has two or more syllables, form the superlative by using *least* or *most* before it: *most recent, soonest, most clearly, least fortunate*. Use superlatives sparingly.

super.
adj.

The set for *The Passion of Dracula* was the **most attractive** one I have seen.

Of all the plays done this year, *Dracula's* scene changes were

super.
adv.

made the **most quickly**.

Note: Some adjectives form the comparative and superlative in an irregular way. They use neither suffixes nor helping words. Instead, they change their spellings completely.

Positive	Comparative	Superlative
bad	worse	worst
good	better	best
little	{ less { littler	{ least { littlest

many
much $\Big\}$ more   most

16h Do not use double comparatives or superlatives.

Only one change of an adjective or adverb is needed to form the comparative or superlative. To use both a suffix and a helping word is incorrect.

> Kliban's cartoons about cats are the ~~most~~ funniest ones I have seen.

> Madonna rose to superstardom ~~more~~ faster than even she expected.

16i Do not use comparatives and superlatives for incomparable adjectives and adverbs.

A few adjectives—for instance, *central, dead, empty, impossible, infinite, perfect, straight,* and *unique*—under most circumstances cannot suggest comparisons of any kind. For instance, the universe is either *infinite* or it is *finite*. It cannot be more or less infinite than something else. Use only the positive form of such modifiers.

Illogical

James Joyce's *Ulysses* is the **most unique** book I have read. (Unique *clearly means "one of a kind." It cannot be made more so.*)

Logical

James Joyce's *Ulysses* is a **unique** book. (*This uses* unique *in its proper positive form.*)

James Joyce's *Ulysses* is the **most unusual** book I have read. (Unusual *is a quality that can be compared among books.*)

216

EXERCISE ☐ *Adjective and Adverb Forms*

Select the appropriate adjective or adverb forms in the following sentences. Be ready to explain your choices.

1. The members of Andretti's pit crew worked (good/well) together because they were all (experienced/more experienced/most experienced).

2. Although pre-fab houses can be constructed (easily/more easily/most easily) than a house built totally on the site, the quality of the work is often (real/really) good.

3. Baroque architecture made use of (intricate/more intricate/most intricate) scrolled molding.

4. Brick houses are (expensive/more expensive/most expensive) than frame houses, but brick houses are virtually (trouble-free/more trouble-free/most trouble-free).

5. Shamir felt (bad/badly) because his scores on his College Boards were (bad/worse/worst) than he expected.

6. When we compared features for microwave ovens, we found that Quasar models have the (long/longer/longest) warranty period: five years.

EXERCISE ☐ *Adjectives and Adverbs*

The following paragraph contains errors in adjective and adverb use. Locate the errors, correct them, and be prepared to explain any corrections.

I began doing needlework six years ago, and from my hours of work I have created some real attractive decorations. On my couch, I have seven cross-stitched pillows, the more beautiful of which has flowers and butterflies on it. Of my framed needlework, my most favoritest is a forest scene with pine trees of various shades of green. The lightest green is so pale it is almost white, and the darker shade is almost black. The contrast in the picture is striking. A most unique project I recently finished is a crewel-worked cover for a Queen Anne's chair I inherited from my great-grandmother. The original fabric on the chair had been damaged by cigarette ashes, and every time I used to look at it, I felt badly. Now, the embroidered cover fits perfect and makes me feel proud of my heirloom. I have spent hundreds of hours working on these projects and hundreds of dollars buying fabrics and thread, but when someone says, "*You* did that. It's beautiful!" I always smile. I know that I sew good, but the compliments make me feel even better about my time and effort.

SENTENCE VARIETY AND EMPHASIS

Writers frequently repeat sentence patterns, sometimes without realizing that they are doing so. In some writing, for instance, simple sentences predominate, while complex or compound-complex sentences are characteristic of other prose. Each type has its strengths, but when writers consistently use sentences of the same kind or length, their work can become monotonous. On the other hand, writers can stimulate interest in their ideas by varying sentences.

When readers comment that sentences "are not varied enough," they often mean that the writer has used too many simple sentences. A progression of simple statements isolates each thought from the next, ignoring the connections between ideas. To achieve sentence variety, consider several of the strategies discussed here.

17 Sentence Length

Sentence length, the number of words in a sentence, is a useful but somewhat subjective standard by which to judge sentence variety. Too many short sentences make writing seem immature and choppy, whereas too many long sentences make it dense and often difficult to read. By considering the number of words in your sentences, you can get a general idea of where to begin working on variety. Several brief statements in a row may signal the need for some coordination or subordination (see **18** and **19**). A succession of very long sentences may need to be broken into briefer, more readable units. Using sentence length to judge sentence variety is not a sure-fire method, but it is one way to watch for a series of sentences that are too similar.

17a Use brief sentences for emphasis.

Sentences with few words normally present one clear, simple idea, uncluttered by clarifications or limitations. Although too many in succession will make writing seem simplistic, a few well-placed brief sentences can add variety and needed emphasis.

Our senator maintains two elaborate residences, one in our state and one in the Washington area. Although I understand the reasons for having two homes, a pair of $300,000 residences seems needlessly extravagant. **In short, I disapprove.**

17b Use sentences of moderate length under most circumstances.

Sentences of moderate length make appropriate connections among ideas, add pertinent facts and details, and, at the same time, keep writing accessible.

Although I enjoy televised boxing, I am often dissatisfied with network commentaries. All too often, sportscasters' comments superficially point out the obvious—like who is winning—rather than help me understand the sport.

17c Use lengthy sentences to link complicated ideas.

Lengthy sentences make complex connections among ideas and include a good deal of clarification.

For nearly a century, the Statue of Liberty, in all its majesty, has stood at the entrance to New York Harbor, welcoming immigrants, travelers, and returning Americans and justly symbolizing the freedoms we value.

Because long sentences are so complicated, write them carefully. For the most part, you are better off reserving them for times when you *need* them. Do not unnecessarily burden readers with too many in any one paragraph.

No sentence length is perfect for every idea. No sentence length is best. The point is that writers should vary sentence lengths to create emphasis and make reading more pleasant.

EXERCISE □ *Sentence Length*

To practice sentence modification, expand the brief sentences below and break up those that seem excessively long.

Example
Medieval castles, *were* typically made of native stone, *. They* served as fortresses as well as homes for the nobility, and the peasants who lived nearby also took shelter there.

1. I enjoy traveling.

2. Although Caleb sometimes rides the bus when the weather is especially bad, he usually walks the mile to work, enjoying the scenery and people and saving money on transportation as well.

3. Rise and Shine, a restaurant that specializes in breakfast menus, is open every day, twenty-four hours a day, and a steady stream of customers who enjoy the good food makes it a lively place to eat.

4. I disagree.

5. The large Victorian houses on Chestnut, built at the turn of

the century, exemplify ornate architecture at its best and reflect a time when craftsmanship was very highly valued.

6. Although riding six mounts a day can be tiring for a jockey, such experience is important in establishing a reputation as a rider, and it also, of course, means the jockey will earn even more money than he or she otherwise might.

7. Owning a goat is frustrating.

8. Because airline fares are currently very low, many people are buying tickets that they will not use for several months, and, as a result, airline revenues will be disproportionately high in the short term and then low in the long term.

9. Janice was fired from her job.

10. Sybil, who is very particular about her appearance, always has Ricardo cut her hair because he has learned what her preferences are and is appropriately meticulous.

18 Coordination

Coordination is forming compound sentences by using a comma and one of the coordinating conjunctions: *and, but, for, nor, or, so,* or *yet* (see Coordinating Conjunctions, **5f,** page 127, and Compound Sentences, **7b**). Coordination joins two independent clauses of equal importance and makes several kinds of important connections.

18a Use coordination to link or contrast roughly equivalent clauses.

Compound sentences use coordinating conjunctions to balance ideas of equal importance, giving the parts of the sentence the same emphasis. Used selectively, coordination is an effective way to join ideas and improve upon the repetitiousness of too many simple sentences.

> Sarah loaned Carla a tea service, **and** Rachel loaned her three serving trays.

> Tamiko does not like watching television, **but** she does like shooting video tapes.

> The weather in Colorado was suitably brisk, **but** Katarina postponed her skiing trip.

18b Use coordination for different effects.

Although there are only seven coordinating conjunctions, they provide some degree of variety in the way writers present ideas. For instance, *but* and *yet* both present contrasts between clauses and are therefore roughly interchangeable. They do, however, create slightly different impressions.

> Estella was a heartless girl, **but** Pip loved her anyway.

> Estella was a heartless girl, **yet** Pip loved her anyway. (*Yet gives this sentence a slightly more formal sound than* but *does.*)

Both *for* and *so* establish cause-and-effect relationships between the clauses in a compound sentence, but the order in which the clauses appear differ from one to the other. When *so* is used, the cause is presented first, followed by the effect. When *for* is used, a description of the effect comes first, followed by a description of the cause. Writers can therefore change the emphasis of a sentence by choosing between *for* and *so*.

> The cattle were grazing in the north pasture, **so** we rode our three-wheelers in the south meadow. *(With so, the cause precedes the effect, and emphasis is placed on the cattle.)*
>
> We rode our three-wheelers in the south meadow, **for** the cattle were grazing in the north pasture. *(With for, the effect precedes the cause, and emphasis is placed on riding three-wheelers.)*

Writers can make this kind of choice and, as a result, change the emphasis in a sentence and often the impact that a sentence has on readers.

18c Avoid overusing coordination in a series of sentences.

Because of the balance of clauses in compound sentences, overusing coordination creates an undesirable teeter-totter effect. Look, for instance, at this series of coordinated sentences:

> Several weeks before the last snowfall, the ground begins to thaw, and the wintered-over spinach starts to turn green. Some of the leaves begin to grow, but most remain dormant for a few weeks more. The plants begin to grow rapidly in the middle of March, and by April we are eating fresh spinach salad.

After the second sentence, an annoying rhythm emerges. Unfortunately, readers often become more attuned to the repetitious balance of the sentences than to the ideas. To avoid such problems, use coordination selectively to join related ideas and consider other alternatives for achieving sentence variety.

Several weeks before the last snowfall, when the ground begins to thaw, the wintered-over spinach starts to turn green. Although some of the leaves begin to grow, most remain dormant for a few weeks more until the middle of March, when the plants begin to grow rapidly. By April we are eating fresh spinach salad.

18d Avoid excessive coordination within single sentences.

Although coordination can effectively link ideas, too many coordinated clauses in a row create a predictable rhythm and suggest a balance that is not always appropriate. If three or more clauses have identical structures, such parallel coordination can create interest. When clauses are dissimilar, however, try other methods to join the ideas.

Awkwardly Coordinated

Americans have become concerned about stimulants in foods, and they have started using products without caffeine, and to accommodate them restaurants now regularly serve decaffeinated coffees and teas. *(These clauses lack balance. The first two explain trends Americans follow, but the third describes an effect of these trends.)*

Suitably Subordinated

Because Americans have become concerned about stimulants in foods and have started using products without caffeine, restaurants now regularly serve decaffeinated coffees and teas to accommodate them. *(Here the first two clauses are joined and then related to the effect. Slight rewording is necessary.)*

Americans, concerned about stimulants in foods, have started using products without caffeine, and to accommodate them restaurants now regularly serve decaffeinated coffees and teas. *(One clause has been reshaped as a verbal phrase. Again, some rewording is required.)*

Coordination is a potentially useful way to balance ideas and to create sentence variety. Be aware, however, that using excessive coordination is as ineffective as using too many simple sentences.

EXERCISE ☐ *Coordination*

Combine these pairs of sentences using commas and coordinating conjunctions: *and, but, for, nor, or, so,* and *yet.* Also revise sentences containing too many independent clauses.

1. Public Television can consider running advertisements. It can continue to rely on generous donations.

2. Five construction firms presented bids for the First National Bank Annex, and the board of directors selected the best one, and construction begins next week.

3. Abbie did not like reading history. He changed his mind when he began *All the President's Men.*

4. Darren intended to fish for only two hours. By dark he had caught only two small bluegill.

5. Isaac did not smoke, and he bicycled twenty-five miles per day, and he would not allow guests to smoke in his apartment.

227

19 Subordination

Subordination is forming complex or compound-complex sentences by using subordinating conjunctions or relative pronouns (see Subordinating Conjunctions, **5f,** page 127; Relative Pronouns, **5b,** pages 107–108; and Sentences, **7c** and **7d**). Subordination joins at least one independent clause with one or more dependent clauses to suggest important relationships among ideas. Additionally, it improves sentence variety.

19a Use subordination to establish the varied importance of clauses.

Complex sentences use subordinating conjunctions (*after, because, when, until,* and so on) to indicate the varied importance of clauses. Because the subordinate clause relies for meaning on the independent clause, the idea in the independent clause is grammatically most important. The meaning and emphasis, however, depend on the subordinating conjunction.

> Jessica lightly rubbed the chair with fine steel wool **before** she varnished it. *(This sentence emphasizes Jessica's sanding of the chair, incorporating varnishing as a subsequent action).*

> Jessica varnished the chair **after** she lightly rubbed it with fine steel wool. *(This sentence emphasizes the varnishing and incorporates sanding as a preliminary step.)*

As these sentences demonstrate, writers can alter the emphasis and effect of clauses in sentences by choosing among related subordinating conjunctions and varying the order of the clauses. Other subordinating conjunctions establish other kinds of emphasis, and by carefully selecting these conjunctions, writers can construct sentences that serve their purposes well.

Newswriters for television must plan brief news stories **since** broadcasts are normally limited to thirty minutes. *(Here the cause-and-effect connection is clear, and in this case, the emphasis is on newswriters.)*

Because broadcasts are normally limited to thirty minutes, newswriters for television must plan brief news stories. *(The cause-and-effect relationship is still clear, but the reordering of the clauses and change in subordinating conjunction place the emphasis on time limits.)*

19b Use relative pronouns to embed secondary information.

Relative pronouns *(that, which, who,* and so on) allow writers to embed clauses within existing sentences to add clarity and produce variety. The embedded information is called a relative clause, and it is clearly less important than the information in the independent clause.

The bird bath **that** Gary bought for the flower garden is sitting behind the garage. *(Who bought the bird bath is less important than where it is sitting.)*

Often relative clauses help to establish the meaning of the main sentence. In such instances, relative clauses are grammatically secondary to the independent clause, but they add important information. Writers can use relative clauses to incorporate this information without having to write related but separate sentences. (See Clauses, **6e**.)

T. S. Eliot was a famous writer. *(The independent clause presents a simple statement.)*

T. S. Eliot, **who** was born in St. Louis, was a famous writer. *(The relative clause embeds some secondary but useful information.)*

T. S. Eliot was a famous writer **who** valued his privacy. *(Here, the relative clause distinguishes Eliot from other famous writers, some of whom relished public life.)*

19c Avoid excessive subordination.

Many ideas can be grammatically subordinated in a sentence. When too much secondary information is included, however, all of the ideas in a sentence can become muddled. For instance, consider this excessively subordinated sentence:

> Although many films about adolescence concentrate on the awkward and often unsatisfying relationships that exist between teenagers and their parents, most of these films take a satiric approach that presents parents as fools or tyrants and that, as a result, defuses through laughter much of the tension in the relationships because the relationships are so extreme, so absurd.

Because too many ideas are piled into this single sentence, it is difficult to read. It *is* grammatically correct, but it is also poorly planned, placing too much material in a single sentence. Several sentences could more smoothly and more stylishly present the same ideas.

> Many films about adolescence concentrate on the awkward and often unsatisfying relationships that exist between teenagers and their parents. Most of these films, however, take a satiric approach, presenting parents as fools or tyrants. Because the relationships in these films are so extreme, so absurd, much of the tension is defused through laughter.

With a large number of subordinating conjunctions to choose from, suggesting so many possible relationships, writers can vary sentences considerably. In addition, relative pronouns allow writers to embed useful information. These possibilities make subordination an especially useful method of varying sentences (but see Logical Consistency, **21e**).

EXERCISE □ *Subordination*

Combine the following groups of sentences, using subordinating conjunctions to create varied connections between ideas. Also use relative pronouns to embed useful information.

Example

If *we*

∧Wheat prices ~~may~~ continue to fall, ̷ M̷any more families could lose their farms.

1. Marie struggled through a two-hour aerobics class twice a week. Her doctor had advised her to start attending.

2. Zen Buddhism is a deeply internal discipline. The practitioner seeks harmony with external things.

3. The Tina Turner concert was supposedly sold out. I bought tickets the day before the performance.

4. Two police officers were in charge of the investigation. They questioned the bank tellers. The rest of the squad searched the building.

5. Lillian Hellman's roots were deeply southern. Her plays succeeded in New York.

EXERCISE □ *Coordination and Subordination*

The following paragraph contains all simple sentences. Establish the importance of ideas and improve the variety of the sentences by using coordination and subordination.

Dermatologists continually warn people about the danger of ultraviolet rays. Many people seem intent on getting dark suntans. During the summer, beaches and pools are crowded with people. These people want to "catch some rays." They smear on creams, lotions, and oils. They can accelerate the sun's natural modification of skin pigments. They want to get deep tans. They lie on towels or stretch out on lounge chairs for hours, oblivious to doctors' stern advice. In most cities, tanning salons are quite popular. "California" tans are not always possible everywhere. For a fee, usually between three and ten dollars, people can lie down and subject themselves to artificial sunlight. This artificial sunlight is produced by ultraviolet bulbs. The tanning beds in these salons are isolated and private. They do not even allow for social contact like that at a beach or pool. Many people think being tanned looks healthy. Overly dark tans, in fact, cause serious skin damage. This damage can last a lifetime.

20 Sentence Structure

Sentence structure refers, at least in part, to the four basic sentence types: simple, compound, complex, and compound-complex (see Kinds of Sentences, **7**). Beyond these classifications, however, sentences are identified as *loose, periodic,* and *balanced.* Writers can vary sentences by alternating among these types. Beginning sentences in different ways will also improve writing.

20a Use loose sentences to emphasize the main clause.

Loose sentences present their major ideas (subject and verb) first and then add clarifications and other information. These are the most common kinds of sentences.

> *Dr. Zhivago* is a typical David Lean film, with panoramic scenes, larger-than-life characters, and universal implications.

> Steve trained vigorously for the competition, running 120 sprints per week and spending four hours a day in the weight room.

20b Use periodic sentences to emphasize subordinate clauses.

Periodic sentences create some degree of suspense by placing the main idea or some part of it at the end of the sentence. Such sentences are less common than loose sentences but are often very effective. Although the emphasis is on the main clause in a periodic sentence, subordinate elements usually seem to receive added emphasis.

> His face flushed, his voice calm but soft, his eyes glancing downward as if he were sharing an embarrassing secret, Nathan proposed to Jessica.

233

After having spent thousands of dollars and hundreds of hours renovating the house, the Petersons sold it.

20c Use balanced sentences for equivalent ideas.

Balanced sentences have parallel elements: words, phrases, and sometimes whole clauses that are in the same form (see Parallelism, **22**). Balanced sentences are fairly common.

> She approached the abandoned farmhouse tentatively, opened the front door cautiously, and entered the dusty parlor hesitantly.

> I practiced; I ran; I lost.

> One brother was refined, intelligent, and persuasive, and the other was crude, shrewd, and domineering.

EXERCISE □ *Types of Sentences*

Label each of the following sentences as loose, periodic, or balanced.

Example

Mesquite is to a Texan as heather is to a Scot. *(balanced sentence)*

1. Happiness is a matter of perspective, in that ignorance can prevent dismay.

2. After several fruitless onslaughts on the herd, with bruises to show for it, the coyote finally trotted away panting.

3. The motorcycle Rick wanted to buy was attractive, powerful, and expensive—sure to be a status symbol.

4. Democracy demands responsibility, whereas tyranny demands obedience.

5. Snorkle divers must proceed intuitively, knowing that reefs contain many surprises.

6. Vito likes novels, short stories, and poetry, but Jessie prefers nonfiction, newsmagazines, and biographies.

7. Having played, for a change, with energy, commitment, and skill, the Blazers won the game by eleven points.

8. Boston ferns require regular watering and filtered sunlight, but philodendrons require infrequent watering and moderate sunlight.

9. Natural gas prices will continue to rise, perhaps drastically, if the government further deregulates them.

10. The 1981 inaugural celebration was well organized, with large public celebrations, elaborate private parties, and intimate gatherings.

20d Use varied sentence beginnings.

Subjects and verbs, in subordinate or independent clauses, begin most sentences. Writers can create variety in sentence beginnings, however, by repositioning some elements. When moving sentence elements, make certain not to create grammatical errors or distort meaning.

Reposition adverbs.

Because adverbs can appear in many positions in sentences, consider using them at the beginning to create needed variety.

The children quietly tiptoed past their parents' bedroom.

Reposition adjectives.

When adjectives immediately follow the subject of the first clause, they can be moved to the beginning of the sentence to create variety.

Jason, exhausted and dirty, collapsed in the armchair.

Reposition prepositional phrases.

When prepositional phrases are adverbial, they can also be moved to the beginning of the sentence.

The Pope did not restrict his travel after the attempt on his life.

Reposition participial and infinitive phrases.

Verbal phrases can introduce sentences. Make certain, however, that the phrases modify the subject of the first clause, or you will create a dangling modifier (see **25e**).

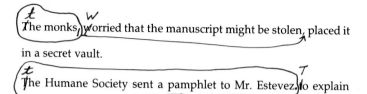

t
The monks, *w*worried that the manuscript might be stolen, placed it

in a secret vault.

t
The Humane Society sent a pamphlet to Mr. Estevez, *T*to explain

the procedures for adopting a pet, ✓

Reposition conjunctive adverbs and transitional expressions.

Like adverbs, conjunctive adverbs and transitional expressions can shift position within sentences. Use them at beginnings of sentences to create variety.

t
The subscription price for *Sports Illustrated*, *F*for instance,

is almost half the news stand price.

Monica refused the nomination, *H*however,

Selectively begin sentences with coordinating conjunctions.

Although coordinating conjunctions are conventionally used to join independent clauses in compound sentences, a coordinating conjunction can be used to introduce a sentence. This introductory position occurs when writers divide a compound sentence into two sentences. Because some readers object to this practice, however, use it selectively.

International terrorism has made many world travelers more cau-
B
tious than they used to be, but some travelers seem naively indifferent to potential threats from terrorists.

EXERCISE □ *Varying Sentence Structures and Beginnings*

In the following paragraph, loose sentences predominate. To make it more varied and interesting, combine some sentences, restructure some to form periodic or balanced sentences, and experiment with different sentence beginnings.

The kinds of checks people order from their banks interestingly illustrate their personalities. Some people are businesslike and unconcerned with appearances, ordering stock checks with faintly striped paper and simple block lettering. Others choose to spend extra money on "designer" checks. Checks with flowers and script print appeal to the ultrafeminine, sentimental, and normally pleasant. Checks with woodland scenes and rustic-looking print appeal to the reserved, private, and normally serene. Other people choose checks that have an antique look, with parchment-colored paper and Gothic printing. These people seem to be fairly sophisticated and nostalgic. Yet others choose novelty checks with cartoons and stylized printing. These people are fun-loving and impulsive. Checks, of course, are used primarily for paying bills or transferring money. They can also be used to discover a person's character and temperament.

USAGE

The purpose of this section of the handbook is to help you learn to *use* principles of grammar and style to produce effective prose—hence the heading *usage*. Knowing parts of speech, parts of sentences, or types of sentences is useful only if you apply that knowledge to your writing. This section will address some key issues of writing—predominantly at the word and sentence levels. The guidelines here should help you learn strategies to improve your usage and allow you to explore some of the impressions that word choices make.

21 Sentence Sense

The sentences that you write should present a uniform impression. For instance, when writing in the first person (*I, we, my,* and so on), do not shift to the second person (*you, your,* and so on). When writing in the past tense, do not shift to the present tense unless you have a specific reason. Such violations of the principles of consistency are quite distracting and suggest that you, as a writer, have not thought carefully enough about what you want to say. Note the four common errors in consistency discussed here, and also look at Pronoun-Antecedent Agreement (**11**), which treats some particularly troublesome problems with consistency.

21a Maintain a consistent point of view.

Point of view describes the way information is presented. Use of the *first person* (*I, we,* and other forms) concentrates attention on the writer: *you* when you are writing about yourself. The *second person* (*you* and other forms) concentrates the attention on readers, establishing their close connection to the information. The *third person* (*he, she, it, they,* and other forms) concentrates the attention on third parties; the writer is addressing the readers about someone or something else. Deciding on a point of view and maintaining it are crucial to clear writing. Watch especially for shifts between second- and third-person point of view, usually the most common problem.

Inconsistent

Golfers should be considerate of other players. You should not linger over minor shots because you will unnecessarily delay another player's game. Golfers who are inconsiderate quickly become annoying and distracting. *(The shift from the third person,* golfer, *to the second person,* you, *breaks the unity of the sentences. The abstract golfer becomes the readers and then becomes abstract again. To correct this inconsistency, decide which point of view suits your purpose and use it consistently.)*

Consistent

Golfers should always be considerate of other players. They should not linger excessively over minor shots because they will unnecessarily delay another player's game. Golfers who are inconsiderate quickly become annoying and distracting.

When you play golf, you should be considerate of other players. You should not linger excessively over minor shots because you will unnecessarily delay another player's game. If you are inconsiderate, you will quickly annoy and distract other players. *(This change requires some slight revision, but revision may be necessary to achieve your purpose.)*

21b Maintain consistent verb tenses.

Verb tenses indicate for readers when things happen (see Using Verb Tenses, **13,** and Consistent Use of Tenses, **14).** Once you select an appropriate tense for a series of clauses or sentences, maintain it throughout your discussion. If you do not, readers will not understand your time references.

went
Immediately after the ceremony, the wedding party ~~goes~~ to the
went
photographer's for a photo session, and the guests ~~go~~ to the Stratford Hotel for the reception. Once at the Stratford, small groups
of people sat down at tables to enjoy the music, while others
danced or nibbled on hors d'oeuvres. Within an hour, the bride,
d
groom, and others make their appearance, and the dinner began.
*(The shifts in tense made it impossible to tell whether the sentences
describe a hypothetical situation—in which case the present tense
might be appropriate—or whether this is a narrative of an actual reception, in which case the past tense would be appropriate. Either
way, the tenses need to be consistent throughout.)*

21c Maintain consistent mood.

Mood is used to show the intent of a sentence (see **15**). *Indicative mood* presents facts and opinions and asks questions.
Imperative mood presents commands or directions. *Subjunctive
mood* presents conditional situations, statements contrary to
fact, and wishes. Because each serves a separate purpose,
moods should seldom be mixed.

Collecting bisque china dolls, Mrs. Harris explained, can be very
She suggested that beginners buy
costly. ~~Buy~~ small, inexpensive dolls first, over a period of months,
they
to make sure that ~~you~~ are truly interested in collecting. *(Here the
shift from indicative in the first sentence to imperative in the second
sentence was confusing: the first sentence described, while the second
advised. The revisions give the sentences a consistent focus.)*

21d Maintain consistent voice.

Verbs appear in two voices: active and passive (see **26**). In
an active sentence, the subject completes an action; in a passive

sentence, the subject receives the action. Because these two voices establish two different kinds of emphasis, they should not be mixed.

> In diving competitions, judges use multiplication to arrive at
> *they multiply that number by another*
> scores. They first record a number score for a dive. Then ^a
>   ⊘
> number indicating the degree of difficulty ^~~is multiplied by the~~
> ~~number score.~~ The result is the total number of points a diver re-
> ceives. *(The second sentence is active, explaining what the judges do;*
> *the third sentence, however, was passive—leaving the judges out of*
> *the process. To show the involvement of the judges throughout, it is*
> *better to maintain the active voice.)*

EXERCISE □ *Consistency*

Revise the following sentences to eliminate inconsistencies in point of view, tense, mood, and voice.

> Example
>   *be*
> A person who drives while intoxicated should ~~have been~~ arrested.
>   ^

1. When a tutor begins to feel frustrated or angry, you should stop the lesson and take a break.

2. If you are dissatisfied with a paper, revise it, or you can try a whole new strategy.

3. After the paint dried in the plastic bucket, I simply throw it away to avoid a messy cleanup.

4. Turner Broadcasting System tried unsuccessfully to take over CBS in June 1985. In August 1985, however, MGM/

United Artists was taken over by TBS without any resistance.

5. Shortly after the accident on runway seven, a camera crew from a local news network arrives on the scene and begins filming.

EXERCISE □ *Consistency*

Revise the sentences in the following paragraph to correct inconsistencies in point of view, tense, mood, and voice.

Performing minor maintenance on a car is one way everyone can save a little money. As a matter of fact, car owners will discover that in the course of a year you can save a considerable amount. Begin by examining your owner's manual to see which procedures you can manage, and then you can buy a few simple supplies. Buy a tool for changing spark plugs and a special funnel for motor oil. Spark plugs, coolant, and oil can also be purchased cheaply at a discount store—usually at half the price one will be charged at a repair shop. Use your manual carefully as you service your car the first time. If you are like most people, you had no problems, and you can spend the money you saved on something special instead of on car maintenance.

21e Maintain logical consistency.

Logical consistency depends, in large part, on clear relationships among subjects, verbs, and complements (see **6a, 6b,** and **6c**); this close connection is normally called *predication*. To examine a sentence for logical consistency, mentally eliminate all words except the subject and verb, and the complement if there is one. Then decide if this core sentence makes sense alone. If it does, the predication is logical. If it does not, the predication is faulty, and the sentence needs to be revised.

Illogical

All aspects of gerontology strive to improve the lives of the aged. *(Core sentence:* aspects strive. *This is illogical, since parts of a study cannot sensibly do anything.)*

Logical

People working in gerontology strive to improve the lives of the aged.

Illogical

The World Series, All-Star Games, and Hall of Fame members are institutions in the sport of baseball. *(Core sentence:* series, games, and members are institutions. *This is illogical. Series and special games may be seen as institutions, but members clearly cannot be seen this way.)*

Logical

The World Series, All-Star Games, and the Hall of Fame are institutions in the sport of baseball.

Players in the World Series, players in All-Star Games, and members of the Hall of Fame represent the best in the sport of baseball.

Illogical

By working in summer stock productions gives well-known actors a chance to experiment with unusual roles. *(The opening preposi-*

tional phrase cannot work as a subject. Consequently, this sentence has no subject. It is therefore ungrammatical as well as illogical.)

Logical

By working in summer stock productions, well-known actors get a chance to experiment with unusual roles.

Working in summer stock productions gives well-known actors a chance to experiment with unusual roles.

EXERCISE □ *Logical Consistency*

The following sentences are illogical. Identify what kind of inconsistency interferes with clear communication, and correct the sentences.

1. The proponents of busing and the antibusing groups frequently share many disagreements about the value of mandatory desegregation.

2. According to some studies, the ages of eleven to sixteen are subject to the most peer pressure.

3. By listing nutritional information on packaging enables shoppers to compare two competing brands quickly.

4. In owning a Rolls-Royce is a symbol of prestige.

5. I have recently desired the idea of visiting Naples.

22 Parallelism

Parallelism in sentences means that ideas of equal importance are expressed in similar ways or that separate clusters of words appear together in identical grammatical form. Parallelism requires that nouns be used with other nouns, verbs be used with other verbs of the same tense, predicate adjectives be used with other predicate adjectives, and so on. Parallelism is important because readers expect symmetry among coordinate sentences and sentence elements.

22a Maintain parallelism in constructions using coordinating conjunctions—*and, but, for, nor, or, so,* and *yet.*

When a coordinating conjunction is used in a sentence, make doubly sure that the elements joined appear in identical grammatical form.

All her employers found Judy to be intelligent, able, and a~~ ~~hard worker. *(Intelligent and able are predicate adjectives; hard worker, a predicate noun, was not parallel.)*

To have dreams is important, but living them is even more important. *(To have dreams is an infinitive phrase; living them was a gerund phrase, and the two were not parallel.)*

Because Isaac memorizes, acts, and ~~can~~ sing well, he is a musical director's ideal performer. *(Memorizes and acts are simple verbs expressing an action; can sing was an auxiliary construction expressing a condition.)*

22b Maintain parallelism in sentences using correlative conjunctions: *both . . . and, either . . . or, neither . . . nor,* and *not only . . . but also.*

Janet could either go to the library or ~~could~~ develop photographs. *(Since could appears before either, it is not part of the correlative con-*

struction. If an auxiliary like could *does not appear* immediately *before the first verb, it should not appear before the second one.)*

The aim of a teacher should be both to inspire and ^to^ educate. *(Infinitive forms must be repeated, not mixed with present-tense verbs in correlative constructions.)*

Remember that certain conjunctions—either coordinating or correlative—signal the need for parallel elements within sentences. When using these conjunctions, double-check sentences carefully. If necessary, list parallel elements in the margin of your draft to check them against one another.

22c Repeat prepositions and subordinate conjunctions when they help clarify the meaning of a parallel construction.

In brief sentences, prepositions and subordinate conjunctions often can be omitted from the second part of a parallel structure. In longer sentences, however, repeating prepositions or subordinate conjunctions clearly stresses parallel relationships.

When the summer days grow longer and hotter and ^when^ work becomes frustrating, I head to the cabin at Bishop's Point for a cool and relaxing break. *(The length of the opening subordinate clause made the parallel construction difficult to follow without the repeated subordinating conjunction.)*

22d Consistently match *and that, and which,* or *and who* with an earlier use of *that, which,* or *who* in the sentence.

My brother coached Natalie O'Rourke, ^who is^ an exceptional skier and who is also a fine ice skater. *(And who is* matched to no previous *pronoun in the sentence. The sentence could also have been corrected by deleting* and *in the original.)*

22e Use parallelism among successive
sentences for clarity, emphasis, or effect.

Although varied sentences are usually effective, sometimes
a series of parallel sentences can convey an idea in an especially
interesting way.

> The tremor in his voice was audible. The blush on his face was
> plain. The microphone in his hand was shaking.

These sentences maintain parallel form because similar sentence structures are repeated, and similar sentence elements are used in similar ways. Consider these parallel elements:

Subjects	Prepositional Phrases	Verbs	Predicate Adjectives
The tremor	in his voice	was	audible.
The blush	on his face	was	plain.
The microphone	in his hand	was	shaking.

EXERCISE □ *Parallelism*

The following sentences all contain nonparallel constructions. First locate the nonparallel elements, and then revise the sentences to improve them. There are different ways to modify the sentences.

1. To design her own clothes and making them are two of Rebecca's goals.

2. After George is discharged from the Navy, he plans to use the GI Bill to go to college, finish in three years, and will get a job on the East or West Coast.

3. Not only are migrant workers exploited in the Southwest but also in other parts of the Sunbelt.

4. Jack Paar, an early host of the *Tonight Show*, was a dazzling interviewer and who was controversial.

5. Not only do children learn teamwork playing league soccer, but they will also stay physically fit.

6. Either Professor Going gave lengthy exams or they were too difficult.

7. The city's sidewalks, extremely narrow and which needed repair, were even more troublesome in the rain.

8. To complain is easy, but finding solutions is difficult.

9. Even at an early age, Raquel could walk on her hands, do forward flips, and showed excellent balance.

10. Although modeling is often perceived as an easy job, it requires talent, patience, and models must have stamina.

EXERCISE □ *Parallelism*

The following paragraph contains many examples of nonparallel constructions. First, locate the nonparallel elements. Then correct them.

Once, not so very long ago, amusement parks were poorly supervised, dirty, and they were rather tasteless. On hot summer Saturdays, American families would head to places with names like Chain-of-Rocks Park to have a good time. Once there, they found that the parking facilities were not only randomly planned but also no guards patrolled the area. The parks themselves were poorly maintained, with litter on the sidewalks, with oil running on the sidewalks, and with food having been left to spoil on the tables. The attendants appeared to be people with nothing better to do and who wash or shave only infrequently. They seemed to be alternately indifferent, callous, or they sometimes appeared to be threatening. Probably because of these unappealing qualities, the amusement parks of an earlier time have been replaced by well-maintained, clean, and attractiveness of today's Six Flags, King's Island, and Disney parks.

23 Comparisons

23a Include all the words needed to make a comparison clear and complete.

A common problem among writers is that they omit words in comparisons, making the comparisons illogical or unclear. To avoid this problem, ask yourself whether the sentence compares similar things.

Illogical

Riding a bicycle to work can be more convenient than a car. *(Here riding is compared with car; that is illogical.)*

Logical

Riding a bicycle to work can be more convenient than driving a car. *(two activities compared)*

A bicycle can offer a more convenient way to get to work than a car can. *(two modes of transportation compared)*

Unclear

The testimony was based more on emotion than the facts.

Complete

The testimony was based more on emotion than on the facts.

23b Use *other,* when necessary, to make a comparison clear and complete.

Incomplete

A Rolls Royce is more prestigious than any car. *(This suggests that a Rolls Royce is not a car.)*

Complete

A Rolls Royce is more prestigious than any **other** car.

23c Do not write an implied comparison.

An implied comparison begins to present a comparison but fails to supply the whole context. Words formed with the suffix *-er* or modified by *more, less,* or similar expressions present comparisons that must be completed to be clear. Use *than* and explain the comparison completely.

Ambiguous

The London Symphony's interpretation of "*Tommy*" was more sensitive. *(More sensitive than what?)*

Clear

The London Symphony's interpretation of "*Tommy*" was more sensitive than The Who's original version.

Ambiguous

The group that brushed with Crest had 30% fewer cavities. *(Fewer than who?)*

Clear

The group that brushed with Crest had 30% fewer cavities than the group that brushed with a generic toothpaste.

EXERCISE □ *Comparisons*

The following sentences contain ungrammatical, illogical, or incomplete comparisons. Revise each sentence to make it effective.

Example

A word processor helps Sara write more efficiently*ₜ* *than she used to.*

1. I do not dance as well.

2. A robin's song is not as shrill as a cardinal.

3. The cost of attending a private college usually exceeds a state-supported school.

4. Capezios are worn by more ballerinas than any dancing shoes.

5. Chiffon made of silk feels infinitely softer.

6. Most teachers agree that learning Latin does not help students understand grammar any more than French or German.

7. Although it is unfortunate, forgetting a friend is easier than a letter.

8. The gasping recruit's boots no longer shone as brightly.

9. A poor mixture of nitrogen, phosphorus, and potash in fertilizer is worse for lawns.

10. Working at the San Diego Zoo was different.

EXERCISE □ *Comparisons and Contrasts*

The following paragraph contains faulty comparisons. Identify the problems, and then revise the paragraph to eliminate them.

In recent years, the winners of the Grammies for best new performer have illustrated a wonderful variety of musical styles. In 1970, for instance, The Carpenters received the Grammy in response to their easy-listening songs. Three years later, Bette Midler received the award; her sometimes bawdy but always entertaining style certainly contrasted with The Carpenters. Marvin Hamlisch's music from *The Way We Were* and

The Sting (1974) also differed greatly from Midler. Later groups
that won were also highly individual. Men at Work presented a
sound that was hard to compare with any group. Culture Club
offered a melodic sound revolving around the talents of Boy
George; and Cyndi Lauper's musical diversity resulted in a
more successful debut year than any performer's. That Grammies have gone to such different individuals and groups only
emphasizes the range of exceptional music on the American
airwaves.

24 Pronoun Reference

Pronouns help writers vary their word choices, because pronouns can substitute for overused nouns. For these substitutions to be clear, however, writers must follow certain patterns
of usage (see Agreement, **11**).

24a Avoid ambiguous pronoun references.

An ambiguous reference occurs when a single pronoun
feasibly refers to more than one word (antecedent). When that
happens, readers are justifiably confused.

Ambiguous

The scuba instructor gave Patrick a detailed lecture on water
safety. **He** thought it was a waste of time. *(Did the instructor feel
dissatisfied, or did Patrick?)*

Clear

Although he thought it was a waste of time, the scuba instructor gave Patrick a detailed lecture on water safety.

Ambiguous

While Liz and Rae watched, the dog nuzzled the orphaned racoon, and then **they** went to sleep. *(Who went to sleep?)*

Clear

Liz and Rae watched as the dog nuzzled the orphaned racoon, and then the animals went to sleep.

24b Avoid vague pronoun references.

A vague pronoun reference occurs when a pronoun (often *this, that,* or *which*) refers broadly to a general idea presented in a whole sentence or clause.

Vague

The members of Israel's Knesset requested more military aid from the United States. **This** was approved by Congress. *(Did Congress approve of the request, or did Congress approve the aid?)*

Specific

The members of Israel's Knesset requested more military aid from the United States. Congress approved the aid.

24c Avoid unclear references using *it, you,* or *they.*

The pronouns *it, you,* and *they,* like all pronouns, require specific antecedents. They should not refer vaguely to implied antecedents. Instead, use only pronouns with specific antecedents.

Unclear

The Theater-in-the-Round is not very innovative, but **they** usually do technically polished productions. (They *has no direct antecedent in the previous clause.*)

Clear

Although the directors at the Theater-in-the-Round are not very innovative, they usually do technically polished productions.

24d Use reflexive pronouns (those ending in -*self* or -*selves*) to refer only to nouns stated in the same sentence.

If no specific antecedent is present in the sentence, use a personal pronoun instead.

Incorrect

Wilbur and **myself** scrambled over the chain-link fence.

Correct

Wilbur and **I** scrambled over the chain-link fence.

Carlotta Monterey gave **herself** credit for the stability in Eugene O'Neill's last years.

24e Do not use pronouns that refer to a single antecedent through a long succession of sentences.

Because pronouns are substitutes for nouns, readers must be able to remember the noun (antecedent). When pronouns and antecedents are separated by too many words, the references become awkward or unclear.

Charlie Chaplin began his work in American films with the Keystone Cops. His early roles were limited, giving him little chance

to demonstrate his considerable talents. However, ~~he~~ *Chaplin* later show-
cased his talents in a one-reeler titled *The Tramp*. In that film, he

introduced the character that was to win him wide acclaim. ~~He~~ *Chaplin*
later produced, wrote, directed, and starred in such films as *The
Kid, City Lights,* and *Modern Times*. *(Although the entire paragraph
is about Chaplin and consequently is not confusing, it is improved by
alternating Chaplin's name with the pronouns.)*

24f Do not use pronouns to refer to antecedents in previous paragraphs.

For clarity, restrict pronoun references to sentences within
the same paragraph, even when a reference may seem clear.
This is a matter of conventional usage.

> . . . Chaplin later produced, wrote, directed, and starred in such
> films as *The Kid, City Lights,* and *Modern Times*.
>
> ~~His~~ *Chaplin's* importance in Hollywood soon became clear. In fact, he,
> Mary Pickford, and Douglas Fairbanks split from their studios to
> form the studio United Artists. . . .

EXERCISE □ *Pronoun Reference*

The following sentences contain unclear pronoun references.
Identify the kinds of reference problems and then correct them.

Example

Although *Out of Africa* presents a compelling story, ~~they~~ *the director* concen-

trate*s* too much on panoramic views of the African plains. *(no
antecedent for they since no people are mentioned.)*

1. In Washington, they are approached by lobbyists from special interest groups.

2. The reporter asked Selina and myself to describe the boating accident in great detail.

3. In the last act of *Macbeth,* it implies that conditions in Scotland will return to normal.

4. I enjoyed the conference's opening meeting and individual sessions. It made me want to attend another one.

5. In the *Wall Street Journal,* it said that deregulating telephone service would eventually result in lower rates for consumers.

6. The American Olympic Team boycotted the Moscow Games because of the Russian invasion of Afghanistan. It was very unfortunate.

7. The diamond appraisers reassured us that they were genuine.

8. OPEC failed to set a price because they could not agree on profit margins.

9. The locker room guard roughly shoved the reporter. He felt that his behavior was threatening.

10. The ambassador met with the Prince of Wales when he was

    in Washington last week.

25 Positioning Modifiers

Modifiers explain, describe, define, or limit a word or group of words. Place modifiers so that it will be clear what words they modify.

25a Try not to place a long modifier between the subject and verb in a sentence.

To understand a sentence, readers must understand the relationship between the subject and verb. Avoid delaying that understanding.

A

Detective Meredith, **after he reviewed the sixty-three-page Etheridge-Martinez file several times and spoke with the**

arresting officers, asked to be assigned to the case.

25b Try not to place a long modifier between a verb and its complement.

Understanding the idea in a sentence often depends on understanding the connection between the verb and its complement. To interrupt that connection with a long modifier is often awkward or confusing.

H

Poe's "The Telltale Heart" is, **However disturbing its main**

premise may be, a spellbinding story.

25c Seldom interrupt a verb phrase with a long modifier.

For smooth reading and easy comprehension, verb phrases should work as a unit. Place long modifiers elsewhere in the sentence.

The barrel   race for quarter horses had to be͜ **because of heavy**

rain, (delayed,)

25d Place prepositional phrases and dependent clauses as near as possible to the words they modify.

Readers instinctively use nearness as a guide to modification. Placing modifiers near the proper words will help readers interpret sentences correctly.

Unclear

They planned the honeymoon they would take **before the wedding.** *(The honeymoon preceded the wedding?)*

Clear

Before the wedding, they planned the honeymoon they would take.

Unclear

Huck and Jim were impressed by the view of the mansion, **sitting on the raft.** *(The mansion was on the raft?)*

Clear

Sitting on the raft, Huck and Jim were impressed by the view of the mansion.

**25e Make sure opening and closing modifiers
clearly refer to the subject of the sentence.**

Grammatical structure suggests that a verbal phrase at the
beginning of a sentence modifies the subject of that sentence.
When it does not modify the subject of the sentence, it is called
a *dangling modifier.* Correct a sentence with a dangling modifier by repositioning the misplaced phrase so that its modification is clear, or else revise the sentence.

Leaping high above the waves, ~~w~~e watched the dolphins. *(We
were not leaping; the dolphins were.)*

When ^(I was) still in high school, my father expected me to be home by
midnight. *(You were not out that late when he was in high school.
You were not even born.)*

~~Smelling of oil,~~ Jeanette tossed the rag ^(, which smelled of oil,) into the trash. *(The rag,
not Jeanette, smelled of oil.)*

**25f Never place a modifier between two
words if it could modify either one of them
equally well.**

Sometimes a modifier feasibly modifies the words before it
or the ones after it. To avoid confusing readers, revise the sentence to clarify meaning.

Ambiguous

Armand said **before ten o'clock** he would reach the summit. *(He
spoke before ten o'clock? Or would he arrive before then?)*

Clear

Armand said he would reach the summit **before ten o'clock.**

Ambiguous

Nicholas said **sometimes** he could see no hope. *(He said it once in a while? He saw no hope at some times?)*

Clear

Sometimes Nicholas said he could see no hope.

25g Use the pronoun *that* when needed to eliminate confusion.

Often, when a modifier appears in an ambiguous position, the meaning of the sentence can be made clear by inserting *that* in the appropriate location.

Ambiguous

Walter said **during the meeting** Monica misrepresented her case. *(Did he make his comment then? Or is that when she distorted her case?)*

Clear

Walter said **that during the meeting** Monica misrepresented her case. *(This use of* that *links* during the meeting *to Monica.)*

Walter said **during the meeting that** Monica misrepresented her case. *(This use of* that *links* during the meeting *to Walter.)*

25h Place limiting modifiers where they create your intended meaning.

Limiting modifiers—*hardly, nearly, only,* and others—substantially change the meaning of a sentence. Place them cautiously, and double-check to make certain the meaning of the sentence is clear.

He **simply** stated the problem. *(That is all he did.)*

He stated the problem **simply.** *(He made it easy to understand.)*

We had time **only** to meet him. *(We did not have time for anything else.)*

We had time to meet **only** him. *(We did not get to meet anyone else.)*

25i Avoid splitting an infinitive with a modifier.

Although people sometimes separate infinitives with modifiers in conversation, and although some linguists find such usage acceptable, it is still best to avoid split infinitives in formal writing.

Questionable

After rereading *Hamlet,* Ralph began to **quickly** prepare his report.

Always Acceptable

After rereading *Hamlet,* Ralph **quickly** began to prepare his report.

Modifiers of all kinds are useful in sentences because they add information and clarification. Yet for this positive purpose to be served, modifiers must be suitably placed within their sentences. Misplaced modifiers will confuse rather than help readers, so follow the preceding guidelines and give your writing the clarity that well-placed modifiers can provide.

EXERCISE □ *Positioning Modifiers*

The following sentences contain misplaced and dangling modifiers. Find the problem elements and move them to positions that make the sentences clear and grammatical.

1. Television documentaries on the Vietnam War have failed to completely and fairly analyze the major issues.

2. Dented and rusty, we watched the truck tow away our old car.

3. People who drink often have liver trouble.

4. Raging out of control, the tenants escaped from the fire.

5. The evening gown, designed by Galános and studded with three thousand sequins and seed pearls, cost twenty-two thousand dollars.

6. Coca-Cola, because it is made with the water in each distinct production region, tastes different in different cities.

7. Nuclear fusion could, if its proponents are even moderately accurate in their forecasts, be our major source of energy someday.

8. Sarah tried to put the sandal on her right foot, which was obviously too small.

9. Amanda Wingfield was, biographers and literary critics tell us, a dramatic portrait of Tennessee Williams' mother.

10. Scientists studied the effects of microwave communications at Bell Laboratories.

EXERCISE □ *Positioning Modifiers*

The following paragraph contains a variety of misplaced modifiers. Locate and identify the kinds of problems, first of all, and then revise the sentences to improve their clarity.

Helping my uncle with his one-acre garden taught me that victories in the garden are won the hard way. My uncle and I, each morning before it got too hot, would do maintenance work. We would pull small infestations of weeds by hand and then spray, with a postemergent herbicide, larger growths of weeds. Then we would mulch the plants whose foliage did not protect the soil from the sun's drying rays. Using straw and sometimes black plastic sheets, we would, trying not to damage low leaves, encircle the stalks of the plants. Covered with parasitical bugs, we would sometimes have to spray plants with a pyrethrin mixture. Once we got started, we worked often without talking. A few comments seemed to be enough on the growth of the asparagus or the tomatoes. Once, however, Uncle Charles told me during our work sessions I was a conscientious worker when he felt talkative. As the days passed, I began to, because of my own hard work, realize how much effort goes into gardening. I must say that grown with so much care, I now appreciate my fruits and vegetables more than I used to.

26 Active and Passive Sentences

Active sentences are "doing" sentences, explaining who does what through their use of subjects, verbs, and optional complements.

subj. *verb* *d.o.* ⌐——— *phrase* ——⌐
Lin Su invested two-thousand **dollars** in the commodities market.

Direct kinds of sentences, active sentences place emphasis on the people and things responsible for actions and conditions. Passive sentences, on the other hand, are descriptive sentences that deemphasize the actors involved and instead focus on people or things that do not act. A passive sentence places in the subject position what would be a complement in an active sentence. Auxiliaries are then added to the verb. These sentences are called passive because their subjects complete no action but are instead acted upon.

subj. *verb* ⌐——— *phrase* ———⌐
Two thousand dollars was invested in the commodities market
⌐*phrase*⌐
by Lin Su.

Notice that the person completing the action can be totally absent from a passive sentence. If the person is mentioned at all, it will be in a prepositional phrase beginning with *by*.

26a Use active sentences most of the time to emphasize the people responsible for actions and events.

Because human choices and actions determine much of what goes on around us, give the credit or blame to the people

responsible. Using them as subjects will stress their importance.

Active

Mr. DeGaetano damaged a gas line when he planted a shade
tree. *(Here Mr. DeGaetano's error in judgment is suitably noted.)*

Passive

A gas line was damaged when Mr. DeGaetano planted a shade
tree. *(This almost suggests that the damage was not Mr. DeGaetano's
fault.)*

26b Use active sentences to make writing forceful.

The relationship between the subject and verb is stronger
in an active sentence than in a passive sentence. This fact is
another reason to use active sentences most of the time.

Active

The 1980 eruption of Mount St. Helens destroyed over sixty million dollars' worth of property. *(Combining* eruption *with the active verb* destroyed *emphasizes the violence of nature.)*

Passive

Over sixty million dollars' worth of property was destroyed by the
1980 eruption of Mount St. Helens. *(This sentence shifts the emphasis to loss of property—certainly unfortunate, but less dramatic.)*

26c Use active sentences to save words.

Because passive sentences require an auxiliary verb and,
often, the preposition *by* (to include the person or thing responsible for the action), they are always slightly longer than active

sentences containing the same information. With a single sentence, this may not seem important, but in paragraphs and papers the additional number of words can be significant.

Active

In less than ten minutes, the plumber repaired the leaking faucet. *(eleven words)*

Passive

The leaking faucet was repaired by the plumber in less than ten minutes. *(thirteen words)*

26d Use passive sentences when the people responsible for actions are unknown or can be only vaguely identified.

Sometimes we see only the results of actions. When that is the case, passive sentences are the logical ones to write.

Passive

Graffiti were scribbled on the walls of the subway station. *(We see the results but not the actions.)*

Active

Somebody had scribbled graffiti on the walls of the subway station. *(The use of an indefinite pronoun does not substantially improve the sentence.)*

26e Use passive sentences to emphasize the receiver of the action instead of those responsible.

At times, the receiver of the action is more important than the one responsible for the action. In those circumstances, passive sentences highlight what is most important.

Passive

Michelangelo's *Pietà*, the exquisite statue of Mary and Jesus, was damaged by a vandal in 1981. *(Here, the emphasis is on the statue.)*

Active

In 1981, a vandal damaged Michelangelo's *Pietà*, the exquisite statue of Mary and Jesus. *(Here, the emphasis is on the criminal— certainly of less interest than the statue itself.)*

26f Use passive sentences to emphasize actions that are more important than any specific person who might be responsible.

Although people usually are important, sometimes universal or widespread actions deserve more emphasis. In those cases, passive sentences focus attention where it ought to be.

Passive

Open-heart surgery to repair faulty valves is now commonly performed across the United States. *(It is the surgical procedure that is most important here, not the doctors who perform it.)*

Active

Doctors across the United States are now commonly performing open-heart surgery to repair faulty valves. *(This construction emphasizes doctors more than procedures.)*

Note that in some scientific writing, a procedure, process, or method of research may be more important than the people who complete it. In those cases, passive sentences are useful because they emphasize the important technique.

Writers usually agree that active sentences are more effective than passive ones. As a general guide to usage, then, remember that when "who is doing what" is most important, you should write active sentences. But also remember that passive sentences serve specific purposes as well and are effective if used selectively.

EXERCISE ☐ *Active and Passive Sentences*

The following sentences are all written in the passive voice. Most could be improved if they were rewritten in the active voice. Change sentences to the active voice when they can be strengthened that way, and explain why some sentences should remain in the passive.

Example

Paleontologists often make

∧ ~~P~~laster molds of dinosaur footprints~~are often made by paleontologists.~~

1. Dogs and cats should not be used by scientists to test chemicals for products as trivial as cosmetics.

2. Solar panels should only be installed by workers experienced in the procedures.

3. Litter of all kinds—paper plates, plastic utensils, paper napkins, and food wrappers—was scattered in the park at the end of the day.

4. The soccer ball was kicked with great force into the goal.

5. Snow should not be shoveled by people with respiratory ailments.

6. Thousands of people, mostly the poor, have been left homeless by urban redevelopment.

7. Red Dye no. 5 has been banned from food manufacturing by the Food and Drug Administration.

8. The delicate chess pieces were carved by Joshua for his woodcraft project.

9. Wren houses can be built with inexpensive materials and simple tools by almost anyone.

10. The package apparently was delivered while we were at work.

27 Conciseness

Conciseness means presenting ideas in as few words as possible. Concise writing avoids needless repetition and useless words, saving time and work for the reader.

To write concisely, eliminate all words, phrases, and clauses that do not add to your meaning. This does not mean all sentences must be short, for some long sentences are concise and some short ones are not.

As writers make a first draft of a paragraph or a paper, they seldom trouble themselves with issues of conciseness. Instead, they are trying to connect their ideas in a logical way. During revision of the draft, the issue of conciseness becomes especially important. Working toward conciseness in a rough draft of a paragraph or paper means searching for a word here, two words there, or a phrase elsewhere that can be eliminated or reduced without altering ideas.

Creating concise writing is challenging, and no exact set of rules can guide you. Some basic principles, however, can help make your writing economical.

27a Do not repeat words needlessly.

Sometimes words can be repeated for emphasis, in which case they serve a useful purpose. But when repeated words serve no specific purpose, strike them out and, if necessary, rearrange the remaining words to create a smooth sentence.

~~The book~~ John wanted ~~was~~ a book describing Aztec and Mayan cities. *(twelve words/nine words)*

During the thirties and forties, MGM studio became ~~the studio~~ renowned for film musicals. *(fourteen words/twelve words)*

27b Do not repeat ideas that are already understood.

When specific word choices have already made an idea clear, do not needlessly elaborate. Not only will such redundancy use more words, but readers will become annoyed by restatements of the obvious.

Karina's
~~The~~ smile ~~on Karina's face~~ showed that she was ~~pleasantly~~ elated by the reception of her poem. *(Where else could a smile be but on her face? Could elation be anything else but pleasant? seventeen words/twelve words)*

S
~~Magazine~~ subscription rates for *Esquire* will increase ~~in price~~ next year. *(Would anyone think Esquire was anything but a magazine? Can rates increase in anything but price? eleven words/eight words)*

27c Eliminate expletive constructions whenever possible.

Expletive constructions (it is, here is, here are, there is, and there are) provide patterned subjects and verbs that use words needlessly. Because sentences with expletives generally contain words that can be used as primary subjects and verbs, strike out the expletive construction and examine the remaining words. You may discover a more concise way to present the same idea by adding a verb, or you may need only to strike out a relative pronoun.

~~There are~~ *T* three kinds of peppers *are* planted in my garden. *(ten words/nine words)*

~~There is a~~ *A* man in my apartment building ~~who~~ jogs every morning at five o'clock. *(fifteen words/twelve words)*

27d Write active sentences whenever possible.

Active sentences tell who is doing what and present ideas more concisely than do passive sentences, which require additional words to create the same meaning (see Active and Passive Sentences, **26**). Therefore, when active sentences create proper emphasis, as they do most of the time, use them. They will always be at least two words shorter than passive sentences containing the same information.

David took The slides of Okefenokee Swamp ~~were taken by David~~ during his field study. *(thirteen words/eleven words)*

Sarah found The solid oak door ~~was found by Sarah~~ in an abandoned farmhouse. *(twelve words/ten words)*

27e Replace wordy phrases with brief expressions and remove empty phrases.

English contains many equivalent expressions: words or groups of words that convey the same ideas. Such expressions can vary noticeably in length. When alternatives exist and when the ideas truly match, choose the briefest version to save words. Besides, the shorter forms are usually less pretentious.

Because
^ ~~Due to the fact that~~ a train blocked the road for twenty minutes, I was late for work. *(eighteen words / fourteen words)*

to
Paul Newman has used his fame as an actor ^ ~~for the purpose of~~

e
advanci̱ng ~~worthy~~ causes. *(sixteen words / thirteen words)*

Watch out for these other wordy expressions that have briefer counterparts:

Wordy	Concise
at this point in time	now
by means of	by
in order to	to
in the event that	if
of the opinion that	think
until such time as	until

Some phrases—such as *in my opinion, I believe, it seems,* and *I suppose*—add very little meaning to a sentence. Because readers expect to find writers' opinions and educated guesses in writing, such phrases serve no real purpose (unless the writer's opinion is clearly being compared with someone else's). Unlike the wordy phrases noted earlier, however, these empty phrases can be dropped completely.

D
~~I believe that~~ dating services prey upon the insecure and lonely. *(eleven words/eight words)*

A   *seem*
~~It seems that~~ athletes in triathlons ~~are~~ masochistic. *(eight words/ five words)*

27f When possible, eliminate *to be* verbs in favor of stronger ones.

Many words in English have several forms. For instance, *maintain* is a verb, *maintenance* is a noun, and *maintaining* is a gerund. Using these word modifications wisely can reduce the number of words in your sentences. To achieve conciseness in this way, look closely at sentences using *to be* in any of its forms. If possible, transform the words following the *to be* verb into a more forceful verb and reduce the number of words in the sentence. These transformations are not always possible, but when they are, sentences can be made more concise.

can   *e*
Satellite dishes ~~are capable of~~ providing excellent television reception in rural areas. *(twelve words/ten words)*

e
Research assistants ~~are responsible for~~ completing most of the day-to-day experiments and recording the results. *(fifteen words/ twelve words)*

27g Change nonrestrictive clauses into appositives to save words.

Nonrestrictive clauses are not essential to the meaning of a sentence. When these clauses contain *to be* verbs, they can be reduced to appositives, phrases restating a noun or pronoun. Because appositives contain no subject or verb, sentences changed this way will be shortened by two words.

Miloš Forman, ~~who was~~ the director of *Amadeus*, also directed the film musical *Hair*. *(fourteen words/twelve words)*

Chemicals found in aerosols have damaged the earth's ozone layer, ~~which is~~ our main protection from solar radiation. *(eighteen words/sixteen words)*

27h Change modifying phrases into modifying words.

Prepositional and verbal phrases (see **6d**) supply modification in sentences, working as adjectives and adverbs. When possible, eliminate these modifying phrases and substitute one-word or multiword modifiers. Note, however, that when multiword modifiers precede a noun, they are often hyphenated (see **43c**).

ᴧ *Copper* ~~s~~ Skillets ~~of copper~~ conduct heat evenly. *(six words/five words)*

The ᴧ *carpet's* color ~~of the carpet~~ was distorted by a ᴧ window ᴧ *stained-glass* ~~made of stained glass.~~ *(fourteen words/nine words)*

EXERCISE □ *Conciseness*

The following sentences are wordier than they should be. Through revision, make them more concise and note the number of words saved.

1. Falling from the sky, the heavy summer rain replenished the water supply in the reservoir. *(fifteen words)*

2. In spite of the fact that there were 150 people invited to the art gallery opening, there were only forty people who came. *(twenty-three words)*

3. Until such time as we can save money for a down payment on a house, we will continue to live in a rented apartment. *(twenty-four words)*

4. The leftover croissants were left on the kitchen table until noon. *(eleven words)*

5. Engines made for diesel fuel are capable of getting better mileage than engines made for normal gasoline. *(seventeen words)*

6. The budget for our Christmas pageant in December was prepared by Mr. Marcus. *(thirteen words)*

7. Thomas à Becket, who was the Archbishop of Canterbury, was murdered on the altar of his church by four of the king's knights. *(twenty-three words)*

8. The spices oregano, basil, and garlic flavored Uncle Paul's spicy spaghetti sauce. *(twelve words)*

9. I am of the opinion that we should have our taxes prepared by an accountant. *(fifteen words)*

10. Leontyne Price, who was one of America's great opera stars, ended her operatic career playing Aida, who was a doomed Egyptian princess. *(twenty-two words)*

EXERCISE □ *Conciseness*

The following paragraph is bloated with useless words. Make it much more concise. Take your time, try a variety of strategies, and see how much the paragraph improves when it is concise.

To be capable of understanding the development and use of paper and how that use came about, we must make our way back hundreds of years to China. By most estimates, paper was invented by the Chinese, who created it in 105 B.C. As a matter of fact, it was kept as a secret by the state for hundreds of years. As far as we know, most transcriptions were done on bamboo sheets. The Moors discovered the Chinese invention in A.D. 750. They became aware of it when they were at war with the Chinese. The Moors established and forged the link to Europe. In 1100, there was a paper mill for making paper established in Toledo, Spain. Gradually, the use of paper began to spread across Europe in a slow manner. Paper was able to reach Rome in approximately 1200, and it was a cause for the Catholic Church to feel threatened by the new invention. The Church opposed the introduction of something that was so new. According to the Church, documents written on paper were not legally binding due to the fact that the Church did not consider paper permanent. Still, paper began to be used by people instead of parchment, which was treated animal skin. People were greatly intrigued and fascinated as well by the new medium, which was cheaper and more convenient than parchment had ever been or could ever be. The use of paper reached English soil by 1400, and then it reached America by 1690. Soon, paper became a universally accepted writing surface that was used everywhere. At this point in time, we take paper for granted and use it daily. We do not even acknowledge the fact that it was once a revolutionary new invention.

DICTION

Diction is **word choice.** The term refers to the words we use in speech and writing. The most important features of diction are these: word choice helps establish the tone of a piece of writing; word choice implies how writers perceive themselves, their readers, and their purposes in writing; and word choice determines how interestingly and accurately writers communicate ideas. These features are especially important in writing—often determining whether readers understand and appreciate what they read.

28 Levels of Diction

In the largest sense, word choices are considered standard or nonstandard. *Standard* English, the appropriate language in most academic and professional writing, is just what it says it is: standard. Based on grammatical principles and accepted word choices, it is expected by educated people in most of what they read. *Nonstandard* English, in contrast, deviates from this expected standard in its use of ungrammatical constructions and of colloquial or regional expressions.

In early stages of writing—in planning, organizing, and writing a rough draft—most writers do not or cannot attend to matters of diction, standard or otherwise. However, when the writer revises a rough draft to prepare a final copy, word choices are of special concern. The following guidelines, some general and some very specific, will help, but if you encounter specific problems with word choice, consult a dictionary for further advice.

28a Use formal diction when subjects, readers, or purposes require it.

Formal diction is somewhat removed from the word choices in everyday conversation. It should be used for writing that serves serious purposes. Certain kinds of subjects (death, fraud, science, philosophy, and literature, for example) are usually treated formally in any context. Most readers— teachers, employers, and professional colleagues among them —expect some degree of formality in writing. Finally, certain purposes—persuasion, for instance—usually require a formal presentation.

Formal diction usually excludes slang and contractions. In addition, it is often written in the third person. It is putting the best words forward in the writer's most educated and controlled way. The following paragraph, originally very informal, has been revised to make it more suitably formal.

The effects of divorce on children ~~change with the kids'~~ *vary depending on the children's* ages. ~~Lit-tle kids,~~ *Very young children,* one to four, often ~~don't get it when their parents yell at each other,~~ *do not fully comprehend the problems between their parents,* but they usually ~~know something's wrong.~~ *sense the tension.* ~~Bigger kids,~~ *Older children,* from four to eight, ~~have a better idea of what's going on. Be-cause they don't know any better, they're always asking~~ *more clearly recognize relationships in turmoil. Lacking social adeptness, they often ask* embarrassing questions like "Why are you and Mommy yelling at each other?" *and candid*

This abstract discussion of a serious subject needs formality. The changes in word choice create a more appropriate match between the subject and the diction.

28b Use informal diction when subjects, readers, and purposes require it.

In conversation, *informal diction* is more natural than formal diction for most people. Some readers, too, prefer informality, and some subjects are more appropriately presented with informal diction. Professional writers, for instance, usually treat certain subjects informally: camping, travel, sports, amusing personal experiences, and so on. In addition, certain kinds of writing—essays in popular magazines, for instance—are usually written informally.

Informal diction often includes contractions, uses first person pronouns (*I, me, my,* and so on), and sometimes includes slang and regionalisms. Essentially, it presents ideas in a conversational manner. As such, it is usually inappropriate for most college and on-the-job writing. It might serve your purposes well, however, in a "nonacademic" composition, such as a personal-experience paper. The following paragraph, with its personal point of view, is suitably informal.

> When I was about eleven, my parents got a divorce. I wasn't surprised. For months I had known something was wrong, although I wasn't sure what. Mom and Dad would alternately argue about trivial matters and then turn silent, not speaking to each other for days.

28c Consider your audience as you choose words.

Good writing communicates clearly with readers, and it does that, in large part, through careful word choices. A good idea, organized logically and supported with examples and facts, will still not be clear if the word choices do not accurately convey the intended meaning to readers. As a writer, then, you must select your words to insure that your ideas are clearly presented for your reading audience. To assess the appropriateness of your diction, consider these questions:

How well developed are your readers' vocabularies? If your readers are well educated or well read, their vocabularies are probably fairly extensive, and you will have the freedom to use sophisticated word choices to present your ideas. On the other hand, if your readers' vocabularies are not well developed—for any number of reasons—then you will have to adjust your word choices to make sure that your ideas are presented in a fairly uncomplicated way.

Do your readers understand the technical vocabulary of your subject? If your readers are familiar with your subject, chances are good that they know its technical terminology. You will be able to present a discussion in "specialist's" language. If your readers are unfamiliar with your subject, however, you cannot assume that they know the specialized vocabulary of the field. To insure that they understand your discussion, you will have to use everyday equivalents for technical terms or define key words.

How do your readers feel about levels of diction? All readers will expect standard diction in your writing, but some will prefer formal diction, while others will prefer informal diction. If your readers expect formal diction, you will have to omit slang, contractions, and regionalisms from your writing. In contrast, if your readers expect informal diction, you will have a good deal more freedom as you choose your words.

You cannot completely match your word choices with your readers' knowledge, needs, and expectations, but you should make a serious effort to analyze your readers and write to them in language that they can understand and appreciate.

EXERCISE □ *Formal and Informal Diction*

The following sentences are too informally written, considering their subjects. Revise them to make them more suitably formal.

Example

In *Prizzi's Honor,* each of the married assassins ~~cooked up~~ *developed* a plan to ~~bump off~~ *kill* the other one.

1. Maybe Temperance leaders got strung out because cops couldn't enforce the Eighteenth Amendment.

2. People in old folks' homes sometimes get ripped off because they're unable to control their own money.

3. Only a fool would get into anything as dangerous as cocaine.

4. Gina Frenoza was sent up the river because she got nabbed while dipping into the till at First National Bank.

5. In *A Native Son,* Bigger Thomas took off after he did Mary in.

29 Issues of Diction

29a Use words with connotations that match your purpose.

Words are defined in two ways, by their *denotations* and by their *connotations*. Denotations are dictionary meanings—

short, specific definitions. Because denotations are fairly direct, they do not usually cause problems for careful writers. Connotations, the secondary and sometimes emotional meanings of words, create more difficulties, because the connotations of words create added impressions, ones not always planned on by writers. Make sure these secondary meanings match your purposes (see Euphemisms, **29h**).

Two words often share the same denotation (synonyms) but have clearly distinct connotations. *Assertive* and *pushy*, for example, both mean "forward," but their connotations differ greatly.

Positive

Javid was the **most assertive** salesperson on the staff. (Most assertive *implies hard working and persuasive.*)

Negative

Javid was the **pushiest** salesperson on the staff. (Pushiest *implies aggressive and domineering.*)

Neutral

The **group** of students protested outside the administration building. (Group *means "a number of people" but does not imply a threat.*)

Negative

The **gang** of students protested outside the administration building. (Gang *also means "a number of people," but it suggests lack of control and implies a threat.*)

EXERCISE □ *Connotations*

In the following sentences, the words in boldface type have essentially negative connotations. Replace them with more positive words and explain how the alternative words change the meanings of the sentences.

Example

Mr. Bumble ~~glared~~ *gazed* down at the ~~blubbering~~ *sobbing* child. *(These choices make Mr. Bumble and the child more sympathetic.)*

1. The teenagers **badgered** the old woman who was sitting on the park bench.

2. While **dawdling** through the shopping mall, Naomi decided to go see a movie.

3. The **reckless** pilot made one more bombing run over the city.

4. The loose-fitting dress accentuated that Carla was **skinny.**

5. President Reagan seemed **flabbergasted** by the public's response to his visit to Bitburg Cemetery.

29b Use the specific words most suited to your purposes.

The specificity of word choices is often determined by whether the words are abstract or concrete. *Abstract* words name concepts, qualities, or conditions—things intangible: *truth, loyalty, honesty, laziness, freedom, poverty.* *Concrete* words name tangible things: *hydrant, bagel, razor, detonator, rabbit, silo.* In some writing, abstract words can suitably present general ideas. The vividness of concrete words, however, adds interest and specificity to writing. Readers will be able to visualize ideas more clearly when they are illustrated more concretely and specifically.

Abstract

Poverty demoralizes people.

Concrete

Being unable to pay bills, buy suitable clothing, feed one's children well, and buy some small conveniences must surely demoralize parents who want a comfortable standard of living for their families.

Words can also be loosely classified by how specific or general they are and can be seen in something like a continuum.

General Words			Specific Words
game	card game	complicated card game	bridge
tool	power tool	expensive power tool	radial arm saw
soap	laundry soap	liquid laundry soap	Liquid Tide

Words do not always exist in this kind of progression, but use the most specific word possible to clarify your exact meaning.

1. **Heroines** in **fiction** are sometimes shrewder than **men.**
2. **Heroines** in **novels** are sometimes shrewder than **men.**
3. **Heroines** in **nineteenth-century novels** are sometimes shrewder than **their lovers.**
4. **Catherine,** the heroine in *Wuthering Heights,* is shrewder than **Heathcliff.**

Sometimes a generalization is necessary, in which case a sentence like number 3 above may be the best one. However, do not overlook the importance of specificity. Readers of sentence number 1 could easily and justifiably supply their own details, thinking wrongly, for instance, that heroines in modern short fiction are sometimes shrewder than their fathers. To avoid such misinterpretation, use specific diction to make your meaning clear.

EXERCISE □ *Specific Words*

The following sentences present only the most general of ideas. Give them clearer meanings by adding specific words to replace or clarify the general ones.

Example

Politics is expensive.

Running for Congress can cost over a million dollars.

1. The boat was big.

2. Entertainers often have personal problems.

3. The skater won the competition.

4. Television influences people's lives.

5. Children learn important lessons through sports.

29c Use the accepted forms of idioms.

Idioms are groups of words that work together to establish meaning and that are often illogical if examined word for word. The expression "Break it up," for example, is commonly understood to mean "Stop fighting," but examined a word at a time it is somewhat nonsensical. *Break*, in the sense of splitting into two or more pieces, creates a visual image of several fighters separating. *It* is an indefinite but moderately clear reference to *fight*. *Up*, however, defies explanation when considered apart from the brief but still idiomatic phrase *break up*. Idioms like this one have developed along with our language, and although they may not make literal sense, these expressions have become universally recognized. You must follow their accepted patterns of usage.

Some standard idioms:

agree with (someone)

agree to (a proposal)

angry with (not "angry at")

charge for (a purchase)

charge with (a crime)

die of / die from

differ with (meaning "to disagree")

differ from (meaning "to be unlike")

in search of (not "in search for")

intend to (not "intend on")

off (not "off of")

plan to (not "plan on")

search for (something or someone)

similar to (not "similar with")

sure to (not "sure and")

try to (not "try and")

type of (not "type of a ")

wait for (someone or something)

wait on (meaning "to serve")

Other kinds of idioms have also emerged, but they seem to defy explanation or guidelines for usage:

break down the door

fall in love

open up the door

pick up the house

take a shower

When working with idiomatic expressions, be aware that most problems arise because of prepositions. If you are in doubt about which preposition to use, check the list above or refer to a dictionary for expressions not included here.

EXERCISE □ *Idioms*

Circle the appropriate idioms for the following sentences.

1. Although I (agree to/agree with) Councilman Marcello that the rates for trash collection are too high, I cannot (agree to/agree with) his plan to reopen the bids.

2. Before I read Dickens's *Great Expectations*, I (planned on keeping/planned to keep) a list of major and minor characters.

3. Eisenhower's easygoing style of governing (differed from/differed with) Truman's confrontational manner.

4. The National Geographic Society often goes (in search for/ in search of) exotic flora and fauna to describe in its broadcasts.

5. The (charge for/charge on) taking flowers from the funeral home to the cemetery was one hundred dollars.

29d Avoid using phrases that have become clichés.

A *cliché* is an overused expression that has lost its original freshness and often its meaning. Although most of these phrases once presented original and clear connections between ideas, they have now become predictable, stale, and sometimes unclear.

Consider these phrases with the last element omitted:

last but not _____

smart as a _____

time will _____

tried and _____

don't beat around the _____

rough and _____

fit as a _____

in the final _____

red as a _____

dead as a _____

The fact that you can supply the last element of most of these expressions suggests that they are predictable. Such predictability in writing not only bores readers but also suggests that writers are not examining their subjects in original ways.

Now consider these comparisons:

cute as a button (*Some buttons are far from cute, don't you think?*)

cool as a cucumber (*How cool are cucumbers, anyway?*)

as white as snow (*Although this was once a striking image, it has been used too much to add freshness to current writing. Besides, have you ever seen snow in an industrial area?*)

as neat as a pin (*In what sense is a pin neat?*)

like a bull in a china shop (*Once a vivid comparison, this phrase has been overused by everyone, and who except Merrill Lynch has ever witnessed such a phenomenon?*)

Because these kinds of phrases no longer add liveliness or insight to writing, they serve little real purpose. In fact, they often detract from an otherwise good paper. Do not use them in your writing.

29e Avoid using modifiers that have become clichés.

Certain modifying words or phrases have been used so often, and so thoughtlessly, that they have lost their appeal and interest. When selecting modifiers for a sentence, consider whether they clarify the sentence or make the sentence sound prefabricated with ready-made modifiers. Often, choosing more specific words will make sentences substantially clearer.

Cliché

Marge Johnson did an **in-depth** study of the use of asbestos in local school construction. (*In-depth is such a common term, used in so many contexts, that it hardly clarifies the meaning of the sentence.*)

Improved

Marge Johnson did a **two-hundred-page** study of the use of asbestos in local school construction. *(Although we know nothing of her methodology, the length implies that the study was thorough.)*

Cliché

Unlike those of most college students, Mai's clothes were **weird.** *(People perceive weird in so many ways, and the word is used so regularly and thoughtlessly, that this description is unclear.)*

Improved

Unlike most college students, Mai **wore dashikis and cowboy boots.**

EXERCISE ☐ *Clichés*

The following sentences contain examples of worn out comparisons and ineffective modifiers. Identify the clichés and revise the sentences to make them clear.

Example

After an hour-long photo session, Tamita still looked ~~fresh as a daisy.~~ *cool and relaxed.*

1. Rachael studied the Boer War as if her life depended on it.

2. They scrubbed the poor child until she was as clean as a whistle.

3. Stranded at the airport by the snowstorm, the student was as angry as a tiger in a cage.

4. Even though we were as poor as church mice, my family was as close as sardines in a can.

5. Although Arnulfo was scared silly by the idea of white-water rafting, he clearly had a great time once he tried it.

29f Avoid pretentious language.

Even in formal writing, avoid using words to impress readers rather than to communicate effectively. Typically, writers use pretentious diction when they have not carefully considered their readers or purpose—or when they want to sound like experts. Not only is pretentious diction dishonest in this respect, but it often makes simple ideas difficult to grasp and complicated ideas impossible to understand. Translate any pretentious diction into more natural words. If you do not, your readers will have to do so (see also Jargon, **29g**).

Pretentious

Prior to the purchase of the **abode,** the Enricos carefully **ruminated** about how **residential payments** would affect their **cash flow.** *(The artificial word choices here, some poorly selected synonyms and some jargon, require a translation.)*

Natural

Before the Enricos purchased the **house,** they carefully **thought** about how **mortgage payments** would affect their **finances.** *(This sentence uses natural diction and is therefore more easily understood on a first reading.)*

Note: Although a thesaurus, a book of synonyms, is helpful when writers are searching for alternative ways of stating something, it should be used selectively. Use only those words that are a natural part of your vocabulary, beware of clichés, and never choose words whose connotations you do not understand. Using a thesaurus to find impressive or unusual words is the cause of much pretentious writing, so use one intelligently.

EXERCISE □ *Pretentious Language*

The following paragraph uses especially pretentious language to describe a rather commonplace event. Revise it so that the word choices are more natural. (Suggestion: make this a personal narrative.)

When one participates in commencement ceremonies, one is often fraught with a mixture of emotions. One senses relief because one's time in high school is terminating. Conversely, one feels uncertain about what lies ahead. Some students will seek employment immediately, other students will approach matrimony, and yet other students will pursue additional academic studies. For this diversity of students, commencement exercises symbolize an uncertain transmutation in their lives.

29g Avoid jargon.

Jargon is the technical vocabulary or slang of a specialized group. Doctors, mechanics, weather forecasters, teachers, carpenters, and publishers all have special words or expressions that they use in their own contexts. When you write for such a group only, using its jargon may be acceptable. However, when you write outside such specific contexts—as you usually will—translate any jargon into common terms.

Jargon	Translation
urban open-space (city planning)	a city park
investment returns (business)	profits
precipitation (weather forecasting)	rain, snow, sleet
combat situation (military)	battle, skirmish, attack
telephone surveillance (law enforcement)	wire-tapping
economy sedan (car sales)	the cheapest four-door car
cost-efficient (business)	economical
merchantable dwelling (real estate)	a salable house

With Jargon

The city council recommends a systematic program of greening for our arterials as a means to revitalize our declining streetscape.

Translated

The city council recommends that we plant trees along our main streets to make them appear less neglected.

29h Avoid euphemisms.

Euphemisms are "nice" words used to substitute for specific words whose connotations are negative, unpleasant, or unappealing. Instead of saying soldiers were *killed,* a press release will say they *gave their lives;* instead of saying people are *fired,* a notice will say they are *let go;* instead of saying someone is *fat,* a salesclerk will say *full-figured* or *hard-to-fit.* Readers are seldom fooled by euphemisms, which they often translate instinctively. They know what the euphemisms *really* mean. Thus, it makes sense to avoid euphemisms most of the time and save readers from the annoyance of having to interpret sentences. In rare instances, though, euphemisms may acceptably buffer highly unpleasant feelings about a subject, but such use should be selective (see Connotations, **29a**).

Euphemism	Translation
passed away	died
financial enticements	bribes
the oldest profession	prostitution
marriage dissolution	divorce
deferred-payment plan	credit
corporal punishment	whipping, spanking
placed in custody	arrested
hair-color enhancer	dye or bleach

EXERCISE □ *Pretentious Diction, Jargon, and Euphemisms*

The following sentences are all artificial because of poorly chosen words. Translate these pretentious sentences so that they are more natural and clearer.

Example

The house at the corner of Seventh Street and Maple ~~is a handy-~~ *needs extensive but minor repairs.* ~~man's delight.~~

1. More consistent use of passenger restraints in automobiles could reduce the number of fatalities on major thoroughfares.

2. You are cordially invited to attend the nuptials of Mary Freese and Carlos Fernandez at seven in the evening on the twenty-third of May.

3. Because of his hard work as a postal deliverer, Jerrold received a salary increment.

4. At the social gathering, Bryan imbibed so many distilled spirits that he became inebriated.

5. The Congress voted to approve a package of budget enhancements, including higher surcharges on liquor and smoking materials.

EXERCISE □ *Pretentious Diction, Euphemisms, and Jargon*

The following paragraph is full of pretentious diction, including euphemisms and jargon. Translate it so that it expresses its ideas in a more natural way.

Working as a steward in an eating establishment requires knowledge of certain accepted procedures. As patrons are seated by the maitre d', one must welcome them, give them menus, and inquire if they would like to partake of any beverages. Then, having served the beverages, one must record the diners' cuisine preferences, recording any special instructions for the chef. When the orders are ready, one must serve the food with style and assurance. During these procedures, one must carefully observe the table arrangements to make sure that eating utensils are properly placed and that condiments are present. If one serves one's patrons well, one is likely to receive a substantial gratuity.

29i Keep slang and regionalisms to a minimum.

Slang is very informal language that often stays in use for only a brief period. Generally, slang begins as an expression that becomes popular as part of the speaking vocabulary of a close-knit group. Its currency makes it enjoyable in speech—showing that speakers are aware of current language trends—and if the use of the slang expression becomes broad enough, the term may be absorbed into acceptable English. Until that happens, however, slang has little place in writing. Slang is so quickly dated and so informal, and its meaning is so often inexact to those outside the originating group, that it does not communicate very clearly (see Neologisms, **29n**).

> That class was **the pits.** *("Seeds," as in peach pits? "A cavity in the ground," as in the La Brea Tar Pits?)*

Hang gliding is **out of sight.** *("Beyond the rest," as in unseen solar systems?)*

When I saw how far ahead I was, I felt **wicked.** *("Evil"? Wickedly good? Wickedly bad?)*

Regionalisms are expressions that are common only in particular locales. Within their regions, they are understood, but in other areas their meaning is lost. As with slang, avoid regionalisms because they are inexact and muddle communication.

Early in November, we ordered the **tags** for our car. *(Although this makes perfect sense on the East Coast, use the more universal expression* license plates *to guarantee understanding elsewhere.)*

EXERCISE □ *Slang*

Make a list of five slang terms or phrases in current use. Then write two sentences for each—one using slang and one translating it into standard English.

Example

rip-off (noun)

The insurance plan to supplement Medicare was a **rip-off.**

The insurance plan to supplement Medicare was a **fraud.**

29j Carefully distinguish between homonyms, words that sound the same but have different meanings and spellings.

The English language contains many pairs and trios of words that are often confused because of their similar pronunciations. Because the words have different meanings, however, carefully choose the proper one to convey your intended meaning (see Glossary of Usage, **65,** for some commonly confused words).

accept (be willing to receive)

except (all but)

I will not **accept** the blame for you.

Everyone **except** Cheng submitted the assignment on time.

affect (to influence)

effect (the result of an action or to bring about an action)

The medication **affected** Mrs. Bradshaw's vision.

The **effects** of using Agent Orange have been far-reaching.

threw (past tense of *throw)*

through (by way of)

Diana **threw** the Publishers Clearinghouse envelope in the trash.

We silently walked **through** the museum, awed by the splendor of the exhibits.

29k Use figures of speech judiciously.

Figures of speech are words, phrases, and expressions that add uniqueness to writing, most often by making unexpected or suggestive connections between things that are different from each other. *Metaphors,* comparisons that do not use any connective words, are common figures of speech: *Dr. Mantera's criticism of the proposal was all thunder and no lightning.* (The core sentence, *criticism was thunder,* establishes an implied comparison, stressing noise. *No lightning* extends the figurative comparison, stressing that there was no illumination, no insight.) *Similes,* comparisons using the connective words *like, as* or *as if,* are also common: *Rob accelerated his car, shifting lanes quickly and rounding corners at high speed, as if he were making a final lap at the Indianapolis 500.* Figures of speech can enliven writing, but make sure that the connections are fresh. A figure of speech that is a cliché will add no interest or originality to writing (see Clichés, **29d** and **29e**).

Effective Metaphor

Ron's enthusiasm for trickery and adventure always reminds me of Tom Sawyer's.

Ineffective Metaphor

After the laughter stopped, Bernice gave Rinaldo an **icy** stare. *(This modifier is a cliché.)*

Effective Simile

Cleo is like a Duracell battery: she's always starting something, and it lasts longer than we ever expect.

Ineffective Simile

Darryl's grades are **solid as a rock.** (Solid as a rock *is a cliché.)*

29l Do not mix unrelated associations in figures of speech.

Multiple figures of speech must present a uniform impression, drawing on related images, locales, experiences, or circumstances. If the impressions do not fit together logically, the meaning will be confused—often laughably so.

Confusingly Mixed

Like an agile deer, the politician took the wind out of his opponent's sails. *(Deer and ship's sails are seldom associated. Besides,* wind out of his opponent's sails *is a cliché.)*

Logically Linked

Like an agile deer, the politician deftly maneuvered past the questions with which his opponent hoped to trap him. *(Both images relate to deer and woodland activities.)*

EXERCISE □ *Figures of Speech*

The following sentences contain ineffective figures of speech. Revise the sentences to make them better.

Example

Like a delicate flower on a hot summer day, Angela ~~smoldered~~ *wilted* in the afternoon sun.

1. Like a train rushing down the track, Mrs. Matheson ran through the flowers, leaving broken blossoms in her wake.

2. Wilma dived into *War and Peace,* determined to reach the top of her class.

3. Flying down the stairs and then stampeding down the front hallway, the students escaped from the burning school building.

4. Like a kangaroo, Larry Bird jumped for the ball and then fired it down the court.

5. Following Valerie's map, which looked like a spider's web, we continued down the ribbon of highway.

EXERCISE □ *Clichés and Figures of Speech*

The following paragraph contains a variety of figures of speech, many of them clichés. Revise the paragraph to eliminate clichés and clarify figures of speech.

When I sit in the waiting room at my dentist's office, I feel as if I am waiting to be executed. I sit in a chair that is hard as a rock, and I usually have to look at magazines that are as old as the hills. No music is piped in because the speakers are never working, so it is as quiet as a morgue. The only sounds are infrequent ones from the work areas. Sometimes a frightened child will squeal like a stuck pig, and sometimes the dentist and hygienist will chuckle quietly, the way kids do at the back of a classroom. When the receptionist comes through the door to get me, I always feel the way I did in second grade when I was called to the principal's office.

29m Do not use sexist language.

Sexist language implies, generally through choices of key nouns and pronouns, that certain activities are restricted to either males or females. Because such usage is inaccurate, contemporary writers have developed strategies for removing sexism from writing. Some strategies relate specifically to pronoun use (see Pronoun-Antecedent Agreement, **11,** pages 184–185), while others deal with noun usage. Generally, in working with nouns, learn to notice the subtle—and sometimes not so subtle—implications of word choice.

> *ancestors*

According to my family records, my **forefathers** came to the United States from France. (*Foremothers had to come, too, or there would not have been any children. Ancestors includes everyone.*)

> *Chairperson*

The chemistry department needed a **chairman** who could unite the divided faculty. (*Chairman implied that a woman could not do the job. Chairperson applies to both men and women.*)

29n Use as few neologisms as you can.

Neologisms, recently created words or word forms, appear in current speech (and some journalistic and technical writing) and then very often fade away. Many neologisms are part of the technical jargon of specific groups, and some are used so widely that they become universally acceptable. *Stereo, fallout, refrigerator,* and *light bulb* were once newly coined words but have long since become standard. Avoid using new terms in your writing until their use is universally acceptable.

Questionable

Personal computers must be **user-friendly.** (*Computer was once a neologism; it has since become standard. User-friendly, a current sample of computer jargon, is still questionable. Do not use that term yet.*)

Better

Personal computers must be **easy for people to use.**

Questionable

Parenting requires patience, perseverance, and good humor. (*The use of* parenting, *a newly coined term in child care and education, is still questionable.*)

307

Better

Being a parent requires patience, perseverance, and good humor. *(The gerund phrase offers more acceptable usage.)*

Note: Many of the nouns currently used to avoid sexist language are neologisms: *middleperson* and *houseperson*, for instance. Wait to see if such words stand the test of time. Do not use them in your writing yet.

29o Avoid archaic words.

Archaic words were once commonly used (and can be seen in British and American literature) but are no longer in standard use. They add little to current writing because they seem clearly out of place. Words like *yon* ("over there"), *betwixt* ("between"), or *methinks* ("I suspect") only make writing seem artificial and pretentious.

Artificial

We adults sat and reminisced **whilst** the children played along the lake. *(No one says* whilst *anymore; no one should use it to describe a normal situation.)*

Natural

We adults sat and reminisced **while** the children played along the lake. *(This is more in keeping with modern usage.)*

EXERCISE □ *Neologisms and Archaic Words*

The following sentences contain words that are either too new or too old to be acceptable in standard usage. Revise the sentences to make them standard.

1. Ofttimes, I relax on rainy evenings by reading a murder mystery ere I go to bed.

2. Before Professor Gallo assigned *The Affluent Society,* she asked the economics class for some input.

3. Mr. Sabaria always discusses affordability with his clients before he renews their stock options.

4. Mother really need not worry about Vince's hunting in the cedar swamp. He will be home anon.

5. My erstwhile friend had become too clever a wag for my taste.

PUNCTUATION

Marks of punctuation help convey meaning to readers. Punctuation shows where complete thoughts end, where ideas are separated, and where pauses occur. In addition, correct punctuation helps signal the meaning of individual words in sentences.

Because punctuation is governed by a complex system of rules, be ready to double-check usage. Some rules of punctuation will probably be second nature to you, but others will be less familiar. When you have a question about punctuation, find the rule to govern your usage. Do not punctuate without knowing why you do so, and remember that too much punctuation can be as confusing as too little punctuation.

30 End Punctuation

There are three kinds of end punctuation: the period (.), the question mark (?), and the exclamation point (!). Although they serve a few additional purposes, these forms of punctuation usually end a sentence after it has expressed a complete thought.

> ### 30a Use a period after a sentence that makes a statement or gives a conversational command.
>
> Cigarette smoking is hazardous to your health. *(a statement)*
>
> Stop smoking today. *(a command)*

Most sentences will end in periods unless they ask questions or present a truly emphatic observation. Be especially careful of sentences that incorporate indirect questions. Because their main subjects and verbs present statements, they must still end with periods.

Marian asked Walter if he wanted to go sledding. *(Although Marian's question is implied, this sentence simply reports that she asked Walter. The main subject and verb are* Marian asked, *which make the sentence a statement.)*

30b Use a period with most abbreviations.

The period in an abbreviation indicates that letters have been omitted (see Abbreviations, **45**). It is standard practice to abbreviate titles like *Mr., Mrs.,* or *Dr.* with a period. It is also standard to omit periods in abbreviated names of companies and organizations like the *FBI, IBM,* or the *NAACP.*

Dr. Daubs received his Ph.D. in engineering in 1981. He began working for NASA immediately.

30c Use a question mark after a direct question.

Because a question mark should be used only after a direct question—not after an indirect one—analyze a sentence for the other signal for a question: inverted word order. If part of the verb precedes the subject, then the sentence is a direct question. End such sentences with a question mark.

Would you **grab** that lizard and return it to the aquarium? *(The verb* would grab *is divided by the subject* you. *The question mark is correct.)*

Jamie asked if I would grab the lizard and return it to the aquarium. *(The main verb is* asked, *and* I would grab *is in the normal order, indicating that this is a direct statement. A period is correct.)*

Writers occasionally use a question mark in parentheses to indicate an uncertain fact. This use is correct but somewhat questionable, because facts require validation in most cases.

Where facts themselves are uncertain, a few well chosen quali-
fiers (*approximately, around, near, probably, by the best estimates,
and others*) will more smoothly express the uncertainty.

Questionable

The Chinese invented paper in A.D. 105 **(?),** but it was kept as a
state secret for hundreds of years.

Better

By most estimates, the Chinese invented paper in approximately
A.D. 105, but it was kept as a state secret for hundreds of years.

30d **Use an exclamation point only to express
the strongest of feelings or to indicate
special emphasis.**

An exclamation point can follow either a sentence or an interjection, but not many interjections or sentences deserve the
emphasis that exclamation points imply. Use them selectively.

Help! My son has fallen off the dock!

Get out of my house before I throw you out!

If you end too many sentences with exclamation points,
you defeat the purpose of using this form of punctuation.
When every sentence is emphasized, none stands out.

Overused

The wailing sirens seemed to stop right below Martell's office
window! He ran and looked out! People were running from the
first-floor exits into the street! Some firefighters were putting on
gas masks! Suddenly, Martell began to smell smoke! The building was on fire! *(This series of descriptive sentences, with exclamation points, seems excessively frantic. Such overuse of exclamation*

points contradicts Martell's delayed response and emphasizes nothing in particular.)

Better

The wailing sirens seemed to stop right below Martell's office window. He ran and looked out. People were running from the first-floor exits into the street. Some firefighters were putting on gas masks. Suddenly, Martell began to smell smoke. The building was on fire! *(By reserving the exclamation for the last sentence, the writer emphasizes Martell's realization appropriately.)*

EXERCISE □ *End Punctuation*

The following paragraph contains no periods, question marks, or exclamation points. Add the appropriate end punctuation.

Nassar Imports, Inc, which sells carpets, small statuary, and gifts, adds an Eastern flair to the otherwise American business district in my town When old Mr Nassar greets me at the entrance to the display room, he always asks if he can assist me in any way He is a charming man of fifty or sixty A first-generation immigrant, he speaks English with some irregularity, but he seems genuinely interested in helping me find the right item to buy On the other hand, if young Mr Nassar, the son, meets me, he offers help with a more American idiom: "May I help you" He is the Americanized one in the family, with a BS in business from a local college and with a typical American brashness If you show any interest in particular items, he will riddle his speech with his most enthusiastic summary: "A great buy" Although the younger man is more adept with the English language—and probably will make the business even more profitable—I prefer the older, more gentlemanly Mr Nassar

31 Commas

The comma is an internal form of punctuation that separates sentence elements to make meaning clear. If commas do not appear where needed, thoughts can overlap in confusing ways or become altogether incomprehensible.

Confusing

As Ira was shaving the dog barked suddenly, causing the young man to nick his chin. *(Without a comma after* shaving, *the sentence might momentarily imply that Ira was shaving the dog.)*

Clear

As Ira was shaving, the dog barked suddenly, causing the young man to nick his chin.

Confusing

After we finished packing Dad took the suitcases to the car. *(The first impression might be that the packers put Dad in a suitcase.)*

Clear

After we finished packing, Dad took the suitcases to the car.

The following guidelines will help you use commas where they are needed.

31a Use commas to separate three or more items in a series.

When three or more roughly equivalent words, phrases, or clauses are used together in a sentence, commas should separate them. Some writers omit the comma immediately preceding the conjunction (the word that joins the items), but a comma there is always correct and may prevent confusion.

> The recipe called for cinnamon, nutmeg, and allspice. *(Commas separate all nouns in the list; if a fourth spice were added, yet another comma would be needed.)*

> We did not find the hidden money box, although we searched in the barn, under the house, and in the pigsty. *(The commas separate a series of prepositional phrases.)*

> Lela carved the woodblock, Todd printed the cards, and Rachael and I delivered the final versions. *(Three independent clauses are separated by commas and joined by the coordinating conjunction* and. *The commas effectively separate the three related ideas, and the coordinating conjunction keeps the sentence from being a comma splice. Note the confusion that would occur without the comma after* cards.*)*

31b In a compound sentence, use a comma before a coordinating conjunction.

Compound sentences join two or more independent clauses with a coordinating conjunction *(and, but, for, nor, or, so, or yet)* (see **7b**). Because each clause is independent, the ideas must be clearly separated by the conjunction. A comma further emphasizes the separation of the clauses. Essentially, the comma separates ideas so that readers will not be confused when reading a sentence. When the clauses are brief and when no confusion is likely, the comma may be omitted. However, using a comma will always be correct.

Making mistakes is common but admitting them is not. *(Because these clauses are very brief and because confusion is unlikely, the comma may be either omitted or used.)*

Players in the NBA may demand high salaries‸but high ticket prices may drive away the fans who pay for the salaries. *(This long sentence needs the comma to help separate its two independent clauses.)*

Price supports for dairy farmers greatly help the farmers‸and con-sumers benefit as well. *(Without a comma after* the farmers, *the initial reading might inappropriately link* the farmers *and* consumers *as direct objects.)*

When applying this comma rule, do not mistakenly place a comma before *every* coordinating conjunction. Some conjunctions connect only two words, phrases, or dependent clauses, in which case a comma may not be required. Commas are generally required only when the conjunction joins two independent clauses (see Unnecessary Commas, **32a**).

EXERCISE □ *Commas*

The following sentences contain no commas. Supply commas where necessary and explain why commas should or should not be used.

1. Yeats O'Casey Synge Gonne and Gregory were responsible for the success of Dublin's Abbey Theatre.

2. San Francisco's plan to control architectural designs is admirable in theory but it will be difficult to put into practice.

3. Computerized cash registers are now common in grocery stores movie houses discount stores and gas stations.

4. Dana visited with Toby and Jessica continued with her work.

5. Taxes support government programs but taxpayers often do not.

31c Use a comma after an introductory subordinate clause in a complex or compound-complex sentence.

In normal order, a complex sentence begins with its independent clause and ends with its subordinate clause (see **7c**). As writers vary their sentences, however, they often alter this pattern and begin sentences with subordinate clauses. Because of this inversion, a comma must show where the subordinate clause ends and where the independent clause begins. Watch for sentences beginning with subordinating conjunctions. They will require at least this one comma.

Because mosquitoes are such a problem at the camp site∧the owners spray the area with insecticides each evening. *(The comma shows where the clauses meet.)*

When I get ready to clean∧my apartment becomes my mortal enemy. *(Without the comma,* my apartment *can mistakenly be interpreted as the object of* to clean.)

31d Use a comma after introductory prepositional phrases that function as adverbs.

In many sentences, opening prepositional phrases answer the questions when? where? or under what conditions? Such phrases are adverbial, often modifying the entire sentence. To make their meaning clear, separate these phrases from the rest of the sentence with a comma (see Prepositional Phrases, **6d,** pages 143–144).

> After five hours of surgery, Dr. Teranashi stretched out on the sofa in his office. *(The comma signals where the adverbial informa- tion ends and where the main idea of the sentence begins.)*

> After training ⌄the dog was much better behaved than before.
>
> *(Without a comma, the prepositional phrase* after training *may be misread as a gerund phrase:* after training the dog.)

Since the primary purpose of using a comma in this posi- tion is clarity, the comma can be omitted if the prepositional phrase is brief and if the meaning is clear.

> Deep inside I felt sure she would win. *(This sentence is not poten- tially confusing.)*

31e Use a comma after an introductory verbal phrase.

When an introductory infinitive or participial phrase func- tions as an adjective—typically modifying the sentence's sub- ject—it should be set off from the rest of the sentence by a comma (see Verbal Phrases, **6d,** pages 146–149).

> To guarantee that her money was wisely spent, Mrs. Fairchild su- pervised her own household accounts. *(The opening phrase modi- fies* Mrs. Fairchild. *The comma indicates where the modification ends and where the name of the person is introduced.)*

> Crouching in a makeshift hut of sticks and grasses, Jane Goodall observed the chimpanzees at play. *(The introductory participial phrase is adjectival. The comma signals that the person being de- scribed is going to be named.)*

31f Use a comma to set off an introductory adverb.

Introductory adverbs (*first, finally, then, afterward,* and others) should be separated from the rest of the sentence by a comma, especially when they might be joined confusingly to the next word in the sentence.

Subsequently ‚relocating the people of Times Beach was found to cost too much. (*Without a comma,* subsequently *modifies* relocating, *rather than the entire sentence.*)

31g Use commas to set off absolute phrases.

An absolute phrase modifies an entire sentence rather than any single part of the sentence (see **6d,** page 151). Since it is grammatically separate from the rest of the sentence, the phrase must be set off by a comma or commas, depending on where it is positioned.

Her gear carefully packed in her knapsack, Pam headed up the trail. (*Appearing at the beginning part of the sentence, the absolute phrase must be followed by a comma.*)

Jeff, his chores finished, sat by the pool reading a magazine. (*Embedded in the sentence, the absolute phrase must be set off a pair of commas.*)

Marcello left the office, his work for the day completed. (*Appearing at the end of the sentence, the absolute phrase must be preceded by a comma.*)

EXERCISE □ *Commas*

The following sentences contain no commas, although some sentences clearly need them. Place commas where they are appropriate and explain why you used them.

1. Although rowing is a truly amateur sport it attracts partici-

   pants who have the commitment of professional athletes.

2. Generally reading the ingredient labels on convenience foods can be eye-opening.

3. After four attempts to write about the experience Gabriella gave up.

4. Even though learning a foreign language is difficult it has numerous advantages in business as well as personal life.

5. Their fear heightened by the ghost stories the young campers huddled close together.

6. Its head high the show horse cantered past the prospective buyer.

7. When the survivors finally considered rationing water was their prime concern.

8. Her eyes stinging from the chlorine Desirée climbed out of the pool.

9. Inevitably overusing credit cards destroys an individual's sense of money management.

10. Before 9:30 A.M. each weekday Schulmeister's Bakery is crowded with customers.

> **31h** Use a comma or a pair of commas to set off nonrestrictive phrases and clauses, but not restrictive ones.

Nonrestrictive phrases and clauses supply additional information about a word in a sentence. This information can be omitted without making the sentence more general or substantially changing its meaning. Nonrestrictive phrases and clauses are set off by commas.

Restrictive phrases and clauses also supply information about a word in a sentence, but the information is required to make the meaning clear. Because these phrases *restrict* the meaning of the sentence, they are not set off by commas.

Nonrestrictive

The bicycle, **which cost two hundred dollars,** was stolen from the rack. *(The information about price adds a useful detail, but it is not absolutely necessary in order to understand that the theft took place.)*

Restrictive

The bicycle **stolen from the rack** was worth two hundred dollars. *(Here the clause adds clarifying information that is necessary. The restrictive clause separates the purloined bicycle from other bicycles.)*

Relative clauses that function as adjectives

Relative clauses use *that, when, where, which, who, whoever,* and *whomever*—plus a verb—to embed information in sentences (see Subordinate Clauses, **6e,** pages 154–156). Functioning as adjectives, these clauses may or may not be restrictive. Phrases using *that* are always restrictive, but phrases with the other relative pronouns can be either restrictive or nonrestrictive. You must carefully interpret sentences with adjective clauses to decide whether the subordinate information is essential or optional. If it is optional, commas are necessary.

Nonrestrictive

Sasha's best painting, which is prominently displayed in his dining room, has bold colors and brushwork. *(The information in the clause is helpful, but it does not add to the idea of the painting's colors and technique. The sentence would still mean the same thing without it. It is therefore nonrestrictive and must be set off by commas.)*

Restrictive

The painting that earned Sasha first prize at the Artists' Guild Competition was displayed in the foyer. *(Here the modification separates this painting from others Sasha has done. It is therefore restrictive and should not be separated by commas.)*

Prepositional and verbal phrases

Functioning as adjectives or adverbs, these word groups can be either restrictive or nonrestrictive (see Phrases, **6d**). Decide whether the information is essential or optional and use commas accordingly.

Nonrestrictive

Marc pulled his convertible, gleaming from a fresh coat of wax, into the parking space next to mine. *(The participial phrase—* gleaming from a fresh coat of wax—*adds information but does not clarify the action in the sentence. The phrase is thus nonrestrictive and needs to be set off by commas.)*

Restrictive

The convertible with the racing stripes down the side belongs to Marc. *(The prepositional phrases—*with the racing stripes, down the side, *and* to Marc—*are restrictive because they single out this convertible from others apparently nearby. As a result, commas should not be used.)*

A car next to a fire hydrant in our city will be towed away within an hour. *(The prepositional phrases—*next to a fire hydrant *and* in

our city—*are restrictive because they identify which particular car
will be towed away. Consequently, no commas are required.)*

31i Use commas to set off nonrestrictive appositives, but not restrictive ones.

Appositives are words that restate or define a noun or pronoun (see **6d**, page 150). When the appositive provides additional but nonessential information, it is nonrestrictive and
should be set off by commas. When the appositive provides
information essential to the meaning of the sentence, though, it
is restrictive, and no commas are required.

Nonrestrictive

''Thriller,'' the title song of Michael Jackson's album, topped the
charts in a matter of weeks. *(Here the proper noun is clear on its
own. Because the appositive adds nonessential information, it is nonrestrictive. Commas are required.)*

Restrictive

The music video ''Thriller'' was a make-up artist's dream come
true. *(Here the commas are unnecessary because the appositive is essential to the meaning of the sentence. Without it, the sentence would
be too general to be clear.)*

EXERCISE □ *Commas*

Most commas have been omitted from the following sentences. Insert them where necessary to set off nonrestrictive elements. One sentence is correct.

1. A symbol of Agatha's long but unhappy marriage the satin

   wedding gown wrinkled and yellowed with age hung in

   the attic.

2. The miniseries *Shogun* did little to make Americans truly aware of Japanese culture.

3. "A Christmas Memory" a recollection of Truman Capote's childhood presents the bittersweet relationship between a young boy and an old woman.

4. Halogen headlights those used on European cars provide excellent visibility in bad weather.

5. *Beowulf* which is one of the earliest examples of Anglo-Saxon literature still appeals to those who like adventure stories.

EXERCISE □ *Commas*

The following paragraph contains some but not all of the commas needed to make its sentences clear. Supply the commas necessary to set off nonrestrictive elements correctly.

Although zoos provide my only opportunity to see many exotic animals up close, I often object to the facilities for the animals. Rhesus monkeys very small primates do not seem cramped in small places; they do not appear to suffer or experience any ill effects from their confinement. Chimpanzees, however, seem noticeably depressed in areas that do not allow them to move about freely. Orangutans highly intelligent primates also seem despondent. However, the jungle cats tigers and leopards seem to suffer most. They pace in their cages or lie inactive and inattentive. These large primates and big cats which are usually among a zoo's main attractions need more space and some distance from the crowds of eager spectators. In recent years, zoo keepers who have the animals' best interests in mind have begun building habitats for these larger animals. Most zoos have paid for these building projects which can be quite elaborate from general funds. Other zoos have launched major advertising campaigns, hoping for individual donations. Still others stressing commitment to a community have appealed to major corporations. These large building projects should continue, for they provide improved living conditions for large wild animals. As we maintain zoos that entertain and educate people, we must also remember that the animals that live there should not suffer for our benefit.

31j Use commas to separate coordinate adjectives and adverbs.

Adjectives modify nouns and pronouns. Adverbs modify verbs, adjectives, and other adverbs (see **5d** and **5e**). When several adjectives modify a single noun, commas indicate that each modifies the noun separately. Similarly, coordinate adverbs each modify a verb or adjective separately and equally. Commas should appear between such adjectives and adverbs, but no comma is placed between the last modifier and the word it modifies.

> The ancient, dilapidated house on Third Street is going to be demolished next week. (Ancient *house*; dilapidated *house*; *each adjective functions independently.*)

> Jessica slowly, calmly, carefully approached the injured goose. (Slowly *approached*; calmly *approached*; carefully *approached*; *each adverb functions independently.*)

To test the independence of coordinate modifiers, reverse the order of the modifiers or insert *and* between them. If the sentence is still logical, the adjectives or adverbs are coordinate, and commas should separate them. If the modifiers cannot be sensibly inverted, then they are *cumulative* (see **32e**).

> The dilapidated and ancient house on Third Street is going to be demolished next week. *(The modification is still clear, and the sentence is still logical. "Dilapidated, ancient house" also makes sense.)*

> Jessica slowly, carefully, and calmly approached the injured goose. *(The modification is still clear. "Calmly, carefully, slowly approached" also makes sense.)*

31k Use commas to set off transitions or words that provide parenthetical comments.

Transitional words or phrases link ideas, creating smoother writing. Because transitional words do not serve specific grammatical functions in sentences, they should be set off by commas.

> Dr. Foulkes, for example, walks up Spruce Hill to watch the sun set. *(When the transitional phrase falls within the sentence, place a comma before and after it.)*

In fact, he walks up there every clear evening. *(When the transitional words begin or end a sentence, a single comma separates them from the rest of the sentence.)*

31l Use commas to set off conjunctive adverbs.

Conjunctive adverbs—*however, therefore, nevertheless,* and *consequently,* for example—make logical connections between ideas but do not grammatically link words as conjunctions do (see **5f,** pages 128–129). As a result, they generally must be separated from the rest of the sentence by commas. Commas can sometimes be omitted, but only when the sentence reads very smoothly.

> Newspaper reports suggested the president's involvement in Watergate. Nixon, however, claimed he had committed no crimes. *(Placed within a sentence, a conjunctive adverb requires a pair of commas.)*

> Subsequently, testimony proved he was deeply involved in illegal activities. *(One comma separates a conjunctive adverb that begins or ends the sentence.)*

When a pair of independent clauses is joined by a semicolon, a conjunctive adverb often provides a logical connection between clauses. In such a construction, a comma follows the conjunctive adverb as if it were at the beginning of a separate sentence.

> Impeachment proceedings seemed imminent; therefore, Nixon resigned from office.

EXERCISE □ *Commas*

The following paragraph contains some commas but not all that are required for the sake of clarity. Supply the needed commas to separate coordinate adjectives and to set off transitional words and conjunctive adverbs.

In years past recovery from an operation was a sedentary activity. Patients stretched out on clean starched white sheets for days or weeks and passively dully waited to be active again. Today however physical therapists and doctors stress that the sooner patients try to resume normal active routines the better off the patients will be. For instance after having a cesarean section (an operation to deliver a baby through the mother's abdominal wall), a woman used to be bedridden for a week at least. Now such a patient is expected to be mobile the next day. With the assistance of a nurse or a nurse's aide, today's cesarean mother can be seen taking slow sometimes uncomfortable strolls around the maternity ward within twelve hours after her operation. Her early activities help her to return to normal life quickly, and she is as a result able to return home in a matter of days. This emphasis on immediately resuming activities however is by no means restricted to women who have had cesareans. In fact such activity helps patients recover more quickly from gallbladder surgery, appendectomies, and even open-heart surgery. The long-standing tradition of slow boring lethargic recuperation has been replaced by the new tradition of a quick purposeful challenging recovery that gets patients out of hospital beds and back into their daily routines.

31m Use commas to set off contrasting details.

Phrases that provide contrasting details do not grammatically function as parts of sentences. They should therefore be separated from the rest of the sentence by commas.

Dad's first love was philosophy, not economics.

The BBC, unlike American television stations, is completely financed by the government.

31n Use commas to set off the words *yes* and *no*, mild interjections that begin sentences, and names used in direct address.

Interjections function apart from the grammatical structure of a sentence. The words *yes* and *no* also function separately. For especially strong emphasis, interjections and *yes* and *no* can be separated from sentences by a period or exclamation point, but for normal emphasis they are joined to a sentence with a comma.

Okay, buy the white or blue Nikes if you want.

Yes, I think I will.

Jan, will you loan me some money so I can buy two pairs?

31o Use commas to set off statements that signal direct quotations.

Writers use a wide range of phrases when they quote other people: *he said, she commented, they replied,* and so on. Commas should separate these expressions from the quotations they clarify.

Expressions of this sort can be used at the beginning, in the middle, or at the end of a quotation. Note that the comma is placed first, then the quotation mark (see Quotation Marks, **41a**).

Ahliah said, "If you notice prowlers, please call the police." *(The quoted material begins with a capital letter. Also notice that the comma and the period are placed* before *the quotation marks.)*

"Under most circumstances," Tron added, "they will arrive within five minutes." *(When the "someone said" expression interrupts the quotation, a pair of commas must be used.)*

"I will not hesitate to call them," I replied. *(When a quotation begins the sentence, it requires a comma at the end unless it is a question or an exclamation.)*

31p Use commas with numbers, dates, addresses, place names, and titles according to conventional style.

For easy reading, *numbers* are divided by thousands, millions, billions, and so on. Place commas every three digits, moving from the right.

1,271

1,300,000

Dates written in month-day-year order require a comma between the day and the year, and in sentences a comma must follow the year. If dates are written in day-month-year order, however, or if only the month and year are given, no comma is needed.

On December 7, 1941, Japanese planes attacked Pearl Harbor.

On 7 December 1941 Japanese planes attacked Pearl Harbor.

December 1941 was a month of many contradictions.

Addresses require commas after street address and between city and state when they are written on one line. Zip codes follow two spaces after the state, without a comma.

709 Sherwood Terrace, Champaign, Illinois 61820

Parts of *place names* are separated by commas, even when they include only city and state or city and country. Within a sentence, a comma also follows the last item in the place name —essentially making the state or country function like an appositive.

Marietta, Georgia

Ontario, Canada

Nestled in the bluffs along the Mississippi River, Elsa, Illinois, is always 10 to 15 degrees cooler than surrounding towns and cities.

Titles or degree designations can be seen as nonrestrictive appositives or parenthetical identifications, offering useful but nonessential information about a person. Like nonrestrictive appositives, titles and degree designations should be set off with commas.

Adele Zimmerman, professor emerita, spoke at the alumni luncheon on Saturday.

Fernando Rivera, M.D., and Blair Mullican, Ph.D., coordinated the county's alcohol-abuse program.

Arthur Emmanuel McHenry**,** Jr.**,** lost an arm in the Spanish-American War.

Note: When the designations *III, IV,* and so on follow a name, no commas are required.

Louis XIV of France was known as the "Sun King."

EXERCISE □ *Commas*

The following sentences do not include all necessary commas. Insert them where appropriate and explain why they are needed.

1. The families of the thirty-nine hostages were flown to Wiesbaden West Germany to greet their newly freed sons, husbands, and fathers.

2. Peggy Fleming won the gold medal in figure skating at the 1968 Olympics in Grenoble France.

3. William Buckley Jr. is known for his conservative criticism and his caustic wit.

4. Cleopatra's lover in Shakespeare's play is named Antony not Anthony.

5. Rembrandt's *Aristotle Contemplating the Bust of Homer* sold for an unprecedented $1230000 in 1963.

6. Okay, if you need to write to me during August, send your letters to Rural Route 6 Box 24 Whiteridge Minnesota.

7. Professor Marcellos said "Yes it is generally agreed that December 7 1941 marked the beginning of America's active involvement in World War II."

8. No James Entavio D.D.S. lives in Ashburn Virginia. His brother Jeremy lives in Claremont.

9. As the saying goes Jimmy Carter put Plains Georgia on the map.

EXERCISE □ *Commas*

The following paragraph needs commas. Insert them and be ready to explain why they must be used.

Alaska the forty-ninth state joined the Union on January 3 1959. The largest state geographically covering 586412 square miles Alaska is also the least populated with only 479000 people. In fact the entire state has fewer people than many American cities of moderate size let alone Chicago Los Angeles or New York. Yes the contrast in physical size and population presents a seeming contradiction but Alaska's history is full of contradictions. Juneau its capital city has approximately twenty thousand people making it roughly the same size as Texarkana Arkansas; Augusta Maine; and Winchester Nevada.

Alaska has fewer schools than many other states but has the highest teachers' salaries in the nation. Contradictions such as these have always been present. In 1867 when William H. Seward Secretary of State arranged the purchase of Alaska for $7200000, most people thought the purchase was a foolish one. "Seward's Folly" as the acquisition was called turned out not to be so foolish. Rich deposits of minerals oil and natural gas have made Alaska one of America's greatest assets. (For more information on Alaska write to the Alaskan Chamber of Commerce 310 Second Street Juneau Alaska 99801.)

32 Unnecessary Commas

32a Do not use a comma before a coordinating conjunction that joins only two words, phrases, or dependent clauses.

Compound sentences require a comma before a coordinating conjunction because the two clauses are independent (see **31b**). Do not, however, use commas with all compound constructions.

Toby ran toward the net ⌀and used his head to drive the soccer ball past the goalie. *(This sentence contains a compound verb: Toby ran and used.)*

I offered the popcorn first to Jonathan̸and then to Abie. *(This sentence contains two prepositional phrases joined by* and: to Jonathan *and* to Abie.)*

The rising sales of exercise machines demonstrate that people want to work out at home̸and that they are willing to pay dearly to do so. *(This sentence contains two relative clauses:* that people want to work out *and* that they are willing to pay dearly to do so.)*

32b Do not use a comma between a subject and verb.

With sentences in their simplest form, no punctuation should separate the subject and verb (see Subjects, **6a,** and Predicates, **6b**). If you add other information—appositives, nonrestrictive clauses, coordinate modifiers, and so on—you may need commas, but only as required by other comma rules.

The desperate fugitive̸swam the canal in no time. *(The comma interrupts the subject-verb pattern.)*

The desperate fugitive, an unfortunate victim of politics, swam the canal in no time. *(Here the pair of commas is required because a nonrestrictive appositive has been added.)*

32c Do not use a comma between a verb and its complement.

Unless commas are required because of intervening elements, no punctuation should break the verb-complement pattern in a sentence (see Complements, **6c**).

Jessica will stay up to see̸any movie that stars Bette Davis. *(The comma interrupts the verb-complement pattern.)*

Jessica will stay up to see any great, good, mediocre, or bad movie that stars Bette Davis. *(Here the commas are required because of the series of coordinate adjectives.)*

32d Do not use a comma before the first or last item in a series.

Items in a series often function as subjects, verbs, or complements. Unnecessary commas interrupt subject-verb or verb-complement patterns.

Linda worked as a substitute teacher͵/to earn extra money, to get more experience, and to make some important contacts. *(The infinitive phrases all modify the verb* worked. *The commas after* money *and* experience *separate items in a series. The first comma, though, creates an unwanted break in the normal verb-complement pattern of the sentence.)*

Cove molding, crown molding, and OG doorstop͵/are all used extensively in home construction. *(The comma after* doorstop *violates rule 32b. It places a comma between the subject and the verb.)*

32e Do not use commas to separate cumulative adjectives and adverbs.

Some adjectives and adverbs build upon each other to create meaning. Such cumulative modifiers should not be separated by commas, unlike coordinate adjectives and adverbs, which function separately and therefore require commas (see **31j**).

Lance added four͵/small͵/white roses to the flower arrangement. *(These adjectives create meaning through linked modification:* white *modifies* roses; small *modifies* white roses; four *modifies* small white roses.)*

Linda very͵/skillfully maneuvered the car to avoid hitting the boy on the bicycle. *(These adverbs also create meaning through linked modification:* skillfully *modifies* maneuvered; very *modifies* skillfully maneuvered.)*

32f Do not use commas between adjectives or adverbs and the words they modify.

Adjectives and adverbs are closely connected to the words they modify (see **5d** and **5e**). This relationship should never be interrupted by unnecessary commas.

We carried the mortally⌇wounded⌇soldier to the field hospital.

32g Do not use commas to set off restrictive elements in sentences.

Because restrictive elements—whether they are appositives, phrases, or clauses—are essential to the meaning of a sentence, they should not be set off by commas. Commas should set off only nonrestrictive elements (see **31h** and **31i**).

The musical play⌇*West Side Story*⌇is based on Shakespeare's *Romeo and Juliet*. (West Side Story *is necessary to the meaning of the sentence. Without it, the sentence would be unclear.*)

Writers⌇who misuse commas⌇make their prose difficult to decipher. *(The clause* who misuse commas *is essential because it identifies a group of writers who confuse their prose. The sentence does not mean that all writers make their prose difficult to decipher.)*

32h Do not use a comma before a concluding prepositional phrase or subordinate clause that restricts the meaning of a sentence.

Closing phrases and clauses that further clarify the meaning of a sentence—identifying when, where, how, why, or under what conditions the action took place—can be restrictive or nonrestrictive. When they add essential information, they should not be set off by commas. When these elements begin sentences, however, they are typically followed by a comma (see **31c** and **31d**).

> Audience members continued to arrive͵ until well into the first act. *(The comma incorrectly implies that the information in the phrase does not limit the sentence. In fact, the meaning of the sentence depends on the phrase.)*
>
> Whale watchers sometimes weep͵ after they see the huge mammals break water. *(The subordinate clause that ends the sentence is crucial to the meaning. Without it, the sentence states, "Whale watchers sometimes weep," which is less than the writer means.)*

32i Do not use a comma before a parenthesis.

Information in parentheses clarifies words that come immediately before it in a sentence (see **36a**), so commas must not separate the words and the parenthetical explanation. If a comma is necessary for some reason, it should follow the closing parenthesis.

> To protect his home from winter winds, Mr. Osborne planted
>
> conifers͵ (pines, spruces, and junipers)‸ but even they did not help. (Pines, spruces, and junipers *clarifies what* conifers *means, so the comma should follow the second parenthesis, keeping* conifers *and its explanation together.)*

32j Do not put a comma after *such as* or *like*.

Such as and *like* are prepositions that introduce examples in prepositional phrases; the examples serve as the objects. Separating a preposition from its object with a comma interrupts a normal grammatical pattern.

> Some "humanistic" studies—such as ̸economics, history, and sociology—require a more scientific approach than most people think. *(The commas are necessary after* economics *and* history *because three items are listed in a series. The comma after* such as, *however, inappropriately separates the preposition from its objects.)*

32k Do not put a comma before *than.*

Than is used as part of a comparative construction, and it is illogical to separate with a comma the two items to be compared (see Comparisons, **23**).

> The human tongue has more power to persuade ̸than the fangs of the most ferocious beast do.

32l Do not use a comma before an indirect or direct quotation introduced by *that.*

Because a quotation preceded by the word *that* functions as a direct object, no comma should be used. To use one violates the principle outlined in **32c**.

> Jenny said ̸that she believes in reincarnation. *(The entire clause* that she believes in reincarnation *is a direct object, not a direct quotation.)*
>
> *But:* Jenny said, "I believe in reincarnation."

Remember that this rule also applies when *that* is understood.

> Jenny said ̸she believes in reincarnation.
>
> *But:* Jenny said, "She believes in reincarnation."

**32m Do not place a comma after a
question mark or exclamation point in a
direct quotation.**

Question marks and exclamation points within quotations
stand by themselves. They supersede the comma normally required after a direct quotation that does not end a sentence (see
Quotation Marks, **41a**).

"How many people can we squeeze into that Volkswagen?" Joan
asked. *(The question mark, as end punctuation, is enough.)*

EXERCISE □ *Unnecessary Commas*

The following sentences contain far too many commas. Eliminate those that unnecessarily break the flow of the sentences or
violate the logical connections between ideas.

1. Gila monsters, (lizards that grow up to thirty inches long)
   thrive in northern Mexico, and in the southwestern United
   States.

2. "How can we control pornography without infringing on
   the rights of individuals?," Dr. Mitrionne asked in an effort
   to encourage a lively, but purposeful discussion.

3. In justifying the United States' invasion of Grenada, President Reagan said that, "a brutal group of leftist thugs, violently seized power."

4. By scientific estimates, the sun, is 400,000 times brighter,
   than the full moon.

5. Travelers, who visit the wildlife preserves in Kenya, are sure to be impressed by the diverse animal population.

6. Byzantine architecture is characterized by large, central, domes, elongated windows, and intricate mosaic work.

7. The national flag of Malaysia has a blue field in the upper left corner, with a gold half-moon and star. The rest of the flag is covered with seven, red stripes, and seven, white stripes.

8. Bob Pettit, Bill Russell, Wilt Chamberlain, Kareem Abdul-Jabbar, Moses Malone, and Larry Bird, have all been named the NBA's most valuable player at least twice.

9. Groups of animals are described in English with a host of unusual names, such as, a *brace* of ducks, a *gaggle* of geese, a *band* of gorillas, and a *mob* of kangaroos.

10. The actor, Alan Alda, was named Alphonso D'Abruzzo when he was born.

EXERCISE □ *Unnecessary Commas*

Remove the unnecessary commas from the following paragraph. Be ready to explain why some commas are not necessary.

P.T. Barnum reportedly said that, "a sucker is born every minute." If the ploys of advertisers on television really work, then Americans are proving the truth of Barnum's humorous, but scornful statement. Do women really believe they will be magically transformed into beautiful, poised, athletic, examples of womanhood, if they drink Crystal Light? Do men, who watch television, truly think they will become instantly appealing, if they use Old Spice after-shave? Do people of both sexes, imagine blissful romance is the result of using toothpastes like, Ultra Brite or Close-up? I would like to think they do not, but the evidence is against me. A 1983, issue of *Advertising Age*, (a trade publication of the ad industry) reported, the annual advertising expenditures of the top seven toiletries and cosmetics firms. Together, they spent $1,529,000 advertising their products. Sales indicate that ads, that appeal to people's wish fulfillment, more than to their sense of logic, succeed best. Welcome to the world of suckers!

33 Semicolons

A *semicolon* is a multipurpose form of punctuation, sometimes functioning like a comma (separating items in a series) but more often functioning like a period (showing that independent clauses are closely related). More importantly, semicolons normally indicate a full stop when they end an independent clause, so that they resemble end punctuation. Do not consider them fancy commas, or you may produce grammatical errors— typically, sentence fragments.

33a A semicolon without a coordinating conjunction can join closely related independent clauses.

When independent clauses are closely related but you do not wish to use a coordinating conjunction, link the clauses with a semicolon (see Independent Clauses, **6e**). With this usage, the semicolon is like a period. (Note, though, that the word following the semicolon is not capitalized.) Make certain that each clause is, in fact, independent, or you will create a sentence fragment (see **8c**).

> Only a few hundred people in the United States know how to work with neon tubing; most of them are fifty or older. *(Each clause in this sentence can function as an independent sentence. The semicolon emphasizes the close relationship between them. Using a semicolon, instead of a comma and a coordinating conjunction, adds emphasis to the second clause.)*

33b A semicolon can join independent clauses linked with a conjunctive adverb, unless you use a period.

Conjunctive adverbs logically connect ideas in sentences, but they do not grammatically join independent clauses as co-ordinating conjunctions do (see Conjunctions, **5f**). When you want to stress a logical relationship by using a conjunctive adverb without starting a new sentence, join the two independent clauses with a semicolon. Do not do so with a comma, or you will create a comma splice (see **9b**). Also remember to include a comma after the conjunctive adverb.

> Women who desperately want to have children can try fertility drugs; however, they should understand that these drugs increase the chances of multiple births. *(The semicolon in this sentence functions like a period but emphasizes the close relationship of the clauses. The conjunctive adverb establishes that the relationship is a contrast. Notice the comma after* however.)

33c Semicolons can separate items in a series when one or more of the items requires commas.

When separating items in a series, the semicolon works as a comma. It is more emphatic than the comma within the items, however, and shows where the items are separated. This usage, though, can create too many pauses for smooth reading. It is sometimes better to break the sentence into briefer, more manageable ones.

Correct but Awkward

In his travel kit, Martin keeps a small pair of scissors; black, white, and blue thread; and three needles. *(The semicolons separating the three items are necessary because the second item includes coordinate adjectives that require commas. This use of semicolons helps readers keep the items in the travel kit separate, but the sentence still seems hard to read.)*

Better

Martin keeps a small pair of scissors and three needles in his travel kit. He keeps black, white, and blue thread there as well.

33d A semicolon can separate independent clauses in compound sentences when one of the clauses requires commas.

In compound sentences, too, the semicolon can function as an emphatic comma to show where clauses are separated (see Compound Sentences, **7b**). Although this use will show readers where the primary break is, the heavy use of punctuation can be difficult to interpret. It is often best to divide the complicated sentence into several simpler ones.

Correct but Awkward

Much of the sculpture commissioned for public plazas is artistically innovative, visually exciting, and technically impressive; but it often does not appeal to the general public. *(In this sentence, the semicolon indicates where the two independent clauses are joined—an issue that might be confused by the commas in the first clause. The semicolon establishes the balance of the two-part sentence.)*

Better

Much of the sculpture commissioned for public plazas is artistically innovative, visually exciting, and technically impressive. However, it often does not appeal to the general public. *(Separating the compound sentence into two sentences makes the ideas easier to follow.)*

33e Do not use a semicolon in place of a comma with a subordinate clause.

Subordinate clauses must be linked to independent clauses (see **6e**). This relationship is never indicated by a semicolon. When a sentence begins with a subordinating conjunction, use a comma, not a semicolon, to indicate the connection in the sentence.

Because Mrs. Chan worked until 5:30 each evening;⟍ her children had to prepare dinner. *(The relationship between the clauses is broken by the semicolon. In addition, the clause that begins the sentence, now isolated, is a sentence fragment. Use a comma instead.)*

33f Do not introduce a list with a semicolon.

Lists should be introduced with either a colon or a dash. The semicolon imitates a period or a comma and will not help to introduce a list (see Colons, **34a,** and Dashes, **35d**).

Historians cite several reasons for the decline of Rome;⟍expanded citizenship, the deterioration of the army, barbarian invasions, economic decentralization, and inefficient agriculture.

EXERCISE □ *Semicolons*

Use semicolons to join the following groups of sentences effectively or to separate items in a series clearly.

1. U. S. aid to Israel amounts to more than two billion dollars annually. However, aid to *all* nations in Africa is only slightly more than one billion dollars.

2. The Suez Canal provides a major link in European and Eastern trade. It joins the Mediterranean and Red seas.

3. Bjorn Borg led Sweden to its first Davis Cup championship in 1975. He later earned individual recognition by winning at Wimbledon five times.

4. Water boils at 212 degrees Fahrenheit. That translates to 100 degrees Celsius.

5. Vermont entered the Union on March 4, 1791, Louisiana entered on April 30, 1812, and Nebraska entered on March 1, 1867.

EXERCISE □ *Semicolons*

The following paragraph contains some sentences that could logically be joined. Use semicolons to establish connections between ideas and be ready to explain why the sentences work sensibly together.

Studying for exams is a very important part of being a student. Unfortunately, many students do not study well. Some never consciously organize their time or make studying for tests an important part of their day-to-day work. Instead, they postpone studying until it is too late. I confess. I was one such student. Lately, however, I have acquired some better study habits. Now I begin to prepare early, at least one week in advance. I organize my notes every few days, and I review, very briefly, my notes each week. Then, three days before an exam, I finally start to concentrate on details. I regularly make long lists of important names and dates. I carefully define key terms. In other words, I concentrate on the very specific. This system has relieved much of my anxiety about tests. I do not dread them now. I just wish my friends and fellow students would consider my plan. I suspect they would complain a good deal less about tests and perform a good deal better as a result.

34 Colons

A *colon*, which can be translated as "note what follows," is used to introduce a list or clarification in a formal way. Selective use of colons can add clarity and emphasis to writing, but excessive use of colons can be more distracting than helpful.

34a Use a colon to introduce a list or a series of clauses.

Make sure that the part of the sentence that precedes the colon is an independent clause (see **6e**). The items in the series should never be direct objects, predicate nouns or adjectives, or objects of prepositions (see **6c** and **6d**).

> The names of six of the Seven Dwarfs reflect their personal habits: Bashful, Dopey, Grumpy, Happy, Sleepy, and Sneezy. *(Here the list is used to emphasize each name. The words before the colon form a complete sentence without depending on the items in the series.)*

34b Use a colon between two independent clauses when the second explains the first.

Sometimes a complete sentence is needed to explain the meaning of a preceding sentence. In that case, a colon clarifies the relationship. Under most circumstances, the first word following the colon appears with a lower-case letter to stress the sentence's purpose as clarification.

> Good song lyrics are like good poetry: both express ideas in rhythmic, elliptical form. *(Without the second sentence, the first would not be completely clear. The colon stresses this interrelationship.)*

34c Use a colon to emphasize an appositive that comes at the end of a sentence.

Appositives, restatements of nouns or pronouns, can be given special emphasis by introducing them with colons. This colon usage stresses that the appositive is a necessary explanation of a key word in the main sentence.

> Elementary education still depends on three basic skills: reading, writing, and arithmetic. *(The colon introduces the specific skills and gives them special emphasis.)*

34d Use a colon to introduce a direct quotation that is presented formally.

Direct quotations can be informally introduced with a comma or may be introduced formally with a full independent clause and a colon. In this special circumstance, the first word following the colon is capitalized. Other rules for direct quotations also apply (see Quotations, **57d**).

> The educational sentiment Mark Twain espoused would shock many humorless educators: "It doesn't matter what you teach a boy, so long as he doesn't like it." *(The colon, preceded by a complete sentence, serves to emphasize Twain's comment.)*

351

34e Use a colon between numerals for hours and minutes, after formal salutations, between titles and subtitles, and between city and publisher in works cited entries.

Certain special uses of colons are generally accepted. Follow these styles carefully.

Hours and minutes are divided by a colon. When the reference is to hours only, spell out the words.

> The second flight to Des Moines leaves at 2:15 A.M.
>
> *But:* We expect to be home by nine o'clock.

Salutations in formal letters are followed by a colon.

> Dear Ms. Gooch: Dear Dr. Sanborne:

Titles and subtitles of written works are divided by a colon. Follow other conventional rules of punctuation as well.

> *Virginia Woolf: A Biography*
>
> *The Book of Insults Ancient and Modern: An Amiable History of Insult, Invective, Imprecation, and Incivility (Literary, Political, and Historical) Hurled through the Ages and Compiled as a Public Service*

The names of the *city and publisher* are separated by a colon in works cited entries (see Entries for the Works Cited Page, **53**).

> Bloomington: Indiana UP
>
> New York: Doubleday

34f Do not use a colon between a verb and its complement or between a preposition and its object.

Colons introduce clarifications that function apart from the main sentence. They should not separate basic sentence elements (see Complements, **6c,** and Prepositional Phrases, **6d,**

352

pages 143–144). To test this usage, change the colon to a period and drop the words that follow. If the remaining sentence is complete, the colon is correctly placed. If the sentence is incomplete, omit the colon or rephrase the sentence.

Incorrect

Enrico named his cats after: Winston Churchill, T. S. Eliot, Eleanor Roosevelt, and Eudora Welty. *(Change the colon to a period, drop the list, and the sentence reads* Enrico named his cats after. *That is an incomplete construction.)*

Correct

Enrico named his cats after Winston Churchill, T. S. Eliot, Eleanor Roosevelt, and Eudora Welty. *(Here the names are all objects of the preposition* after).

Enrico named his cats after famous historical figures and writers: Winston Churchill, T. S. Eliot, Eleanor Roosevelt, and Eudora Welty. *(Here the prepositional phrase is complete. Then the list adds clarification.)*

Incorrect

The names of Enrico's cats are: Winston Churchill, T. S. Eliot, Eleanor Roosevelt, and Eudora Welty. *(Here the colon separates the verb from its direct objects—the names—leaving an incomplete thought before the colon.)*

Correct

The names of Enrico's cats are Winston Churchill, T. S. Eliot, Eleanor Roosevelt, and Eudora Welty.

35 Dashes

A *dash,* made by typing two hyphens with no spaces before or after, is used to set off parenthetical information, to show interruptions in thought or action, and to introduce clarifications.

Frequently, the dash serves purposes similar to those of commas, colons, parentheses, and semicolons.

35a Use dashes to set off appositives that contain commas.

A complicated appositive (a phrase that renames a noun or pronoun) may contain commas. In such a case, use dashes to show where the appositive begins and ends. The use of dashes in this circumstance will save the sentence from being cluttered with too many commas.

> Rita Moreno—winner of Tony, Grammy, Emmy, and Academy awards—can make even a pizza commercial entertaining. *(Because the appositive contains three commas, commas at the beginning and end would make the sentence confusing. The pair of dashes, as a result, marks the appositive more clearly.)*

35b Use a dash to set off a series that introduces a sentence.

Rarely, a sentence may begin with a series of items for special effect. When this strategy is used, either a colon or a dash is acceptable, although the dash is more common.

> The Tiger, the Mako, the Great White—these "man-eating" sharks deserve our respect as well as our fear.

35c Use dashes, selectively, to introduce parenthetical interpretations and evaluations.

Parenthetical comments present ideas that are only loosely related to the main idea of the sentence. When such comments offer interpretations or evaluations that deserve special emphasis, use dashes to show where the additional information begins and ends.

> American military advisers did not fully understand the Viet Cong's strength or tenacity—a costly error by any standard.

35d Use a dash to introduce a list.

A list can be introduced with a dash instead of a colon. The use of the dash is somewhat informal; the use of the colon is formal.

> Everything I needed to build the model was on the table—newspaper, glue, toothpicks, tweezers, and the model parts themselves. *(The informality of the subject makes the use of the dash acceptable. A more serious style for a more serious subject, however, would be better served by a colon.)*

35e Use dashes, selectively, to show shifts in thought or action.

Darryl spent hours shaving, showering, selecting his clothes, and dressing for the dance—and then stayed home.

35f Use the dash selectively.

Dashes serve two primary purposes in most writing: setting off appositives that contain commas and setting off introductory series. Beyond those uses, other forms of punctuation often work as well. Incorporate the dash in your writing when it serves a specific purpose; use it without overusing it.

The thunderstorm—coming from the southwest—looked threat-

ening,—with black and blue clouds and flashes of lightning.

Within ~~a matter of minutes~~ _minutes,_ $\mathcal{L}$~~five to be exact~~ $\mathcal{L}$ it was upon us.
Around our house, the trees—tall maples, stout pines, and deli-

cate dogwoods—bent in the heavy winds $\mathcal{L}$ their branches sway-
ing violently. The black sky, the growing roar, the shaking

house—all signaled the approach of a tornado $\mathcal{L}$ $\underset{w}{\text{we}}$ headed for
the basement. _(Only two uses of the dash are required in this para-
graph, one with the appositive and one with the introductory list. The
other uses were technically correct, but fewer dashes will draw less attention to the mechanics of the paragraph.)_

EXERCISE □ _Colons and Dashes_

Revise these sentences, using colons or dashes to make them
clearer or more emphatic.

Example
Several word-processing programs are leading the market $\underset{\wedge}{;}$ $\overset{t}{\text{T}}$hese
programs are WordStar 3.1, PC = Write 3.1, Pfs.Write 3.1, and
Volkswriter Deluxe 3.1.

1. Petroleum or petroleum by-products form the basis of the

   industrial products of several major companies. These

   companies include Ashland Oil, Exxon Corporation, and

   Uniroyal, Incorporated.

2. In Beirut, on the morning of 23 October 1984, a bomb ex-

   ploded at twenty-two minutes after six, killing 241 Ameri-

   can soldiers.

3. Correcting punctuation and mechanics in an essay is like

tuning an engine. Both require skill and attention to detail, and both result in better performance.

4. Boris Spassky was heralded by some as the premier chess player of the century. He won world titles in 1969, 1970, 1971, and 1972.

5. Tuskegee Institute was founded in 1881. This college for blacks is located in Tuskegee, Alabama.

EXERCISE □ *Punctuation Review*

The following paragraph is written in predominantly simple sentences. Revise it using semicolons, colons, and dashes to emphasize relationships between ideas and to embed information. Add commas where necessary.

Courtroom scenes have provided intensity and interest for years on American television. In the early 1950's several shows concentrated on legal scenes in the courtroom. *They Stand Accused* was one such program. *The Verdict Is Yours* was another. Considered in retrospect, these programs seem artificial but they were informative. In production between 1957 and 1966 and continuing today in reruns *Perry Mason* re-created the format of Erle Stanley Gardner's best-selling novels. Numerous plot complications a wide range of intriguing witnesses a reversal by a witness on the stand and a patterned climax in the courtroom were common. These common features established the standard pattern for virtually all of today's dramas in the courtroom. Later programs continued to transport everyday television viewers into courtrooms. Some of these programs were *The Defenders Slattery's People* and *The Trials of O'Brien.* Gradually the scenes began to get grittier and truer to life. This was a way of making such scenes more credible more sensational. Today trial sequences are part of many police and detective shows. Even though many viewers have never been in a courtroom themselves they have gained a sense of courtroom procedures from programs like these.

36 Parentheses

Parentheses are used to set off secondary information in sentences or, with numbers, to indicate numerical sequence of items. Parentheses are used in pairs, with one curved line indicating where secondary information begins and another curved line showing where the information ends. Because information in parentheses breaks the flow of a sentence, this form of punctuation should be used selectively.

36a Use parentheses to set off information that is only casually related to the flow of ideas in the rest of the sentence.

Do not include long explanations parenthetically. If the information is important, it deserves direct treatment.

Bryant Gumbel (an extremely hard worker, some say) coanchors *The Today Show* on NBC. *(The information about Gumbel's work habits is a supplemental afterthought and is appropriately set off by parentheses.)*

36b Use parentheses around numbers or letters that indicate a sequence of events or processes.

Although numbers can help clarify a complicated sequence, numbered lists can be as distracting as they are helpful. Use them only for special purposes. Notice that the numbers should be enclosed by pairs of parentheses. One parenthesis is not sufficient.

Freezing green beans involves six steps: (1) snap the ends off the beans; (2) wash the beans thoroughly in water; (3) blanch the beans for two or three minutes in boiling water; (4) cool them in ice water; (5) drain them for several minutes and then pack them into freezer containers; (6) seal the containers, label them, and put them in the freezer.

36c Do not overuse parentheses.

Parentheses signal a sharp break in a sentence. They call attention to themselves and, if overused, make writing seem uneven, incoherent, or immature—as if a writer could not decide what to include and what to leave out. To avoid such problems, use parentheses only when no other strategy or punctuation will serve your purposes.

Choppy

The compass (scratched and cracked) should have been replaced (years ago), but Joaquin (reluctant to spend money) preferred to keep it as it was. *(The rhythm of the sentence is broken by the intervening details. In addition, some of this information is potentially important.)*

Better

The scratched and cracked compass should have been replaced years ago, but Joaquin, reluctant to spend money, preferred to keep it as it was.

37 Brackets

Brackets indicate when alterations have been made in direct quotations. If your typewriter or word processor does not have brackets, leave spaces as you type and insert them by hand.

37a Use brackets in direct quotations to add clarifications or to substitute for a general noun or pronoun.

Direct quotations that appear out of context may not always be clear. Brackets are used to clarify information in such quotations, but you should add only information that makes the original clearer. Never add contradictory information or negative comments (see Quotations, **57d**).

Davies commented, ''The army nurses' judgment in triage [where the medical staff decides which patients to treat first] is paramount, for they must determine a soldier's medical stability in a matter of seconds." *(The bracketed material explains a key term that might cause confusion. The brackets clearly indicate that the writer, not Davies, defined* triage.*)*

"If architectural preservationists are unsuccessful in their efforts, most [theaters built in the early 1900's] will probably be demolished by the end of the century," noted Walter Aspen. *(The original reads "of these fascinating buildings." Out of the context of the original, this phrase is unclear. The specific information in brackets is a good substitution.)*

37b Do not overuse brackets.

We use quotations because other writers have expressed ideas better than we can. Do not quote anything that requires too much clarification or substitution. If you have to add too much to a quotation, paraphrasing is preferable (see **57d** and **57e**).

Overuse

Professor Cooke offered this closing comment: "That [Japanese Americans] could maintain their dignity in [prisonlike] conditions [during World War II] is a testament to their spirit." *(Three added clarifications suggest that this should not have been quoted in the first place.)*

38 Ellipsis Points

Ellipsis points are three spaced periods that indicate omission, usually in quoted material. A highly specialized form of punctuation, ellipsis points should be used sparingly.

38a Use ellipsis points to show where words
have been omitted in a direct quotation.

Generally, use ellipsis points to leave out extraneous information, parenthetical details, or unnecessary clarifications.
Never omit words in order to change the meaning of your
source.

Original

"This is a great movie if you enjoy meaningless violence, gratu-
itous sex, inane dialog, and poor acting. It is offensive by any
standards."

Dishonest

"This is a great movie ... by any standards." *(Obviously, this is a
complete misquotation.)*

Original

"The Ninth Street Station is a superb example of ornate wood-
working and stonework. Typical of Steamboat-Gothic architecture, it was designed in 1867 by Fielding Smith. It is a landmark
we should endeavor to preserve."

Acceptable

"The Ninth Street Station is a superb example of ornate wood-
working and stonework. ... It is a landmark we should endeavor
to preserve. *(This omits secondary details. Note that when ellipsis
points follow a complete sentence, the sentence's own end punctuation precedes them.)*

38b Use ellipsis points to indicate
hesitation, a trailing off of thought, or an
incomplete statement.

This usage is more standard in fiction than in other kinds of
writing, but it can be employed for special effect. If the ellipsis

points are used to replace the end of a sentence, they are still considered part of the sentence and a period is needed after them to end the sentence—resulting in *four* spaced periods.

Woody Allen's *Stardust Memories* was . . . boring.

As the elevator doors closed, Chie shouted, "Call me after. . . . " Unfortunately, the doors shut before I heard the time.

EXERCISE □ *Parentheses, Brackets, and Ellipsis Points*

Revise the following sentences, correcting the faulty use of parentheses, brackets, and ellipsis points.

1. Roger Marston summarized the situation this way: "As long as seasonal crops are harvested by migrant workers...prices for produce will stay low, but the savings are earned at the expense of exploited people."

2. New York City, (population: 7,071,639) has the highest population density of any city in North America: 23,494 people per square mile.

3. Simply follow these directions: 1) remove the converter from the box; 2) attach the blue adapter wires to your television set; 3) plug the converter into an electrical outlet; 4) select a channel and test the equipment by turning it on.

4. "The benefits (of out-patient care) are reduced paperwork, limited use of hospital facilities, and reduced time for treat-

ment—all of which lower medical costs,'' explained Professor Fulbright in her opening remarks.

5. County Supervisor Estivez added, ''Without substantial improvements in our road systems, we will not attract investors . . . That will result in economic stagnation.''

EXERCISE □ *Punctuation Review*

Correctly punctuate the following paragraph.

The Postal Reorganization Act signed into law by President Nixon on August 12 1970 created a government-owned postal service operated under the executive branch of the government The new US Postal Service is run by an eleven-member board with members appointed by the president of the Senate for nine-year terms The Postmaster General who is no longer part of the president's cabinet is selected by the members of the board Since 1971 when the system began operating four men have served as Postmaster General Winton M Blount E T Klassen Benjamin F Bailer and William F Bolger But has the postal system changed substantially since the PRA went into effect on July 1 1971 No not to any great extent First class second class third class and fourth class these still represent the most commonly used mailing rates However some services have been added For instance Express Mail which tries to rival Federal Express Purolator and other one-day delivery services guarantees that packages will arrive at their destinations by 300 the day after mailing the prices are steep as one might expect In addition the Postal Service has instituted nine-digit zip codes in some areas For all practical purposes however the business at 29990 post offices throughout the US continues in much the same way it did before the PRA

MECHANICS

Each aspect of mechanics—capitalization, italics, quotation marks, apostrophes, hyphens, abbreviations, and number style—signals meaning in sentences. Mechanical errors create distractions and confuse readers, so observing the rules of mechanics will help you not only to be grammatical but also to be clear.

39 Capitalization

Capitalization serves a variety of purposes: it indicates the beginning of a sentence; it identifies important words in titles; and it signals when nouns or adjectives refer to specific people, places, or things. Although appropriate capitalization is important, unnecessary capitalization is confusing and annoying. Before capitalizing a word, make sure that a rule justifies a capital (upper-case) letter.

39a Capitalize the first word in every sentence.

This rule of mechanics may be the earliest learned. Remember, however, that when a complete sentence follows a colon, capitalizing the first word is optional.

> The Declaration of Independence presents an idea we should remember: All people are created equal. (*A lower-case* a *after the colon would also be correct.*)

39b Capitalize the first word and other important words in titles.

A, an, and *the;* coordinating conjunctions; and prepositions of four or fewer letters are not normally capitalized unless they begin or end a title. When the word *to* is part of an infinitive, it is capitalized.

> William Faulkner's *The Sound and the Fury*
> Anne Frank's *The Diary of a Young Girl*

When a colon is used to separate a two-part title, the first word following the colon is capitalized. When words in titles are hyphenated, capitalize nouns and adjectives, even in the second position.

> Dan Greenburg's *How To Make Yourself Miserable: Another Vital Training Manual*
>
> R. C. Bald's *Seventeenth-Century English Poetry*

39c Capitalize the pronoun *I*, whether it is used by itself or as part of a contraction.

I want to sail to the Bahamas, but I've got to earn the money first.

39d Capitalize the names of people, races, nationalities, languages, or places.

This rule applies whether the names are used as nouns or adjectives.

Nouns	Adjectives
Samuel Johnson	Shakespearean sonnet
Caucasian	Jewish holiday
New Yorker	of German descent
Jupiter	Portuguese trade
Kenya	Lilliputian steak

39e Capitalize the names of historical periods, movements, events, and documents.

the Industrial Revolution

the Suffrage Movement

the Battle of Bull Run

the Bill of Rights

39f Capitalize the names of days, months, and holidays.

Monday   Memorial Day

August   Hanukkah

Seasons used by themselves are not capitalized. If another rule of capitalization applies—a rule relating to titles, for instance—then seasons may be capitalized.

I despise winter weather.

But: Amos read Steinbeck's *The Winter of Our Discontent.*

39g Capitalize the names of organizations or government departments.

Sigma Tau Delta

Greenpeace

the United States Senate

the Department of Agriculture

39h Capitalize the names of educational institutions, departments, specific courses, and degrees.

Brandeis University

Edward Sheridan High School

Department of Anthropology

Home Economics 421

Master of Arts

General references to courses do not require capitalization unless they are language courses (English, Spanish) or courses using proper nouns or adjectives (American history). When course numbers appear, however, capitals must be used.

Armand got *A*'s in every speech course he took, but he was proudest of his *A* in Speech 363.

39i Capitalize the names of religions and religious terms.

Islam	Christians
God	Buddhist traditions
Allah	the Resurrection

39j Capitalize titles used with proper names.

Mr. Morris Winston

Dr. Martin Luther King, Jr.

Professor Angela Cambridge

Secretary-elect Marcellas

President Roosevelt

When a title is used in a general way, it should not be capitalized.

My history professor is always late for class.

Jefferson was the third president of the United States.

39k Capitalize nouns indicating family
relationships only when they are used
as proper names or as titles used with
proper names.

Do not capitalize words that describe family relationships
when they are used after possessives.

My grandmother and grandfather spend four months in Arizona
each year.

Jim called his parents **Mother** and **Father** rather than **Mom** and
Dad.

Sarah selected the present for **Aunt Jetta.**

39l Capitalize abbreviations of organization
and business names, time designations, and
documents; also capitalize the letters that
name radio and television stations.

100 B.C.	ERA
seven P.M.	WZZQ radio
NAACP	KTVI

39m Carefully distinguish between specific
names (which require capitalization)
and general names (which do not
require capitalization).

The teacher's union voted to strike.

But: The Benton Teachers' Association voted to strike.

The shoe repair shop is located three blocks south of the bank.

But: Axton's Shoe Repair Shop is located three blocks south of the
Merchants' National Bank.

39n Capitalize the first word of a direct quotation if the quotation is a complete sentence or an interjection that can stand alone.

Melissa said, "We should invest in grain futures." *(Here the quotation is an independent sentence.)*

But: Melissa said that we "should invest in grain futures." *(Here the quotation is not a complete sentence, so no capitalization is needed.)*

If a long quotation is interrupted by a "someone said" construction, capitalize only words that begin sentences.

"Prospects for peace in the Middle East exist," the senator reiterated, "only if leaders negotiate in good faith." *(Because the quoted sentence is divided, no capital is needed to begin the second part of the quotation.)*

Her only response was "Oh my!" *(Here the quotation is an interjection that functions apart from a sentence.)*

EXERCISE □ *Capitalization*

Correct capitalization in the following sentences. Identify the rule that guides each correction.

1. the epa, under the direction of anne burford, was always the subject of controversy.

2. although marty had been raised a presbyterian, he chose to attend St. John's united methodist church while at College.

3. the Invitation's printed cover read dr. and mrs. Arnold j. Bennett.

4. ms. green, loni's Academic Advisor, suggested that she sign up for either russian or italian.

5. December is my favorite Winter month, not only because of christmas but also because of the Winter Carnival dance.

6. The new foreign students first attended an Orientation Meeting in Patterson Hall and then went to a Reception at the foreign students' Union.

7. The twenty-four-year-old Fitsimmons had already written two unpublished novels: *a whimper in the urban wilderness* and *yuppie madness.*

8. The Editor was not a Sociologist, a Political Scientist, or a Historian, but he could recognize inhumane Government.

9. ever since we were small, we have always called my Grandmother *Mom.*

10. Yvonne felt deeply satisfied by her work for catholic charities.

40 Italics

Italics normally identify the titles of complete or independent works, but they can also be used to draw special attention to words or groups of words. In a printed text, italics are indicated with slanted type *(like this)*, but in a typed or handwritten text, italics are indicated with underlining (<u>like this</u>). The meaning is the same.

40a Italicize the titles of complete or independent works, such as books, periodicals, newspapers, pamphlets, plays, films, television programs, radio shows, long poems, long musical compositions, albums, paintings, and statues.

Books

Ernest Hemingway's *The Sun Also Rises*

Zora Neale Hurston's *Their Eyes Were Watching God*

Periodicals

Discover

Education Digest

Newspapers

the *Kansas City Star*

the *New York Times*

Pamphlets

NCTE's *How To Help Your Child Become a Better Writer*

ISU's *Traffic Regulations*

Plays

Neil Simon's *Brighton Beach Memoirs*

Bernard Shaw's *Mrs. Warren's Profession*

Films

Terms of Endearment

The Wizard of Oz

Television Programs

Cheers

Hill Street Blues

Note: Although italic type is required for the name of an entire television program, episodes (daily, weekly, or monthly segments) are indicated with quotation marks (see **41b**).

"Antarctica: Earth's Last Frontier" from *NOVA*

Long Poems

John Milton's *Paradise Lost*

Henry Wadsworth Longfellow's *Evangeline*

Long Musical Compositions

Igor Stravinsky's *Firebird Suite*

Giacomo Puccini's *Madam Butterfly*

Albums

Tina Turner's *Private Dancer*

the Beatles' *Abbey Road*

Paintings

Pablo Picasso's *Guernica*

James Whistler's *Study in Black and White*

Statues

Claes Oldenburg's *Soft Hamburger*

Michelangelo's *David*

Note: The Bible, the Koran, the Talmud, divisions of these religious works, and legal documents are not italicized—although they are capitalized.

40b Italicize the names of ships, trains, airplanes, and spacecraft.

Although types (or models) of ships, trains, airplanes, and spacecraft are capitalized, italicize only those references to individual craft, ones with individual names.

Ships

Australia II

Andrea Doria

Trains

Orient Express

Stourbridge Lion

Airplanes

The Spirit of St. Louis

The Spruce Goose

Spacecraft

Apollo I

Voyager II

40c Italicize foreign words and phrases used as part of your own writing.

Although the use of foreign terms is acceptable in writing, such a vocabulary often sounds pretentious and stuffy. Keep such use to a minimum. Also note that some foreign terms—*blitz, cinéma vérité, cliché, haute couture,* and *kindergarten,* for instance—are standard in American usage and no longer require italics. Consult a dictionary for specific guidance.

40d Italicize words used as words, letters used as letters, numbers used as numbers, and symbols used as symbols.

Ms. Jojuma says I use *okay* too often when I speak.

Because the child was left-handed, her *q*'s looked like *g*'s and *p*'s.

Carolyn always writes her 7's with horizontal lines through them.

When I want to emphasize a paragraph in a letter, I put a ¶ in the margin.

40e Italicize words selectively for emphasis.

Do not overitalicize to create emphasis, because too many italicized words detract from the natural emphasis that good word choices should create.

Overuse

We had a *great* time when we visited Six Flags, the one in *St. Louis.* We rode the Screaming Eagle *four* times and spent $26 on food. Add that cost to the admission price, and it was an *expensive* day; nevertheless, it was *really* enjoyable. *(With so much emphasized in these few sentences, the writer seems too emphatic, too excitable. With all these italics, nothing stands out.)*

Effective

Our graduating class had *five* valedictorians. *(A simpler use, as in this sentence, is more appropriate.)*

41 Quotation Marks

Outside their use to set off quotations (see **57d**), *quotation marks* serve a limited purpose as a form of mechanics: they identify the titles of short works or sections of long works. They can also be used to highlight words used in a special way.

41a Place punctuation with quotation marks consistently, depending on the kind of punctuation.

Periods and *commas* always appear before closing quotation marks.

> Brian reread the article "Success Is Counted Sweetest."
>
> "The Circus Animals' Desertion," a poem by William Butler Yeats, was Don's favorite.

Semicolons and *colons* always follow closing quotation marks.

> For the *Beverly Hills Cop* soundtrack, Glenn Frey wrote "The Heat Is On"; the song was subsequently used in numerous television programs and commercials.
>
> One word describes Lewis Carroll's "Jabberwocky": nonsense.

Question marks and *exclamation points* must be placed to maintain the logic of the sentence. If you are quoting a question, for instance, the question mark is followed by the closing quotation marks. If your sentence is a question that happens to contain a quotation, then the question mark is placed *after* the closing quotation marks. The same principles apply to the use of exclamation points with quotation marks.

> Nelson Riddle arranged the music for Linda Ronstadt's version of "What's New?" (*Here the question is part of the material in quotation marks.*)
>
> Have you read "A Diamond as Big as the Ritz"? (*Here the question follows the quotation marks because it applies to the entire sentence.*)

41b Use quotation marks with the titles of
brief works or parts of complete works.

Articles, short stories, poems, essays, and songs are brief
works whose titles should appear in quotation marks. Chapter
or unit titles, and episodes of television programs require quotation marks because they are parts of complete works. In addition, titles of unpublished papers or dissertations are placed
in quotation marks.

Articles

"Running on Empty?" in *National Wildlife*
"Daughters of Divorce" in *Glamour*

Short Stories

Flannery O'Connor's "Good Country People"
J. D. Salinger's "A Perfect Day for Bananafish"

Poems

Robert Browning's "My Last Duchess"
Robert Frost's "The Death of the Hired Man"

Essays

Michael Korda's "What It Takes To Be a Leader"
James Thurber's "University Days"

Songs

Bette Midler's "The Rose"
Irving Berlin's "What'll I Do?"

Chapters or Unit Titles

"Theatre of the Orient" in Oscar Brockett's *History of the Theatre*
"Nightmare" in *The Autobiography of Malcolm X*

Episodes of Television Programs

"The Death of Chuckles the Clown" from *The Mary Tyler Moore Show*

"Captain Tuttle" from *M*A*S*H*

Unpublished Papers and Dissertations

"Prohibition in the New England States"

"The Poetic Heritage of Emily Dickinson"

41c Use quotation marks judiciously to highlight words used in special senses.

Words, most of the time, should be used according to their normal meanings. Do not overuse quotation marks to highlight special meanings or you will quickly annoy readers.

Who needs enemies with "friends" like these? *(Clearly* friends *is being used here in a special sense.)*

EXERCISE □ *Quotation Marks and Italics*

The following sentences contain no quotation marks or italics. Insert quotation marks where needed, and remember to place them accurately in relation to other punctuation. Underline any words that should be italicized.

1. Huxley's essay, The Scientific Method, can be found in Amos Emerson's A Beginner's Book of Scientific Principles.

2. Discover magazine explained in some detail the reasons for the Statue of Liberty's extensive and expensive renovations.

3. Billy Joel's first big hit was Piano Man, from the album with the same name.

4. Well-detailed prints of Van Gogh's Sunflowers and Starry Night illustrated the article When Madness Creates Meaning.

5. Sandra O'Connor's appointment to the Supreme Court was described in a Time article titled Justice at Last!

6. The first episode of For Love and Honor, The Bay of Pigs, had the highest Nielsen rating of the week.

7. The slang word macho, which has negative connotations in America, is free of connotations in Spain, where it simply means male.

8. Over the Rainbow, the most famous song from The Wizard of Oz, won the 1939 Oscar for best song.

9. I found the information in an unpublished MSU dissertation titled The Last Revolution: Religious Cults in the Sixties and Seventies.

10. The Jazz Singer, with Al Jolson, was the first commercial film that used sound.

11. For Thursday, Chuck has to read Site Preparation, a seventy-five-page chapter in his text for Engineering 267.

12. Scattered next to Jon's bed were recent copies of Time, Newsweek, and U.S. News and World Report, a clear sign he was preparing for a debate.

13. Many unsuspecting readers assume that Mary Shelley's novel Frankenstein will be like the film.

14. Ambiance, a French word that roughly translates as atmosphere, is frequently used in advertisements for fine restaurants.

15. Norman Lear produced All in the Family, Maude, Good Times, and The Jeffersons, a series of trend-setting programs.

42 Apostrophes

Apostrophes are used (usually with an *s*) to show possession, to indicate that letters have been omitted, and to form some plurals. Errors in the use of apostrophes, although common, are easily corrected.

> **42a** Use an apostrophe and an *s* to form the possessive of a singular noun or indefinite pronoun that does not end with an *s*.

A noun (**5a**) is a word that names a person, place, thing, or idea. An indefinite pronoun (**5b**, pages 106–107) is a general pronoun that has no particular antecedent (examples are *all*, *everybody*, *nobody*, and *none*).

> Chuck's favorite sport
>
> Mrs. Eldred's final examination
>
> everybody's last choice
>
> the children's party
>
> a week's wages

42b Use only an apostrophe, without an *s*, when a noun already ends with an *s*.

Many nouns have *s* as their last letter: *boss, Chris, albatross.* Nouns may also end in *s* because they are plural: *clocks, scientists, cats.* Either way, use an apostrophe at the end, without an additional *s*, to show possession.

> Silas' Camaro Z28
>
> the boys' new clothes

To double-check this usage, mentally eliminate the apostrophe and the *s*, or just the apostrophe. The word form that remains should be the one needed for the sentence.

> teacher's room (teacher['s] *is singular; only her room*)
>
> teachers' room (teachers['] *is plural; a room for several teachers*)

42c Use an apostrophe with only the last noun in a compound word or to show joint possession.

> brother-in-law's
>
> Lydia and Rob's new apartment
>
> Madelyn and Erin's Hitachi stereo

Note: It is also acceptable to use an apostrophe with each of the compound nouns. Whichever pattern you choose for treating possessives of compound nouns, use it consistently in your writing.

Lydia's and Rob's new apartment

Madelyn's and Erin's Hitachi stereo

To show separate possession of the same thing, make each noun in a series possessive.

Angel's, Bert's, and Lionel's fingerprints *(Each person has separate fingerprints, so separate possessive forms must be used.)*

42d Use an apostrophe to show that letters have been omitted in contractions or to show that numbers have been left out of dates.

shouldn't	should not
I'll	I will or I shall
it's	it is
the '83 champions	the 1983 champions

42e Use an apostrophe and an *s* to form the plurals of numbers, letters, or words used as words.

Remember as well to italicize the numbers, letters, or words, but not the '*s*.

Clearly distinguish between *1*'s and *7*'s.

Q's are always followed by *u*'s, except in *qintar* and *qoph*.

Too many *very*'s can ruin good sentences.

42f Do not use apostrophes with possessive pronouns such as *hers, yours, its,* and *theirs.*

Incorrect

a dog with it's bone *(The apostrophe makes this a contraction. A dog with it is bone is nonsense.)*

Correct

a dog with its bone

Incorrect

a comment of their's

Correct

a comment of theirs

EXERCISE □ *Apostrophes*

In the following sentences, insert apostrophes where appropriate. Delete any apostrophes that are incorrect.

1. Lois and Thomas son began to stutter just after he started nursery school.

2. The secretaries typewriters were repaired by Commercial Business System's, the company that held the offices' service agreement.

3. Having gotten seven 9.5s in preliminary rounds of competition, Leslie was not surprised to win the state gymnastics' meet.

4. During the winter of 1984, peoples utility bills climbed dramatically as families' tried to keep their homes' warm.

5. Jan and Stacys' trip to Europe had to be rescheduled because of Stacys mothers surgery.

6. The divers form breaks in the final round cost him his' Olympic medal.

7. After the accident, Kirbys bridgework needed only minor repairs.

8. Mrs. Beruttis final comment before we started our tests was always "Make sure I can distinguish between your *T*s and *F*s."

9. Before one'oclock, I've got to eat lunch, read a chapter, and revise a paragraph.

10. The couples reaction to losing the lawsuit was violent. The defendants lawyer insisted that they be escorted from the courtroom.

43 Hyphens

Hyphens are used to divide words at the ends of lines, to form compound words, and to create written forms of some numbers.

43a Hyphenate a word that must continue on the next line.

Since hyphens must go between syllables, check a dictionary when you do not know where to divide a word. Do not break one-syllable words and do not isolate one or two letters on any line. Do not divide proper nouns. Instead, move the whole word to the next line.

The old farmer could bare~~ly~~ *ly* ∧
~~ly~~walk by the time he
finished making hay.

Every year some natural disaster seems to strike ~~Ca-~~ *Ca*
∧lifornia.

Although Rebecca and Jason talk~~ed~~ *ed* ∧
~~ed~~ on the phone often, they didn't
talk for long.

43b Hyphenate some compound nouns.

A compound noun is a pair or group of words that together function as a single noun. Many compounds are hyphenated, but some are not. When unsure about a compound noun, consult a dictionary. If the compound does not appear there, it should be spelled "open," without a hyphen.

mother-in-law	*But:* beer mug
master-at-arms	living room
razzle-dazzle	Swiss cheese

Some compound nouns are spelled as one word: *snowflake, bookkeeper, stationmaster*. The best strategy remains checking a dictionary when you are unsure.

43c Hyphenate words that precede a noun and combine to modify it.

When modifiers that precede a noun cannot be sensibly separated but must work as a unit, use hyphens to emphasize their unity. Adverbs (see **5e**) generally will not be part of these clustered modifiers, and adverbs ending in -*ly* are never followed by a hyphen.

out-of-the-way resort

down-at-the-heels inventor

When the clustered modifiers follow a noun, however, they are not normally hyphenated.

The resort was out of the way.

The unemployed inventor seemed down at the heels.

43d Hyphenate compound numbers from twenty-one to ninety-nine and fractions.

eighty-two recipes

three-fourths of the taxpayers

But: two hundred tulips

their third demand

43e Hyphenate words using the prefixes *all-*, *ex-*, and *self-*; also hyphenate words using the suffix -*elect*.

all-consuming ambition

ex-department chairperson

self-satisfied athlete

president-elect of the school board

Note: If prefixes like *non-*, *un-*, *pre-*, or *post-* appear with proper nouns, hyphens are required. Remember to capitalize the proper nouns.

    un-American   post-World War II

    pre-Columbian   non-Cubist

43f Hyphenate words that could be confusing.

With a few words in English, a prefix without a hyphen can create a spelled form that is identical to another word. To make sure that readers can sensibly interpret sentences on a first reading, use a hyphen to avoid confusion.

    release (let go)

    re-lease (to lease again)

    prejudicial (showing prejudice)

    pre-judicial (before that which is judicial)

EXERCISE □ *Hyphens*

The following sentences contain no hyphens, although each sentence needs at least one. Insert hyphens where they are needed. Also make sure that all compound nouns are spelled correctly—hyphenated, spelled as two words, or spelled as one word. Use a dictionary.

1. Greg's self discipline amazed everyone—his parents, his teachers, his boss, his teenage friends, and his girlfriend.

2. You can make a chaircushion with three fourths of a yard of that polyester knit fabric.

3. The Abberly mansion on South Sherwood has twenty six rooms and four bath rooms.

4. Looking at the first day handouts, we clearly understood that our instructor was protest. From the class' groans, it was clear that we were antitest.

5. My father always called himself a dyed in the wool conservative.

6. All chemical engineering students admitted to the program had scored in the ninety third percentile, or better, on the test.

7. Nora, Vicki, and Monica made the all state volley ball team.

8. The six pointed buck moved cautiously into the right of way and then lowered his head toward the saltlick.

9. Even after the court awarded Evan custody of the children, his ex wife asked permission to say good bye.

10. If there is a rain storm on the day of the Jones family reunion, everyone in Witcherville will be eating fried chicken for a week.

44 Numbers

Whether to write out numbers or use digits depends on the form numbers take in a paragraph or paper and on their specific use. Follow these guidelines when using numbers.

44a Write out numbers that can be written in one or two words.

This principle clearly applies to numbers *one* through *one hundred,* but it also applies to larger round numbers like *four thousand* or *nine million.*

> Eugene O'Neill wrote over fifty plays, four of which won Pulitzer Prizes.

44b Use digits for numbers that would require three or more words if written out.

The number 101 is the obvious starting point at which most numbers are presented in this fashion.

> Celina indexed 257 recipe cards on her personal computer.

44c Write out a number that begins a sentence.

In this primary position, a number must be spelled out—no matter how many words are needed. If possible, revise the sentence to shift the numbers' position.

Incorrect

715 seniors attended graduation.

Correct

Seven hundred and fifteen seniors attended graduation.

Better

There were 715 seniors at graduation.

44d Use digits for addresses, dates, divisions
of books and plays, exact amounts of money,
identification numbers, percentages, scores,
and times.

These accepted conventions save time and space and specifically emphasize the numbers.

Addresses

316 Ridge Place, 1111 West 16th Street

Dates

24 December 1948 (or December 24, 1948), 150 B.C., A.D. 1066

Divisions of Books and Plays

chapter 3, volume 9, act 2, scene 4

Exact Dollar Amounts

$3.12, $7,279,000, $546 million

Identification Numbers

337–44–7709, UTC 88 22495

Percentages

82 percent, 26 percent

Scores

101 to 94

Times

3:15 A.M., 7:45 P.M.

45 Abbreviations

Abbreviations are shortened forms of words. Because abbreviations must be easy to recognize, do not use them unless they are conventionally accepted. When in doubt, consult a dictionary or spell out the words.

45a Abbreviate titles used before or after people's names.

Most titles are so standard that abbreviations are perfectly clear. They also save space.

John Walton, Jr.	Rebecca Santos, Ph.D.
Ms. Denise Beirbaum	Harold Blankenbaker, M.D.
Dr. Asha Wan Mustapha	the Rev. Joshua Felten

45b Use standard abbreviations for the names of organizations, corporations, and countries.

Many abbreviations are readily recognized, and many common ones can be written without periods.

UNESCO	GE	USA (or U.S.A.)
MADD	AT&T	UK (or U.K)

45c With an unfamiliar abbreviation, first use the complete name and then use the abbreviation.

Write the full name the first time you use it, followed by the abbreviation in parentheses. Then use the abbreviation throughout the rest of your paper.

The Potato Chip/Snack Food Association (PC/SFA) is an international trade association. Like other trade associations, the PC/

SFA is concerned about government regulations that affect business.

45d Use standard abbreviations to refer to specific numbers and times; the dollar sign is also acceptable with specific amounts.

$9.86

part no. 133 (or No.)

1:05 P.M. (or p.m.)

Note: When referring to dates, place the abbreviation B.C. following the date, but place the abbreviation A.D. before the date.

The Trojan War took place around 1200 B.C.

The Roman Empire fell in A.D. 476.

45e Use Latin abbreviations only in lists of works cited.

Latin abbreviations were once quite common in English writing, but most contemporary writers use English equivalents instead. *Et al.* (presented without italics) is the one form retained in most usage, but even that is restricted to entries on a works cited page (see **53**). (Notice that no period follows *et*, since it is a complete word; the period after *al.* signals an omission, however.)

Latin Abbreviation	English Equivalent
cf.	compare
e.g.	for example
et al.	and others
etc.	and so on, and others
i.e.	that is

45f In most writing, do not abbreviate
business designations (unless the company
does), units of measurement, calendar names,
courses, divisions of books and plays,
geographical names (except in addresses), or
personal names.

Although certain kinds of specialized writing—for instance, recipes, technical directions, entries for a works cited
page, and résumés—logically use abbreviations to save space,
academic writing should not include these kinds of abbreviations. Instead, write the words out completely.

	Not	But
Business Designations	Co., Inc.	Company, Incorporated
Units of Measurement	lb., tbs.	pound, tablespoon
Calendar Names	Fri., Oct.	Friday, October
Courses	psych., Eng.	psychology, English
Divisions of Books and Plays	chap., vol.	chapter, volume
Geographical Names	L.A., VT	Los Angeles, Vermont
Personal Names	Wm., Robt.	William, Robert

EXERCISE □ *Numbers and Abbreviations*

The following sentences contain mechanical errors resulting
from misuse of number forms and abbreviations. Correct the
sentences.

1. Doctor Ruth Waller, an econ. prof. at UCLA, has written 26

   articles and 2 books about Asian-American trade relations.

2. In 1971, the Baltimore Colts beat the Dallas Cowboys in the closest game in Super Bowl history: the final score was sixteen to thirteen.

3. My flight, Trans World Airlines flight number three hundred and seven, is scheduled to arrive in N.Y. at twenty minutes till midnight. I hope Robt. remembers to meet me.

4. PepsiCo, Inc., in addition to owning a soft drink company, owns Frito-Lay, Pizza Hut, Taco Bell, Wilson (the sporting goods manufacturer), and N. Am. Van Lines.

5. To receive a free copy of " 'He' Is Not 'She,' " write to Westside Women's Comm., Post Office Box twenty-four-D, Village Station, L.A., California 90024. For additional materials on sexist language, send two dollars and fifty cents.

6. 10 public libraries serve the people of Hartford, CT.

7. By Fri., Sept. twelfth, we are supposed to read chap. one through four for our psych. class.

8. *Hair*, the brash rock musical, was performed one thousand seven hundred and fifty times on Broadway.

9. Japan's labor force is well diversified, with eleven percent in agriculture, thirty-four percent in manufacturing, and forty-eight percent in services.

10. 227 people applied for the management position at National Biscuit Company's main plant.

EXERCISE ☐ *Mechanics Review*

The following paragraph contains a wide range of mechanical errors—both omissions and additions. Correct all errors.

Walter e. Disney, better known as *Walt*, was born Dec. fifth, 1901 in Chicago. After early work at the Chicago Academy of fine arts and at a Commercial Art firm in Kansas City, he moved to Hollywood in nineteen-twenty-three. It was there that he revolutionized american entertainment. In 1928, his short cartoon *Steamboat Willie* introduced "Mickey Mouse," as well as the use of sound-tracks with cartoons. 10 years later, his studio produced the 1st feature length animated cartoon, Snow White and the seven dwarfs, and 2 year's later, Pinocchio. The success of Disneys films stemmed from their innovative use of animated forms, color, music, voices, and story. In Song of the South, he added yet another innovation by combining live actors with animation. Although far less original than the cartoons, Disney studios conventional films—treasure island, robin hood, pollyanna, and others—appealed to the young and the young at heart. disney began work in television in 1950, and the fact that so many people can still sing M I C K E Y M O U S E attests to the success of his programming. Begun in 55 with the opening of *Disneyland* outside L.A., Disneys theme parks created a new standard for amusement parks and continue to attract millions each year. Few would have suspected, in 1926, that the man whose first cartoon creation was "Oswald the Rabbit" would change the way americans were entertained.

46 Spelling

Incorrect spelling interferes with good writing because misspelled words distract readers, who, as a result, lose track of the connections among ideas. Such interference is unfortunate because it shifts the reader's focus from ideas to mechanics. To deal effectively with spelling problems, writers have developed a number of strategies.

One strategy is to learn basic spelling rules (*i* before *e*, except after *c*, for example). Although such rules can prove helpful, spelling rules in English have many exceptions because English words are derived from many language groups. It is often more expedient, then, to concentrate on words that are particularly troublesome *to you* and to develop practical rather than theoretical strategies for overcoming individual spelling problems.

46a Use a spelling dictionary for words whose meanings you understand.

Spelling dictionaries are collections of words, nothing but words. These small, specialized dictionaries—intended only for finding spellings—dispense with pronunciation guides, discussions of word origins, definitions, and synonyms. Instead, they include page after page, list after list of words. Most of these dictionaries indicate syllable breaks in words with symbols, which are often helpful when hyphenating at line ends (see **43a**).

Spelling dictionaries are ideal for people with good vocabularies but poor spelling skills. They offer a quick way to make sure that *separate* is spelled with two *a*'s and two *e*'s or that *develop* does not end with an *e*.

46b Use a standard dictionary to check the spellings of words with similar meanings.

Sometimes you will need to know the meaning of a word to spell it correctly, especially when several words share a similar root word. Then you will need to use a standard dictionary to make sure that you have chosen the proper word and spelled it correctly. For instance, *domestic* and *domesticated* share similar meanings, but their uses are distinct. *Domestic* is either an adjective (*Domestic animals offer companionship.*) or a noun (*Jeffrey worked as a domestic at the Farrington's house.*), while *domesticate* is a verb (*You can domesticate a wild racoon, but it will not make a good pet.*). To make sure that you use the proper spelling, you must first make sure that you are using the proper word. That is when a standard dictionary will help you.

The sample dictionary entry from *Webster's II: New Riverside University Dictionary* (Boston: Riverside, 1984) shown in Figure 1 illustrates a universally used format.

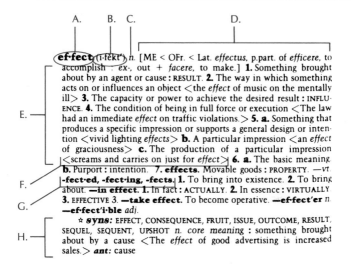

A. Spelling and syllabification
B. Pronunciation (guide at bottom of dictionary page)
C. Part of speech
D. Word origins
E. Numbered definitions
F. Sample illustrating usage
G. Spelling variations (past tense, present participle, plural)
H. Synonyms and antonym

Figure 1 A sample dictionary entry.

When reading a dictionary definition to select the proper word and spelling, be sure to read all the definitions, because words in English often have a variety of meanings.

46c Differentiate carefully among words that have similar pronunciations.

English contains many pairs and trios of words that sound the same—or almost the same—in speech (*cite/sight/site* or *rain/reign*). These words, technically called homonyms, present stumbling blocks for many uncertain spellers. Use the Glossary of Usage (**65**) to select and spell the word you need, or consult a dictionary to check for meaning and appropriate spelling.

46d Pronounce troublesome words to stress all the letters.

In speech, some letters are naturally omitted as words are pronounced. The omission causes no real problem in conversation, but in writing it often leads to incorrect spelling. To ensure correct spelling, exaggerate (with definite stress) the letters that you often omit in speech. Such practice with selected words will enable you to spell them correctly. In speech, for instance, we pronounce the word *accidentally* as if it were spelled "accident*ly*," even though the root word is *accidental* rather than *accident*. Slowing down to sound out all the letters —even though we don't use them in normal speech—will help you avoid spelling problems.

46e Make a list of words you frequently misspell.

Like most people, you will have an individual set of words that you regularly use and misspell. You should therefore take your own steps to avoid special problems. On a note card or sheet of paper, type or write favorite but troublesome words.

This record will save you the time needed to look them up when you want to use them.

46f Use a spelling program with your word processing program.

If you use a word processor to prepare your paragraphs and papers, use a spelling program with it. A spelling program will search through your manuscript for words that do not appear in its dictionary of correctly spelled words. Be aware, though, of several potential problems when using spelling programs.

First, a spelling program cannot distinguish between homonyms, words that have the same sound but different meanings (see Words with the Same Sounds, **29j**, and Glossary of Usage, **65**). As long as the spelling of a word appears in the program's dictionary, the program will move on. For instance, the following spelling errors would go unnoticed:

> The flight attendant wore a **pail** yellow jacket with navy **blew** slacks.

Pail (although this spelling means "bucket") and *blew* (although this spelling is for the past tense of *blow)* would both appear in the dictionary of a standard spelling program, and these errors would go undetected. You must therefore remain attuned to the meanings of your word choices to guarantee that the spellings are accurate.

Second, a spelling program cannot identify errors in typing if such errors produce words included in the dictionary of the spelling program. For instance, the following errors would go unnoticed:

> Even after the speaker finished her speech, **the the** audience remained **quite,** in awe of her talents and insights.

The inadvertent repetition of *the* would go unchecked because a spelling program moves a word at a time to check spelling—and is incapable of interpreting meaning. *Quite* would go unnoticed, too, because the inversion of the *t* and *e* in typing still produces a recognizable English word. You must therefore proofread for errors in spelling that are related to meaning.

Third, spelling programs are, according to computer jargon, "capitalization and punctuation insensitive." They check clusters of letters with spaces before and after them, but they cannot interpret capital letters or specialized punctuation, like hyphens. For instance, a spelling program would note two "errors" in the following sentence, even though they are not actually errors.

> **NASA** planned a rocket test in an **out-of-the-way** region of Arizona.

Unable to interpret the acronym *NASA* because it cannot recognize capitalization, a spelling program would check its dictionary for *nasa*, find nothing, and note an error. Similarly, *out-of-the-way* would stump a spelling program because it would read this hyphenated modifier as *outoftheway*—a group of letters that clearly would not appear in a standard dictionary.

Fourth, the dictionary for a spelling program must be necessarily general so that a wide variety of people can use it. Highly specialized words—proper names or technical terms, for instance—may not be included. In such cases, you can add these specialized words to the word list of the dictionary or check them individually.

Finally, spelling programs seem remarkably inconsistent in their quality. Some list only one spelling for words that have several alternative spellings, any of which is acceptable. Other programs even contain errors in spelling. For these reasons, you must use spelling programs judiciously.

Spelling programs are a wonderful aid in preparing a manuscript, but because of their limitations, they cannot substitute for your own careful proofreading for spelling errors that depend on meaning and context.

46g Carefully check the spelling of technical terms.

If you need to use specialized words in a paragraph or paper, check them carefully. Their spellings are sometimes difficult because we use such words infrequently. To ensure correct spelling, look these words up. Do not guess at them and hope no one will notice their misspelling.

46h Use American rather than British spellings.

A number of commonly used words will be listed in the dictionary with alternative spellings. Many times you can use either one. When such alternatives are identified as American (Am.) and British (Brit.), however, use the American spelling. These words are a sampling of such alternative spellings:

American	British
center	centre
color	colour
encyclopedia	encyclopaedia
judgment	judgement

Note: When you are referring to a proper name in your writing, maintain the original spelling even if it is British. Words that are not proper names, however, should appear with American spelling.

The **Labour Party** in Great Britain, being somewhat socialist, favors the nationalization of many industries. (*Although the American spelling is* labor, *the proper name of the political party must maintain the British spelling.*)

46i Check your spellings against this list of commonly misspelled words.

The following list contains words that many people misspell. If you do not have access to a spelling dictionary as you write, this list may be helpful.

abbreviate	allotted	arouse	becoming
absence	allowed	arranging	before
absolutely	although	article	beggar
absurd	altogether	association	beginning
accelerate	always	athlete	believe
accidentally	amateur	athletics	beneficial
accommodate	ambiguous	attempt	benefited
accomplish	among	attractive	biscuit
according	amount	audible	breath
accumulate	analysis	audience	breathe
accustom	analyze	authorities	brilliant
achievement	annual	automobile	bulletin
acquaintance	anxiety	auxiliary	buoyant
acquire	apartment	awkward	bureau
across	apparatus		buried
address	apparent	bachelor	burying
adoption	appearance	balance	business
aggravate	appropriate	balloon	busy
aggression	argument	barring	
alleviate	arising	bearing	cafeteria
alley	arithmetic	because	calendar

candidate
carrying
casualties
category
ceiling
celebrity
cemetery
certain
changeable
changing
characteristic
chief
choose
choosing
chose
chosen
climbed
column
coming
commission
commitment
committed
committee
companies
comparatively
compel
compelled
competent
competition
complaint
completely
compulsory
concede

conceivable
conceive
condemn
condescend
condition
conjunction
conquer
conscience
conscientious
conscious
considered
consistent
contemptible
continuous
control
controlled
convenient
cooperate
copies
corner
corpse
costume
countries
courteous
courtesy
cozy
cries
criticism
criticize
cruelty
cruise
curiosity
curriculum

custom
cylinder

dealt
debater
deceitful
deceive
decide
decision
defendant
deferred
deficient
definite
definition
democracy
dependent
descendant
describe
description
desirable
despair
desperate
destruction
develop
developed
development
diary
dictionary
diet
difference
digging
disappearance
disappoint

disastrous
discipline
discussion
disease
dissatisfied
dissipate
distribute
doctor
dominant
dormitory
dropped
drunkenness

echoes
ecstasy
efficient
eighth
eligible
eliminate
embarrass
eminent
emphasize
employee
encouraging
encyclopedia
enthusiastic
environment
equipment
equipped
equivalent
especially
eventually
exaggerate

exceed
excel
excellent
exceptional
excitement
exercise
exhaust
exhilaration
existence
experience
explanation
extensive
extracurricular
extremely
exuberance

fallacy
familiar
fascinate
February
fiery
finally
financial
financier
forehead
foreign
foremost
forfeit
forty
frantically
fraternity
freshman
friend

fulfill
furniture

gaiety
generally
genius
genuine
glorious
government
grammar
grandeur
grieve
guarantee
guard
guardian
guess
guidance

handicapped
handkerchief
harass
hearse
height
heroes
hesitancy
hindrance
hoarse
hoping
human
humane
humorous
hundredths
hurries
hygiene

hypocrisy
hysterical

illiterate
illogical
imaginary
imagination
imitative
immediately
implement
impromptu
inadequate
incidentally
incredible
indefinitely
independent
indicted
indispensable
inevitable
influential
innocent
inoculate
intellectual
intelligence
intentionally
intercede
interest
interpret
interrupt
irrelevant
irresistible
irreverent
itself

judgment
judicial

khaki
kindergarten
knowledge

laboratory
laid
later
latter
legitimate
leisure
library
lightning
likable
likely
literature
loneliness
losing

magazine
magnificent
maintain
maintenance
maneuver
manual
manufacture
mathematics
mattress
meant
medicine
messenger
millionaire

miniature
minute
mischievous
misspelled
modifies
modifying
momentous
mortgage
mosquitoes
mottoes
mountainous
murmur
muscle
mysterious

naive
naturally
necessary
necessity
neither
nervous
nevertheless
nickel
niece
ninety
ninth
noticeable
notorious

obedience
obliged
obstacle
occasionally
occur

occurred
occurrence
o'clock
official
officious
omission
omit
omitted
opinion
opportunity
optimistic
organization
original
orthodox
ought
outrageous
overrun

paid
pamphlet
parallel
parliament
particularly
partner
pastime
peaceable
perceive
perform
perhaps
permissible
perseverance
persuade
phrase

physical
physician
pierce
planed
planned
playwright
pleasant
politics
possess
possessive
possible
potatoes
practice
prairie
precede
predominant
prefer
preference
preferred
prejudice
preparation
procedure
primitive
privilege
probably
proceed
professor
prominent
pronounce
pronunciation
propaganda
propeller
protein

psychology
pursue
pursuing
putting

quantity
quarantine
quarter
questionnaire
quiet
quizzes

realize
really
recede
receipt
receive
receiving
recognize
recommend
refer
reference
referred
referring
regard
regional
relevant
religion
religious
remembrance
reminiscence
rendezvous
repetition
replies

representative
reservoir
resistance
restaurant
reverent
rhetoric
rheumatism
rhythm
ridiculous

sacrifice
sacrilegious
safety
salary
sanctuary
sandwich
scarcely
scene
scenic
schedule
scrape
secretarial
secretary
seize
sense
sensible
sentence
separate
severely
shining
shriek
siege
sieve
similar

sincerely
sincerity
skeptical
slight
sophomore
source
specifically
specimen
sponsor
spontaneous
statement
statue
stature
statute
stomach
stopped
strength
strenuous
stretch
struggle
studying
subordinate
subtle
succeed
success
successful
suffrage
superintendent
supersede
suppress
surely
surprise
suspense
swimming

symmetry
synonymous

taboo
tangible
tasting
technical
technique
temperament
tenant
tendency
than
therefore
thorough
though
thought
till
tired
together
tournament
toward
traffic
tragedy
transferred
tremendous
tries
truly
twelfth
typical
tyranny

unanimous
undoubtedly
unnecessary
until

usage
useful
using
usually

vacancy
vacuum
valuable
vengeance
victorious
view
vigilant
vigorous
village
villain
volume

warrant
warring
weird
welfare
where
which
whole
wholly
whom
wiry
woman
women
won't
worried
worrying
writing
written

yacht

WRITING A
RESEARCH PAPER

In some ways, a research paper is similar to any other paper. It must be logically organized, clearly developed, grammatically accurate, effectively written, and ultimately interesting and convincing. In some ways, however, it is different. Essentially, it is developed from information (ideas, facts, examples) taken from outside sources, rather than from personal experiences. Because you must clearly identify where or how you gathered information, research papers must also include precise documentation—specialized forms for identifying sources.

Importantly, writing a research paper is more than compiling facts and mastering the mechanics of documentation. It is a strategy for gathering information from outside your experience, interpreting the value of the information, and using it selectively to make a point. The research paper is, in essence, an expansion of basic writing and reasoning skills.

47 Choosing a General Topic

To begin work on a research paper, select a topic to research and write about. Any number of subjects are possible, of course, but a topic must have special qualities to be suitable for a research paper. Here are some useful techniques for deciding whether a topic will work well.

47a Consider your interests.

A well-chosen topic must interest you, first of all, because you will be spending many hours reading and learning about it. You will not want to spend hours in the library researching the Boston Marathon, for instance, if you are uninterested in long-distance running. But your interest in a subject is not the sole consideration. Other, more specific criteria are also important.

47b Consider length.

In most writing courses in college, the research paper is between ten and fifteen pages long, not counting documentation. You will not find or read everything written on a subject nor explain every facet of it, but you must present a relatively complete discussion. Therefore, a topic must be narrow enough to be discussed thoroughly in a moderately short paper (or moderately long one, if that is how you perceive ten to fifteen pages). Forget about topics like "The Holocaust," "Gandhi and Passive Resistance," and "Professional Basketball: The American Dream." Such topics are too broad to be treated adequately in a ten-to-fifteen page paper.

47c Consider your library.

Because facilities often determine the quality of research, pick a topic that you can research suitably in your library. There is little point in selecting sports medicine as a topic if you do not have access to a library with a strong section on either sports or medicine, or subscriptions to current magazines and journals in that area. Consider doing some preliminary research to see what is available in your library or ask your instructor for advice.

47d Consider the potential controversy of the topic.

Since most research papers support a thesis statement, select a moderately controversial topic. Remember, however, that some topics seem to preclude rational, balanced discussion. Emotionally charged topics—like abortion, the death penalty, and euthanasia—beg for problems because source materials are often biased. In addition, you may not be able to distance yourself enough from the controversy to write a clear, fair paper. Other kinds of topics offer almost no controversy because virtually everyone agrees about them. The ethics of Watergate can elicit little real discussion, since people universally agree that the actions leading to the break-in and cover-up were unethical. In selecting a topic, then, consider those for which controversy is possible but emotional reactions controllable.

47e Consider your knowledge of the topic.

Although one primary purpose of completing a documented paper is learning more about a subject, do not research a subject that is too technical or too advanced for you. Researching some subjects, like computer programming, requires sophisticated, technical skill because the materials are so complex. In the process of researching you could feasibly develop that skill, but learning new skills will be very difficult and time-consuming. Therefore, you might be better off working with a less technical topic—for instance, the use of computers in secondary classrooms.

47f Consider methods of development.

Research papers, like any other writing, can be organized in a variety of ways. They can use facts and examples to illustrate a thesis statement, they can present problems and their possible solutions, or they can explain a process. In addition, research papers can be organized using traditional methods like description, comparison and contrast, cause and effect, classification, definition, or a combination of these (see Paragraphs, **2e–2h**). Since you write more effectively with some strategies than others, consider a topic whose natural pattern of development is one of your favorites. After all, learning to research, document, and incorporate source material will be enough of a challenge. Do not further complicate the process by struggling with a writing strategy you have not mastered.

47g Consider the popularity of the topic.

Because some topics have long aroused curiosity or sparked the public's imagination, they have been overused and probably offer few possibilities for reaching new conclusions or for producing new patterns of development. How tired teachers have become of "UFO's," "Analysis of Dreams," "Anorexia Nervosa," "The Bermuda Triangle," and "Cloning" as topics. But beyond the worn-out approaches to such topics, their popularity suggests that the library's sources on them may very soon be depleted, and unnecessary and avoidable problems may arise.

47h Use a topic checklist.

When considering topics for a research paper, use the following questions about topic selection:

1. Am I honestly interested in the topic, interested enough to give it my time and energy?

2. Is my topic narrow enough to be treated adequately?

3. Can I find enough materials to make my research fairly complete?

4. Is my topic at least slightly controversial (so I can construct a workable thesis statement) but not so emotionally charged that a fair, balanced discussion is unlikely?

5. Do I have the technical knowledge to research the subject well?

6. Can I effectively do the kind of writing the topic requires?

7. Is my topic overused?

47i Consider this sample approach to choosing a topic.

One useful approach for selecting a topic is to focus on your major or minor field of study, or on a subject with which you have or plan to have some experience. Consider, first of all, general kinds of subjects, and then begin to narrow them.

For instance, Yasuko, a Japanese exchange student majoring in history, considered these general topics:

1. Japanese-American trade relations
2. the differences in Japanese and American education
3. American treatment of Japanese Americans
4. the bombings of Hiroshima and Nagasaki
5. American stereotypes of Japanese culture

Yasuko eventually dropped topic 1 (Japanese-American trade) because she did not have the specialized knowledge of trade patterns to research the subject well. She decided that topic 4 (Hiroshima and Nagasaki) was too emotionally charged for her to present a balanced discussion. She also eliminated topic 5 (stereotypes) because she felt her argument that American stereotypes of Japanese culture are wrong would not have the controversial edge that a research paper needs. That left Yasuko with two potential topics: the differences between Japanese and American education and American treatment of Japanese Americans. To deal with a comparison and contrast of the two educational systems, Yasuko would have to narrow the topic considerably—selecting, for instance, an educational level to discuss. With that kind of necessary restriction of the original topic, she might have difficulty finding materials. To work with American treatment of Japanese Americans, Yasuko would also have to narrow the topic considerably. Yasuko eventually chose the treatment of Japanese Americans because she could narrow the subject easily, could find a suitable range of source materials, and could write with personal commitment on a subject that especially interested her.

EXERCISE □ *Topics to Test*

Listed below are five sets of topics. Read them and think about how well they could be treated in a ten-to-fifteen-page research paper. Would they fit the checklist for choosing a topic? Which ones would probably produce the best papers? Also note what is wrong with poor topics.

Example

Topics from an agriculture major:

1. The farmer as businessperson—too broad.
2. Are small farms dying?—too broad, but has promise.
3. Government price supports—too broad.
4. Soil lab testing and crop production—too technical.
5. Water conservation and western farming—too broad, too controversial.

A. Topics from a computer science major:

1. The boom in computer software.

2. Computerized library systems.

3. Developing computer languages.

4. Computers and education.

5. Video games: the result of computer advances.

B. Topics from a music major (piano specialty):

   1. Choosing the best piano: cost and performance.

   2. The effects of major music awards on musical careers.

   3. Professional options for a piano major.

   4. Van Cliburn and the popularizing of classical piano music.

   5. Conservatory versus teacher-college training.

C. Topics from an elementary-education major:

   1. Educational games in the classroom.

   2. Sex education in grade school.

   3. Physical training in grade school.

   4. I.Q. testing in grade school.

   5. Children's television and learning.

D. Topics from a business major:

   1. Affirmative action in business.

   2. Creating a company image.

   3. A typical young executive.

   4. Computerized bookkeeping.

   5. Marketing a product for successful sales.

E. Topics from an English major:

1. The importance of setting in the stories of Edgar Allan Poe.

2. Feminist themes in Virginia Woolf's *Mrs. Dalloway.*

3. A survey of major poems in high school anthologies.

4. Job prospects for an English major.

5. Stoppard's *Rosencrantz and Guildenstern Are Dead* and Shakespeare's *Hamlet.*

EXERCISE □ *Topics*

On a 3-by-5 note card, type your standard paper heading and then list *five* possible topics for a research paper. Make sure that you are interested in working on any of the topics and are not writing one good topic and then padding the list. Test the topics against the checklist on pages **415–416,** making sure they have promise.

Example

Carla Walters

English 105

Dr. Potter

1. Should black history be taught in high school?
2. The NAACP on college campuses.
3. The Ku Klux Klan in Mississippi.
4. The rise of the black comedian.
5. Why is Martin Luther King's birthday a national holiday?

Note: If you are having difficulty finding topics, skim the index of one of the textbooks in your major or minor field of concentration. The headings may suggest interesting topics.

48 Narrowing Your Topic

Having identified a topic of general interest, the next step is to narrow your focus, to limit your options. Here are some helpful strategies.

48a Consider time.

Most subjects span a number of years, making complete discussion difficult or impossible. One way to narrow a topic is to set time limits. A fairly narrow subject, like assembly-line production of cars, can be made even narrower, and so more approachable, by adding a time limit like "during the 1920's" or "during the 1970's." This technique will focus research and reduce the amount of information to read.

48b Consider place.

Some subjects, like revitalizing cities, apply to a wide variety of circumstances and locales, and these varied conditions could present contradictions. To discuss effectively a subject where place is important, consider limiting the topic to a region or perhaps to a specific location. Gathering materials on revitalizing *midwestern* cities or on revitalizing *St. Louis* would be workable because the topic is focused.

48c Consider special circumstances.

Almost any subject can be further narrowed and clarified by defining special circumstances. A subject like renovating houses is too broad to be discussed thoroughly. By identifying special circumstances, however, you make the topic more manageable: renovating houses for resale, renovating houses for energy savings, or renovating houses to use for private business, for instance.

48d Do some preliminary reading in general reference books.

When you have special difficulty narrowing a topic, do some preliminary reading. Use the general sources in the library's reference room—encyclopedias, specialized dictionaries, and fact books. Skimming such materials may highlight times during which your topic was especially important, places where the influence was the greatest, or circumstances that influenced the topic. (See **50b** for a brief discussion of sample reference books.)

48e Consider this sample approach to narrowing a topic.

Yasuko's general topic, she had decided, would be American treatment of Japanese Americans. She could then further narrow the subject by examining American treatment of Japanese Americans during the late 1800's, the 1920's, or some other particular period. In addition, Yasuko could narrow the topic of the paper by discussing American treatment of Japanese Americans in particular parts of the country: the East,

South, Midwest, Southwest, or West. Yasuko could also consider special circumstances to narrow her topic. She could consider problems resulting from cultural differences, laws that specifically affected Japanese Americans, or financial pressures placed on Japanese Americans. Eventually, Yasuko could consider combining several of these approaches and discuss, for instance, American laws that affected Japanese Americans in the late 1800's.

To get a general perspective on her topic and to help her decide how to narrow her topic, Yasuko skimmed some reference materials in her library—encyclopedias, fact books, and bibliographies. From those reference materials, she discovered that a large number of laws, agreements, and proclamations had been directed over a number of years at Japanese Americans. She also discovered that during World War II, Japanese Americans on the West Coast were placed in detention camps in western states. Those discoveries from preliminary reading helped her narrow her topic in an accurate, realistic way. Yasuko tentatively planned to discuss the legal ways that Americans discriminated against Japanese Americans. She was not sure whether to address only those actions during World War II or whether to discuss laws over a number of years. What is important, however, is that she had begun to restrict her topic and could then search for specific kinds of materials.

You, too, will need to narrow your topic to avoid wasting valuable research time reviewing and reading materials that will not fit into your final paper. An hour or two of skimming reference books often saves many hours in the longer process. Such preliminary work limits the amount of detailed reading you have to do later. This does not mean that everything you read will be helpful (none of us can be sure of that), but you will be selectively beginning your research and productively using your time and energy.

EXERCISE □ *Narrowed Topics*

Select one of the broad topics from among the sets of topics on pages **417–419,** and narrow it by identifying a particular time, place, or special circumstance. Then write a combined, narrowed topic.

Example

(From Student A, Topic 1)

topic	The farmer as businessperson.
time	The farmer as businessperson in the 1970's.
place	The midwestern farmer as businessperson.
special circumstance	The wheat farmer as businessperson.
combined	The Kansas wheat farmer as a business-person in the 1970's.

EXERCISE □ *Specific Topics*

Select the best three topics presented on your note card from the exercise on pages **419–420,** and narrow them by identifying a particular time, place, or special circumstance. Then, on another 3-by-5 note card, type your heading and the three combined, narrowed topics.

Example

Carla Walter

English 105

Dr. Potter

1. The increasing influence of the NAACP on southern college campuses in the 1960's

2. The rise of Mississippi's Ku Klux Klan in the late 1800's

3. Introducing legislation in the 1980's to require units on black history in high school American history classes

49 Writing a Working Thesis Statement

Reading general materials, narrowing your topic, and considering your background with the topic should help you write a working thesis statement—a statement of the specific point to make in your paper.

49a Consider the purpose of a working thesis statement.

A working thesis statement is one written at the onset of research, presenting a narrowed topic and your opinion of it. Its primary purpose is to guide early research and reading, not to present a foregone conclusion to support with manipulated evidence. Use a working thesis statement to select and evaluate materials, but do not lock yourself into an unsupportable thesis statement.

49b Plan deductively, but be ready to work inductively later.

Early in your research, balance carefully between deduction and induction. By establishing a working thesis statement, you are researching deductively (starting with a general conclusion and finding support material). But also work inductively (looking for information that might lead in a new direction). Always research with an open mind, looking for new and important material that will influence your views about the subject. (See Deduction, **2c,** and Induction, **2d.**)

49c Consider this sample approach to writing a working thesis statement.

From her general reading and from some subsequent discussions with a history teacher she knew, Yasuko decided that a whole series of laws had probably led to the extreme treatment of Japanese Americans during World War II. She therefore began her careful reading of material with this working thesis statement to guide her research: "The harsh treatment of Japanese Americans during World War II was not a sudden reaction to the bombing of Pearl Harbor but was instead based on long-developing resentment." This thesis statement would allow Yasuko to eliminate some potential sources because they treated other aspects of the Japanese American experience, and it would require her to read other sources thoroughly because they treated legal issues.

As Yasuko gathered materials, however, she had to be open-minded. If enough sources contradicted her working thesis statement, she would have to revise it (Her new thesis statement, for instance, might read "Although Japanese Americans were always a racially conspicuous group, their harsh treatment during World War II was an isolated reaction to the bombing of Pearl Harbor.") Recognizing that her working thesis statement was tentative—at least until she found proof during her research—and recognizing that it would have to be further refined even if it proved true, Yasuko began her thorough exploration of the topic.

As you begin your work, do not consider a working thesis statement an absolute standard by which to gather information. Instead, think of it as a controlling idea to be confirmed, refuted, or modified based on the materials you will be reading in the weeks or months ahead.

EXERCISE □ *Working Thesis Statements*

On another 3-by-5 note card, type your heading and three working thesis statements from which your research might begin. If possible, discuss with other students or with your instructor which working thesis statement will probably lead to the most productive work and the best paper.

Example

Carla Walters

English 105

Dr. Potter

1. Influenced by the NAACP, black students in southern colleges became more politically active in the 1960's.

2. In spite of political and moral pressure against it, Mississippi's Ku Klux Klan became more active in the late 1800's.

3. Because of the long exclusion of black history from traditional American history courses, students are receiving a limited view of black achievement. It is therefore necessary to introduce legislation to require units of black history in high school American history courses.

50 The Library

With a good sense of what your research topic will encompass and with a working thesis statement, begin active work in the library, the place where you will gather most information.

50a Get to know your library.

Most library staffs offer tours of their facilities, either during student orientation or during the first few weeks of each term. If your school's library is very large—with departmental libraries or separate buildings or a sprawling library complex—then definitely take a tour. Even if your campus library is of moderate size, consider touring the facilities with a staff guide. After a twenty-minute walk through, though, do not assume that you know the library. Rather, investigate closely the most important areas: the card catalog area, the main reference room, the periodical section, the newspaper section, the stacks (the areas where the books are shelved), and the main circulation desk (where you will check out books). Familiarize yourself with any microfilm, microfiche, or other viewing devices. Talk to library staff members about the services the library offers. Some libraries now include terminals that allow researchers to complete computerized searches for sources on a topic. Ask for special instructions about using computers and remember that they often give you easy access to the library's holdings. Also ask whether the library can obtain materials for you through interlibrary loan from other libraries.

50b Use general reference works to gather background information.

Many general but useful sources are found in a library's main reference room: major encyclopedias, almanacs, atlases, recent biographical volumes, books of quotations, and dictionaries. Because these volumes are often more general than either books or articles, they probably will not provide much material for your final research paper. They can, though, provide useful background information before you begin more extensive research, and they can help you narrow a topic and write a working thesis statement. The following list is a brief sampling of available reference works:

The Cambridge Ancient History. 3rd ed. 12 vols. 1973.

Current Biography. 1940 to date.

Dictionary of Education. 3rd ed. 1973.

A Dictionary of Politics. Rev. ed. 1974.

Encyclopaedia Britannica. 14th ed. 24 vols. 1973. Yearbooks.

Encyclopedia Americana. 30 vols. 1980. Yearbooks.

Encyclopedia of Philosophy. 4 vols. 1973.

Encyclopedia of World Art. 15 vols. 1959–1968.

English, Horace B., and Ava C. English. *A Comprehensive Dictionary of Psychological and Psychoanalytical Terms.* 1958.

Facts on File. 1940 to date.

International Encyclopedia of Film. 1972.

International Encyclopedia of the Social Sciences. 17 vols. 1968.

The Interpreter's Dictionary of the Bible. 5 vols. 1976. Supplement.

Literary History of the United States. 4th ed. 2 vols. 1974.

McGraw-Hill Dictionary of Modern Economics: A Handbook of Terms and Organizations. 2nd ed. 1973.

The New Grove Dictionary of Music and Musicians. 20 vols. 1980.

The Oxford Companion to the Theatre. 3rd ed. 1967.

Times Atlas of the World. 1972.

Van Nostrand's Scientific Encyclopedia. 5th ed. 1976.

Who's Who in America. 1899 to date.

The World Almanac and Book of Facts. 1868 to date.

50c Use the card catalog or a computer cataloging system to locate books.

As you begin your research, consult the card catalog to find what books the library has and where they are. Arranged in alphabetical order, the cards themselves will be typed in three consistent forms—author cards, title cards, and subject cards—and some libraries separate the cards into three catalogs by these classifications. Thus, each book in the library's collection will be catalogued on at least three cards, making your search for materials easier. For instance, if you need a book by Carl Sagan but cannot remember the title, go to the *S* section of the catalog (perhaps in the "author" section), find the series of cards headed with Sagan's name, and check for the particular book you need. Similarly, if you need a book titled *The Unheavenly City* but cannot remember the author's name, go to the *U* file (*a, an,* and *the* do not figure into the alphabetization) and locate the book.

It is also possible to locate a subject like "solar energy" to find a complete set of cards for related books. Subject catalogs are usually organized according to Library of Congress subject headings. To find the heading for a subject, use the index to Library of Congress headings, which is most often located near the card catalog.

The individual cards (author, title, and subject) offer a great deal of technical but helpful information. They contain basic information about authors, titles, publishing companies, and call numbers. The call number (the general numbered category into which the book fits and the appropriate subclassifications within the larger category) will provide the information needed to find the book in the stacks. In addition, card catalog cards indicate when books include maps, illustrations, lists of sources, and so on. Even if you do not use all such information, you can use the card catalog efficiently as long as you recognize the card formats shown in Figure 1.

If your library includes computer terminals, you will have an optional method for finding books. The computer systems used in libraries vary. Your introduction to a specific system may be in the form of printed instructions (usually located near the terminals) or demonstration lessons provided by the library staff. All computer searching systems, however, depend on the same basic information that is provided on catalog cards: call number, subject classification, author's name, book title, and so on.

The major difference between card and computer searching is that when you work with a computer, the computer system will instantly retrieve the information you need from its memory and display it on the screen. For instance, suppose you are planning a paper on insomnia. You will type a series of operating commands and then type your subject, *insomnia*. Within a matter of seconds, the computer screen will display the names of the books the library has on that subject. (If the library's collection contains more titles than will fit on one screen, you will see them one group at a time.)

The quickness of computer searching is very helpful for researchers, but working from a screen rather than from cards can be initially confusing and fatiguing. If you continue to use a computer system to search for information, however, you will soon adjust to working from a screen. Then the computer will save you a great deal of time during early research.

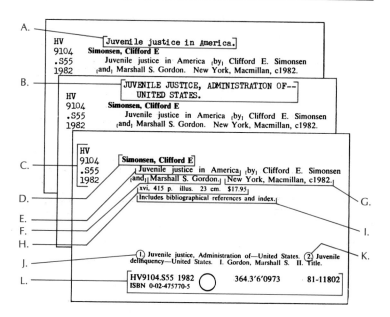

A.   Juvenile justice in America.
HV 9104 .S55 1982
Simonsen, Clifford E
Juvenile justice in America ₍by₎ Clifford E. Simonsen ₍and₎ Marshall S. Gordon. New York, Macmillan, c1982.

B.   JUVENILE JUSTICE, ADMINISTRATION OF-- UNITED STATES.
HV 9104 .S55 1982
Simonsen, Clifford E
Juvenile justice in America ₍by₎ Clifford E. Simonsen ₍and₎ Marshall S. Gordon. New York, Macmillan, c1982.

HV 9104 .S55 1982
Simonsen, Clifford E
Juvenile justice in America₎ ₍by₎ Clifford E. Simonsen ₍and₎₎ Marshall S. Gordon.₎ ₍New York, Macmillan, c1982.₎
xvi, 415 p. illus. 23 cm. $17.95₎
Includes bibliographical references and index.₎

① Juvenile justice, Administration of—United States. ② Juvenile delinquency—United States. I. Gordon, Marshall S. II. Title.

HV9104.S55 1982   364.3'6'0973   81-11802
ISBN 0-02-475770-5

A.   Title card heading
B.   Subject card heading
C.   Library of Congress number
D.   Author card heading
E.   Title of book
F.   Name of second author
G.   Publication information: city, company, date
H.   Technical information: number of pages in preface, number of textual pages, illustrations, book size, price
I.   Additional information: textual apparatus
J.   First subject classification
K.   Second subject classification
L.   Library of Congress number, ISBN number, Dewey Decimal number, On-Line Computer Library Center number

Figure 1 Author, title, and subject cards.

431

50d Use indexes and bibliographies to locate articles in periodicals.

Another general source for your research paper will undoubtedly be periodicals: magazines, journals, and newspapers. Because these sources are published more frequently than books, they offer very recent discussions of subjects. In addition, their discussions are often very specialized.

Magazines, trade publications written for wide audiences, are sold at newsstands and provide current but nontechnical and often general information. Journals, on the other hand, are professional or scholarly publications written by and for practitioners in a given field. They are usually published for members of organizations and contain specialized, technical information.

Instructors will usually explain whether magazines or journals will fit the requirements of a particular research assignment. If you receive no specific guidance, use both, to investigate the general viewpoints of magazines and the sophisticated information and analysis of journals.

A guide for magazine articles

The *Readers' Guide to Periodical Literature* provides the easiest access to articles in magazines. Normally located in either the reference area or in the periodicals section, the *Readers' Guide* is printed regularly, is bound yearly, and contains references to articles in popular magazines.

Like the card catalog, the *Readers' Guide* is arranged alphabetically and includes author, title, and subject entries. Presented without standard punctuation, the entries rely heavily on abbreviations to save space. The abbreviations are generally clear, but lists at the front of each volume identify the full titles of magazines and explain sequences of information in case a reader might have trouble interpreting an entry. Figure 2

A. ——[**Furniture, American**
       See also — B.
       House decoration, American]
   American furniture [special issue] il *Antiques* 129:1044-99
    My '86

               Exhibitions

C. ——[Boston japanned furniture in the Metropolitan Museum
   of Art. M. H. Heckscher and others. bibl f il *Antiques*
   129:1046-61 My '86 — D.
   Museum accessions [acquisition of the Bybee Collection
   of American furniture by Dallas Museum of Art] E.
   H. Gustafson. il *Antiques* 129:956+ My '86 — E.
Furniture, Built in
   It's the everything-built-in bedroom. il *Sunset* 176:128+ — F.
    Ap '86
   Pocket hides curtain's bulk. il *South Living* 21:225 Ap
    '86
Furniture, Painted
   Country painted. il *Redbook* 166:114-15 Ap '86
Furniture finishing *See* Furniture—Finishes and finishing

A. Subject heading
B. Cross reference
C. Article title
D. Special information: bibliography, footnotes, illustrations
E. Author
F. Publication information: magazine title, volume number, page numbers,
   month, year

Figure 2 Sample entries from the *Readers' Guide to Periodical Literature.*

shows an extract from the *Readers' Guide.* You can see that a
good deal of information is presented in very little space.

Guides for journal articles

To find the more expert information in journals, use specialized indexes and bibliographies, which are normally located
in a library's reference room. As with the card catalog and the

Readers' Guide, indexes and bibliographies present entries in alphabetical order—listing authors, subjects, and sometimes titles. Because so many indexes and bibliographies exist and because they all follow slightly different patterns of presentation, no standard format can be described. However, the extract from *The Education Index* shown in Figure 3 provides a fairly typical sample. Most indexes and bibliographies will follow a similar pattern.

Using the call number of a subject, you can locate specific indexes and bibliographies in the library's reference room. The following are but a few of the guides you may find:

Agricultural Index, 1919–1964

The American Humanities Index, 1975 to date

American Indian Index, 1953–1968

Applied Science and Technology Index, 1958 to date

The Art Index, 1929 to date

Bibliography and Index of Geology, 1961 to date

Biography Index, 1949 to date

Biological and Agricultural Index, 1964 to date

Book Review Index, 1965 to date

Business Periodicals Index, 1958 to date

Catholic Periodical Index, 1930–1933, 1939 to date

Cumulated Drama Index, 1909–1949

Dramatic Index, 1909–1949

The Education Index, 1958 to date

Engineering Index, 1884 to date

Film Literature Index, 1974 to date

General Science Index, 1978 to date

A. —————[Camping

            See also

B. ————— Camps

            Outdoor life

            Wilderness survival

                 Educational aspects

         ⌊Archaeology camp.⌋J. R. White. ⌊il por(inside cover) ⌊*GCT*

C. —————   no35:2-4 N/D '84   — D.

         Early adolescence: a camp-out—conference style. B. S.

            Tubertini. il *Sci Child* 22:41-3 O '84

         Okefenokee notes [visit to swamp in southeast Georgia

E. —————   and northeast Florida] ⌊P. E. Burton.⌋il ⌈*Sci Child* 22:5-9 ⌉

            My '85   — F.

     Camping for the handicapped

         Choosing a summer camp. il *Except Parent* 14:37-9 Ap

            '84

         Parents creating recreational experiences: Kamp for Kids.

            il *Except Parent* 14:40-2 Ap '84

         Summer camps and schools for deaf and hard of hearing

            persons. *Am Ann Deaf* 129:252-4 Ap '84

A.   Subject heading
B.   Cross references
C.   Article title
D.   Special information: illustrations, portraits
E.   Author
F.   Publication information: journal title, volume number, page numbers, month, year

Figure 3 Sample entries from the *Education Index.*

Humanities Index, 1974 to date

Index to Legal Periodicals, 1908 to date

Index to U.S. Government Periodicals, 1974 to date

Industrial Arts Index, 1913–1957

MLA International Bibliography of Books and Articles on Modern Language and Literature, 1922 to date

Music Index, 1949 to date

Social Sciences Index, 1974 to date

United Nations Documents Index, 1950 to date

A guide for newspaper articles

In the general reference collection or in the newspapers section, a number of indexes will help you locate articles in newspapers. The *New York Times Index, Wall Street Journal Index, London Times Index,* and *Washington Post Index* are several prominent ones. They are compiled yearly and alphabetized by subject. Although references are for articles published in only one newspaper, checking other newspapers printed on the same day will yield other coverage of the event. The section from the *New York Times Index* shown in Figure 4 is typical of other newspaper indexes.

51 | Compiling a Preliminary List of Sources

Once you feel comfortable in the library and know where materials are located, begin to identify possible sources for your research paper. With your narrowed topic in hand, gather materials to use.

51a Write a preliminary list of sources.

Compile a preliminary list of useful sources that are available in your library. Include books on your list because books offer solid, thorough presentations of a subject. Include a variety of journal, magazine, and newspaper articles to provide recent and specialized discussions of your subject. Also consider

A. — **NIKE Inc**
B. — Nike Inc co-founder, chairman and chief executive officer, Philip H Knight, to reassume post of president, which he relinquished just over year ago; will replace Robert L Woodell, who remains with company. Knight photo (S). — C.
S 24,IV,2:5 — D.

E. — **NIKKO Hotels International. See also** Hotels, O 29 — F.
NIKOLAI, James. See also Farmers Group Inc, F 14
NIKOLAIS, Alwin. See also Dancing, Ja 16, F 12,26, O 28
NIKOLAIS Dance Theater. See also Dancing, F 12,17,19
NIKOLIC, Milan. See also Yugoslavia, D 3,12,15
NIKON Gallery (NYC). See also Botanic Garden, Brooklyn, Ap 21
NIKON Inc
  Nikon Inc elects Yutaka Sasaguchi president to succeed Herbert Sax (S), Jl 19,IV,2:5
  Nikon Inc appoints Walter Buhrmann executive vice president and director-instrument group, and Jack Abrams executive vice president and director-photo group (S), S 11, IV,2:3
NILE River. See also Fish, Je 17. Ships and Shipping, Ag 9. Sudan, D 4

A. Subject heading
B. Abstract of an important news story
C. Photograph information
D. Note on length of the article: (L) means over three columns; (M) means one to two columns; (S) means less than one column
E. Publication information: month, day, newspaper section number, page number, column number
F. Cross reference

Figure 4 Sample entries from the *New York Times Index.*

a variety of nontraditional sources—for instance, interviews, pamphlets, filmstrips, or class notes—to present a very complete review of potential material about your subject. Not all of these sources will be incorporated in the final paper, but this original work will reveal the range of materials available and indicate how much reading lies ahead.

Using separate 3-by-5 note cards for each source, begin to jot down key information on potential sources. For a book, write down the complete call number, the author's name (spelled correctly), and the book's title. For an article in a periodical, write down the complete entry from an index or bibliography, and do not use abbreviations unless you will be able to decipher them later. (A return trip to a reference book wastes valuable time, so be thorough and accurate the first time.)

Before beginning detailed research, briefly examine your potential sources to discover what they contain. Sometimes you can eliminate a source quickly because it does not include needed information, or you can identify an especially useful source from a quick preliminary examination.

51b Annotate your source cards.

Annotations, comments on or evaluations of books or periodicals, are a useful part of a preliminary list of sources. For instance, if a source includes maps—and if they would be useful for your topic—jot a note on the source card. If a source includes a bibliography, note that, too. When appropriate, be highly subjective and record personal responses to sources: "nice pictures," "well written," "clear diagrams," and so on. Basically, record any information that will help you decide later whether a source is worth reading thoroughly.

Sometimes instructors will ask that you later complete a formal *annotated list of works cited*. Such work combines the specific information from a works cited entry with the comments that evaluate the quality of a source. Your initial comments on source cards will supply you with basic evaluations, but you will need to present them in full sentence form.

When instructors ask for annotations, they often want evaluations of all the sources you examine, not just the ones you use in the paper. Such an annotated list is labeled *Works*

438

Consulted. The annotations that follow each entry will clarify why some sources were useful for the paper and why some were not.

The sample card in Figure 5 shows a standard approach for completing an annotated entry for a list of works consulted.

51c Begin to evaluate the quality of sources.

Even at an early stage in research, evaluate sources based on key information. Use these questions as guides and add evaluative comments to your source cards.

1. Does the author have special expertise? An *M.D.* after an author's name can indicate authority in medical matters. A university listed with an author's name may also suggest special expertise in a particular subject.

2. Does the title suggest a focus suitable for your work? Sometimes the phrasing of a title (or subtitle) will indicate how specifically a source covers a topic. A title like *Drug Abuse* may not help much, while *The Cocaine Connection* might.

3. Is the publishing company a reputable one? You may not feel totally prepared to evaluate publishing companies, but you can establish some sense of their importance. University presses usually publish major theoretical works, and you will soon recognize the important publishing companies in your field. Company names alone will not always guarantee high-quality sources, but they are effective as general guides.

4. Are the periodicals well respected? Again, you may not be able to evaluate this question thoroughly, but you should sense that an article from *Time* probably has more credence than one from *Mother Earth News.*

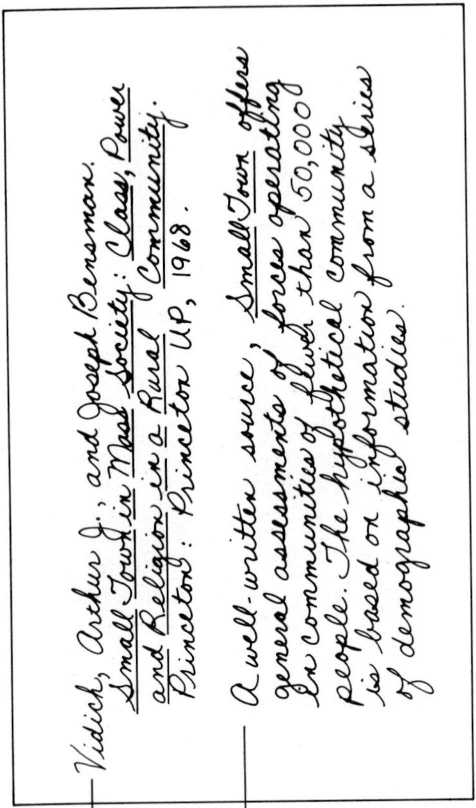

Vidich, Arthur J., and Joseph Bensman.
_Small Town in Mass Society: Class, Power
and Religion in a Rural Community._
Princeton: Princeton UP, 1968.

A well-written source, _Small Town_ offers
general assessments of forces operating
in communities of fewer than 50,000
people. The hypothetical community
is based on information from a series
of demographic studies.

Full entry form

Evaluation

Figure 5 An annotated source card.

5. Is the publication date recent? With some topics, the currency of a source will be unimportant, but many times information must be up to date. In those cases, sources older than ten or twenty years may be of little use.

Early in your work, get a sense of how valuable your materials will be. These general guidelines can help you begin, but carefully reading sources is the best way to test their quality.

Yasuko, for instance, considered using a book titled *Minorities in American Society* by Charles F. Marden and Gladys Meyer (New York: Van Nostrand, 1968) for part of her research. A brief look at the book's title page provided some useful information for evaluating the book. Charles F. Marden, Yasuko found, was affiliated with Rutgers University and Gladys Meyer with Barnard College. That information assured Yasuko that Marden and Meyer had the expertise needed to write a reputable book on her subject. That the book was a third edition suggested that its ideas had been well received and that its views and information had been brought up to date. Van Nostrand Reinhold, the publishing company, was one that Yasuko recognized, and that made her secure about the book's general quality. A copyright date of 1968 was sufficiently recent, since the events related to Yasuko's topic ended with the mid-forties. This information—from the title and copyright pages—indicated that *Minorities in American Society* was a promising source.

By looking at the book further, however, Yasuko discovered that it would have only limited value for her work. The title suggested, first of all, that the book treated many minorities, not just Japanese Americans. A review of the table of contents revealed that many large divisions of the book concentrated on general sociological issues: "The Significance of Minorities in American Society," pages 1–19; "Introduction to the Sociology of Minorities," pages 20–53; "Race: Myth and Science," pages 54–69; and others. Chapter 9, the single chapter devoted exclusively to Japanese Americans, was only twenty-three pages long (pages 197–220). By examining the divisions within Chapter 9, Yasuko discovered one small section called "Native Reaction to the Japanese," but the forty-five lines devoted to the topic seemed too brief to be useful.

Yasuko decided to skim the book for general ideas that might help her think about her topic. From her quick look at *Minorities in American Society*, however, Yasuko knew the book would not provide the kind of detailed information she would need to develop her paper.

You, too, will need to evaluate your potential sources briefly and thoroughly. You will need to decide whether a book is worth reading for background ideas or for detailed information. Sometimes you will decide that a source is not worth using, for one reason or another. Early evaluation of sources will save you time and energy and will give you a clear idea of their usefulness.

51d Ask the library staff for special help.

If problems arise at any time during your work in the library, ask a member of the library staff for help. Librarians are specially trained to help people find materials and can help you save time and energy as you search for unusual sources. Do not exploit the staff, however, by asking them to solve easy problems or to do simple work for you. Instead, consider yourself an independent researcher and use your instincts to find materials. Only when you have exhausted the options you can identify should you ask the library staff for help. That way, you can tell them where you have looked and what searching system you have followed. Then they will be able to identify any searching errors or recognize where you became confused. The library staff will be willing to locate hard-to-find materials, help you interpret especially confusing indexes and bibliographies, and explain special procedures. Use their expertise.

52 General Guidelines for Documentation

Documentation includes two basic kinds of entries: works cited entries and notes. Both explain for readers where you got the facts, quotations, or ideas in your paper. Documentation can become complicated, but if you work carefully, it should be manageable.

Although there are various formats for entries and notes, both kinds of documentation provide readers with as much of the following information as is available:

1. *author(s):* of the book or article

2. *title:* of the book, of the chapter and the book, or of the article and the periodical in which it appears

3. *necessary additions:* edition number, volume number, name of the series, editor, compiler, or translator

4. *facts of publication:* for a book, this will include city of publication, publishing company, and the year of publication; for a periodical it will include the volume number and date of publication

5. *page numbers:* for articles; for material that forms a part of a larger work

Because most readers have grown accustomed to basic patterns of documentation, present information in a consistent and accepted form.

52a Use the style of the Modern Language Association (MLA) unless advised otherwise.

The works cited entries and note forms presented here are derived from Joseph Gibaldi and Walter S. Achtert's *MLA Handbook for Writers of Research Papers,* 2nd ed. (New York: Modern Language Association, 1984). The MLA style is simple and clear, eliminating much of the confusion caused by Latin abbreviations in other documentary styles. Other forms of documentation, however, are required in certain subject areas. So, before submitting a paper in a non-English class, always ask the instructor if MLA style is acceptable or if another style of documentation is expected. If you are required to follow another style guide, it will probably be one of these:

CBE Style Manual. 5th ed. Bethesda: Council of Biology Editors, 1983.

The Chicago Manual of Style. 13th ed. Chicago: U of Chicago P, 1982.

Handbook for Authors. Washington, D.C.: American Chemical Soc., 1978.

Publication Manual of the American Psychological Association. 3rd ed. Washington, D.C.: American Psychological Assn., 1983.

Style Manual for Guidance in the Preparation of Papers. 3rd ed. New York: American Inst. of Physics, 1978.

Turabian, Kate. *A Manual for Writers of Term Papers, Theses, and Dissertations.* 4th ed. Chicago: U of Chicago P, 1973.

The American Psychological Association (APA) style is described in section **60,** including guidelines for preparing manuscripts and sample note forms. (See pages **549–555.**)

52b Complete a works cited page to show where you gathered information.

The works cited page is the most general form of documentation in a research paper. It provides a complete list of sources incorporated in the paper (but it does not indicate how many times a writer has referred to each work). It is placed at the very end of a research paper. (See pages **541** and **543** for a sample.)

52c Carefully follow format guidelines when preparing entries for the works cited page.

The works cited page (or pages) is alphabetized using the first word in each entry, usually the author's last name, and each entry is typed following this very specific format:

1. The first line of an entry begins at the normal left margin. All subsequent lines are indented five spaces.

2. The author's name is inverted so that the last name appears first (to make alphabetizing easier).

3. The title must appear in complete form, including subtitles.

4. The major sections of entries are separated by periods.

5. Entries are double-spaced.

52d For books, gather information for each entry from the title page and copyright page.

When searching for information to include in a works cited entry, check the beginning pages of a book. On the title page—a page typically located near the front of the book—you will find the complete title of the book, including any subtitles, the author's name presented as it should be listed in the entry, and the name of the publishing company and the city where it is located. Names of editors, compilers, and translators—as well as indications of edition, volume, and series—will also appear on the title page.

Copy the book's title from the title page rather than from the cover, because the title page is the only place where the complete title must be listed. Also copy the author's name from the title page. When several authors are listed, always copy their names in the order in which they appear—from top to bottom—rather than in alphabetical order. Shorten the publisher's name as much as possible while still keeping it recognizable (the *MLA Handbook* suggests useful shortened forms for major publishers). Do not, for instance, include words like *the, publishers, press, company,* and *incorporated.* If several cities are included with the publishing company's name, use the one listed first. Although the publication date is sometimes listed on the title page, always double-check it against the date on the copyright page (a page printed on the back of the title page). Find the copyright symbol (©) and use the most recent date. In addition, read the copyright information to see if the book is a reprint of an older edition. All this information will be important in preparing a works cited entry.

> **52e** For periodicals, gather information for each entry from the masthead and the article itself.

The masthead is the listing of important information about a periodical, such as the periodical's title, volume number, and date of publication. A newspaper's masthead runs across the top portion of the first page, making it especially easy to locate. The masthead for a magazine or journal, however, is not always easy to find. It is normally located in the first few pages of the publication but may be surrounded by advertisements or may be combined with a table of contents. Look for the title of the magazine or journal in bold letters (often in the same style as is used on the cover) and then search for the accompanying facts of publication that you need.

Turn to the article itself to record the full title, author, and the page numbers. In some periodicals, authors' names are listed at the end rather than the beginning of an article, so check both places. If no author is listed, note that fact on your card to avoid confusion later on. Then note the inclusive page numbers for the article, omitting pages that are more than half advertisement.

52f For nonprint sources, gather information carefully.

Finding information for an entry for a nonprint source is usually easy, but sometimes it requires ingenuity. Phonograph records are easy to work with because album jackets contain printed information. A lecture is fairly easy, too, because a printed program for a formal lecture or a syllabus for a course lecture provides essential information. Films and television programs always include the necessary information for an entry in their opening or closing credits, but you may not be able to record this information quickly enough. In such cases, consult reference books, such as *Facts on File* or *American Film Record.* Printed sources like these will include pertinent information. If you have any special problems with nonprint sources, ask your instructor or a librarian for help.

53 Entries for the Works Cited Page

The most frequently used forms for works cited entries appear next. If you need other, more specialized forms, consult the *MLA Handbook.* Pay special attention to punctuation, since these forms must be reproduced precisely.

53a Complete entries for books depending on general publishing information.

A Book by a Single Author

Corbett, Edward. *Classical Rhetoric for the Modern Student.* 2nd ed. New York: Oxford UP, 1971.

- The author's last name appears first, followed by a comma and the first name.
- A period follows the author's name, the title, and the date.
- A colon follows the city, and a comma follows the name of the publishing company.
- The edition of a book—clearly noted on the title page—is included after the title.
- Note that the letters *U* and *P* are used to abbreviate *university* and *press.*

A Book with Multiple Authors

Vidich, Arthur J., and Joseph Bensman. *Small Town in Mass Society: Class, Power and Religion in a Rural Community.* Princeton: Princeton UP, 1968.

- A comma follows the initial author's first name.
- The second (or third) author's name is not inverted.
- Note that the authors' names are not in alphabetical order. They are presented as they appear on the title page.
- A colon is used to separate a title and subtitle.

Lewis, George L., et al. *Teaching Speech.* Columbus: Merrill, 1969.

- To save space, use *et al.,* which means "and others" and is not italicized in the note form, when a work has more than three authors. In this entry, using *et al.* eliminates the names of Russell I. Everett, James W. Gibson, and Kathryn T. Schoen from the entry.

A Book with a Corporate Author

1900–1910. Vol. 1 of *This Fabulous Century.* 6 vols. New York: Time-Life, 1969.

- Because no authors or specific editors are mentioned, move the next piece of information—the title—forward and continue the entry as usual.

A Work in Several Volumes

Churchill, Winston S. *A History of the English-Speaking Peoples.* 4 vols. New York: Dodd, 1966.

- Notice that *volumes* is abbreviated.

- In this entry, the placement of *4 vols.* immediately after the title emphasizes the entire collection rather than any one volume. An entry as general as this will probably not apply to most of your work.

- You do not need two periods after *S.* One kind of end punctuation will do.

Churchill, Winston S. *The Birth of Britain.* Vol. 1 of *A History of the English-Speaking Peoples.* 4 vols. New York: Dodd, 1966.

- Here the entry emphasizes one titled volume in the complete series.

- Notice that *Vol. 1* begins with a capital, since it follows a period.

Granville-Barker, Harley. *Prefaces to Shakespeare.* 2 vols. Princeton: Princeton UP, 1975. Vol. 2.

- This entry emphasizes one volume of a complete work without separate titles for each volume.

- Notice that the number of volumes follows the title, while the particular volume reference ends the entry.

A Work in a Collection by the Same Author

Salinger, J. D. "The Laughing Man." *Nine Stories.* New York: Bantam, 1964. 56–73.

- The title of the short work comes first, followed by the title of the complete work.

- Notice that the period precedes the quotation marks.

- The once-accepted abbreviation, *pp.* for *pages*, is eliminated, implying that everyone will understand that *56–73* refers to the paging.

A Work in a Collection by Different Authors

Shaw, George Bernard. "The Technical Novelty in Ibsen's Plays." *Essays in the Modern Drama.* Ed. Morris Freedman. Boston: Heath, 1964. 9–18.

- Editors' names must be included for collections like this because they are responsible for selecting and bringing together the shorter works.

- Again, note that the title of the short work comes first, followed by the title of the complete work, and that inclusive pages are listed.

Articles in Encyclopedias and Other Reference Works

Napier, J.R. "Primates." *Encyclopaedia Britannica: Macropaedia.* 1980 ed.

- When an author is listed for an encyclopedia article, the name must be included in the entry. Sometimes initials only will be listed at the end of the article *(Britannica* listed *JRN* for this article). To find the author's full name, consult the table of contributors and remember to begin your entry with his or her last name. *Britannica* lists names at the back of a volume titled *Outline of Knowledge.*

- Reproduce the spelling of titles exactly. The *ae* instead of *e* in *Encyclopaedia* is a British spelling that must be reproduced accurately.

- Notice the small *e* in *ed.,* because it does not follow a period.

- Also notice that no pages are needed because the reference work is arranged in alphabetical order.

"Spock, Benjamin," *Who's Who.* 1981–1982.

- People's names are normally inverted in reference works. You must follow that pattern in your entries.

- Distinguish carefully among general reference works, especially those with alternative editions. This entry is from the international *Who's Who,* rather than *Who's Who in America* or *Who's Who in Great Britain.*

- Because reference books are so well known, no other information is required except the title, edition number, if any, and date.

A Work in a Series

Strachey, Lytton. *Landmarks in French Literature.* Oxford Paperback's University Series 42. New York: Oxford UP, 1969.

- If a work is part of a series, it will be clearly indicated on the title or copyright pages at the front of the book.

A Reprint of an Older Edition

Faulkner, William. *The Unvanquished.* 1938. New York: Vintage, 1966.

- If a work is a reprint of an earlier edition, the copyright page will clearly indicate that.

- List the original publication date first, followed by a period. Consider this part of the publication information.
- The rest of the entry follows the normal pattern.

A Translation

Mann, Thomas. *Death in Venice.* Trans. Kenneth Burke. New York: Modern Library, 1970.

- The translator's name usually follows the title and abbreviation *Trans.*, with a capital *T*.
- It is also possible to emphasize the translator's work by placing his or her name first in the entry. Unless you are discussing the techniques of translation, however, follow the form above.

Aristotle. *Rhetoric.* Trans. W. Rhys Roberts. In *Aristotle: Rhetoric and Poetics.* New York: Modern Library, 1954.

- Placing the translator's name after the short work makes it clear that he or she did not translate all of the material in the book, only part of it.

A Pamphlet

How to Feed Your Baby: The First Year. Evansville: Mead Johnson, 1980.

- The pattern for a pamphlet is like a book's, although the information may not be complete. Standards for printing pamphlets are less consistent than they are for books. Work around missing information. Use *n.p.* for "no place of publication" or "no publisher." Use *n.d.* for "no date." (Neither should be italicized in the entry.)

An Unpublished Dissertation

Shapiro, Barbara. "Structure and Form: The Architectural Development of Frank Lloyd Wright." Diss. U of Illinois, 1984.

- An unpublished dissertation may be bound and therefore resemble a book, but its pages will probably be photocopied on only one side.

- Because these dissertations are bound for the university library collection but are not really published, you should give the title in quotation marks, rather than italics.

- All necessary information can be gathered from a typed title page.

A Published Dissertation

Rollins, Jeremy. *The Philanthropic Legacies of the Robber Barons: Carnegie, Rockefeller, and Vanderbilt.* Diss. Syracuse U, 1979. Ann Arbor: UMI, 1980. 9413756.

- A published dissertation will be identified as such. It will look like a book, however, and will be documented like a book.

- The title is italicized.

- If University Microfilms International (UMI) published the dissertation, the order number must be included in the entry. It is found on the title or copyright page.

53b Complete entries for periodicals depending on publication patterns.

An Article in a Journal with Continuous Paging through a Single Year

Ohmann, Richard. "Reflections on Chaos and Language." *College English* 44 (1982): 1–17.

- Up to the journal's title, all should look familiar. No punctuation follows the title, however, and the volume number is given (without the abbreviation *vol.*), followed by the year in parentheses.

- Notice that page numbers are preceded by a colon and listed without a page abbreviation.

An Article in a Journal with Separate Paging in Each Issue

Sills, Toni. "Socrates Was Executed for Being Innovative." *English Journal* 70.7 (1981): 41–42.

- Notice the addition when each issue is paged separately: a period and the number of the issue. This allows readers to find the volume first and then locate the particular issue.

- Again, abbreviations are eliminated.

An Article in a Weekly Publication, Magazine, or Newspaper

Church, George J. "Paying More for Money." *Time* 8 March 1982: 74–83.

- The date of the issue is written in special form to avoid using a comma.

- Pages, once again, are included to make finding the article easy.

- If no author's name is listed with the article, begin the entry with the article's title.

An Article in a Monthly Magazine

Angier, Natalie. "How Fast? How High? How Far?" *Discover* November 1981: 24–30.

- For this kind of entry, only the month and year are needed to direct readers to the article.

- Notice that when a question mark is used as part of a title, no period is needed, since a question mark is a form of end punctuation.

An Article in a Newspaper

Oppenheim, Carol. "San Francisco Transit Running in the Red." *Chicago Tribune* 19 March 1982, midwest ed.: sec. 1:4.

- Editions must be cited when they are identified. Check the lead page of the paper for information about an edition.

- Section and page are identified to help readers find materials easily.

- Sometimes sections will be identified by letters, in which case no punctuation separates the section from the page (*B4*).

A Letter to the Editor

Benshoof, Steve. Letter. *Newsweek* 1 March 1982: 7.

- Notice that you do not use titles that publishers used to get readers' attention.

- If the letter appears in a journal or newspaper, follow the appropriate format after the designation "Letter."

A Review

Corliss, Richard. " 'Go on—the Limit!' " Rev. of *Reds,* dir. Warren Beatty. *Time* 7 December 1981: 66–67.

- Because it is a form of end punctuation, the exclamation point in the title suitably replaces the period found in normal entries.

- The combination of single quotations within normal quotation marks indicates that the article title was itself a quotation. (See **41b**.)

53c Complete entries for nonprint sources depending on the nature of the source.

A Lecture or Speech

Brent, Harry. "Teaching Composition Theory in the People's Republic of China." NCTE Convention. Boston, 21 November 1981.

- Notice that in citations for lectures, the city follows the description of the circumstance.

- Use materials from course work by following a similar pattern—substituting information about instructor, course title, university or college, city, and date. If a lecture or speech has no title, follow the author's name with a descriptive word *(lecture, address)*, which should not be italicized.

A Film

Fosse, Bob, dir. *Cabaret*. With Liza Minnelli and Joel Grey. Allied Artists, 1972.

- The director is usually given credit in a general reference to a film. If, however, you want to emphasize the film's screenwriter, list his or her name first.

Zemeckis, Robert, and Bob Gale, screenwriters. *Back to the Future*. Dir. Robert Zemeckis. With Michael J. Fox and Christopher Lloyd. Universal, 1985.

- When writers are emphasized, their names come first.

- Additional information begins with the director.

A Television Program

The Great American Fourth of July and Other Disasters. Writ. Jean Shepard. American Playhouse. PBS. WGBH, Boston. 16 March 1982.

- The name of the program comes first, followed by the name of the writer, director, or producer—whichever is appropriate.

- The series title is capitalized but not italicized.

- Include the name of the network and the date on which the program was broadcast.

- To refer to a special episode of a regular program, write the episode title first (in quotation marks). Then, after the writer's name, include the title of the program (italicized).

- Notice that abbreviations of television networks do not require periods.

A Recording

The Beatles. *Sgt. Pepper's Lonely Hearts Club Band.* Capitol, SMAS 2653, 1967.

- This entry would be alphabetized by *Beatles*, not *The*. A single performer's name would be inverted: "Streisand, Barbra."

- The manufacturer's cataloging number can be found on the album cover, on the record label, and usually imprinted on the record itself.

- Look closely for the copyright date—in very small print along the edges of the printed material. If no date is included, use *n.d.*

- A song title from an album would be placed in quotation marks and would precede the title of the complete work.

An Interview

Haroldson, Thomas B. Telephone interview. 15 December 1986.

- The person interviewed—who supplied answers—is listed in the "author" position, even though you composed the questions.

- The date must be included to place the interview in its context.

- If the place of the interview is important, insert the city (followed by a colon), and perhaps the business or institution (followed by a comma) before the date.

53d Shorten second references to works by the same author.

When your works cited list includes several sources by the same author, you need not repeat the person's name in each entry. Instead, use the author's full name in the first entry (the sources should be in alphabetical order by title) and then use three hyphens and a period in place of the author's name in subsequent entries.

Gould, Stephen Jay. *Ever Since Darwin: Reflections in Natural History.* New York: Norton, 1977.

_____. *Hen's Teeth and Horse's Toes.* New York: Norton, 1980.

_____. *The Panda's Thumb: More Reflections in Natural History.* New York: Norton, 1980.

53e Maintain a consistent pattern for all entries.

Learning to transfer information from a book, periodical, or other source into a works cited entry takes practice, patience, and care. Whichever form you use (either MLA style or that of some other recognized group), follow it carefully and vary from it as little as possible. If information is missing for a source, note it and proceed with the next part of the entry. If you must combine forms for different kinds of entries, remember the basic order: author, title of part of the work, title of the complete work, additional information (edition, volume number, name of the series, editor, compiler, or translator), city, publisher, date, and inclusive pages if necessary. Finally, if you have problems writing an entry for a source, ask for help.

EXERCISE □ *Compiling a Works Cited Page*

Listed below in scrambled order and form are thirteen sets of information needed to produce thirteen entries for a works cited page. For each set of material, prepare a card. When you have finished and have double-checked their form, alphabetize the cards, and transfer them to a works cited page. It should look like a finished product, with appropriate heading, proper spacing, and accurate form. (See pages **541** and **543** for a sample.)

1. "Double Talk About Divorce"; Margaret Mead; *Redbook*; May 1968; pages 47–48.

2. "Some Thoughts on Divorce Reform"; Paul Bohannan; in *Current Issues in Marriage and the Family*; edited by J. Gipson Wells; 2nd edition; Macmillan Publishing Company; 1979; New York.

3. *The Road to Reno: A History of Divorce in the United States*; Nelson Manfred Blake; Macmillan Publishing Company; 1962; New York.

4. *Marriage in the United States*; Auguste Calier; Arno Press; 1972; 3rd edition; New York; originally published in 1867.

5. *'Til Divorce Do You Part*; Roberta Greene; KNOW, Inc.; 1972; Pittsburgh; this is a pamphlet.

6. "Data Shows Marriages Up, Divorces Down"; *Washington Post*; section A; page 3; March 16, 1983.

7. "Divorce and Separation"; *Facts on File*; 1984 edition.

8. *Inside Divorce: Is It What You Really Want?*; Edmond Addeo and Robert Burger; Chilton Book Company; 1975; Radnor, Pennsylvania.

9. *Kramer vs. Kramer*; directed by Robert Benton; Columbia Pictures; 1979, starring Dustin Hoffman and Meryl Streep.

10. Personal interview with Rebecca Stahl; February 19, 1986.

11. "The Sorry State of Divorce Law"; *Time*; pages 26–27; February 11, 1966.

12. "Divorce Is a Family Affair"; Jack C. Westman and David W. Cline; *Family Law Quarterly*; March 1971; volume 5; number 1; pages 1–10.

13. "Divorce"; *The American Heritage Dictionary: Second College Edition*; 1982 edition.

54 Notes

In addition to the works cited page, which lists basic but general information about sources, a research paper must include notes to identify clearly which material comes from which sources. Notes further identify the specific page or pages where facts, quotations, or ideas appeared in original sources.

In the past, notes were presented according to a fairly complex pattern: writers placed note numbers (a half-space above the line) at the ends of sentences that included information, ideas, and quotations from source materials. Those note numbers corresponded to full citations either at the bottom of the page (footnotes) or at the end of the paper (endnotes). Numbered notes in either position required a complete relisting of information found in full entries in the list of works cited, although the form varied.

Acknowledging the repetitive nature of full note citations, the MLA has modified its notation form, following the lead of the American Psychological Association. With both forms, sources are now briefly identified in the paper in parentheses, greatly simplifying citations. You should be aware, however, that many of your sources—especially those older than two or three years—will rely on the older forms of notation. Note the differences but simplify your own work by using the parenthetical forms now in standard use.

54a Match parenthetical references to entries from the list of works cited.

Parenthetical references must clearly correspond to works that are included on the works cited page. Follow the pattern you established for each entry, referring to the key information that begins the entry. For instance, if an entry begins with an editor's name, the parenthetical note should begin with his or her name as well—not with the title of the book. If you follow this pattern, readers will be able to match information in parenthetical references with the lead information in works cited entries.

54b Complete parenthetical references, using brief but clear information.

A Book by a Single Author

(Calder 273)

* In most cases, only the last name is needed.

* No punctuation separates the author's name from the page number, and no abbreviation for *page* is required.

A Book by an Author Whose Last Name Is the Same as That of Another Author Listed in Your Bibliography

(Nigel Calder 273)

* To avoid possible confusion in this circumstance, also include a first name.

* Notice that the name appears in normal order, not reversed.

Two Sources by a Single Author

(Calder, *Universe* 22–23)

- Include the author's last name and a short form of the title (properly punctuated).

- Shorten titles by eliminating subtitles, prepositional phrases, or nonessential words. Make sure the shortened title will not confuse readers, however.

A Book with Multiple Authors

(Vidich and Bensman 131–133)

- With fewer than four authors, list all last names.

- The order of the names should match that in the list of works cited.

(Lewis et al. 27)

- No comma separates *Lewis* and *et al.*

- With four or more authors, list the first and then use *et al.*, without italics.

A Book with a Corporate Author

(*1900–1910* 79)

- Since no author's name can be used, use the title or a shortened version of it and follow regular parenthetical form.

A Work in Several Volumes

(Churchill 1: 8)

- Begin with the author's name.

- Identify the volume number, followed by a colon and a space, and then include the page reference.

Articles in Encyclopedias and Other Reference Works

(Napier)

- If an author's name accompanies the reference article, use the name.

- No page notation is required because reference works are presented in alphabetical order.

  ("Spock")

- If the article has no author, use a shortened form of the article's title.

- Again, a page reference is unnecessary.

  Nonprint Sources: a Lecture, a Film, a Television Program, a Recording, or an Interview

  (Brent)

  (Fosse)

  (*Fourth of July*)

  (Haroldson)

- Use the name or title from the works cited entry: lecturer, director, writer, producer, performer, or respondent.

- No page can be cited.

54c Incorporate parenthetical references directly in your paper.

As you include facts, quotations, and ideas in your research paper, parenthetical notes will allow you to place citations as closely as possible to the source material, normally at the end of the appropriate sentence.

Facts, Summaries, or Paraphrases

Jefferson and Latrobe modified the original design of the White House by adding terraces in 1807 (Pearce 17).

- Note the space between the last element of the sentence and the opening parenthesis.

- The period follows the second parenthesis.

- Pearce, Mrs. John N. *The White House: An Historic Guide.* Washington: White House Historical Assn., 1963.

Quotations in the Text

Individual occupants, from Jefferson to Roosevelt, have each modified the building to suit their tastes. Thus, present features of the White House "form a living link with the building's past" (Pearce 17).

- Note the placement of the punctuation: quotation marks, then parenthetical information, and then the period— breaking the normal pattern of placing punctuation before the closing quotation marks.

Set-Off Quotations

The limited press coverage of the Kitty Hawk flight was probably the result of other notable failures:

> Just nine days before Kitty Hawk, the secretary of the Smithsonian Institution, Samuel Langley, had tried to launch a winged contraption from the roof of a house-boat on the Potomac River in Washington, D.C. . . . But while boatloads of reporters and government officials watched expectantly, the craft had left its catapult and plunged nose first into the Potomac. (*1900–1910* 88)

- When a long quotation is set off (indented ten spaces), a period is placed immediately following the quoted material. No quotation marks are used.

- The parenthetical note follows after a space, without additional punctuation.

- Notice the use of the ellipsis points (the three spaced periods); see **38** for a discussion of their use.

- *1900–1910.* Vol. 1 of *This Fabulous Century.* 6 vols. New York: Time-Life, 1969.

54d If information is already clear in the
text of the paper, do not repeat it in a
parenthetical reference.

When you supply source information in your sentences, do
not repeat that information in the parenthetical references. For
instance, if you clearly identify an author in a sentence, omit his
or her name in the reference, as in the following example, taken
from Dee Brown's *Bury My Heart at Wounded Knee: An Indian
History of the American West* (New York: Bantam, 1972):

> As Dee Brown notes, between 1851 and 1861, approximately
> 150,000 white settlers moved westward into land previously
> claimed by the Santee Sioux (38).

Besides simplifying the preparation of the references themselves, this strategy improves the flow of the paper, because
sentences are not cluttered with repetitious information.

Parenthetical notation provides a simple and clear system
for citing pages. In preparing notes, however, make sure to
supply enough information and to punctuate carefully.

55 Note Taking

Once you have compiled a tentative list of sources and have
learned basic procedures for documentation, begin reading materials and taking notes. This process takes considerable time,
but you can simplify it by taking notes in a systematic way.

55a Before taking any notes from a source,
prepare a works cited entry.

Before using a source, write a complete and accurate entry
for the works cited page on a 3-by-5 note card. Writing the

complete entry in correct form (following all the intricacies of spacing and punctuation noted earlier in this unit) will save a good deal of time in the later stages of preparing the research paper.

55b Use a uniform format for note taking.

When writing down information from sources, establish a uniform system. Many writers, for instance, take notes on 4-by-6 index cards. This size is easy to handle and can be easily rearranged when it is time to organize materials for writing. In addition, 4-by-6 cards are easily distinguished from the 3-by-5 source cards. Other writers prefer to use legal pads or notebook paper for their notes. These writers feel that paper provides more space than cards for recording information.

Your instructor will advise you on which pattern—using note cards or using paper—will be acceptable for your work. Either way, use a consistent format for note taking. (All of the following suggestions relate to using note cards, but with slight modification they could also apply to using paper.)

As much as possible, write on only one side of the cards to avoid having to flip them over to find information. Also, fit material on one card if possible. If a second card is necessary, however, note in the heading that it is the second of two cards. Finally, write closely related information on each card and use new cards for new ideas. Because you will sort cards later into subject or subtopic categories, do not cover more than one subject per card. Doing so will complicate later attempts to organize materials.

Since each note card works independently, certain information should appear on each: the author's name, a short title for the source, and a page citation. In addition, marking on each card the kind of note will help you gauge whether you are overusing quotations, recording little besides bare facts, and the like.

Using a uniform system that is simple, clear, and complete will make note cards easy to use later. Use abbreviations sparingly (even though they might save time in note taking) because several weeks later, when writing the paper itself, you may not remember exactly what you were abbreviating. Returning to original sources to supply incomplete information wastes valuable research time.

55c Take the kinds of notes that seem appropriate for the material you are recording.

As you read materials and prepare note cards, you will discover a number of useful ways to take down information. Often they will overlap. Notes can be classified in four general ways:

1. facts
2. summaries
3. quotations
4. paraphrases

Do not use one kind of note exclusively. Instead, record whatever kind of information the source presents best. Some sources supply facts, while others contain excellent quotations, and still others contain useful ideas to express in your own words.

The sample note cards in Figures 6, 7, 8, and 9 present information from Stephen Jay Gould's *The Mismeasure of Man* (New York: Norton, 1981).

Recording facts

Factual notes are clearly the easiest kind to take because they include bare pieces of information: dates, names, figures, examples, and so forth. Because factual notes emphasize only information, without interpretations, consider using condensed forms: make lists and avoid writing factual information in full sentences (although you will have to sometimes). Carefully check your information for accuracy, however. Also make sure that your notes include no errors in transcription: misspellings, dropped digits in numbers, and so on. Figure 6 shows a sample fact card.

EXERCISE □ *Taking Factual Notes*

Using the following paragraphs, take down factual notes. Practice selecting only the most important information and writing it down in brief form.

Richardson, Doug. *F-16: Fighting Falcon. Vol. 2 of Modern Fighting Aircraft.* 12 vols. New York: Arco, 1983. [page 6]

> Following industrial submissions by five companies, General Dynamics and Northrop were chosen to develop flight-test hardware, and a contract was awarded to General Dynamics on April 13, 1972. This was a "cost plus fixed fee" contract worth $37.9 million and covered the design, construction and test of two prototypes under the USAF designation YF-16, plus one year of flight testing.
>
> Although development and test of these light fighters was a technology-demonstration programme, the USAF retained the option of carrying on to develop the design into a service aircraft. The contract with GD specified an average flyaway unit cost target of $3.0 million in 1972 dollars (rather more in 1983 prices), assuming a production run of 300 examples at a rate of 100 per

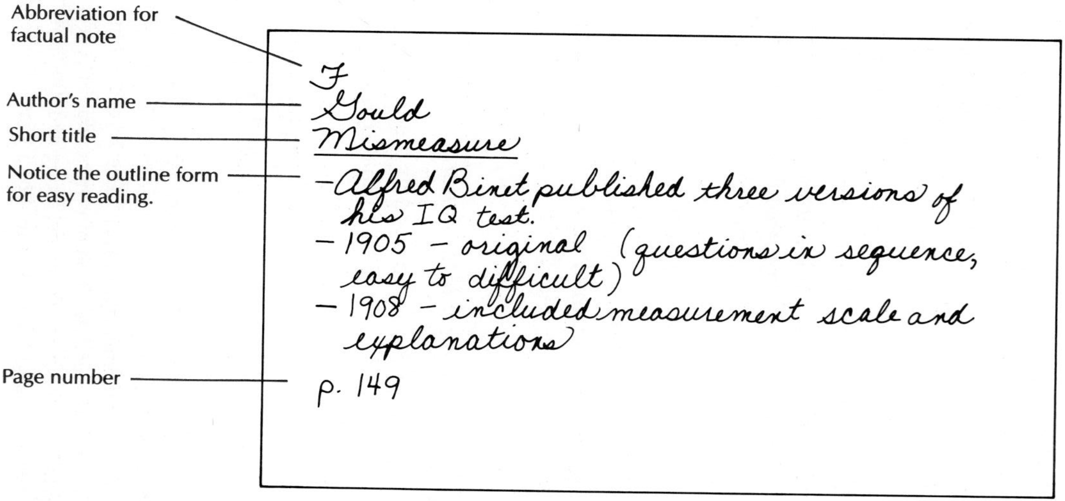

Abbreviation for
factual note

Author's name

Short title

Notice the outline form
for easy reading.

Page number

F
Gould
Mismeasure

- Alfred Binet published three versions of
  his IQ test.
- 1905 - original (questions in sequence,
  easy to difficult)
- 1908 - included measurement scale and
  explanations)

p. 149

Figure 6 A fact card.

year. Complete design responsibility for the aircraft lay with the contractors, in order to reduce paperwork and maintain the pace of the programme, under the direction of the Aeronautical Systems Division at Wright-Patterson AFB, which monitored both projects throughout subsequent development.

Summarizing general information

Sometimes sources include general but useful information on a topic. Perhaps a chart or diagram presents a general observation worth noting, but you do not want to painstakingly record all the information. That is the time to summarize, to write a brief comment or series of comments that record, in greatly reduced form, the impression the information creates. Avoid unintentionally taking words or phrases from the original source (see Plagiarism, **55d**). Figure 7 shows a sample summary card.

EXERCISE □ *Summarizing General Information*

Summarize the general information provided in the following paragraph. Practice recording the impression that this general information presents.

Granger, Richard H. *Your Child from One to Six*. Washington, D.C.: U.S. Department of Health, Education, and Welfare, 1979. [page 8]

One to six might be called the civilizing years. The 1-year-old is still self-centered and unreasonable, making demands and expecting these demands to be met right away. The 1-year-old has no patience and little or no consideration of others. But by 5 or 6 the child is going to have to enter school, get along with the other children and the teachers, and learn. In this 4 or 5 years children

Abbreviation for
summary ———————

Author's name —————

Short title ————————

Page number —————

S

Gould

Mismeasure

— The Beta retest — an Army IQ test for soldiers who mis-took the first one — includes a visual part that requires test takers to identify missing parts in pictures: letters without stamps, pigs without tails, violins without strings, lightbulbs without filaments, and so on.

p. 211

Figure 7 A summary card.

have to go from thinking only of themselves to being considerate of the needs and priorities of other individuals and the group. That is what being civilized means.

Quoting from sources

Quoting—writing down someone else's work word for word—is perhaps the kind of note writers most overuse, mainly because they fail to assess the value of a quotation before copying it. Before taking down a quotation—especially a long one—ask yourself the following questions:

1. Is the author's style so exceptional that I could not say the same thing as well or as clearly in my own words?

2. Is the vocabulary technical and therefore difficult for me to translate into my own words?

3. Is the author well-known or important enough to quote simply because his or her reputation or position will lend authority to the passage?

If you answer "yes" to at least one of these questions, then the quotation is probably worth copying. If the material does not fulfill any of these criteria but is significant nonetheless, paraphrase it instead. Doing so at the note-taking stage will save time later.

Copy quotations carefully. Always use quotation marks to indicate where quoted material begins and ends, and double-check your copy with the original. Your copy must be *exact*. Figure 8 shows a sample quotation card.

EXERCISE □ *Quoting Effective Passages*

Record any notable quotations from the following paragraph. Select only quotations that meet the criteria we have discussed.

Abbreviation for
quotation

Author's name

Short title

Quotation marks

Q.uld

Gould

Mismeasure

"Not only did Binet decline to label IQ as inborn
intelligence; he also refused to regard it as a
general device for ranking all pupils according
to mental worth. He devised his scale only
for the limited purpose of his commission by
the ministry of education; as a practical guide
for identifying children whose poor performance
implicated a need for special education — those
who we would today call learning disabled
or mildly retarded."

Page number

p. 152

Figure 8 A quotation card.

Mowry, George E. *The Era of Theodore Roosevelt and the Birth of Modern America: 1900–1912.* New York: Harper & Row, 1958. [page 38]

> Confronted with the turbulent world of 1900, fairly seething with economic and technological change, with strange new scientific and religious ideas, with the growth of giant industry and organized labor, with the rapid and uproarious rise of "the alien city," thinking Americans divided politically into ideological groups which in their bewildering diversity almost defy analysis. At either end of the political spectrum the pattern was the classical one of conservative and radical, two strains that had much in common and were to alter very little in the first two decades of the new century. The middle ranges of political thought, however, were to feel the full impact of the new ideas and conditions, with the result that the old strains of agrarianism, individualism, and humanitarianism were disrupted and sharply altered. Collectively and inexactly labeled "liberalism," these traditions after strong infusions of the new thought underwent a process of mutation and hardened into a political creed that eventually became known as "progressivism." In this readjustment of political values many one-time conservatives became progressives or radicals, and some men, torn between old memories and loyalties and the new conditions and the impact of the new thought, never could decide just what they believed and why.

Paraphrasing sources

Paraphrasing someone else's work, using the ideas but not the exact wording, is a good alternative to overquoting. If, for instance, a book or article contains an important idea but if the material does not stand up to the test questions for quotations, transfer the ideas into your own words. Select significant points and express them more briefly than the original does. Do not, however, use phrases or sentences from the original source without placing them in quotation marks. Intentional or not, such borrowing from an original source is called plagiarism, a serious error by any standard (see **55d**). Not only the language but also the structure and sequence of sentences should be entirely your own. Once again, check your notes against the original source—this time to see if the idea is truly stated in your own words. Figure 9 shows a sample paraphrase card.

EXERCISE □ *Paraphrasing a Source*

Paraphrase the main ideas in the following paragraph. Remember that you can combine selected use of quotations with a paraphrase.

Kitto, H. D. F. *The Greeks.* Baltimore: Penguin, 1951. [pages 64–65]

> "Polis" is the Greek word which we translate "city-state." It is a bad translation, because the normal polis was not much like a city, and was very much more than a state. But translation, like politics, is the art of the possible; since we have not got the thing which the Greeks called "the polis," we do not possess an equivalent word. From now on, we will avoid the misleading term "city-state," and use the Greek word instead. In this chapter we will first inquire how this political system arose, then we will reconsti-' tute the word "polis" and recover its real meaning by watching it in action. It may be a long task, but all the time we shall be improving our acquaintance with the Greeks. Without a clear conception of what the polis was, and what it meant to the Greeks, it is quite impossible to understand properly Greek history, the Greek mind, or the Greek achievement.

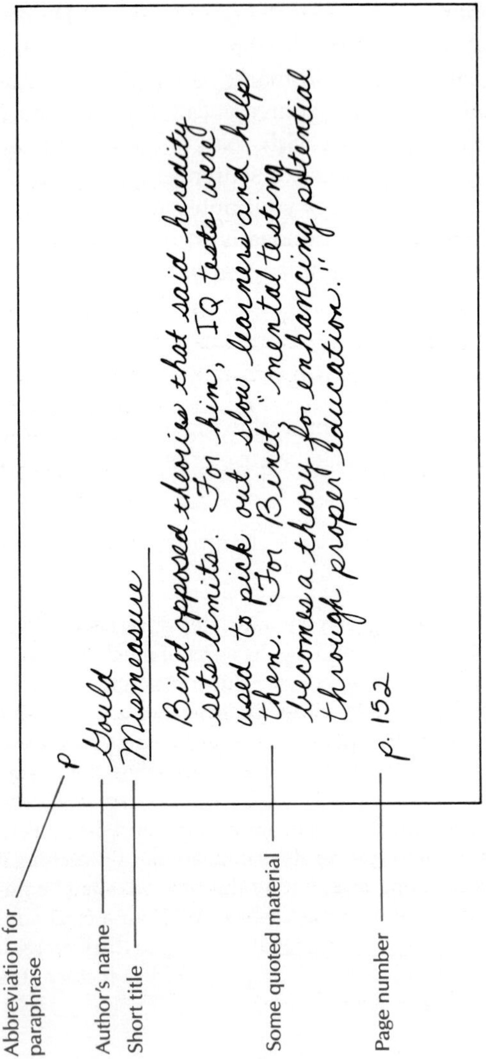

Abbreviation for paraphrase

Author's name

Short title

Some quoted material

Page number

p

Gould

Miomeasure

Binet opposed theories that said heredity
sets limits. For him, IQ tests were
used to pick out slow learners and help
them. For Binet, "mental testing
becomes a theory for enhancing potential
through proper education."

p. 152

Figure 9 A paraphrase card.

55d Avoid plagiarism by carefully evaluating sources and selectively taking notes.

Plagiarism is using someone else's words or ideas without giving proper credit. The most flagrant form of plagiarism is the wholesale use of someone else's complete paper, but such theft is not very common. In cases of that magnitude, however, the penalties are extremely severe: at many schools students fail not only the paper but also the course and may well be dismissed from school or have their degrees withdrawn.

Unintentional plagiarism is more common but is also serious. Sometimes writers do not document sources or do not clearly indicate an author's words with quotation marks. Even when such plagiarism is the result of careless or uninformed work, the work is still dishonestly presented, and the penalties are severe. But how can you avoid problems with plagiarism? How can you separate your words and ideas from those of other people? In large part, avoid plagiarism by being aware of particular qualities in source materials and following some specific guidelines in note taking.

Look, for instance, at this paragraph from Stephen Jay Gould's book:

> Goddard introduced Binet's scale to America, but Terman was the primary architect of its popularity. Binet's last version of 1911 included fifty-four tasks, graded from prenursery to mid-teen-age years. Terman's first revision of 1916 extended the scale to "superior adults" and increased the number of tasks to ninety. Terman, by then a professor at Stanford University, gave his revision a name that has become a part of our century's vocabulary—the Stanford-Binet, the standard for virtually all "IQ" tests that followed. (175)

What characterizes this paragraph? What makes it distinctly Gould's?

1. *The word choices and phrases.* Some phrases stand out particularly because of their special word combinations, their distinct sounds: *the primary architect of its popularity, a name that has become a part of our century's vocabulary.*

2. *The sentence structure.* The last sentence, especially, has an elaborate structure with three appositives. This is a structural pattern that indicates a sophisticated style.

3. *The factual information.* The paragraph contains some important facts about the number of tasks involved, the levels of skills tested, the date of Terman's revision, and some information about Terman himself. This information is specialized enough that it is not common knowledge. It is particularly Gould's.

4. *The idea presented.* Gould's assessment of Terman's role is a fairly common one, since most educators realize that the sweeping use of IQ tests began with the Stanford-Binet. Although this paragraph presents no highly original ideas, its presentation is particularly Gould's.

Recognizing these four features of an author's work, you can honestly record the author's words and ideas—and therefore avoid subsequent problems with plagiarism, even unintentional plagiarism.

Record bare facts

When taking notes, concentrate on information and make sure not to include unmarked words or phrases that are distinctly the author's. If you do not mark these notes with quotation marks at the note-taking stage, such wording can inadvertently work its way into your paper later.

Unacceptable Factual Notes

—Binet's 1911 test, 54 tasks, **graded from prenursery to mid-teen-age years**

—Terman's 1916 revision, **extended the scale to "superior adults,"** 90 tasks

—Terman, professor at Stanford U.

(The phrases in boldface type are clearly Gould's. You would probably not describe these features of the tests in the same way. To avoid this kind of unintentional plagiarism, either place key phrases in quotation marks or translate them entirely into your own words.)

Acceptable Factual Notes

—Binet's 1911 test, 54 tasks, toddlers to teenagers

—Terman's 1916 version, upward to "superior adults," 90 tasks

—Terman, professor at Stanford U.

(Here, phrases have been rewritten, presenting key information without copying key phrases.)

Quote any particularly unusual or stylish words or phrases

When words, phrases, or whole sentences stand out, include them in your notes. But make doubly sure to place them in quotation marks so that you will not incorporate them inappropriately in your paper.

The unacceptable recording of facts, noted previously, could be acceptable if quotation marks suitably identified Gould's phrasing.

Summarize and paraphrase blindly

To summarize or paraphrase without inadvertently including an author's phrases or sentence patterns, reread the useful

479

portion of a source, turn the page, and then describe the information or ideas on your note card. That way, the wording will be truly yours. Then return to the source to quote a few pertinent phrases if you wish and doublecheck your notes against the original once again—to make sure that you have not accidentally incorporated special wording in your paraphrase.

Unacceptable Paraphrase

Terman, a professor at Stanford, gave his test a name that is now familiar—the Stanford-Binet, the one all IQ tests are modeled after. *(Working a phrase at a time and changing a few words to make them more common is not acceptable paraphrasing. The telltale structure of Gould's sophisticated sentence remains, even when the word choices are less interesting.)*

Acceptable Paraphrase

When Terman was working at Stanford University, he named his revised test the Stanford-Binet. It became the model for later IQ tests.

—the name "became part of our century's vocabulary"

(Here, the paraphrase presents Gould's idea but does not mimic his sentence structure. The quoted material records a special phrase for possible use later.)

Avoiding plagiarism takes conscious effort, and that effort takes time. Mostly, it requires an awareness of special qualities in source material and painstaking, careful note taking. By preparing notes properly and then documenting your paper completely, you will avoid the serious errors of plagiarism that can spoil a research paper.

EXERCISE □ *Practice in Note Taking*

Here are three sets of paragraphs taken from three sources. Take notes from these sources as if you were using them for papers. Include a fact, a quotation, and a paraphrase from each one. Avoid plagiarizing.

A. Pearce, Mrs. John N. *The White House: An Historic Guide.* Washington: White House Historical Assn., 1963. [The paragraphs are from page 17.]

> When the Commissioners for the Federal City chose James Hoban's design for the President's House in 1792, they fully expected the house would be completed when the Government moved to Washington in eight years' time; as we know, it was not. Indeed, it was never completed according to Hoban's original plans. Ever-changing personalities and styles of living and building have inspired the continuing metamorphosis that has marked the history of the White House.
>
> This constant change is symbolized by the development of the wings on either side. L'Enfant had expected that the President's House would have long wings, in the manner of Versailles. Hoban also incorporated wings in his design. This conception was modified, however, by Jefferson and Latrobe, in the low-lying terrace-pavilions which were completed by 1807. Over the years the east terrace was demolished and the west terrace incorporated into the understructure of the Victorian greenhouse. In the 1902 renovation, a new terrace was built on the east, based on the Latrobe-Jefferson design. The original walls of Jefferson's pavilion on the west were repaired and strengthened and were incorporated into the new terrace. Thus, terraces and other elements of the White House form a living link with the building's past.

B. Brown, Dee. *Bury My Heart at Wounded Knee: An Indian History of the American West.* New York: Bantam, 1973. [The paragraphs are from page 38.]

> Almost a thousand miles north of the Navaho country and at this same time of the white men's great Civil War, the Santee Sioux

were losing their homeland forever. The Santees were of four divisions—the Mdewkantons, Wahpetons, Wahpekutes, and Sissetons. They were woodland Sioux but kept close ties and shared a strong tribal pride with their blood brothers of the prairies, the Yanktons and the Tetons. The Santees were the "people of the farther end," the frontier guardians of the Sioux domain.

During the ten years preceding the Civil War, more than 150,000 white settlers pushed into Santee country, thus collapsing the left flank of the once "permanent Indian frontier." As the result of two deceptive treaties, the woodland Sioux surrendered nine-tenths of their land and were crowded into a narrow strip of territory along the Minnesota River. From the beginning, agents and traders had hovered around them like buzzards around the carcasses of slaughtered buffalo, systematically cheating them out of the greater part of the promised annuities for which they had been persuaded to give up their lands.

C. Buckley, Tom. "The Discovery of Tutankhamun's Tomb." *Treasures of Tutankhamun.* New York: The Metropolitan Museum of Art, 1976. [The paragraphs are from page 11.]

Tutankhamun, it appears, ascended the throne at the age of nine or thereabouts in about 1334 B.C., during the Eighteenth Dynasty. His parentage is uncertain, but it is known that he was married while still a child to Ankhesenamun, the third daughter of the famous Nafertiti.

The reign of Tutankhamun lasted only about nine years. It was a period of economic prosperity but of some religious confusion. Tutankhamun had been named Tutankhaton at birth, the last part of his name being a sign of his family's devotion to Aton, the solar disk. During his reign the priestly orders of the kingdom, which still yielded greatest reverence to Amun, "the hidden one," were able to wield enough influence to have the young king change his religious alliance. Tutankhamun died when he was eighteen or nineteen; the cause of his death is unknown.

56 Organization

The basic patterns of organization for a research paper should resemble patterns used for other papers (see Outlining, **1f**). Comparison and contrast, cause and effect, process, classification, and definition are all suitable patterns for research papers. Although the topic, thesis statement, and source material will usually determine which organization will work best, keep an open mind and consider several alternatives.

56a Reassess your source materials.

Before organizing your research paper, review your materials, reconsider your working thesis statement, and group your notes by categories. Rereading all notes is time consuming, but it is still a useful strategy. Rereading will refresh your memory and help you see the range of your materials. Next, reconsider your thesis statement and rewrite it if you need to, so that it presents a valid point. Then, with the revised thesis statement in mind, think about an organizational plan for your paper.

56b Divide your materials into subject groupings.

Go someplace where you can spread out—a large table in the library, the floor in your family room, the bed in your room —and begin to divide your materials according to major topics that might be treated in your paper.

First, stack your note cards into separate but major subject groups, using label cards to help you keep the stacks distinct. For instance, a biographical paper about Norman Rockwell might include stacks of cards relating to "childhood," "adolescence," and "adulthood." A problem/solution paper on industrial pollution might include a stack of cards with information to describe the problem and then other stacks of cards with information about alternative solutions. Almost any kind of topic might require supplying historical background or defining the topic, so some cards might be divided into those subjects.

This organizational stage will seem somewhat chaotic because you will be analyzing notes, sorting them, stacking cards, reconsidering where notes might fit, moving them, and perhaps moving them again. Work flexibly and allow yourself plenty of time to sort and perhaps re-sort materials. If a piece of information (or quotation or paraphrase) might feasibly fit in several groups, complete a card noting "See Parker quotation, p. 219 —in *childhood*" to refer you to a card in another group. You should also expect to have a stack of miscellaneous notes, ones that do not logically fit into a major group. Label them as such and keep them for possible use in the paper itself or in the introductory or concluding paragraphs. Then use large paper clips, clamps, or labeled envelopes to keep materials separated.

Sometimes you will group materials easily, and then you can consider yourself lucky. More often, however, you will arrange and rearrange your materials for hours before you are satisfied with them. Remember, though, that this first stage of organization is important because your groupings develop from the materials themselves and indicate the direction the paper will logically take.

56c Prepare a working, skeletal outline for your paper.

A skeletal outline should include the major divisions of the paper but not the specific arrangement of each part. In fact, at this stage of planning, becoming concerned with the exact arrangement of smaller sections will be counterproductive. After all, you might change a larger organizational pattern and then make your detailed work useless. To save time and energy, arrange large blocks of your paper first.

Examine your subject groupings and let the materials themselves help you decide on a suitable arrangement. What group is largest? That might be worth saving till last in the paper. What group is small? That might need to be dropped. Work *from the materials* to develop a skeletal outline. Never impose an outline that does not logically fit the materials you have gathered. Also consider completing several possible plans and then selecting the best one.

Yasuko, for instance, prepared this skeletal outline for her paper on American treatment of Japanese Americans:

Introductory Paragraph/Thesis statement

—Early immigration: 1866–1908

—Japanese American success in the United States

—7 December 1941: Pearl Harbor

—American reactions

—Relocation camps

—Legal issues involved

Concluding Paragraph/What we have learned

At this stage of planning, Yasuko was not worried about details—for instance, deciding how to present the early laws or how to arrange her discussion of the relocation camps. Instead, she was making more general decisions: Should the paper be developed chronologically? Should the discussion of legal issues come first or last? Should she explain early immigration or Japanese American success in the United States? These were the major discussions that would determine what materials she would use in the paper and in what order she would present them.

Your skeletal outline will be brief, but in completing it you will make decisions that will affect the way your paper takes shape. Remember especially that the skeletal outline is only a plan, even though it is an important plan. You may still need to modify it or change it completely during your later work on the paper.

56d Prepare a detailed outline.

Having decided on the arrangement of the large sections of the paper, organize the material within the sections. Work on one section at a time to develop the specific framework for the whole paper. (At this stage, formal outlining is useful.)

For example, Yasuko began her detailed outline in this way. (A complete outline appears with the sample paper, pages **544–549**.)

Introduction

Thesis Statement: The harsh treatment of Japanese Americans during World War II was not a sudden reaction to the bombing of Pearl Harbor but was instead based on long-developing resentment.

  I. Early immigration by Japanese was slight but steady (1866–1908).

    A. Immigration patterns

        1. 1866–1885

        2. 1866

        3. 1908

    B. General American reactions

II. Early laws were directed against Japanese Americans.

    A. 1905: municipal laws

    B. 1906: San Francisco school laws

    C. 1906: Japanese and Korean Exclusion League

    D. 1907: "Gentlemen's Agreement"

    E. 1913: Webb-Heney Act

    F. 1924: Immigration Act

III. Throughout this early period, Japanese Americans were productive citizens. . . .

Yasuko began making detailed structural decisions at this point, establishing a chronological arrangement for immigration patterns and laws, rather than clustering such discussions by similarities between the actions. You, too, will need to make detailed plans before you begin to write your paper. Remember, though, that these specific plans may also need to be changed as you write. But never begin writing a long and complex paper without a clear, detailed outline.

57 Writing the Rough Draft

After weeks of gathering materials and perhaps days of organizing it, writing the rough draft of a research paper may seem a major step. It is. It is also an exciting step, because at this point your information and ideas are ready to come together to form a clear and convincing paper.

As you write, remember the purpose of the research paper: to present your views, based on outside reading and personal interpretation, on a subject—not just to show that you collected and compiled what others have said about the subject. Besides demonstrating that you can gather materials and manage the mechanics of documentation, you are showing that you can reach valid conclusions of your own. Be a part of your own paper, adding comments on some sources and disagreeing with others, when necessary. Do not be a stenographer. Be a thinker and a writer.

57a Give yourself ample time to write.

Perhaps the biggest mistake writers make is putting off writing the paper—stalling until the last few days before the deadline for submission. Such delays create unnecessary pressures during the process of writing and reduce the time available for careful evaluation, revision, and typing. To avoid such problems, begin writing early, write a portion of the paper each day, and avoid the pressures of writing with time against you.

57b Work on individual sections, not necessarily in order.

Writing a research paper is a complex task. To simplify a difficult process, write the easiest sections first. Doing that will give you helpful momentum. For instance, a background paragraph that requires little original insight may be easy to write, or a paragraph that presents an extended example may be a good place to begin. Work as best you can—in any order—and note new ideas that occur to you as you write. Do not lock yourself into a strict writing pattern that progresses paragraph by paragraph, following the outline.

57c Incorporate facts that support your statements or provide needed background.

Facts are probably the easiest kind of researched material to include, because such information easily fits into your own sentences. Remember to use a note with each sentence containing unique facts, to show that they come from outside sources. Be aware, though, that information that is common knowledge does not require notation. For instance, almost everyone knows that Edison invented the light bulb and the phonograph. Such facts, therefore, need no documentation. Generally, if a fact appears in more than two sources, consider it common knowledge. When facts are not common knowledge, place a parenthetical note at the end of the sentence, as described in **54c**.

Since it is sometimes confusing when a sentence contains two references, avoid placing two facts from separate sources in the same sentence. Instead, write two sentences and then assign them different references.

57d Incorporate quotations that clearly and effectively present ideas.

Incorporating quoted material requires skill because quotations must fit smoothly into sentences and paragraphs, and note references must be clear. It is very important that quotations be used selectively to add clarity and emphasis to a research paper, not to pad the paper's length. Overquoting seriously detracts from a paper. Worse, overquoting of weak sources suggests that the writer has not evaluated materials effectively. Even if quotations are good ones, too many will break the flow of paragraphs and suggest that the writer has depended too heavily on other people's ideas. Therefore, reserve quotations for special times when no other material will work as well.

When quotations will help clarify a part of a paper, use a variety of strategies to incorporate them.

Brief quotations

Include short quotations—ones that take fewer than four typed lines or approximately forty-five words—within a normal paragraph by inserting quotation marks. The Gould sample used earlier in the section could be incorporated this way:

> Binet's IQ test has been under attack for decades. Yet many of the most vocal critics have not objectively considered Binet's intended use for the test. According to Stephen Jay Gould, in *The Mismeasure of Man,* Binet designed his test "as a practical guide for identifying children whose poor performance indicated a need for special education" (152). If critics of the Binet test would consider. . . . *(The Gould quotation used in this example, and in the following ones, is a partial quotation from the note card. Ellipsis points could be inserted after* education *but before the closing quotation marks; the period, as end punctuation, would still follow the parenthetical note.)*

To give research papers the variety they need, also consider incorporating quoted material in other ways—placing references at the end of the quoted material or, if possible, in the middle. The same quotation, for variety, could be presented in the following ways:

> Binet's IQ test has been under attack for decades. Yet many of the most vocal critics have not objectively considered Binet's intended use for the test. "He devised his scale . . . as a practical guide for identifying children whose poor performance indicated a need for special education," explains Stephen Jay Gould in *The Mismeasure of Man* (152). If critics of the Binet test would consider. . . .

Or:

> Binet's IQ test has been under attack for decades. Yet many of the most vocal critics have not objectively considered Binet's intended use for the test. "He devised his scale," Stephen Jay Gould em-

phasizes in *The Mismeasure of Man,* "as a practical guide for identifying children whose poor performance indicated a need for special education" (152). If critics of the Binet test would consider. . . .

These methods allow you to incorporate quotations in varied ways. Notice that they provide the same information—only changing the placement of the information about the source—and notice that the parenthetical note still comes at the end of the *sentence,* even when that is not the end of the quotation.

Brief verse quotations in your own paragraph

Including brief quotations from poetry requires some special attention to form. If the verse quotation runs fewer than four lines, it should be incorporated in your own paragraph, rather than indented. The quotation is enclosed with quotation marks, and the line divisions of the poem are indicated with a slash (/), with spaces before and after. Maintain the poem's pattern of capitalization as well. The following example illustrates how these issues are handled:

Tennyson again stresses Ulysses' youthful longing for unreachable goals, even as he grows older: "And this gray spirit yearning in desire / To follow knowledge like a sinking star, / Beyond the utmost bound of human thought" (137–138). The word choices clarify the dichotomy between Ulysses' youthful spirit and his aging body. . . .

Quoted material in your own sentence structure

To incorporate brief quoted material, especially a few words or a part of a sentence, make the quotation part of your own sentence structure. Although this passage relies on the same quotation as the preceding ones, notice how it uses only part of the quotation:

> Binet's IQ test has been under attack for decades. Yet many of the most vocal critics have not objectively considered Binet's original use for the test. Stephen Jay Gould, in his book *The Mismeasure of Man*, stresses that Binet's primary purpose was to separate "children whose poor performance indicated a need for special education" (152). If critics of the Binet test would consider. . . .

In this case, Gould's comments play an integral part in the sentence structure and, as a result, no comma is needed to begin the quoted material. A comma would not come between *separate* and *children* in your own sentence, so do not use one here.

Long quotations

To incorporate lengthy quoted material (more than four typed lines or forty-five words), set the quotation off from the body of the paragraph by indenting it. Set-in quotations are double-spaced like the rest of the paper, are indented ten spaces, and do not require quotation marks. A colon normally introduces long passages, but other punctuation may be used if it is required by the context of the introductory sentence. If the entire passage copied on the note card on page **473** were used in a paper, the form would look like this:

> Binet's IQ test has been under attack for decades. Yet many of the most vocal critics have not objectively considered Binet's intended use for the test. As Stephen Jay Gould clarifies in *The Mismeasure of Man*:
>
> > Not only did Binet decline to label IQ as inborn intelligence; he also refused to regard it as a general device

for ranking all pupils according to mental worth. He devised his scale only for the limited purpose of his commission by the ministry of education: as a practical guide for identifying children whose poor performance indicated a need for special education. (152)

If critics of the Binet test would consider. . . .

Long verse quotations

If you wish to include more than four lines of poetry in your paper, follow a pattern similar to that used for other long quotations: indent ten spaces, omit quotation marks, and double-space the lines. When poets use unusual spacing for their verse lines, approximate them in your quoted material. Lines that are indented in a poem, for instance, should be set in beyond the ten-space indention for the entire quotation; that means they may be indented fifteen to twenty spaces from the normal left margin to reproduce the form of the original poem, as in this sample:

The abusiveness of miserable parents is evident even in modern poetry. Robert Hayden, for instance, in a narrative poem titled "The Whipping," describes a scene that is painfully familiar to far too many children:

> The old woman across the way
>   is whipping the boy again
> and shouting to the neighborhood
>   her goodness and his wrongs.
>
> Wildly he crashes through elephant ears,
>   pleads in dusty zinnias,
> while she in spite of crippling fat
>   pursues and corners him. (120)

As in life, the pleading of the child does little to alter the adult's behavior.

Quotations that contain quotation marks

When quoting from a source that itself contains some material within quotation marks, punctuate carefully so that the use of quotation marks in both instances will be clear. Place the material you are quoting in standard quotation marks and change the source's punctuation to single quotation marks, as in this example:

> Gould explains Binet's IQ scoring this way: "The age associated with the last tasks he could perform became his 'mental age,' and his general intellectual level was calculated by subtracting this mental age from his true chronological age" (149–150).

Here, readers know that the entire sentence is quoted from Gould's book, and that Gould himself has used quotation marks with the term *mental age.*

Clarifying quoted material

If you must add material—words or phrases—to a quotation to make its meaning clear, use brackets to show that the addition is yours. For instance, in the last example, the reference *he* might confuse readers. A clarification in brackets would eliminate possible confusion:

> Gould explains Binet's IQ scoring this way: "The age associated with the last tasks [a schoolboy] could perform became his 'mental age,' and his general intellectual level was calculated by subtracting this mental age from his true chronological age" (149–150).

The information in brackets can completely substitute for the original word or words, as in the case above, or it can follow the original material in the quotation. If your typewriter or word processor does not have brackets, add them neatly by hand. Remember, though, that a quotation that requires extensive use of bracketed information is probably not a good one to use. (See Brackets, **37b.**)

Omitting part of a long quotation

When you have recorded a long quotation in your notes but only want to include part of it, use ellipsis points (three spaced periods) to show that some of the quotation has been omitted. If the omission comes in the middle of a sentence, the three ellipsis points are all that is needed. If the omission comes at the end of a sentence, however, a fourth period (the end punctuation) is needed. The ellipsis points are separated from it by a space—creating four spaced periods, the first one immediately following the last letter of the last word.

> Gould notes: "[Binet] devised his scale . . . as a practical guide for identifying children whose poor performances indicated a need for special education" (152).

Be especially careful that omissions do not distort a quotation's meaning (see Ellipsis Points, **38a**).

Introducing a quotation

One last note about quotations: always provide sufficient information to introduce a quotation and provide some comment of your own. Never "float" a quotation and expect readers to know automatically why it was worth quoting. The previous samples illustrate one workable pattern for introducing a quotation: mention the person who made the statement, identify where the comment was made (book, article, interview, and so on) unless it is already clear from previous discussion, and explain the quotation's relevance to the discussion. Primarily, keep readers apprised of who said what. Readers appreciate the clarity of this format and have less trouble following a discussion.

57e Incorporate paraphrased material when you want to stress someone else's idea but want to present it in your own words.

If you have put a source's ideas into your own words during note taking, then incorporating those ideas should be fairly easy. Include the ideas in your sentences. The problem, however, is in placing the parenthetical reference. If the paraphrase appears in only one sentence, place the reference at the end. Writers often find, however, that they want to use a whole paragraph to paraphrase material—especially when background information is taken from a single source. In that case, the parenthetical reference appears at the end of the entire paragraph to cover all of the material included. To avoid confusing readers, who may assume that the note applies only to the ideas in the last sentence, emphasize the author and source of the ideas very clearly at the beginning of the paragraph and then end the paragraph with the parenthetical note. Using the paraphrased note from page **476**, this simple background paragraph could be presented:

> Stephen Jay Gould, in *The Mismeasure of Man*, provides a useful summary of Binet's position on IQ testing. According to Gould, Binet opposed theories that heredity set limits on a student's achievement. For him, a student's score on the test did not establish his worth as a student or as a person. Rather, Binet wanted to use IQ tests to pick out slow learners and help them through better planned and better focused education (152).

Although large blocks of paraphrased material will sometimes prove helpful when you must provide background information, use such paraphrased work sparingly. Excessive paraphrasing—especially blocked paraphrasing—may suggest that you have not synthesized material well enough or may imply that you have depended too heavily on a single source for the ideas in your paper. In short, use paraphrases, but use them selectively.

57f Give special attention to introductory and concluding paragraphs.

Ideas for introductory and concluding paragraphs may occur to you at any time during writing. You may, in fact, find yourself thinking about them and working on them during the entire course of writing your rough draft. Or an appropriate introductory or concluding format may come to you in a flash at some unexpected moment. Because these paragraphs serve important purposes in a paper, they should be carefully written. Consider several strategies for each kind of paragraph and select the ones most clearly matched to the tone and purpose of the entire paper (see Introductions and Conclusions, **1g**). Also revise your thesis statement one last time so that it clearly expresses the idea of your paper.

57g Arrange your works cited page.

Since the information for your works cited entries is written on note cards, this process will be easy. Separate the cards for sources *used in the paper* and alphabetize them. Double-check them, and then secure them with a paper clip or rubber band until you type the works cited page.

57h Revise your rough draft for content, style, and technical errors.

After writing the first draft of the paper, set it aside for as long as possible. Then reread it with a fresh outlook and a critical eye. Check the basic organization to make sure that it is logical. Make sure that you have incorporated facts, quotations, and paraphrases smoothly, completely, and accurately. Check sentences to make sure they are clear and well worded. Check punctuation and mechanics. Rework any part of the paper that does not seem sufficiently clear or well written and correct any technical errors (see Revision, **1i–1k**).

57i Evaluate your rough draft.

The following questions can help you test the quality of your rough draft. Use them yourself as a general guide, have a friend use them to evaluate your paper, or, better yet, have someone in your writing class use them to double-check the rough draft before preparing the final copy.

Introduction

1. Is the strategy a good one?
2. Does the paragraph suggest the pattern of organization? Does it need to?
3. Is the thesis statement clear?
4. Is the length balanced to the rest of the essay?
5. Is the title interesting and appropriate?

Organization

1. Is the organizational pattern well matched to the subject?
2. Are topics supported adequately?
3. Is background information well presented?
4. Do all discussions relate to the thesis statement?

Style

1. Are sentences clear and logical?
2. Are the sentences in the active voice when possible?
3. Are the sentence types varied?
4. Is the diction appropriate?
5. Is jargon explained? Is it kept to a minimum?

Content

1. Are sufficient facts used?
2. Are quotations well chosen?
3. Are paraphrases appropriately managed?
4. Is material from sources well incorporated?
5. Is the documentation correct?
6. Is the thesis statement clear throughout?
7. Is sufficient information provided?
8. Is the argument convincing?

Conclusion

1. Are the ideas drawn together?
2. Is an effective strategy used?
3. Is the final impression effective?

58 Final Stages

Preparing a final copy is an especially important stage in researched writing. Having spent a great deal of time thinking, reading, taking notes, rethinking, organizing, writing, and revising, you will not want to submit a badly typed or carelessly prepared final copy.

58a Make last-minute improvements before typing.

Before you begin typing, reread the rough draft one last time to make sure it needs no further revision. Reconsider the quality of the introduction, organization, style, content, and conclusion. If everything is satisfactory, type the final copy.

58b Review the guidelines for preparing a manuscript.

The manuscript format for the research paper varies only slightly from that for other papers (see Manuscript Form, **63**, or the sample research paper, pages **503–543**). The margins, the heading, and the paging are the same, and double-spacing is still required throughout the paper. Because the research paper has additional parts and because documentation complicates the typing process, however, allow yourself extra time to prepare the final copy. Whatever you do, do not assume that typing and proofreading a research paper is a one-night process. If you do, it will probably turn out to be an *all*-night process with a poor result.

58c Type the paper carefully.

Type the paper at an unhurried pace, proofreading for mistakes as you work, making as many corrections as possible on your typewriter or word processor. Keep the pages nearby so you can easily double-check them. When you begin to type the works cited page(s), work one card at a time, paying special attention to form.

Once the final copy is complete, proofread it carefully for typing errors and make any small corrections neatly in black ink. Check especially the use of parentheses, commas, colons, quotation marks, brackets, ellipsis points, and periods.

58d Submit the paper.

With the final proofreading done, take the manuscript to a copy shop and have at least one high-quality photocopy made of all the pages. This is your insurance against damage or loss. After getting a copy, submit the paper to your instructor. If he or she suggests a special way to protect the manuscript, follow those guidelines carefully. If your instructor suggests no special procedure, secure the pages with a paper clip (outline first, then text, and then works cited pages) and place them in a 9-by-12 manila envelope with the information from your paper heading typed on the outside. It *is* important to protect the manuscript.

With the research paper completed and submitted, you can breathe a sigh of relief, for you have completed probably the longest, most involved, and most important paper of the term. In completing that long paper, you have learned how to research, incorporate, and properly document information. Most importantly, you have learned a process for gathering information, insights, and ideas to supplement those of your own. That ability can be useful long after you leave college.

59 A Sample Student Paper

The following sample paper was written by a student in a freshman research class. Although it does not illustrate every feature of research presented in this unit, it does provide illustrations of most of the major issues of writing and documenting a paper based on outside sources.

59a The paper

1. The heading for the research paper is just like that for other papers: it includes the writer's name, course number, instructor's name, and the date. It is double-spaced and is placed within the normal 1-to-1½-inch margin.

2. Following four spaces, the title is centered. In this case, the title runs to a second line and both lines are centered. Notice, also, that the two-part title is separated by a colon. The first title is imaginative (to create interest), and the subtitle is descriptive (to clarify the topic). Four spaces separate the title from the first paragraph of the paper.

3. Yasuko introduces her paper with a long quotation, one over four typed lines. It is indented ten spaces (see **57d**).

4. With a set-in quotation, the parenthetical note follows the end punctuation.

5. In addition to using the quotation as an introductory strategy, Yasuko also uses a series of questions to gain her readers' attention. Use of multiple strategies is a good idea in a lengthy paper (see Introductions and Conclusions, **1g**).

1.   Yasuko Kawamura

English 105

Dr. Robert Perrin

2 May 1986

2.   Declining into Cruelty: The Treatment of Japanese

Immigrants in the United States

3.   The road was very muddy. On the way I saw

many people who had just come in. They were

all dressed in their best. Many of them had no

umbrellas and were soaking wet. Children and

babies were crying. Men were all carrying

heavy luggage, and the women had tears in

their eyes, making their way through the

4.   mud. . . . (McWilliams 197–198)

5.   Is this an account of Jewish prisoners entering

Dachau or Buchenwald? Is this a description of

citizens rounded up by the Khmer Rouge in Cambodia?

No, it is not. Instead, it is a description of what one

young Japanese American woman saw in 1942 as her

people were driven like cattle into the Tanforan Assembly

6. Second and subsequent pages are headed with the writer's last name and the appropriate page number, placed in the upper right hand corner but within standard margins.

7. To place her researched work in a general context, Yasuko discusses the slight attention her subject has received. This technique provides Yasuko with a smooth transition to her thesis statement, which ends the paragraph.

8. Yasuko's thesis statement is written in two sentences. The first sentence presents a general opinion, which her research proved invalid. Because it is a generally accepted view, however, it is important enough to repeat and serves as the qualification for her true thesis statement. Yasuko's statement of her topic and opinion are in the last sentence of the paragraph, and the use of *instead* emphasizes that her thesis statement counters the generally accepted view (see Working Thesis Statement, **1e**).

6.

Center in southern California. They were being
transferred by presidential order to "relocation" centers.

7.   Much has been written about the events that led to
the imprisonment of over 110,000 Japanese Americans
during World War II, and yet many Americans do not
know that it happened. Even in Japan, where we are
very interested in the lives of Japanese people in the
United States, we are not always told of this dark
chapter in American history. But why? Why are these
events so little noted in history classes? Why are they so
often ignored? As a Japanese student studying in
America, I have been driven to research this episode to
try to understand why it happened and to try to
understand its meaning. My reading has led me through
numerous accounts of the events and countless
explanations of the actions, but one thing seems clear.

8. The evacuation and internment of Japanese Americans
was not a sudden reaction to the bombing of Pearl
Harbor. Instead, it was an irrational and
unconstitutional reaction based on a developing
resentment of Japanese Americans that developed over a
period of sixty years.

9. This paragraph provides historical background and is used primarily to establish the context for Yasuko's later discussion. As a background paragraph, it needs little elaboration but still needs a strong grounding in facts. Facts taken from note cards like this one are simply incorporated in Yasuko's own sentences and then documented:

F
Kawakami
a. g. Relations
– 1866 –1885 : 446 immigrants to U.S.
– 1886 : 194 immigrants

pp. 286 - 287

Notice that the parenthetical documentation follows the sentence but precedes the end punctuation (see **54c**).

10. Specialized terms, like *Issei*, are defined when first used, to make sure the ideas of the paper are clear for readers who are nonspecialists. *Issei* is also italicized (underlined) in the paper because it is a foreign term (see **40c**).

9.   Japanese immigration to the United States began

slowly. Between 1866 and 1885, only 446 Japanese came

to the United States, a small number compared to the

immigration figures from other countries (Kawakami

286). In 1886, a year of some importance, 194 Japanese

came to America in hopes of a brighter future (Kawakami

287). Most of the immigrants settled in California,

although some settled in Oregon and Washington. During

the same period, from 1866 to 1886, a very large number

immigrated to Hawaii, which was not then a part of the

United States. The most important immigration year,

however, was 1908. In that year over nine thousand

Japanese men, women, and children came to the

continental United States, some from Japan and some

from Hawaii (Wilson and Hosokawa 125).

10.   During the time of this minimal but steady

immigration, first—generation Japanese, Issei, established

themselves in numerous lines of work—-farming, fishing,

business, and service professions. Many worked as

menial laborers, but a sizable number were professional

or skilled workers. In the same way that immigrants

11. A brief quotation (fewer than forty-five words) is incorporated directly in Yasuko's paragraph. What is important, she identifies the author and source as she introduces the quotation, to make readers aware of who made the comment and under what circumstances. Because Yasuko names the author in the sentence, she has to include only a page citation in the parenthetical note (see **54b**).

12. Yasuko comments on the content of the quotation in a followup sentence, showing how it helped clarify the idea she wants to stress. It is very important that she does not simply use the quotation and expect readers to make the needed connections.

13. Following her brief explanation of immigration patterns and the social conditions of Japanese Americans, Yasuko begins to present the evidence to support her thesis statement: negative reactions to Japanese Americans had a long tradition in the United States. She presents a clear, chronological discussion of laws and agreements.

from Europe lived in groups, the Japanese tended to cluster together in areas that were known as "Little Tokyos," but because of their race, they were more

11. easily distinguishable than other immigrant groups. As Carey McWilliams suggests in <u>Prejudice: Japanese–Americans</u>, "Concentration and visibility increased the prejudice against them and this prejudice, in turn,

12. increased [their] degree of concentration" (85). Easily separated from other Californians because of their appearance, language, and social patterns, the Japanese became easy targets for negative reactions. In addition, they worked longer hours, often for slightly lower pay, than white Americans, and created serious job competition for Americans and European immigrants.

13.   As a result, restrictive laws were introduced that consistently worked against Japanese Americans, suggesting some deep–seated hatred and fear of a people whom Americans seemed to misunderstand. As early as 1905, municipal laws in some cities in California prohibited marriages between the Japanese and people of other races or nationalities (McWilliams 79). The San

14. Yasuko incorporated information and a quotation from one source card but needed two notes to document what she included.

> 3/Q
> Kawakami
> A. J. Relations
> - December 23, 1906 / Japanese and Korean Exclusion League met
> - Mass meeting at Walton Hall, San Francisco
> - Demonstrated against Asians in the U.S.
> - O. A. Tveitmoe presided — and said:
>   "If Americans and Japanese married, the results would be a nation of gas-pipe thugs and human hyenas!"
>
> p. 303

In using information from the note card, Yasuko omitted the specific date and the name of the meeting hall, since they were not essential to her discussion. She documented the date of the meeting, however. Yasuko then introduced the quotation by mentioning who made the comment and under what circumstances. Notice, however, that the parenthetical note refers to the author of the book where Yasuko found the quotation, not the person quoted.

15. To achieve special emphasis, this summary is indented. The note, as with set-in quotations, follows the end punctuation.

Francisco School Board reacted more strongly on 11
October 1906 by ordering Japanese and Chinese students
to attend segregated "Oriental" schools (Kawakami 307).
The irony in this action was that out of roughly 25,000
students in San Francisco, only ninety–three were
Japanese (Petersen 41).

14.   In the same year, 1906, a group that called itself
the Japanese and Korean Exclusion League met in San
Francisco to demonstrate against Asians living in the
United States (Kawakami 303). The organizer, O. A.
Tveitmoe, said at the meeting, "If Americans and
Japanese married, the results would be a nation of
gas–pipe thugs and human hyenas!" (Kawakami 303).
His extremely negative comments clearly represented the
feeling of the group's members, for they introduced a
bill, through a California legislator, that would have set
up four limitations for Japanese Americans:

15.   1. Japanese Americans would be denied the right to
            own land.

        2. No Japanese Americans would be allowed to
            direct a corporation.

16. Yasuko provides a useful comment on the list of four limitations and supplies a logical transition to the next legal action she chooses to discuss.

17. *Gentlemen's Agreement* appears in quotation marks because that is the informal name of the pact Roosevelt and the Japanese agreed to honor.

18. Yasuko placed the word *undesirable* in quotation marks to stress its special sense in her discussion. She, of course, does not feel that Japanese immigrants were undesirable but wants to stress the feelings of most Americans in the early twentieth century.

    3. Japanese Americans would be segregated by law.

    4. Japanese Americans would be permanently labeled aliens and thereby would never be eligible for citizenship through naturalization. (Kawakami 329)

16.   Theodore Roosevelt and his advisors successfully prevented the bill from passing, but the negative reactions to Japanese Americans prevailed, and even Roosevelt himself was later responsible for limiting the numbers of Japanese allowed to come to America.

17.   In 1907, Roosevelt and the Japanese government approved what was known as the "Gentlemen's Agreement." This agreement, intended to pacify the labor unions in California and the Exclusion League, set quotas for the number of Japanese laborers who could come to the United States, although it did not affect the number of skilled laborers and professionals who could

18.   immigrate. The law was intended to exclude "undesirable" Japanese who competed directly with unskilled immigrants from other countries. An unintended but inevitable result was that the Japanese

19. This note refers to the work of three writers. According to standard conventions, all three authors' names must appear (see **54a**).

20. Once again, Yasuko defines a term not commonly known: *Nisei*. It is underlined because it is a foreign word (see **40c**).

who came to the United States were likely to succeed because of family background and training. This influx of highly skilled Japanese did little to ease the tension in California, however.

In 1913, for instance, the Webb–Heney Act, better known as the California Alien Land Law, barred "aliens
19. ineligible for citizenship" from owning land (tenBroek, Barnhart, and Matson 37). Since first–generation Japanese immigrants could not become citizens, they were not allowed to own land. The Japanese American Issei cleverly evaded this law by buying property in
20. their children's names. This was legal, since second–generation Japanese, Nisei, were native–born Americans and could therefore own land. However, circumventing an unfair law did not eliminate the animosity that had created the law in the first place.

Some years later, on 15 March 1924, Congress passed an immigration act that excluded from immigration any aliens who would, according to previous legislation, be ineligible for citizenship (McWilliams 67). The Supreme Court had ruled earlier that the

21. This paragraph serves to establish the financial success of Japanese immigrants in America. The paragraph stresses the irony of the situation, for usually those who succeed are accepted.

22. The quotation is introduced with the name of the writer, but the note directs readers' attention to the book where the comment appears. Brackets are used within the quotation to indicate Yasuko's substitution for an unclear phrase.

Q
Glaser and Possony
Victims

Chester Rowell (progressive journalist) said:
"Right or wrong, our people will not live with those of a physically different race except on the basis of that race's inferiority. Since the Japanese are [in some respects superior], there is friction"

p. 340

The phrase *our people* makes little sense out of context, so Yasuko substitutes more specific words, *white Americans*, that clarify the author's main idea.

Kawamura 8

Constitution allowed only for the naturalization of "free whites" and those of African ancestry, clearly indicating that Asians were ineligible for naturalized citizenship.

21.   In spite of these harsh, discriminatory laws, Japanese American immigrants prospered, mostly through diligence and skill. They often bought acreage that was thought undesirable and through careful work transformed it into vastly productive farmland. By 1941, for instance, Japanese Americans owned only 2.7 percent of all crop land in California, yet they produced between 50 and 90 percent of the crops of celery, peppers, strawberries, cucumbers, artichokes, cauliflower, spinach, and tomatoes (McWilliams 87). This must surely have upset the whites who had, for generations,

22. said the Japanese were inferior. Chester Rowell, a progressive journalist, commented:

> Right or wrong, [white Americans] will not live with those of a physically different race except on the basis of that race's inferiority. Since the Japanese are in some respects superior, there is friction. (Glaser and Possony 340)

23. Although this sentence contains a fact and a specific date, they are both so commonly known that they do not need to be documented.

24.

$\mathcal{F}$
Wilson and Hosokawa
East
December 8, 1941 (day after Pearl Harbor)
  – Funds of <u>Issei</u> were frozen
  – Creditors demanded immediate payment
  – Auto insurance policies canceled
  – Checks not honored

p. 189

Yasuko selectively used and arranged the information from her note card. She chose not to reiterate that 8 December 1941 was the day after Pearl Harbor, assuming that such information was already clear. In addition, she rearranged the four facts when she wrote her own sentence, to create her own order of importance.

As a result, Japanese success in America did not lead to acceptance. Perhaps it even fueled the resentment toward Japanese Americans.

23.   When the Japanese military attacked Pearl Harbor on 7 December 1941, Americans, and especially Californians, reacted strongly. Japanese immigrants, who had long been resented and suspected, became "the

24. enemy." Reactions were swift and devastating. On 8 December 1941, the funds of <u>Issei</u> were frozen in banks, creditors demanded immediate payment, checks were not honored, and even automobile insurance policies were canceled (Wilson and Hosokawa 189). On 11 December, four days after Pearl Harbor, the Western Defense Command declared the western coast a "theater of war" (Wilson and Hosokawa 191). That action authorized military search and seizure of property—and most of the property that was searched and seized was owned by Japanese Americans. Within weeks, the FBI had rounded up 3,600 enemy aliens, half of them Japanese Americans; of this large number, only one received a sentence—of two months—and that was for neglecting to register his business connections in the Orient (Petersen 67).

25. Yasuko again provides an evaluative comment of her own —based on general impressions found in all her sources— to stress her reaction to the factual information that was previously documented.

26. This paragraph summarizes general American reactions to Japanese Americans, providing a transitional assessment of immediate reactions after the bombing of Pearl Harbor. Because it contains commonly known information found in virtually all sources, no documentation is required.

Japanese houses were searched, and such everyday

items as flashlights and cameras were confiscated

25. (Petersen 67). While all this was going on, newspaper

headlines across America announced the FBI roundup of

the Japanese and searches of their homes, but few

newspapers explained later that no Japanese were found

guilty of espionage or sabotage.

26.   As the fires of anti–Japanese reaction raged, some

Japanese were dismissed from their jobs, while others

were evicted from their residences. Some grocery stores

and other businesses refused to sell goods to people of

Japanese ancestry. Government officials encouraged

Japanese Americans to relocate in other parts of the

country, but with their money frozen in banks, the

Japanese did not have the financial resources to move.

They remained in a state of limbo for months, knowing

that they were suspected of great crimes against the

nation and unable to convince most Americans of their

innocence.

          On 11 February 1942, Franklin Roosevelt agreed to

a military plan to evacuate Japanese Americans from the

27. To emphasize this series of proclamations, Yasuko used two forms of indention. The four proclamations are indented five spaces, and further description is set in another five spaces. This pattern makes this information visually distinct.

Kawamura 11

West Coast, and on 19 February 1942 he signed
Executive Order 9066, which gave the military "blank-
check" authority to carry out the plan (Wilson and
Hosokawa 194). Within a matter of weeks, military
actions began, best illustrated by a series of Public
Proclamations:

27.   Public Proclamation 1 (2 March 1942) designated
                the western halves of California, Oregon, and
                Washington and the southern half of Arizona
                as war zones.

        Public Proclamation 2 (16 March 1942) declared the
                rest of California, Oregon, Washington, and
                Arizona as war zones and added the states of
                Idaho, Montana, Nevada, and Utah as well.

        Public Proclamation 3 (24 March 1942) established a
                curfew between 8:00 P.M. and 6:00 A.M. for
                Japanese and limited their travel to five
                miles.

        Public Proclamation 4 (27 March 1942) stated that
                voluntary evacuation from these states was
                illegal. (Wilson and Hosokawa 205–207)

28. Once again, Yasuko offers a summary comment on the proclamations, showing that she has ideas of her own to share.

29. Here Yasuko begins her transition into the discussion of the actual evacuation to detention camps.

Kawamura 12

28. This series of orders was directed exclusively at the Japanese. German and Italian immigrants, even though their native countries were also at war with the United States, were not subject to the controls. The proclamations, in conjunction with earlier orders, left Japanese Americans in a no–win situation. Fred Korematsu, a <u>Nisei</u> who was picked up and jailed during the war, commented, "I was an American and I had as much rights as anyone else" (Maragolick 25). Unfortunately, for Japanese Americans, constitutional rights were not really considered. It was illegal for them to stay where they were, but it was also illegal for them to leave. Many were citizens of the United States, but they were denied citizens' rights. However, as Francis Biddle, the United States Attorney General during the war years, reflected in his memoirs, "The Constitution has never greatly bothered any wartime President" (Zich 526).

29.   In May 1942, Japanese Americans were forced to leave their homes and property to be relocated in what were euphemistically called "evaluation centers" They

30. In this paragraph, Yasuko provides a series of useful facts to establish the context of Japanese American internment.

were given only two days to dispose of their property
and allowed to take only what they could carry. Dorothy
Thomas and Richard Nishimoto described the situation
well in The Spoilage:

> [Japanese Americans could] either turn over
> their businesses to their creditors at great
> loss, or abandon [them] entirely, [while] the
> commercial buzzards [took] great advantage of
> the hardship, making offers way below even
> inventory cost, and very much below real
> value. (8)

The Federal Reserve Bank was later to estimate that $400
million worth of the evacuees' property was lost because
the government made no arrangements for its security
(Petersen 107). Quite obviously, losses of this magnitude
devastated the Japanese subeconomy of California.

30.   The emotional toll was equally high, because
Japanese Americans felt that they had done nothing
dishonorable or illegal. At the time of Pearl Harbor, 3,500
Japanese Americans, mostly Nisei, were in the armed
services (Wilson and Hosokawa 223). They were either

31.

F
Wilson and Hosokawa
East
Location of the camps:
— 1 in Utah   — 2 in Arkansas
— 2 in Arizona   — 1 in Idaho
— 1 in Colorado   — 2 in California
— 1 in Wyoming

p. 212

Because Yasuko is not emphasizing life in the camps—but is instead using the camps to illustrate the unfair treatment of Japanese Americans—the exact number of camps is unimportant. Consequently, Yasuko uses only a portion of the facts included on her note card.

perfunctorily discharged and then sent to relocation
centers, or they were put on permanent K.P. duty or
isolated in "Oriental" units assigned to unpleasant
duties. Of the 112,985 people of Japanese ancestry who
were eventually interned in camps, 60 percent were
<u>Nisei</u>, second–generation immigrants, and <u>Sansei</u>,
third–generation immigrants—all of whom were
American citizens (Peck 910). Of these, approximately
40,000 were under the age of fifteen (Wilson and
Hosokawa 210). That these people were stunned,
shocked, offended, and distressed comes as no surprise
today. One <u>Nisei</u> recalls that he was against the
evacuation policy at first but that he came to think it
would be better for his aged parents to go to an
internment camp and live with their friends than to live
in such a hostile community (Thomas 250). However,
he, and others who agreed with his views on the
evacuation, had not yet known the harsh realities of the
camps.

31.   The camps were located in seven states: Arizona,
Arkansas, California, Colorado, Idaho, Utah, and Wyoming

32. Having visited several of the camps, Yasuko chooses to incorporate details from her own experiences. Such discussion of personal experiences should not dominate a research paper, but selective use of first-hand information can provide interest and immediacy in a discussion.

(Wilson and Hosokawa 212). They were federally owned, self-contained, semipermanent, surrounded by barbed-wire fences, and guarded by the military (Wilson and Hosokawa 211). Each family group was assigned to a barely furnished, 20-by-25-foot "apartment" in a makeshift barracks (Thomas and Nishimoto 109). Although the government allotted 45 cents a day per person for food, usually less was spent. At the Tule Lake Camp, for instance, only 27 cents was spent per person, making the quality and quantity of food below acceptable standards (Thomas and Nishimoto 109).

32.   I have visited several of these campsites since I have been in the United States, and they are extremely desolate. I saw few plants and animals. During the days, it was uncomfortably hot, and, I was told, during the nights it was severely cold. With desert as far as I could see, I imagined the hopelessness of the people who were forced to live in such an environment--the last place where innocent people should spend an average of two and a half years of their lives (Zich 512). It was disgraceful that political and military codes had justified

33. These sentences deemphasize the experience in the camps and again redirect readers' attention to the overall issue of how Americans singled out Japanese Americans for severe treatment.

34. Again, Yasuko introduces the quotation by naming the person and circumstance but documents the quotation using the source where she found the comment.

Kawamura 16

such treatment. As Galden Fisher asked in a 1943 article in <u>Christian Century</u>, "How is that different from the Nazi race laws?" (984).

33. The time Japanese Americans spent in the camps is well chronicled, and some have suggested that their treatment was not that bad. But a basic question remains: Why the Japanese? In part, of course, the American government was giving vent to the country's hostility toward the Japanese nation for the attack on Pearl Harbor. Yet it goes beyond that, for American

34. reactions to the Japanese had long been negative. Even General John L. DeWitt, the Commander of the Western Defense Command, who orchestrated the evacuation, commented in this way as he explained the relocation project: "The Japanese were a mass conspicuous racial group who were tightly knit, culturally unassimilated, and socially isolated" (Kachi 318). Without admitting to a charge of racism, DeWitt as much as said that the Japanese were an easy target because they were easily identified.

35.

Q
Beck
Constitution
Amendment V:
"No person shall be held to answer for a capital, or otherwise
infamous crime, unless on a presentment or indictment
of a grand jury, except in cases arising in the land
or naval forces, or in the militia, when in actual
service in time of war or public danger; nor shall any
person be subject for the same offense to be twice put in
jeopardy of life or limb; nor shall be compelled in any
criminal case to be a witness against himself, nor
be deprived of life, liberty, or property, without due
process of law; nor shall private property be taken for
public use without just compensation."

p. 296

The use of ellipsis marks in the quotation eliminates a large
segment of the Amendment and highlights the portion that
suits the context of the paper (see Ellipsis Points, **38a**, and
57d).

36. This paragraph summarizes the major issues in the paper.
The third sentence effectively, briefly, and specifically
notes the major examples used in the paper.

35.   Amendment V of the Constitution declares: "No person shall be . . . deprived of life, liberty, or property, without due process of law" (Beck 296). The Constitution makes no exception on account of race. Yet because of their race, Japanese Americans were clearly and systematically denied their liberty and property. It is sadly ironic, then, that the Supreme Court and the president justified racism in the United States while Americans were fighting Hitler's racism in Europe (Conroy 199).

36.   The events that led up to the evacuation and internment of Japanese Americans are surely unfortunate. Systematically, Americans sought to isolate and denigrate those of Japanese ancestry. The series of agreements, quotas, bills, executive orders, and proclamations makes that clear. Ultimately, however, it was the internment of Japanese Americans in "concentration camps" that brought the greatest shame to America. As Jacobus tenBroek, Edward Barnhart, and Floyd Matson note: "The Japanese American episode of World War II looms as a great and evil blotch upon our national history" (325).

37. Yasuko uses this paragraph to provide a transition out of the paper, talking about the positive changes that have taken place. The paragraph includes selected facts to illustrate this point.

38. Yasuko uses a challenge as one concluding strategy—asking readers to consider these issues completely and honestly. Her final strategy is a quotation that highlights the desperation that can be prevented (see Introductions and Conclusions, **1g**).

37. With that kind of recognition, however, America has gone some way in rectifying the wrongs of earlier times. Legally segregated residential areas are now a thing of the past, and marriages between Caucasians and Asians are now common. During the 1950's, 2,600 cases were settled that returned to Japanese Americans some of their property losses——in the sum of $38 million (Wilson and Hosokawa 266). Although that amounted to only 10 cents for every dollar lost, it was an attempt to right the wrongs of the past——albeit in a small way. Additionally, in 1952, Congress passed the Nationality Act, which made it possible for <u>Issei</u> to become naturalized citizens (Kachi 322–323).

38. It is important now that people of a new generation learn about these unfortunate events. We must examine these episodes in American history——episodes of long-standing prejudice and harsh reactions——without masking the truth or reaching false conclusions. Events like these do not happen as the result of a single action but are more often the result of a series of small but meaningful reactions. If people——Americans, Japanese,

and others——are more aware of how our treatment of

people can decline into cruelty, perhaps we will not

repeat the mistakes of World War II. Perhaps then we

will not force new victims of prejudice to repeat the

questions and comments of Kiyoshi Hamanaka:

> Why, why did it have to be me? What did I do
>
> to deserve this? What rhyme or reason is
>
> there? I don't know why. . . . I guess I'll never
>
> know all the reasons, all the causes.
>
> (McWilliams 199)

39. Even the works cited page (or pages) requires a paged heading.

40. The heading is centered and specifically indicates that the sources that follow it are used (cited) in the paper itself. (A works consulted page would include not only the sources cited in the paper itself but also any sources read during the process of research.)

41. The list of sources (either cited or consulted) is alphabetized by the first word of each entry, excluding *a, an,* and *the.* Each entry provides complete information and follows exact patterns of punctuation (see Documentation, **52**). Notice that the first line of each entry begins at the normal left margin but that second and subsequent lines are indented five spaces. Also notice that the entire list is double-spaced.

39.

40.   Works Cited

41. Beck, James M. The Constitution of the United States.

New York: Doubleday, 1941.

Conroy, Hilary. "Justice at War: The Story of the

Japanese American Internment Cases." The Annals

of the American Academy of Political and Social

Sciences Sept. 1984: 199–200.

Fisher, Galen M. "Are the Evacuees Being Coddled?"

Christian Century 1 Sept. 1943: 984.

Glaser, Kurt, and Stefan T. Possony. Victims of Politics:

The State of Human Rights. New York: Columbia UP,

1979.

Kachi, Akiko. "The Japanese–Americans: The History

and Culture." The Unity in the Diversity. Ed.

Hidetoshi Kato. American Culture Series 4. Tokyo:

Ministry of Finance, 1970. 287–327.

Kawakami, Kiyoshi K. American–Japanese Relations: An

Inside View of Japan's Policies and Purposes. New

York: Rowell, 1912.

Kawamura 21

Maragolick, David. "Legal Legend Urges Victims to Speak

Out." New York Times 24 Nov. 1984: L 25–26.

McWilliams, Carey. Prejudice: Japanese–Americans:

Symbol of Racial Intolerance. Boston: Little, 1944.

Peck, J. Richard. "Seeking Justice for Japanese–

Americans." Christian Century 4 Oct. 1978: 910.

Petersen, William. Japanese–Americans: Oppression and

Success. New York: Random, 1971.

tenBroek, Jacobus, Edward N. Barnhart, and Floyd W.

Matson. Prejudice, War and the Constitution.

Berkeley: U of California P, 1968.

Thomas, Dorothy Swaine, and Richard S. Nishimoto. The

Spoilage. Berkeley: U of California P, 1946.

Wilson, Robert A., and Bill Hosokawa. East to America: A

History of the Japanese in the United States. New

York: Morrow, 1980.

Zich, Arthur. "Japanese Americans: Home at Last."

National Geographic Apr. 1986: 512–538.

59b An optional outline

Not all instructors will expect an outline with the final copy of the research paper, but some will. On those occasions when you must submit an outline, place it at the beginning of the paper.

Examine the following sample, which might have accompanied the paper presented in **59a**. These features of the outline are of special importance:

1. A standard heading is provided, with the student's name, course, instructor's name, and the date.
2. The full title of the paper is used.
3. The introduction and conclusion are separated from the body of the paper, without Roman numerals.
4. The full thesis statement is presented.
5. A traditional outline form is used, with Roman numerals indicating major divisions of the paper and capital letters, Arabic numerals, and lower-case letters indicating subdivisions of main ideas.
6. Roman numeral divisions are presented in sentence form, with subdivisions presented in topic-outline form.

The most important thing to remember is that an outline presented with a research paper serves as a "table of contents," clearly and completely describing the information presented in the paper itself. (See also Outlining, **1f.**)

Yasuko Kawamura

English 105

Dr. Robert Perrin

2 May 1986

Declining into Cruelty: The Treatment of Japanese

Immigrants in the United States

INTRODUCTION

Thesis statement: The harsh treatment of Japanese

Americans during World War II was not a sudden reaction

to the bombing of Pearl Harbor but was instead based on

long-developing resentment.

   I. Early immigration by Japanese was slight but

      steady (1866–1908).

     A. Immigration patterns

        1. 1866–1885

        2. 1886

        3. 1908

     B. General American reactions

  II. Early laws were directed against Japanese

      Americans.

     A. 1905: municipal laws

   B. 1906: San Francisco school laws

   C. 1906: Japanese and Korean Exclusion League

   D. 1907: "Gentlemen's Agreement"

   E. 1913: Webb-Heney Act

   F. 1924: Immigration Act

III. Throughout this early period, Japanese Americans were productive citizens.

   A. Farmland

   B. Crop production

IV. Immediately following the bombing of Pearl Harbor (7 December 1941), Japanese Americans were treated harshly.

   A. Community reactions

      1. Banks

      2. Other businesses

   B. Military reactions

      1. Searched and seized property

      2. Rounded up suspected aliens

   C. Newspaper accounts

   D. Later reactions

      1. Businesses

      2. Government agencies

3. Banks

V. Executive Order 9066, issued 19 February 1942, began the devastating discrimination against Japanese Americans.

A. Evacuate Japanese Americans from the western United States

B. Complete freedom for the military

C. A series of Public Proclamations

1. Public Proclamation 1—established war zones in western halves of some states.

a. California

b. Oregon

c. Washington

d. Arizona

2. Public Proclamation 2—established war zones in all parts of those states, plus others

3. Public Proclamation 3—restricted Japanese American lifestyle

a. 8:00 P.M.–6:00 A.M. curfew

b. 5–mile limit on travel

4. Public Proclamation 4—said evacuation to other states was illegal

VI. The military evacuation of Japanese Americans

begin in May 1942.

   A. Two–day notice

   B. Property lost through quick sale

   C. Additional discrimination

VII. The camps were bleak and desolate places.

   A. Located in seven states

      1. Arizona

      2. Arkansas

      3. California

      4. Colorado

      5. Idaho

      6. Utah

      7. Wyoming

   B. Conditions

      1. Facilities

      2. Food

      3. Location

VIII. Constitutional issues were ignored when the

military evacuated Japanese Americans to detention

camps.

   A. Race conspicuousness

B. Amendment V of the Constitution—due process
     of law

IX. Efforts to rectify the wrongs were insufficient and
      too late, but at least something was done.

A. Financial restitution

1. 2,600 cases handled

2. Ten cents per dollar lost

B. Nationality Act

1. 1952

2. Issei became nationalized citizens

CONCLUSION

WORKS CITED

60 APA Style

In some fields—for instance, the social sciences, education,
community health, and criminology—writers are expected to
document their work according to the formats outlined in the
Publication Manual of the American Psychological Association,
3rd ed. (Washington: APA, 1984).

APA style is similar to MLA style (presented in the main
portion of the book) in a few key ways: both style manuals
stress brevity in presenting information, parenthetical citations
of sources, and limited use of footnotes and appended materials. Nevertheless, there are important differences in the
organization of manuscripts and in specific kinds of notes,

reflecting the different kinds of work that naturally emerge in different fields.

MLA	APA
No title page (heading and title appear on the first page of the text)	*Separate title page* (includes descriptive title, author's name and affiliation, and a shortened title [running head for later pages] at the bottom)
No Abstract	*Abstract* (a 75–100-word paragraph describing the major ideas in the paper; follows the title page)
Introduction (a discursive paragraph or series of paragraphs used to establish interest and present the major idea of the paper)	*Introduction* (a specialized paragraph or series of paragraphs that defines the problem to be discussed; presents the hypothesis [main idea], explains the plan of the study, and presents its implications)
Body (a series of logically connected paragraphs that illustrate, describe, or discuss the main idea; may be arranged according to a wide range of plans: topical, chronological, problem/solution, cause/effect, comparison/contrast, and others)	*Body* (a series of paragraphs, in required order, that tells how the study was conducted, summarizes the data gathered and the way it was organized, and presents an evaluation and interpretation of the findings)
Works Cited (the MLA name for the list of sources)	*References* (the APA name for the list of sources)

MLA	APA
Appendix (seldom included)	*Appendix* (sometimes included when related materials—charts, graphs, illustrations, and so on—cannot be incorporated in the paper itself)

Beyond these basic organizational differences are variations in the presentation of the manuscript itself.

MLA	APA
Type (any standard type style, typewriter or printer)	*Type* (any standard type style; dot matrix without descending letters is unacceptable)
Margins (wide, at least 1 to 1½ inches)	*Margins* (1½-inch margins expected)
Paging (last name and page number in the upper right corner, ½ inch from top)	*Paging* (short title in the upper right corner; under that, page number; author's name omitted)
Headings in the text (not recommended except for extremely lengthy papers)	*Headings* (recommended for major divisions of the manuscript)
Corrections (neat, preferably typed)	*Corrections* (typed corrections only)

In addition to these variations in organization and presentation of the manuscript are important differences in the way citations are presented in the list of sources and in the text itself. The following APA models will give you some idea of how the style differs from MLA style; comments will stress the differences, and page citations will direct you to comparable MLA forms in the main discussion.

References to works cited in the text

A Book by a Single Author

Corbett, Edward. (1971). *Classical rhetoric for the modern student.* New York: Oxford UP.

- The publication date appears in parentheses immediately following the author's name. A period follows the closing parenthesis.

- Only the first word of a title is capitalized, unless a word is a proper noun.

- See MLA form, page **448.**

A Book with Multiple Authors

Vidich, Arthur J., & Bensman, Joseph. (1968). *Small town in mass society: Class, power and religion in a rural community.* Princeton: Princeton UP.

- All authors' names are inverted, not just the first.

- An ampersand (the *and* sign) is used to join the names.

- A capital letter begins the first word of a subtitle.

- See MLA form, pages **448–449.**

A Work in a Collection by Different Authors

Shaw, George Bernard. (1964). The technical novelty in Ibsen's plays. In Morris Freedman (Ed.), *Essays in modern drama* (pp. 9–18).

- The title of the short work is not punctuated.

- *In* is used to stress where the short work appears.

- The editor of the collection is listed before the title of the complete work. The abbreviation for editor is capitalized and placed in parentheses, followed by a comma.

- Inclusive pages for the short work are included in parentheses, using an abbreviation for *pages.*

- See MLA form, page **450.**

An Article in a Journal with Separate Paging in Each Issue

Sills, Toni. (1981). Socrates was executed for being innovative. *English Journal, 70* (7), 41–42.

- The journal title is italicized, as is the volume number. An unitalicized comma separates them, however.

- The issue number appears in parentheses, followed by a comma.

- Pages for articles are listed without a page abbreviation.

- See MLA form, page **454.**

An Article in a Monthly Magazine

Angier, Natalie. (1981, November). How fast? How high? How far? *Discover,* pp. 24–30.

- The year of publication is followed by a comma and the month of publication. Both are placed in parentheses.

- Page abbreviation is used.

- See MLA form, page **454.**

An Article in a Newspaper

Oppenheim, Carol. (1982, March 19). San Francisco transit running in the red. *Chicago Tribune,* p. 4.

- The day follows the month in the parenthetical information.

- Information on edition or section is not provided.

- See MLA form, pages **454–455.**

A Lecture or Speech

Brent, Harry. (1981, November 21). *Teaching composition theory in the People's Republic of China.* Paper presented at the meeting of the National Council of Teachers of English, Boston, MA.

- The title of the speech is italicized.
- The explanation, following the title, names the organization, the city, and the state—with all elements separated by commas.
- See MLA form, pages **455–456.**

A Film

Fosse, Bob (Director). (1972). *Cabaret* [Film]. Los Angeles: Allied Artists.

- Director (or producer) is written in full form and placed in parentheses following the person's name.
- The kind of medium (film, filmstrip, slide show, tape recording) is listed in brackets following the title.
- The name of the city precedes that of the production company.
- No mention is made of actors.
- See MLA form, page **456.**

References within the text

One Author

Greybowski (1985) noted that . . .

or

In a recent study at USC (Greybowski, 1985), participants were asked to . . .

Multiple Authors

First reference: Calendrillo, Thurgood, Johnson, and Lawrence (1967) found in their evaluation . . .

Second reference: Calendrillo et al. (1967) also discovered . . .

Corporate Authors

First reference: An Environmental Protection Agency (1981) survey showed . . .

Second reference: . . . a close connection between political interests and environmental issues. (Environmental Protection Agency, 1981)

Third reference: . . . in their additional work. (EPA, 1981)

Citations within the text

She stated, "The cultural awareness of a student depends, by implication, on the cultural awareness of the parents" (Hermann, 1984, p. 219).

Hermann (1984) added that "enrichment in our schools is costly and has little bearing on the later lives of the students" (pp. 231–232).

"A school's responsibility rests with providing solid educational skills, not with supplementing the cultural education of the uninterested," stated Hermann (1984, p. 236) in her summary.

These brief comparisons and guidelines are by no means a substitute for reading and using the complete APA style manual if you are required to document according to its style. Rather, these sections are intended as an introduction to the varied patterns of APA form. If you need to use the APA style manual—or some other—read it thoroughly and follow its guidelines carefully.

APPENDIXES

61 Business Letters

Like a good paper, a business letter is a clearly organized, well-presented piece of writing that supports a thesis statement (whether it is stated or implied). A business letter differs from a paper, however, in form and purpose.

As you write a business letter, be especially sensitive to the tone. In most instances, you will be writing to solve a problem or to ask for help. A reasonably formal but friendly tone is therefore appropriate. Do not be harsh or demanding in an initial letter. If the problem continues, of course, a more extreme tone might be suitable in later correspondence.

Although a number of formats for business letters exist, a block-form letter (as in the example) will serve your purposes well. The format is specific, and you should follow it exactly. The guidelines on content in paragraphs is flexible, although these guidelines will serve most purposes.

General guidelines

Use high-quality, $8\frac{1}{2}$-by-11-inch paper.

Type the letter (or print it, using a word processor), using a black ribbon in good condition. You may have to clean keys, elements on a daisy wheel, letters on a ball, or components of a printhead.

Maintain wide margins on all sides.

Single-space throughout the letter, with double-spacing between paragraphs. Do not indent paragraphs.

Use a legal-sized envelope to place the letter in. The letter should be folded in thirds.

Proofread the final copy carefully for spelling, punctuation, mechanics, grammar, and typing errors.

Parts of the letter

Your address: This address clarifies where you wish to receive follow-up correspondence. Notice that your name does not appear with the address, since it is typed beneath the signature.

The date: Include the date on which you plan to mail the letter.

Inside address: Name the person to whom you are writing and include his or her title if you know it. If the letter is addressed to a company, begin this section with the name of the company and then use the complete business address.

Salutation: This greeting should be specific rather than general. Begin with *Dear,* followed by the name of the person and a colon (not a comma). Use general titles *(Mr., Ms., Dr., Professor)* with the person's name, using *Mrs.* or *Miss* only when you know a woman prefers to be addressed in one of those ways. Under general circumstances—when you do not know the name of the person to whom you are writing —avoid the salutary phrase "To Whom It May Concern." "Dear Madam or Sir" is a much more effective way to begin generally directed correspondence.

Introductory paragraph: Like a paper, a business letter needs an introductory paragraph. The first paragraph should establish the context for the letter. The sample, for instance, includes information to answer important questions: *When* did the transaction take place? *What* did she order (including stock numbers for easy identification)? An introductory paragraph needs to supply whatever information is necessary while being concise and specific.

Body paragraph or paragraphs: These important middle paragraphs provide a description of the problem. They should be clearly written, with careful word choices and specific details. Essentially, these paragraphs give you a chance to present your case—and they must therefore be precise and convincing. If you have tried to solve the problem, describe the strategies you have used, again supplying detailed information and descriptions.

Request for action: This closing paragraph should ask for help in solving the problem. Be reasonable. If alternative solutions are acceptable, include them.

Closing: Use a reasonably formal closing: *Sincerely, Sincerely yours,* or *Yours truly* are standard. (The closing should line up directly with your address.)

Signature: sign your name in ink in a space of at least four lines (so that it doesn't look cramped).

Typed name: Lined up under the closing, type your name as you wish it to be in return correspondence.

Parts of the envelope

Return address: Include your full return address in the upper-left corner of the envelope.

Mailing address: Address the envelope fully. Include the person's name and title (if applicable) and the full business address, including zip code.

Postage: Be sure to use sufficient postage.

1627 Lafayette Avenue
Topeka, KS 66603
February 27, 1987

Aaron Steinmann, Service Director
Museum Reproductions, Incorporated
392 Hazelwood Drive
Chicago, IL 60607

Dear Mr. Steinmann:

On November 16, 1986, I ordered several small pieces of statuary
from your Fall 1986 sale catalog: Child with Rabbit, (#097444),
Sleeping Cat (#097118), and Swan (#097203).

On December 3, 1986, my insured package arrived by UPS, and I
excitedly opened the cartons to examine my newest collector's
items. Two of the statues were in excellent shape, but the third,
Child with Rabbit, was not. The glaze on the rabbit and the base was
streaked and irregularly colored. These flaws in the finish
disappointed me greatly, especially since that piece alone had cost
$54 on sale.

I immediately called the service number listed on the invoice. Your
representative instructed me to repack the statue and return it for a
replacement. I did so the next day, December 4, 1986, enclosing a
photocopy of the invoice (#1784229). It has now been over two
months, and I have yet to receive my new Child with Rabbit statue.

I would appreciate receiving my statue soon (since I have already
paid for it) or would like to know the reason for the delay. If you are
unable to send me the statue, I would appreciate your crediting my
MasterCard account (#3275 3014 0011 1846). Thank you for your
help in solving my problem.

Sincerely,

Alicia Hudson

Alicia Hudson

Alicia Hudson
1627 Lafayette Avenue
Topeka, KS 66603

stamp

Aaron Steinmann, Service Director
Museum Reproductions, Incorporated
392 Hazelwood Drive
Chicago, IL 60607

62 The Résumé

A résumé is a brief listing of important information about your academic and work experience. The title *résumé* is acceptable under many circumstances, but it is only one description for such a listing. *Curriculum vitae* is the title often used in academics, although it is generally inappropriate in other circumstances. *Data sheet,* a general title, is acceptable under almost any circumstances. A listing of information, labeled in any of these ways, is usually submitted with a job application and is sometimes submitted with admissions or scholarship applications.

Because a résumé often makes a strong impression on the people who read it—suggesting what caliber of employee or student you are—complete it carefully. Be flexible as you prepare your résumé, modifying the format and information of the sample (see page **566**) to fit your own needs.

Format

Use headings that clearly describe the information used to explain them.

Supply complete information (accurate dates, complete addresses, phone numbers, and so on).

Abbreviate sparingly, using only standard abbreviations.

Make the organization easy to follow and the sectioning logical.

Arrange information in each section so that the section is clear and logical. Chronological order is appropriate when you have only a few items to present (two part-time jobs, for instance). Reverse chronological order is more helpful when you have a larger number of experiences or degrees to present—especially if the most recent one is the most important. Alphabetical order is useful for listing references or names of organizations.

Keep all information parallel (all fragments or all sentences; all capitals for headings or normal capitalization; similar items indented or similar items lined up with the margin).

Include only information that is pertinent to the job (or the scholarship or the admission) for which you are applying. Do not overload your résumé with trivial information.

Leave plenty of white space (wide margins and spaces between sections) to make information as accessible and attractive as possible.

Limit your résumé to one page if possible. A longer résumé may suggest that you have included too much secondary information.

Typing

Type single-spaced with double-spacing between sections.

Make sure your résumé is free of spelling and typing errors. It must be "letter perfect."

Use correction fluid or tape when you make alterations. You will keep the original and submit a photocopy, and these correction aids will not photocopy. Smudges on erasable paper *will* copy.

Type on good-quality paper with a clean, dark ribbon to get the best results in photocopying.

Do not use a typewriter with unusual type.

Photocopying

Always submit the best photocopy available. Avoid "five-cent specials" and instead go to a reputable copy shop.

Insist on copies from the best machine available.

Consider having your copies made on bonded paper. Spending a little more money might be worth it.

Parts of the résumé

Heading: Clearly label your information page with the word *résumé* (or the descriptive word of your choice), making sure to add the accent over both *e*'s by hand. List your name in the form you intend to use on applications.

Personal information: Include pertinent information. Notice that two addresses and telephone numbers are given in this form, suggesting that Sandra spends time at both places and may be reached at either one. Full telephone numbers are provided, including area codes. The information on birth date, marital status, and health are optional, since employers and agencies can no longer demand such information and may not legally use it when assessing applications. Unless you are sensitive about these issues, however, it is best to include this information.

Educational information: Supply basic information about your education, including full names of schools, addresses, dates of attendance, and other important information like majors and minors. Still enrolled as a full-time student, Sandra includes her anticipated graduation date. Notice that the information is presented chronologically.

Extracurricular activities: Include a list of activities that relate to your work, mentioning any special kinds of involvement. Do not clutter your résumé with all your activities, however. Again, notice that the information is presented in chronological order.

Work experience: Supply pertinent information about your work experience: work dates, names of businesses or organizations, addresses, and the title of your position or a description of your work. Once more, notice the chronological presentation.

Recommendations: List the people who can recommend your work. Include their full names, titles when appropriate, addresses, and telephone numbers. Arrange the list either in alphabetical order or by the importance of the recommendations. Include only names of people you have contacted first for permission to use them as references.

RÉSUMÉ
Sandra K. Royer

PERSONAL

School: 363 Maehling Terrace   Home: 431 N. Seventh St.
        Alton, IL 62002   Waterloo, IL 62298
School phone: (618) 465-7061   Home phone: (618) 686-2324
Date of birth: 15 August 1965   Marital status: Married
                                      Health: Excellent

EDUCATION

1979–1983:   Benjamin Thomas High School, Waterloo, IL
1983–   :   Freemont College, Alton, IL; will graduate May
                1987. Major: Music education. Minors: Music
                theory and business

EXTRACURRICULAR ACTIVITIES

1979–1983:   Benjamin Thomas High School Orchestra (1st
                violin, 1981–1983)
                Benjamin Thomas High School String Ensemble
                (student coordinator, 1982–1983)
1983–   :   Freemont College Orchestra (2nd violin,
                1983–1984; 1st violin, 1984–present)
                Pi Kappa Lambda, music honorary society
                (secretary, 1984–1985)

WORK EXPERIENCE

1982–1983:   Carter's Music Shop, Waterloo, IL 62298; part-
                time appointment secretary and sales clerk
1983–   :   Hampton Music, Alton, IL 62002 (837 Telegraph
                Square); sales clerk

REFERENCES

Dr. Glendora Kramer, Professor of Music and Orchestra Director,
   Freemont College, Alton, IL 62002   (618) 461-6299, ext. 2110
Mr. Philip Sheldon, Manager, Hampton Music, 837 Telegraph,
   Alton, IL 62002   (618) 466-6311
Mrs. Rhonda Travis, Music instructor, Benjamin Thomas High
   School, Waterloo, IL 62298   (618) 686-5534

63 Manuscript Form

Over the years, writers have developed fairly consistent methods for presenting manuscripts (papers, articles, short stories, proposals, reports, and books). These methods, although not inflexible, have become a standard that is expected. It is wise to adhere to them.

Accepted guidelines for typed manuscripts (on typewriters and word processors) and handwritten manuscripts are included below.

Paper

Typed manuscript: Use white, $8\frac{1}{2}$-by-11-inch paper; 16-pound bond is best. Avoid onion-skin paper because it is flimsy and difficult to work with. When possible, avoid "erasable" paper because it smudges easily and is difficult for instructors to write comments on. (If you need to type on erasable paper, submit a high-quality photocopy.) If you are using a word processor and printing a copy of your manuscript, be sure to use letter-quality paper rather than flimsy, draft-quality paper. Or submit a good photocopy.

Handwritten manuscript: Use good, white paper, preferably with lines. Again, use paper of standard size, not legal size or steno-notebook size. Never submit work on torn-out spiral-notebook paper without first trimming the edges (over a wastebasket!).

Ribbons and pens

Typed manuscript: Use a black ribbon to type your manuscripts. Do not use an old, light ribbon, and remember to clean your typewriter keys periodically. (No one likes to squint to read, especially writing instructors with large stacks of papers to grade.) If possible, use a letter-quality printer with your word processor to produce a manuscript that looks as if it has been typed. If you must use a dot-matrix printer, use its letter-quality mode rather than its draft mode, or ask your instructor if copies printed in the draft mode are acceptable.

Handwritten manuscript: Use a black pen for handwritten work unless advised otherwise. Make sure your pen does not blob or skip.

Typing and handwriting formats

Typed manuscript: Always double-space throughout every paper. Double-spacing makes papers easier to read and allows space for corrections and additions. Use only one side of each sheet of paper.

Handwritten manuscript: Write on every other line unless given other advice. Write on only one side of each page, clearly and carefully forming your letters.

Margins

Typed manuscript: Always use ample margins, 1 to $1\frac{1}{2}$ inches *on all sides* of the page. Instructors need that space to make comments and corrections, so do not force them to squeeze advice into too little space. Word-processing programs will automatically establish even and consistent margins.

Handwritten manuscript: The same standards apply to handwritten work—leave substantial margins.

Indentions

Typed manuscript: Indent paragraphs five spaces. Do not skip extra lines before beginning a new paragraph.

Handwritten manuscript: Make sure that your indentions are obvious (one inch from the left margin) and consistent.

Headings

Typed manuscript: In the upper left corner of your paper, but within the margins, type your name, the course number, your instructor's name, and the date. (Your instructor may also ask you to include the section number and the assignment number.) Then double-space twice and type your paper's title, centered. Capitalize all important words in your title, but do not italicize or use quotation marks for your own title (see Capitalization, **39**, Italics, **40**, and Quotation Marks, **41**). Then double-space two more times and begin your first paragraph. In some cases, your instructor may ask for a separate title page (see APA Style, **60**, page 550).

Handwritten manuscript: Include the same information on handwritten work, and follow the same guidelines for your title. Begin your heading, however, on the top line of your paper.

Paging

Typed manuscript: On the second, third, and other pages, type your last name and the page number, separated by a space in the upper right corner of the page but within the regular margins. Then continue the text of your paper on

Samples

Ronald Davis

English 000

Dr. J. Frazer

6 September 87

Title of the Paper

....

....

....

....

Davis 2

....

....

....

....

the next line. If you are using a word-processing program that normally centers page numbers at the bottom of the page, you will have to use additional commands to place your last name and the page number at the top.

Handwritten manuscript: Indicate paging in the same way on handwritten manuscripts, using the top line to begin the page.

Proofreading

Typed manuscript: Proofread typed manuscripts for grammar, usage, and mechanics, to make sure that no errors slip by. Use this handbook. Look carefully for typing errors, because a word misspelled because of poor typing is still misspelled, no matter how it got that way. (See Technical Revision, **1k**.)

Handwritten manuscript: Proofread handwritten manuscripts to catch errors and also to make sure that all your words are legible. If your handwriting is bad, make a conscious effort to re-form any letters that may be confusing— and consider typing the manuscript even if that is not required.

Corrections

Typed manuscript: Make corrections cleanly—using correction fluid or tape. Draw a single line through words you must omit at the last minute. Words accidentally omitted may be inserted *above the line* using a caret (∧) to indicate where the material goes. Type corrections whenever possible or use black ink. If you are using a word processor, make all revisions in the original manuscript and then print out a corrected copy to submit.

Handwritten manuscript: Follow the same guidelines as for typing, except, of course, you will write in corrections.

Submitting the manuscript

Typed manuscript: Most instructors like to have manuscripts presented in specific ways, so follow their guidelines carefully. If your instructor gives no guidelines, then staple your pages together in the upper left corner (never the right) or secure the pages with a small paper clip. Never fold down the corners to secure the pages, and do not place the paper in an acetate binder. With longer papers, though, it is wise to place the paper in a manila envelope with your name and course information on the outside, if your instructor does not object. Whatever the case, always photocopy your paper before handing it in.

Handwritten manuscript: The same basic rules apply for handwritten manuscripts.

A final word on manuscript form

If for some reason you are having difficulty following these manuscript guidelines or those specifically presented by your instructor, see him or her before you prepare the final copy of a paper. Preparing a final typed or handwritten copy takes time, and redoing a final copy because of some inconsistency will take even more time. So, if you feel insecure about manuscript form, do not trust your luck. Instead, get help and *then* prepare the final copy.

64 Using a Word Processor

The availability of computers and the introduction of various word-processing programs have dramatically altered the way many people write. In the past, many writers wrote a draft of a paper, revised it any number of times, and then typed a single final copy if possible. When that final copy worked well, there were no problems. Sometimes, however, a writer might be satisfied with a final manuscript that honestly needed further revision, simply because he or she wanted to avoid typing one more copy.

Computers and word processors have changed the process of writing because writers can now modify selected portions of a paper without retyping the whole manuscript. But word-processing programs can do a good deal more than reproduce previously typed and slightly altered manuscripts, and much of what they can do frees writers to experiment with formats and substantially revise their work.

64a Approach word processing in a realistic and practical frame of mind.

Using a computer with a word-processing program for the first time will be somewhat unnerving because so much about using computers will be new to you. In fact, the arrangement of the primary keys on the keyboard may be the only thing that seems remotely familiar. But the novelty of using a word-processing program need not be intimidating if you follow some simple and practical advice:

- Have someone *show* you how the word processor works. Find out how to turn on the computer and how to activate the program so that you can begin typing.

- Write down on an index card the exact sequence of steps for convenient reference. Printed instructions in user's manuals generally include more details than you need, often explaining how the system works. You can operate the word processor without knowing such information, just as you can drive a car without knowing how a combustion engine works.

- Start the program *yourself* with someone knowledgeable nearby, an experienced friend or an experienced tutor in a computer center. If you cannot operate the program yourself, ask for help immediately. Do not frustrate yourself (which you are likely to do if you repeat the same mistake).

- Remember that a computer is not a typewriter. As obvious as that sounds, making direct associations between the two kinds of machines causes unnecessary frustration. For instance, if you strike a key on a typewriter and nothing happens, something is clearly wrong—a broken key, a locked bearing, or something else mechanical. Computers, on the other hand, operate by electronic impulses created by typed commands. If you type a nonexistent command (or an inappropriate one), nothing happens. Nothing is broken; the machine is simply waiting for a correct command to carry out. If you do not expect a computer to be just like a typewriter, your transition into word processing will be easier.

- Make reference cards (5-by-7 index cards work especially well) listing the most common commands. Most word processing programs provide lists of frequently used commands in the upper or lower portions of the screen. It is often easier, however, to prepare and use your own list. At first these commands will seem alien, and you will have to refer to your card frequently, but as you work, you will quickly memorize common commands.

- Practice word processing by completing a simple, real-life project. Although some user's manuals include practice lessons, such work sometimes seems counterproductive. After all, it is *only* practice. Instead, practice word-processing skills by doing everyday kinds of writing, like personal letters or summaries of class notes. That way your practice time will serve two purposes.

- Expect to have some problems. In other words, be realistic. Word processing is not impossible to learn—thousands of working writers have demonstrated that—but it is not easy, either. Mostly, it takes commitment to learning basic skills, but it also takes practice, lots of practice. The more practice you get, the more proficient you will become. Then you can take advantage of a wonderful tool for writing and revision.

64b Use a word processor to prepare an early draft of a paragraph or paper.

People use the word processor at different stages in writing. Some writers (typically, proficient typists) work directly at the keyboard, composing freely while at the same time realizing that they can later modify the text. Other writers prefer to complete a draft by hand and then type it, following a pattern similar to that of using a typewriter for a final copy. You should follow, naturally, whichever pattern works best for you.

64c Reread your draft and plan revisions.

Again, writers work according to various strategies. Some read from the screen and make revisions instantly. Others print out a copy of the manuscript and write in additions, corrections, and changes. Still others—most writers, probably—

work both ways, making some changes immediately and some on a printed manuscript. As you work with a word processor, you will discover which strategy (or strategies) works best for you.

64d Be aware of how word processing simplifies revision.

Revision is never easy because it involves making choices —choices between words, phrases, sentences, examples, explanations, paragraphs, and structural patterns in whole papers. But once you have made your decisions, word processing makes it easy to incorporate them in your writing. By using a variety of commands, you can

change words, phrases, or sentences.

make corrections in punctuation and mechanics.

delete material (from a single letter to a paragraph to a whole series of pages).

move material (words, sentences, paragraphs, pages, or more) around.

locate a misspelled or misused word throughout an entire manuscript and change it wherever it has been used. (Be aware, however, of the limitations of spelling programs. See **46f**.)

copy portions of the manuscript (or all of it, for that matter) to use for other purposes.

check for correct spelling if your word processing program has a supplementary spelling program (see **46f**).

What you do not alter or move remains in the original form and need not be retyped, saving you from the tedious work that often makes serious revision troublesome. Clearly, the ability of a word processing program to make selected changes in a manuscript without altering other portions makes revision easier and more efficient.

64e Consider the flexibility word processing will give you in preparing the format of a manuscript.

Beyond the correction-substitution-modification abilities of word processing, there are other possibilities for changing the way a manuscript looks. For instance, using most word processing programs and a good printer, you can

change the spacing of a manuscript (single, double, triple, quadruple, and so on).

change the margins of a manuscript (to make them wider or to make them narrower).

justify both margins (making the right as well as the left margin perfectly straight) so that the manuscript resembles a printed text.

re-form paragraphs to close up any spaces left by deletions or substitutions.

automatically page a manuscript so that bottom margins are consistent.

automatically center material on a page.

automatically italicize words and titles without having to backspace to underline them individually.

incorporate boldface (darker letters) in a manuscript.

automatically produce superscript (characters a half-space above a line, as in note numbers) and subscript (characters a half-space below a line, as in mathematical and scientific notation).

change print characters to incorporate different styles of type (if an available printer can do that).

change print colors (if an available printer can do that).

With these and other possibilities for changing the format of a manuscript, you can be much more creative with presentation.

64f Remember that you make yourself a good writer; a word processor only makes revision easier and more efficient.

Word processors are tools—powerful tools, certainly. They allow writers to revise manuscripts easily and quickly, but using a word processor cannot, by itself, make you a good writer. Only you can do that. You will still need to bring to your work all the interest, commitment, selectivity, and skill you can muster. You must still plan carefully, write a draft clearly, and evaluate the draft critically. But using a word processor will simplify preparing and revising the manuscript, and therein lies its value.

65 Glossary of Usage

This brief glossary contains words and phrases that often cause problems for writers. The explanations are intended as quick guides to usage, and the sample sentences are used to illustrate how the words and phrases can be used in sentences. If you are unsure of the appropriate use of a word or phrase not included here, consult a dictionary.

A, An Use *a* before a consonant sound; use *an* before a vowel sound. Be especially careful to "listen" to words beginning with *h*.

a locket   **an** umbrella

a historical event   **an** honorable mention

Accept, Except *Accept*, a verb, means "to receive"; *except*, a preposition, means "all but."

I will **accept** the blame for the accident.

Everyone signed the petition **except** Charles.

Accidentally, Accidently Use *accidentally*, the correct word form. The root word is *accidental*, not *accident*.

Jason **accidentally** tore the cover page of the report.

Advice, Advise *Advice*, a noun, means "a suggestion or suggestions"; *advise*, a verb, means "to offer ideas" or "to recommend."

Rachel's **advice** is always sensible.

Mr. Jones plans to **advise** new students in the Mathematics Department.

Affect, Effect *Affect*, a verb, means "to influence"; *effect*, a noun, means "the product or result of an action"; *effect*, a verb, means "to bring about, to cause to occur."

The smallness of the audience did not **affect** the speaker's presentation.

One sure **effect** of decontrol will be stronger competition.

Marsha intends to **effect** a change in her students' behavior before the end of the semester.

Agree to, Agree with *Agree to* means "to accept" a plan or proposal; *agree with* means "to share beliefs" with a person or group.

The workers would not **agree to** the contract offer.

Most of the members **agreed with** the advisory council.

A lot, Alot Use *a lot*, the correct form. Generally, however, use more specific words: *a great deal, many,* or *much*.

The long lines at the market frustrated **a lot** of people.

The long lines at the market frustrated **many** people.

All ready, Already *All ready*, a pronoun plus a verb, means "all (were) prepared"; *already*, an adverb, means "previously."

Ten minutes before curtain time, the performers were **all ready.**

We have **already** arranged for the loan.

All right, Alright Use *all right*, the correct form.

Mel said it was **all right** to use his stereo.

All together, Altogether *All together* means "all (act) in unison"; *altogether* means "totally" or "entirely."

Synchronized swimming requires participants to swim **all together.**

Rob's reactions were **altogether** different from Todd's.

Among, Between Use *among* to describe the relationship of three or more people or things; use *between* for two.

Disagreements **among** the workers disrupted the meeting.

Leave at least three feet **between** the cars.

Amount, Number Use *amount* for quantities that can't be counted separately; use *number* when you can count the people or things. Some concepts, like time, can use both forms, depending on how you identify the elements.

The **amount** of time necessary to finish the building is shocking.

A large **number** of elm trees will need treatment for disease.

An See **A.**

And/or Generally, avoid this construction. Instead, use either *and* or *or.*

Anxious, Eager *Anxious* means ''apprehensive'' or ''worried'' and consequently describes negative feelings; *eager* means ''anticipating enthusiastically'' and consequently describes positive feelings.

For four weeks, Angie was **anxious** about her qualifying exams.

Lew was **eager** to leave for Europe.

As, As if, Like Use *as* or *as if,* subordinating conjunctions, to introduce a clause; use *as* or *like,* prepositions, to introduce a noun. Be especially careful when making these comparisons.

As I listened to the song, I tried to remember where I'd heard it before.

Walt talked to his cocker spaniel **as if** the dog understood every word.

I entered college **as** a sophomore.

Jennifer, everyone agrees, looks **like** her brother, Christopher.

As, Because, Since *As,* a subordinating conjunction, establishes a time relationship; it is interchangeable with *when* or *while. Because* and *since* describe causes and effects.

As the train pulled out of the station, it began to rain.

Because (Since) Karen bowled infrequently, she preferred to rent a ball and shoes.

Awful Generally avoid this word which really means ''full of awe,'' or ''awe-inspiring.'' Instead, use words which probably match your meaning more closely: *bad, terrible, unfortunate,* and others.

Bad, Badly Use *bad,* an adjective, to modify a noun or pronoun; use *badly,* an adverb, to modify a verb.

Whenever Kevin's allergies flare up, he looks **bad.** (Bad *modifies the pronoun* he, *not* looks.)

580

Carla's solutions seem **bad** because she presents them in such an unappealing way. (Bad *modifies the noun* solutions, *not* seem.)

Our volleyball team played **badly** in the regional tournament. (Badly *modifies the verb* played.)

Because, Due to the fact that, Since   Use *because* or *since; due to the fact that* is merely a wordier way of saying the same thing.

Aaron rode the bus to Omaha **because** he could not afford to fly.

Before, Prior to   Use *before* in almost all cases. *Prior to* should be used only when the sequence of events is drawn out, important, and legalistic.

I always make a grocery list **before** I go to the store.

Prior to receiving the cash settlement, the Jacobsons had filed four complaints with the Better Business Bureau.

Being as, Being that, Seeing as   Use *because* or *since* instead of these nonstandard forms.

Beside, Besides   *Beside* means "next to"; *besides* means "except."

In the waiting room, Tom had to sit **beside** a man smoking a cigar.

All the cyclists **besides** Shelley completed the race.

Between   See **Among.**

Borrow, Loan   *Borrow* means "to take something for temporary use"; *loan* means "to give something for temporary use." They describe two sides of the same process.

I'd like to **borrow** your pen to fill out these forms.

Jessie will **loan** no one his favorite albums.

Bring, Take   *Bring* means "to transport from a distant to a close location"; *take* reverses the pattern and means "to transport from a close location to a distant one."

When you come to the meeting, **bring** your written recommendations.

Please be sure to **take** some samples home with you.

Can, May   *Can* means "is able to"; *may* means "has permission to." Keep these two forms distinct. *May* is also used with a verb to suggest a possible or conditional action.

Almost anyone **can** learn to cook well.

According to the sponsors, visitors **may** park in the designated lots.

I **may** learn to like escargot, but I doubt it.

Can't help but   Avoid this phrase which contains two negatives: *can't* and *but*; instead rewrite the sentence omitting *but*.

We **can't help** wondering if Gretchen is sincere about getting married.

Center around, Center on Use *center on*. *Center around* is contradictory because *center* identifies one position, while *around* suggests many possible positions.

> If we can **center** our discussions **on** one topic at a time, we'll use our time more productively.

Compare to, Compare with *Compare to* stresses similarities; *compare with* stresses similarities *and* differences.

> In "The Love Song of J. Alfred Prufrock," T. S. Eliot **compares** the evening **to** an anesthetized patient.

> Lester **compared** the film version of *Amadeus* **with** the original play.

Complement, Compliment *Complement*, normally a noun, means "that which completes"; *compliment*, either a noun or a verb, means "a statement of praise" or "to praise."

> A direct object is one kind of **complement.**

> Philip seems to have a **compliment** for every person he meets.

> Let me **compliment** you on your fine choice of wine.

Continual, Continuous *Continual* means "repeated often"; *continuous* means "without stopping."

> Orienting new workers was a **continual** activity.

> A **continuous** stream of water rushed down the slope.

Council, Counsel *Council*, a noun, means "a group of people that consults and offers advice"; *counsel*, a noun or a verb, means "advice" or "to advise."

> The **council** met in the conference room of the city hall.

> Following the meeting, they offered their **counsel** to the mayor.

> Mrs. Reichmann **counsels** runaway teenagers at the Seventh Street Shelter.

Could of, Should of, Would of Use the correct forms: *could have, should have,* and *would have.*

> We **should have** mixed the concrete in smaller batches.

Different from, Different than Use *different from* with single complements and clauses; use *different than* only with clauses. *Different from* is generally more acceptable in formal writing.

> Angie's career goals are **different from** those of her friends.

> My stay in New York was **different than** I had expected.

Disinterested, Uninterested *Disinterested* means "impartial" or "unbiased"; *uninterested* means "indifferent" or "unconcerned about."

Olympic judges are supposed to be **disinterested** evaluators, but most aren't.

Fred is **uninterested** in classical music.

Due to the fact that   See **Because.**

Each and every   Generally, avoid this double usage, which repeats the same idea. Use either *each* or *every*, not both.

Eager   See **Anxious.**

Effect   See **Affect.**

Enthusiastic, Enthused   Use *enthusiastic*, the preferred form.

William was **enthusiastic** about his summer job.

Etc.   Except in rare instances, avoid the use of *etc.*, which means "and so forth." Normally, either continue your discussion or stop rather than implying—sometimes inaccurately—that you have more of value to add.

Every day, Everyday   *Every day*, an adjective and noun, means "each day"; *everyday*, an adjective, means "typical" or "ordinary."

Sean jogs two miles **every day.**

An argument seems to be an **everyday** occurrence at our house.

Exam, Examination   *Exam*, a conversational form, is acceptable in many situations, but use *examination* in formal writing.

The CPA **examination** is given three times a year.

Except   See **Accept.**

Farther, Further   *Farther* describes physical distances; *further* describes degree, quality, or time.

From our house, it is *farther* to St. Louis than to Nashville.

This report needs **further** work to make it really outstanding.

Fewer, Less   Use *fewer* to describe physically separate units; use *less* for things that cannot be counted.

It took us **fewer** than three hours to drive to Houston.

Rick has **less** faith in himself than I have.

Figuratively, Literally   *Figuratively* means "involving a figure of speech," usually meaning that the statement is not really true; *literally* means "actually," consequently describing true circumstances.

Jessica has **figuratively** reached the "top of the heap."

Mrs. Brandon **literally** fainted when she heard the news.

Finalize, Finish   Generally, use *finish* or *complete*, less pretentious ways of expressing the same idea.

Fun   This noun should not be used before another noun, as if it were an adjective.

The canoe trip down the Black River was **fun.**

Further   See **Farther.**

Good, Well   Use the adjective *good* to describe someone or something; use *well*, the adverb, to describe an action; use *well*, the adjective, to describe a physical condition.

A **good** debater must be knowledgeable, logical, and forceful.

We work **well** together because we think alike.

Tom says he's sick, but he looks **well** to me.

Has got, Have got   Simply use *has* or *have.*

Karl **has** a severe case of measles.

He or she, Him or her, His or hers, Himself or herself   Use these combinations when you are unsure of the gender of an antecedent; avoid awkward constructions, like *he/she* or *s/he*. Generally, however, use plurals when possible or use specific subjects in the first place—which will in turn require specific pronouns.

Each child is responsible for bringing **his or her** own lunch.

Children are responsible for bringing **their** own lunches.

Hopefully, I Hope   Use *hopefully*, an adverb, to describe the *hopeful* way something is done; use *I hope* to describe your wishes.

Al **hopefully** opened the envelope, expecting to find a letter of acceptance.

I hope it doesn't snow before the weekend.

Imply, Infer   *Imply* means "to suggest without stating"; *infer* means "to reach a conclusion based on unstated evidence." They describe two sides of a process.

His awkward movements and tentative comments **implied** that Bill was uncomfortable.

I **infer,** from your tone of voice, that you are displeased.

In, Into   *In* means "positioned within"; *into* means "moving from the outside to the inside." Avoid using *into* to mean "enjoying" or "involved with," a slang expression.

We left a dim light on **in** the house.

As we walked **into** the room, we were startled by the size of the crowd.

Infer   See **Imply.**

Irregardless, Regardless   Use *regardless*, the accepted form.

Child custody is usually awarded to the mother, **regardless** of the father's competence.

Its, It's, Its' *Its,* a possessive pronoun, means "belonging to it"; *it's,* a contraction, means "it is"; *its'* is nonstandard.

The dog licked **its** injured paw repeatedly.

It's going to be a beautiful day.

Kind of, Sort of Use *rather, somewhat,* or *to some extent* instead.

Lay, Lie *Lay* means "to place something"; *lie* means "to recline." Some confusion is typical because *lay* is also the past tense of *lie.*

Jerry **lays** his clothes on the chair before going to bed.

Sharon always **lies** on the couch to watch television.

Lead, Led *Lead* is the present tense verb; *led* is the past tense.

I plan to **lead** a quiet life.

Abbie **led** the tourists through the Logan Mansion.

Learn, Teach *Learn* means "to acquire knowledge"; *teach* means "to give instruction." These are two sides of the same process.

Carla has to **learn** algebraic equations to manage her later classes.

Without realizing that he is doing so, Mr. Whiteside **teaches** the neighborhood children about wild birds.

Less See **Fewer.**

Lie See **Lay.**

Like See **As.**

Literally See **Figuratively.**

Loan See **Borrow.**

Loose, Lose *Loose,* an adjective, means "not tight or binding"; *lose,* a verb, means "to misplace."

The jacket was too **loose** to look attractive.

Linda **loses** her temper over the slightest incident.

May See **Can.**

May be, Maybe *May be,* a verb, means "could be"; *maybe* means "perhaps."

This **may be** my last visit to the orthopedic surgeon.

Maybe Katie will remember my birthday this year.

Number See **Amount.**

Off of Use the preposition *off* by itself; it's perfectly clear.

Some shingles were torn **off** the roof during the storm.

On account of Use *because* or *since,* briefer ways of saying the same thing.

Passed, Past   Use *passed* when you need a verb; use *past* when you need a noun, adjective, or preposition.

Brad **passed** the same people in the halls each morning.

The **past**, as the saying goes, helps determine the present.

Neil continues to be haunted by his **past** actions.

The ambulance raced **past** the cars, hurrying to the hospital.

People, Persons   Use *people* when referring to a group, emphasizing anonymity; use *persons* to emphasize unnamed individuals within the group.

The **people** who demonstrated at the White House were orderly.

Several **persons** at the council session criticized the mayor's dealings with cable companies.

Percent, Percentage   Use *percent* with a number; use *percentage* with a modifier.

Over **fifty percent** of the government's money is spent on social security and defense.

A **large percentage** of the millworkers opposed the union.

Persons   See **People.**

Pretty   *Pretty* means "attractive" or "pleasant looking"; do not use it to mean "rather" or "somewhat."

Principal, Principle   *Principal,* an adjective, means "main" or "highest in importance"; *principal,* a noun, means "the head of a school"; *principle,* a noun, means "a fundamental truth or law."

Tom Gavlin's **principal** difficulty was dealing with the press corps.

Much to our surprise, the school's **principal** was unaware of the problems.

The **principle** of freedom of speech is vital to American interests.

Prior to   See **Before.**

Quotation, Quote   *Quotation,* the noun, means "someone else's material used word for word"; *quote,* the verb, means "to use a quotation." In conversation, *quote* is often used as a noun; for formal writing, however, distinguish carefully between these two forms.

The opening **quotation** was too long to be effective.

Steve frequently **quotes** from Shakespeare and from the Bible.

Reason, Reason why, Reason is because   *Reason,* used by itself, is sometimes unclear; *reason why,* a more complete expression, is generally preferred. *Reason is because* is repetitive, since *reason* itself implies a connection.

I'll never understand the **reason why** Sarah left the city.

Respectfully, Respectively *Respectfully* means "showing respect" or "full of respect"; *respectively* means "in the given order."

Geoffrey **respectfully** declined the nomination.

These comments were made by Joshua Blaney, Andreas Church, and Jessica Meredith, **respectively.**

Seeing as See **Being as.**

Set, Sit *Set* means "to place or position something"; *sit* means "to be seated."

I **set** the alarm for 6:00 A.M. so that I would not be late.

Don't **sit** on that bench; I just painted it.

Shall, Will Past distinctions between these forms are disappearing, and *will* is used in almost all cases. *Shall* remains standard, however, for questions using the first person.

We **will** probably buy a Honda rather than a Toyota.

Shall I start dinner?

Should, Would Use *should* to explain a condition or obligation; use *would* to explain a customary action or wish.

Marilee **should** invest her money more wisely.

When asked a particularly difficult question, he **would** change the subject.

Should of See **Could of.**

Since See **As, Because.**

Sit See **Set.**

Sort of See **Kind of.**

Supposed to, Suppose to Use *supposed to,* the standard form.

Tonya was **supposed to** meet Brian at the restaurant at seven o'clock.

Take See **Bring.**

Teach See **Learn.**

That, Which, Who Use *that* to refer to people or things, but usually things; use *which* to refer to things; use *who* to refer to people.

The boat **that** I want costs eight thousand dollars.

The position **which** we advertised has now been filled.

People **who** cannot control their tempers are irritating and sometimes dangerous.

Their, There, They're *Their,* a possessive pronoun, means "belonging to them"; *there,* usually an adverb, indicates placement; *they're,* a contraction, means "they are."

The Marshalls sold **their** cabin to buy a larger one.

Put the boxes over **there,** and I will open them later.

If Lester and Connie don't see a counselor, **they're** probably going to get a divorce.

Theirself, Theirselves Use *themselves,* the standard form.

The members of Congress voted **themselves** a raise.

There See **Their.**

They're See **Their.**

Threw, Through, Thru *Threw,* the past tense of the verb *throw,* means "hurled an object"; *through* means "by way of" or "to reach an end"; *thru* is a nonstandard spelling of *through.*

Rhonda **threw** bread crumbs outside for the birds.

We walked **through** the shop but saw nothing we wanted.

Till, Until, 'Til Both *till* and *until* are acceptable; 'til, though slightly archaic, is also admissible; watch spellings and punctuation.

Jeremy worked **till** after midnight.

Jeremy worked **until** after midnight.

To, Too, Two *To* is a preposition or part of an infinitive; *too* is a modifier meaning "in extreme" or "also"; *two* is the number.

Shari walked **to** the library **to** find a book for her report.

The popcorn was **too** salty for my taste.

Wilma ordered **two** prints of each picture.

Try and Use *try to,* the accepted form.

Try to have more patience with the children.

Uninterested See **Disinterested.**

Use to, Used to Use *used to,* the standard form.

We **used to** see a film every weekend.

Until See **Till.**

Utilize, Utilization Generally use *use,* a shorter, simpler way of expressing the same idea.

Very The adverb *very* is sometimes used unnecessarily: very central, very unique. In such instances, omit it. At other times, limit your use of *very,* choosing other adverbs instead: *especially, extremely,* and so on.

Wait for, Wait on *Wait for* means "to stay and expect"; *wait on* means "to serve."

We'll **wait for** Jan and Peter ten more minutes.

Carolyn loves to be **waited on** when she's sick.

Weather, Whether *Weather* means "conditions of the climate"; *whether* means "if."

Rapid changes in the **weather** often disrupt airline schedules.

Citizens must pay taxes **whether** they like it or not.

Well See **Good.**

Whether See **Weather.**

Which See **That.**

Who See **That.**

Who/Whom, Whoever/Whomever Use *who* and *whoever* in subject positions; use *whom* and *whomever* in object positions.

Would the person **who** owns the blue Chevrolet please move it?

Would **whoever** owns the blue Chevrolet please move it?

"To **whom** it may concern" is an inappropriate way to begin a letter.

Call **whomever** you wish. You will not change my mind.

Who's, Whose *Who's,* a contraction, means "who is" or "who has"; *whose,* a possessive pronoun, means "belonging to someone."

Who's going to help me clean up this mess?

Whose gloves are these?

Will See **Shall.**

Would See **Should.**

Would of See **Could of.**

66 Glossary of Grammatical Terms

Absolute Phrase See **Phrase.**

Abstract Noun See **Noun.**

Active Voice See **Voice.**

Adjective A word that modifies or limits a noun or pronoun by answering one of these questions: what kind? which one? how many? or whose? Distilled *water makes the* best ice *cubes.* A **regular adjective** precedes the word it modifies: *The blue velvet dress cost* two hundred *dollars.* A **predicate adjective** follows a linking verb but modifies the subject of the sentence or clause: *Ladders should be* sturdy *and* lightweight. An **article** *(a, an, the)* is considered an adjective: A *good friend is* a *good listener.* A **demonstrative adjective** can show closeness *(this, these)* or distance *(that, those)* and singular *(this, that)* or plural *(these, those).* A **pronoun-adjective** is a pronoun that modifies a noun: Somebody's *car is parked in* my *space.* A **positive adjective** directly modifies one noun or pronoun: *Logan's is a* good *restaurant.* A **comparative adjective** compares two subjects: *Logan's* *is a* better *restaurant than Applegate's.* A **superlative adjective** compares three or more subjects: *Logan's is the* best *restaurant in town.*

Adjective Clause   See **Clause.**

Adjective Phrase   See **Phrase.**

Adverb   A word that modifies a verb, adjective, other adverb, clause, phrase, or whole sentence by answering one of these questions: how? when? where? how often? or to what extent? *Roberto enunciates carefully.* (*Carefully* modifies *enunciates,* telling *how.*) *He is* usually *soft-spoken.* (*Usually* modifies *soft-spoken,* telling *when.*) *He sometimes speaks too softly.* (*Too* modifies *softly,* telling *to what extent.*) Frequently, *he has to repeat comments.* (*Frequently* modifies the whole sentence, telling *how often.*) A **positive adverb** directly modifies one verb, adjective, other adverb, or group of words: *Masumi works well in groups.* A **comparative adverb** compares two circumstances: *Masumi works better in small groups.* A **superlative adverb** compares three or more circumstances: *Masumi works best alone.*

Adverb Clause   See **Clause.**

Adverbial Conjunction   See **Conjunctive Adverb.**

Agreement   The matching of words according to number (singular and plural) and gender (masculine, feminine, and neuter). A verb must take a singular or plural form depending on whether its subject is singular or plural. A pronoun must match its antecedent (the word it refers to) in gender as well as number. A **demonstrative adjective** must also match the number of the word it modifies (*this* and *that* for singular, *these* and *those* for plural).

Antecedent   The word to which a pronoun refers. *Rachel changed the tire herself.* (*Rachel* is the antecedent for the reflexive pronoun *herself.*)

Appositive   A word or group of words that restates or defines a noun or pronoun. An appositive is positioned immediately after the word it explains. **Nonrestrictive appositives** clarify proper nouns and are set off by commas: *Crest, the best-selling toothpaste, is recommended by many dentists.* **Restrictive appositives** are themselves proper nouns and require no commas: *The toothpaste Crest is advertised heavily on television.*

Article   See **Adjective.**

Auxiliary Verb   See **Verb.**

Balanced Sentence   See **Sentence.**

Case   The form a noun or pronoun takes when it is used in different ways in sentences. **Subjective case** describes a word used as a subject or predicate noun: *She drives a Mazda GLC.* **Objective case** describes a word used as a direct object, indirect object, or object of a preposition: *The small size is just* *right for* her. **Possessive case** describes a word used to show ownership: Her *Mazda is cherry red.* Most nouns and pronouns change only to form the possessive case (made by adding an apostrophe and an *s: cat's, some-one's).* Personal, relative, and interrogative pronouns, however, change form for all three cases.

Clause   A group of words that has a subject and predicate. An **independent clause** is grammatically complete; when used separately, it is indistinguishable from a simple sentence: *Dinosaurs had small brains.* An independent clause can be joined to another clause with a coordinating conjunction, a subordinating conjunction, or a semicolon. A **subordinate clause** also has a subject and predicate, but it is not grammatically complete; it must be joined to an independent clause: *Although they had enormous bodies, dinosaurs had small brains.* A subordinate clause can function as an adjective, an adverb, or a noun. An **adjective clause** modifies a noun or pronoun: *We want a television* that has remote controls. An **adverb clause** modifies a verb, an adjective, another adverb, a clause, a phrase, or a whole sentence: *Jason gets up earlier* than I usually do. A **noun clause** functions as a noun: Whoever finds the wallet *will probably return it.*

Collective Noun   See **Noun.**

Comma Fault   See **Comma Splice.**

Comma Splice   Independent clauses incorrectly joined by a comma: *Einstein's brain has been preserved since his death, the formaldehyde has damaged the tissue.*

Common Noun   See **Noun.**

Comparative Degree   See **Degree.**

Complement   Words or groups of words that complete the meaning of a sentence. A **direct object** follows a transitive verb and answers these questions: what? or whom?: *Jason rented some skis.* An **indirect object** also follows a transitive verb, is used with a direct object, and answers these questions: to what? or to whom?: *Jason gave me skiing lessons.* A **predicate noun** follows a linking verb and restates the subject of the sentence or clause: *Jason is a patient instructor.* A **predicate adjective** follows a linking verb and modifies the subject of the sentence or clause: *Nevertheless, the lessons were frustrating.*

Complete Predicate   See **Predicate.**

Complete Subject   See **Subject.**

Complex Sentence   See **Sentence.**

Compound   Two or more words, phrases, or clauses that work together as one unit. **Compound words:** *dining room, razzle-dazzle.* **Compound subject:**

Shimita and Amir *were married on Tuesday*. **Compound predicate:** *We* attended *the wedding* but skipped *the reception*.

Compound-Complex Sentence   See **Sentence.**

Compound Predicate   See **Compound.**

Compound Sentence   See **Sentence.**

Compound Subject   See **Compound.**

Concrete Noun   See **Noun.**

Conjugation   A listing of verb forms to indicate changes in mood, number, person, tense, and voice (see Verbs, pages **109–119**). The verb *teach* is conjugated as follows:

PRINCIPAL PARTS

Infinitive: teach

Present Participle: teaching

Past Form: taught

Past Participle: taught

INDICATIVE MOOD

Active Voice		*Passive Voice*	
Present Tense			
Singular	*Plural*	*Singular*	*Plural*
1. I teach	we teach	I am taught	we are taught
2. you teach	you teach	you are taught	you are taught
3. he (she, it) teaches	they teach	he (she, it) is taught	they are taught
Past Tense			
Singular	*Plural*	*Singular*	*Plural*
1. I taught	we taught	I was taught	we were taught
2. you taught	you taught	you were taught	you were taught
3. he (she, it) taught	they taught	he (she, it) was taught	they were taught

Active Voice		*Passive Voice*	
Future Tense			
Singular	*Plural*	*Singular*	*Plural*
1. I will (shall) teach	we will (shall) teach	I will (shall) be taught	we will (shall) be taught
2. you will teach	you will teach	you will be taught	you will be taught
3. he (she, it) will teach	they will teach	he (she, it) will be taught	they will be taught
Present Perfect Tense			
Singular	*Plural*	*Singular*	*Plural*
1. I have taught	we have taught	I have been taught	we have been taught
2. you have taught	you have taught	you have been taught	you have been taught
3. he (she, it) has taught	they have taught	he (she, it) has been taught	they have been taught
Past Perfect Tense			
Singular	*Plural*	*Singular*	*Plural*
1. I had taught	we had taught	I had been taught	we had been taught
2. you had taught	you had taught	you had been taught	you had been taught
3. he (she, it) had taught	they had taught	he (she, it) had been taught	they had been taught
Future Perfect Tense			
Singular	*Plural*	*Singular*	*Plural*
1. I will (shall) have taught	we will (shall) have taught	I will (shall) have been taught	we will (shall) have been taught
2. you will have taught	you will have taught	you will have been taught	you will have been taught
3. he (she, it) will have taught	they will have taught	he (she, it) will have been taught	they will have been taught

SUBJUNCTIVE MOOD

Active Voice   *Passive Voice*

Present Tense

Singular: if I, you, he teach (teaches)   *Singular:* if I, you, she be taught

Plural: if we, you, they teach   *Plural:* if we, you, they be taught

Past Tense

Singular: if I, you, he taught   *Singular:* if I, you, she were taught
Plural: if we, you, they taught   *Plural:* if we, you, they were taught

Present Perfect Tense

Singular: if I, you, he have (has)   *Singular:* if I, you, she have (has)
taught   been taught
Plural: if we, you, they have taught   *Plural:* if we, you, they have been
                                                 taught

Past Perfect Tense

(Same as Indicative)

IMPERATIVE MOOD

Active Voice   *Passive Voice*

Present Tense

teach   be taught

PROGRESSIVE TENSES

Present Progressive: am (is) teaching
Past Progressive: was (were) teaching
Future Progressive: will (shall) be teaching
Present Perfect Progressive: have (has) been teaching
Past Perfect Progressive: had been teaching
Future Perfect Progressive: will (shall) have been teaching

Conjunction   A word that joins words, phrases, and clauses. Conjunctions link compound words, explain alternatives, show contrast, clarify chronology, and explain causal relationships. A **coordinating conjunction** (*and, but, for, nor, or, so,* or *yet)* links equivalent sentence parts: *Stenographic* and *typing skills are required for the job.* A **subordinate conjunction** (*although, because, before, until,* and others) introduces a subordinate clause in a sentence: Although *Todd could type, he could not take shorthand.* A **correlative conjunction** (*either . . . or* and others) links equivalent sentence parts and provides additional emphasis: *He will* either *learn shorthand* or *look for other work.*

Conjunctive Adverb   An adverb used to link ideas logically; it does not make a grammatical connection as a traditional conjunction does and must therefore be used in an independent clause: *The experiment lasted two weeks;* however, *the results were inconclusive.*

Coordinating Conjunction   See **Conjunction.**

Correlative Conjunction   See **Conjunction.**

Dangling Modifier   An introductory modifier that does not logically modify the subject of the sentence: Charred from overcooking, *we could not eat the pork steaks.*

Degree   The form adjectives and adverbs take to show degrees of comparison. **Positive degree** is a direct form, with no comparison: *simple, complex.* **Comparative degree** compares two items. Most one-syllable words form the comparative degree with the suffix *-er;* most multisyllable words form it with the words *more* or *less: simpler, more complex.* **Superlative degree** compares three or more items. Most one-syllable words form the superlative degree with the suffix *-est;* most multisyllable words form it with the words *most* or *least: simplest, most complex.*

Demonstrative Adjective   See **Adjective.**

Demonstrative Pronoun   See **Pronoun.**

Dependent Clause   Same as **Subordinate Clause.** See **Clause.**

Direct Address   A noun used to identify the person or people spoken to; the noun is set off by commas and restricted to speech, or writing that approximates speech: *It is time,* my friends, *for us to voice our opinions.*

Direct Object   See **Complement.**

Direct Quotation   The recording of someone's exact words—either from spoken or written circumstances. Quotation marks indicate where the quoted material begins and ends: *Jim often says,* "Writing is never finished; it is only abandoned." An **indirect quotation** reports what people say without using direct wording; an indirect quotation is often introduced with *that* for statements and *if* for questions: *Jim asked if I understood what he meant.*

595

Elliptical Construction   A construction that omits words (usually verbs and modifiers) that are understood: *Gorillas are more intelligent than chimpanzees* [are].

Expletive Construction   A construction (*here is, here are, it is, there is,* and *there are*) that functions as the subject and verb of a sentence or clause but depends on a complement to create meaning: There are *too many desks in this office.*

Fragment   A group of words improperly presented as a sentence, with a capital letter at the beginning and with end punctuation. A fragment can lack a subject or verb; it can be an unattached subordinate clause; it can be an unattached phrase: *Stood at the baggage claim area for ten minutes.*

Fused Sentence   Two or more independent clauses placed one after the other with no separating punctuation: *The vegetables at Trotski's Market are always fresh those at Wilkerson's are not.*

Future Perfect Tense   See **Tense.**

Future Tense   See **Tense.**

Gender   Three classes of nouns and pronouns based on sex: **masculine** *(Roger, he)*, **feminine** *(Blair, she)*, and **neuter** *(tractor, it).*

Gerund   See **Verbal.**

Gerund Phrase   See **Phrase.**

Helping Verb   Same as **Auxiliary Verb.** See **Verb.**

Imperative Mood   See **Mood.**

Indefinite Pronoun   See **Pronoun.**

Independent Clause   See **Clause.**

Indicative Mood   See **Mood.**

Indirect Object   See **Complement.**

Indirect Quotation   See **Direct Quotation.**

Infinitive   See **Verbal.**

Infinitive Phrase   See **Phrase.**

Intensive Pronoun   Same as **Reflexive Pronoun.** See **Pronoun.**

Interjection   A word that expresses surprise, shows emotion, or provides a conversational transition: Well, *I don't want to go either.*

Interrogative Pronoun   See **Pronoun.**

Intransitive Verb   See **Verb.**

Irregular Verb   See **Verb.**

Linking Verb   See **Verb.**

Loose Sentence   See **Sentence.**

Main Clause   Same as **Independent Clause.** See **Clause.**

Misplaced Modifier   A modifier incorrectly placed in a sentence; what word, phrase, or clause it modifies is not clear.

Modal Auxiliaries   See **Verb.**

Modifier   A word, phrase, or clause used as an adjective or adverb to limit, clarify, qualify, or in some way restrict the meaning of another part of the sentence.

Mood   A verb form that allows writers to present ideas with proper meaning. **Indicative mood** presents a fact, offers an opinion, or asks a question: *The baby* has *a fever.* **Imperative mood** presents commands or directions: Call *the doctor to make an appointment.* **Subjunctive mood** presents a conditional situation or one contrary to fact: *If she* were *feeling better, we* would go *shopping.*

Nominative Case   Same as **Subjective Case.** See **Case.**

Nonrestrictive Element   An appositive, phrase, or clause that supplies information that is not essential to the meaning of a sentence. A nonrestrictive element is separated from the rest of the sentence by commas: *Cabaret, my favorite film, is on Cinemax next week* (appositive); *Michael York, with charm and humor, played the leading male role* (phrase); *Marisa Berenson, who is better known for her modeling than her acting, played the wealthy Jewish woman who came for English lessons* (clause).

Noun   A word that names a person, place, thing, idea, quality, or condition. A **proper noun** names a specific person, place, or thing: *Elijah P. Lovejoy, Versailles,* the *Hope Diamond.* A **common noun** names a person, place, or thing by general type: *abolitionist, palace, jewel.* A **collective noun** names a group of people or things: *team, herd.* A **concrete noun,** either common or proper, names something tangible: *Mrs. Mastrioni, clinic, credit card.* An **abstract noun** names qualities or conditions—things intangible: *honesty, nervousness.*

Noun Clause   See **Clause.**

Noun Marker   Same as **Article.** See **Adjective.**

Number   Two classes of nouns, pronouns, and verbs: **singular** (one) and **plural** (more than one). A noun in the plural form usually ends with *s: problem* (singular), *problems* (plural); a verb in the third-person singular form ends with *s: she cares* (singular), *they care* (plural); a **demonstrative pronoun** in the plural form ends with *se: this rabbit* (singular), *these rabbits* (plural).

Object of a Preposition   A noun or pronoun that a preposition links to the rest of the sentence: *The electrical outlet is behind the* couch (*couch* is linked to *is,* telling *where*).

Objective Case   See **Case.**

Parallelism   The matching of sentence elements so that they appear in the same forms: verbs in the same tense, clusters of similar verbals, clusters of predicate nouns, and so on: *Congressman Hirohito* denied *the charges,* questioned *the evidence,* produced *full records, and* received *a formal apology* (all past-tense verbs).

Parenthetical Expression   A word or group of words that interrupts the pattern of a sentence, separating elements and adding secondary information. Such expressions are separated by punctuation: *Seeing* Cats *on Broadway—the tickets were thirty-five dollars apiece—was very enjoyable.*

Participial Phrase   See **Phrase.**

Participle   See **Verbal.**

Parts of Speech   The eight major classifications of words, explaining how they are used in sentences: **noun, pronoun, verb, adjective, adverb, conjunction, preposition,** and **interjection.** Each is separately defined in this glossary.

Passive Voice   See **Voice.**

Past Participle   See **Verbal.**

Past Perfect Tense   See **Tense.**

Periodic Sentence   See **Sentence.**

Perfect Tenses   See **Tense.**

Person   Three classes of nouns, pronouns, and verbs which indicate the relationship between the writer and the subject. **First person** *(I am, we are)* indicates that the writer writes about himself or herself; **second person** indicates that the writer writes about *and* to the same people *(you are);* **third person** indicates that the writer is writing to an audience *about* someone else *(she is, they are, Mitch is, the cheerleaders are).*

Personal Pronoun   See **Pronoun.**

Phrase   A group of words that cannot function independently as a sentence but instead must be part of a sentence. A whole phrase often functions as a noun, adjective, or adverb. A **prepositional phrase** consists of a preposition *(above, during, under,* and others), its object, and any modifiers: *above the front doorway, during the thunderstorm, under the subject heading.* A prepositional phrase can function as an adjective or adverb: *The woman* next to me *read a book* during the entire flight *(next to me* is adjectival, modifying *woman; during the entire flight* is adverbial, modifying *read*). A **gerund phrase** combines a gerund and its complements and modifiers; it functions as a noun: Conducting an orchestra *requires skill, patience, and inspiration (conducting an orchestra* is the subject of the sentence). A **participial phrase** combines a participle and its modifiers; it functions as an adjective: *From her window, Mrs. Bradshaw watched the children* playing under her maple tree *(playing under her maple tree* modifies *children).* An **infinitive phrase** combines an infinitive and its complements and modifiers; it functions as a noun, adjective, or adverb: To succeed as a freelance artist *is difficult* (noun); To make ends meet, *I work part time at a bank* (adjective); *Art supplies are costly unless I am able* to buy them from wholesale dealers (adverb). An **absolute phrase** modifies a whole sentence or clause. It contains a noun and a participle and is separated from the rest of the sentence by a comma: All things considered, *the recital was a success.*

Positive Degree   See **Degree.**

Possessive Case   See **Case.**

Predicate   A word or group of words that expresses action or state of being in sentences; it consists of one or more verbs, plus any complements or modifiers. A **simple predicate** is the single verb and its auxiliaries, if any: *Iago mercilessly* manipulated *the lives of Othello and Desdemona.* A **complete predicate** is the simple predicate, plus any complements or modifiers: *Iago mercilessly manipulated the lives of Othello and Desdemona.*

Predicate Adjective   See **Complement.**

Predicate Noun   See **Complement.**

Preposition   A word that establishes a relationship between a noun or pronoun (the object of the preposition) and some other word in the sentence: After *his term* in *office, Jimmy Carter returned* to *Plains, Georgia (office* is linked to *term,* which is linked to *Carter; Plains, Georgia* is linked to *returned).*

Prepositional Phrase   See **Phrase.**

Present Participle   See **Verbal.**

Present Perfect Tense   See **Tense.**

Present Tense   See **Tense.**

Progressive Tense   See **Tense.**

Pronoun   A word that substitutes for a noun (its antecedent). A **personal pronoun** refers to people or things: *I, me, you, he, him, she, her, it, we, us, you, they, them.* A **possessive pronoun** shows ownership. Some function independently: *mine, yours, theirs;* some must be used with nouns and therefore function as pronoun-adjectives: *my, your, his, her, our, your, their* (see **5b,** page 105). A **reflexive pronoun** shows that someone or something is acting for itself or on itself: *myself, yourself, himself, herself, itself, ourselves, yourselves, themselves.* An **interrogative pronoun** is used to ask a question: *who, whom, whoever, whomever, what, which, whose.* A **demonstrative pronoun** is used alone: *this, that, these, those.* An **indefinite pronoun** has no particular antecedent but serves as a general subject or object in a sentence: *another, everything, most, somebody,* and others. A **relative pronoun** introduces an adjective or noun clause: *that, what, which, who, whom, whoever, whomever, whose.*

Proper Adjective   An adjective derived from a proper noun: *Belgian lace, Elizabethan sonnet.*

Proper Noun   See **Noun.**

Quotation   See **Direct Quotation.**

Reflexive Pronoun   See **Pronoun.**

Regular Verb   See **Verb.**

Relative Pronoun   See **Pronoun.**

Restrictive Element   An appositive, phrase, or clause that supplies information necessary to the meaning of a sentence. A restrictive element is not set off by commas: *The police show* Cagney and Lacey *was critically successful but only moderately popular; the problems* that two female detectives might face *were dealt with honestly.*

Run-On Sentence   Same as **Fused Sentence.**

Sentence   An independent group of words with a subject and predicate, with a capital letter at the beginning and with end punctuation. It expresses a grammatically complete thought. For most purposes, sentences are classified by their structure. A **simple sentence** contains one independent clause and expresses one relationship between a subject and predicate: *The test flight was a success.* A **compound sentence** contains two or more independent clauses joined by a comma and a coordinating conjunction: *The test flight was a success, and we began production on the jet.* A **complex sentence** contains one independent clause and one or more subordinate clauses: *Although there were some problems, the test flight was a success.* A **compound-complex sentence** contains two or more independent clauses and one or more subordinate clauses: *Although there were some problems, the test flight was a success, and we began production on the jet.* In addition, a sentence can be classified by the arrangement of its ideas. A **loose sentence** presents major ideas first and then adds clarifications: *The bus was crowded with students, shoppers, and commuters.* A **periodic sentence** places the major idea or some part of it at the end: *Although we wanted a car with power steering, power brakes, power windows, automatic transmission, and air conditioning, we couldn't afford one.* A **balanced sentence** contains parallel words, phrases, or clauses: *Jeremy was irresponsible, undisciplined, and rowdy, while his brother Jerod was responsible, disciplined, and reserved.* A sentence can also be classified by its purpose. A **declarative sentence** presents a statement: *Blue whales are the largest mammals.* An **exclamatory sentence** presents an emphatic statement: *There she blows!* An **imperative sentence** presents a command: *Save the whales.* An

interrogative sentence presents a question: *Have international laws sufficiently controlled the whaling industry?*

Sentence Fragment   See **Fragment.**

Simple Predicate   See **Predicate.**

Simple Sentence   See **Sentence.**

Simple Subject   See **Subject.**

Simple Tenses   See **Tense.**

Subject   The people, places, things, ideas, qualities, or conditions that act, are acted upon, or are described in a sentence. A **simple subject** is the single word or essential group of words that controls the focus of the sentence: Oppenheimer and Teller, *participants in the Manhattan Project, disagreed about the development of the hydrogen bomb.* A **complete subject** is the simple subject, plus all related modifiers, phrases, and clauses: Oppenheimer and Teller, participants in the Manhattan Project, *disagreed about the development of the hydrogen bomb.*

Subjective Case   See **Case.**

Subjunctive Mood   See **Mood**

Subordinate Clause   See **Clause.**

Subordinating Conjunction   See **Conjunction.**

Superlative Degree   See **Degree.**

Tense   The modification of main verbs to indicate time references. **Simple tenses** include the **present** *(he plans, they plan)*, **past** *(he planned, they planned)*, and **future** *(he will plan, they will plan)*. **Perfect tenses** include the **present perfect** *(he has planned, they have planned)*, **past perfect** *(he had planned, they had planned)*, and **future perfect** *(he will have planned, they will have planned)*. The **progressive tense** indicates habitual or future action *(he is planning, he was planning, he will be planning, he had been planning; they are planning, they were planning, they had been planning, they will have been planning)*.

Transitive Verb   See **Verb.**

Verb   A word or group of words that expresses action or state of being. For most purposes, verbs are classified by their function. An **action verb** expresses physical or mental action: *The cat* pounced *on the mouse. I* thought *that was cruel.* Action verbs are further classified as intransitive or transitive. An **intransitive verb** does not require a direct object to complete its meaning: *The large white cat* slept *on the roof.* A **transitive verb** requires a direct object to complete its meaning: *Ethel's cat* found *the catnip ball.* A **linking verb** expresses a state of being or condition and joins the subject with a complement: *The cat* seemed *indifferent to my reaction. Cats* are *skillful predators.* An **auxiliary verb** is used with a main verb to form a verb phrase, commonly used to clarify time references, explain states of being, or ask questions: *We* will *stay on schedule. Things* could *be worse.* Can *you play the harpsichord?* **Modal auxiliaries** show ability, possibility, or necessity. They include *can, could, might, must, should,* and *would: Harriet* could *have helped solve the problem, but she* would *not take the time.* All verbs are classified by the way they form basic verb parts. A **regular verb** forms the past tense by adding *-ed, -d,* or *-t* and maintains that form for the past participle: *talk, talked, had talked; close, closed, has closed.* An **irregular verb** follows varied patterns and often changes for each form: *go, went, has gone; sing, sang, had sung.*

Verb Phrase See **Phrase.**

Verbal A verb form used as a noun, adjective, or adverb. A **gerund** is an *-ing* verb that functions as a noun; the form of a gerund is the same as the present participle: Sitting *is my favorite sport.* An **infinitive** is a verb form that uses *to;* it functions as a noun, adjective, or adverb: To open his own shop *is Gerhardt's dream* (noun). *Raising enough money is the biggest obstacle* to overcome (adjective). *Gerhardt is too committed* to give up (adverb). A **participle** is a verb form that uses *-ing, -ed, -d, -n,* or *-t;* it functions as an adjective or adverb. A **present participle** ends in *-ing:* Beaming, *Clancey accepted the first-place trophy.* A **past participle** ends in *-ed, -d, -n,* or *-t;* a past participle can also help form a verb phrase: Broken by a baseball, *the windowpane must be replaced* (adjective). *We have* broken *that window many times* (part of main verb). Also see **Phrase.**

Voice The form of a transitive verb that illustrates whether the subject *does* something or has something *done to it.* **Active voice** indicates when the subject acts: *Roy Hobbs hit the winning home run.* **Passive voice** indicates when the subject completes no action but is instead acted upon: *The winning home run was hit by Roy Hobbs.*

ANSWERS TO SENTENCE EXERCISES

This answer key provides answers for the numbered sentence-length exercises in the text, excluding some exercises in "The Composing Process" and "Writing a Research Paper." For exercises that include six or more items, answers to only the first five items are provided.

Page 98 (Logical Fallacies)

1. *Ad hominem* reasoning: Comments on Jane Fonda as a political activist have nothing to do with her exercise tapes.
2. Fallacy of association: Wealthy and famous cardholders do not give American Express its credibility.
3. Hasty generalization: One extreme example does not justify such a conclusion about food-stamp recipients.
4. *Post hoc* reasoning: Trips do not improve grades, just because one comes before the other.
5. *Non sequitur:* Suits and dishes have little connection.

Page 108 (Nouns and Pronouns)

Antecedents for pronouns appear in brackets.

1. *Nouns:* Economics Department, Clemson Hall, computers, students, course, training. *Pronoun:* everyone *[no antecedent]*.
2. *Nouns:* boys, courtyard, wallet, boy, boy. *Pronouns:* it [wallet], his [boy, wallet], it [wallet].
3. *Nouns:* Democrats, Republicans, deficit. *Pronouns:* other [Democrats, Republicans], Whom [Democrats, Republicans], we *[no antecedent]*.

4. *Nouns:* vengefulness, Ahab, crew, contempt. *Pronouns:* his [Ahab], his [Ahab].
5. *Nouns:* Chinese, language, inflection, form. *Pronoun:* it [Chinese].

Page 112 (Verbs)

Possible additions presented. Labels for verbs appear in brackets.

1. The Kennedy Center program, "Honors for Lifetime Achievement," recognized *[action verb]* over thirty performers.
2. *The Maltese Falcon* is *[linking verb]* a first-rate film.
3. Lea might have *[auxiliary verb]* been a first-rate pianist, but she broke two fingers on her left hand.
4. The EPA has *[auxiliary verb]* long neglected chemical dumps.
5. Has blindness influenced *[action verb]* the music of Ray Charles or Stevie Wonder?

Page 119 (Verb Tenses)

Labels for verb tenses in original sentences appear in brackets. Possible modifications presented.

1. will have been married *[future perfect tense]*. Last April, my wife and I had been married fifteen years.
2. carries *[present tense]*. Plato's, the off-campus bookstore, once carried works by some little-known poets.
3. has interrupted *[present perfect tense]*. Chris interrupts my work frequently.
4. had spoken *[past perfect tense]*; had known *[past perfect tense]*; was *[past tense]*. Margaret speaks often about her family, so we know she is homesick.
5. will drive *[future tense]*; say *[present tense]*. Drive me to the station this evening and say good-by.

Page 124 (Adjectives and Adverbs)

The words the adjectives and adverbs modify appear in brackets.

1. *Regular adjectives:* security [guard], staff [card], identification [card]. *Pronoun-adjective:* your [card]. *Article:* the [guard]. *Adverbs:* forward [stepping], gruffly [said], now [see].

2. *Regular adjectives:* second-year [student], French [horn]. *Articles:* a [student], the [horn]. *Adverbs:* rather [well], well [plays].
3. *Regular adjective:* mountain [nights]. *Predicate adjective:* cold [nights]. *Article:* the [Rockies]. *Adverb:* extremely [cold].
4. *Regular adjective:* originating [flight]. *Predicate adjective:* disastrous [trip]. *Pronoun-adjectives:* our [flight], our [flight], our [connection], our [trip]. *Adverbs:* luckily *[the entire first sentence]*, late [was], not [was], completely [disastrous].
5. *Regular adjectives:* pediatric [dentists], small [children]. *Predicate adjectives:* friendly [dentists], gentle [dentists], patient [dentists], important [qualities]. *Demonstrative adjective:* these [qualities].

Page 129 (Conjunctions)

Possible additions presented. Labels for conjunctions appear in brackets.

1. Because *[subordinating conjunction]* Sports Illustrated and Sport are remarkably similar magazines, I do not understand why Murray subscribes to both.
2. Agatha Christie novels line my shelves, but *[coordinating conjunction]* I have never really enjoyed films based on her works.
3. Mortgage rates were 14 percent when *[subordinating conjunction]* we bought our house, so *[coordinating conjunction]* our monthly payments were less than rent on a similar house.
4. Because *[subordinating conjunction]* Julia and Alexei were adopted when they were quite young, their parents waited a number of years to explain the situation to them.
5. Alison D'Elia, while *[subordinating conjunction]* she worked as an independent landscape architect, completed an internship at Blumfield Nurseries.

Page 136 (Subjects)

1. *Complete subject:* Atlanta and Nashville. *Simple subjects:* Atlanta, Nashville. *Compound subject.*
2. *Complete subject:* you. *Simple subject:* you.
3. *Complete subject:* [you, understood]. *Simple subject:* [you, understood].

605

4. *Complete subject:* all the offices at the city hall. *Simple subject:* all.

5. *Complete subject:* seals, whales, and some types of otters. *Simple subject:* seals, whales, types. *Compound subject.*

Page 138 (Predicates)

1. *Complete predicate:* anxiously awaited the release of *A Passage to India* and were thrilled with it. *Simple predicates:* awaited, were. *Compound predicate.*

2. *Complete predicate:* is growing more popular in the United States. *Simple predicate:* is growing.

3. *Complete predicate:* have ever thought about the history of your family. *Simple predicate:* have thought.

4. *Complete predicate:* arrived three weeks after Nedah's birthday. *Simple predicate:* arrived.

5. *Complete predicate:* buy and recondition used cars. *Simple predicate:* buy, recondition. *Compound predicate.*

Page 142 (Complements)

Labels for complements appear in brackets.

1. runner *[indirect object]*; shot *[direct object]*.

2. sculptor *[predicate noun]*; painter *[predicate noun]*; architect *[predicate noun]*.

3. expensive *[predicate adjective]*; bulky *[predicate adjective]*.

4. canary *[direct object]*.

5. pebble *[direct object]*.

Page 144 (Prepositional Phrases)

The words the prepositional phrases modify appear in brackets.

1. in recent decades [have stressed]; of all specialties [doctors]; of a good diet and daily exercise [importance].

2. into the water [waded]; down the flooded street [rushing].

3. of the dollar [value]; in world money markets [rises]; of imports [price]; from foreign countries [imports]; in the United States [down].

4. to her older sister [talking]; for a short while [talking]; about pledging a sorority [better].
5. at every camping site [found]; for the rock garden [stone]; in his backyard [garden].

Page 146 (Gerund Phrases)

The way the gerund phrase functions in the sentence appears in brackets.

1. *Phrase:* bringing home a pet boa constrictor. *Gerund:* bringing. *Object:* constrictor *[object of preposition].*
2. *Phrase:* eating and getting warm. *Gerunds:* eating, getting *[subject].*
3. *Phrase:* revealing the truth about the meat-processing industry. *Gerund:* revealing. *Object:* truth *[object of preposition].*
4. *Phrase:* sleeping, eating, and sleeping some more. *Gerunds:* sleeping, eating, sleeping *[direct object].*
5. *Phrase:* searching for buildings with unusual architectural styles. *Gerund:* searching *[direct object].*

Page 147 (Participial Phrases)

The word the participial phrase modifies appears in brackets.

1. *Phrase:* glistening against the dark velvet background. *Participle:* glistening [brooch].
2. *Phrase:* hurt by the overly critical comments. *Participle:* hurt [Marlene].
3. *Phrase:* pleased that she had been elected president of the NOW chapter. *Participle:* pleased [Ms. Abernathy]. *Phrase:* promising to lead them well. *Participle:* promising [thanked].
4. *Phrase:* carved of smoky gray marble. *Participle:* carved [sculpture].
5. *Phrase:* excited by the prospect of a new job. *Participle:* excited [Nicole]. *Phrase:* making plans to move to San Diego. *Participle:* making [began].

Page 149 (Infinitive Phrases)

The way the infinitive phrase functions in the sentence appears in brackets.

1. *Phrase:* to prepare for her trip to Europe. *Infinitive:* to prepare *[adjective]*.
2. *Phrase:* to escape from the exploding water balloons. *Infinitive:* to escape *[noun]*.
3. *Phrase:* to be happy in our work. *Infinitive:* to be *[noun]*.
4. *Phrase:* to illustrate how simply one could live. *Infinitive:* to illustrate *[adjective]*.
5. *Phrase:* to be a fine dancer. *Infinitive:* to be *[noun]*.

Page 150 (Appositives)

Possible uses of appositives presented.

1. The quilt, Harriet's project for her crafts class, was done in a star pattern.
2. The arrangement of yellow roses and bronze chrysanthemums, a gift from Cindy's grandmother, made a lovely centerpiece.
3. The deadline for National Merit Scholarship applications, July 15, has already passed.
4. My favorite golf course, the Oakland Park Eighteen, is closed for reconditioning.
5. Mattie places absolute trust in Nathan, her oldest son.

Page 151 (Phrases of All Kinds)

The kind of phrase appears in brackets.

1. giving blood *[gerund]*; of life *[prepositional]*; to help people *[infinitive]*; in need *[prepositional]*.
2. finding time *[gerund]*; to practice *[prepositional]*; of the most difficult aspects *[prepositional]*; of playing *[prepositional]*; playing a musical instrument *[participial]*.
3. suffering from severe headaches *[participial]*; from severe headaches *[prepositional]*; always a cautious person *[absolute]*; to limit her social activities *[infinitive]*; during the winter *[prepositional]*.
4. maintaining dignity even in defeat *[participial]*; in defeat *[prepositional]*; at Appomattox *[prepositional]*; to sign the surrender agreement *[infinitive]*.

5. her brow knitted *[absolute]*; in frustration *[prepositional]*; to approach the bench *[infinitive]*.

Page 156 (Clauses)

The way the clause functions in the sentence appears in brackets.

1. wherever I hang my hat *[noun, subject]*.
2. that we should reschedule our court date *[noun, direct object]*.
3. because he is very tall *[adjective, modifying Nguyen]*; that are long enough *[adjective, modifying jeans]*.
4. that you propose *[adjective, modifying action]*.
5. that the church window needed repairing *[noun, subject]*.

Page 160 (Sentences)

Possible combinations presented. The kind of sentence created appears in brackets.

1. Marx said that religion is the opiate of the masses, but he was just looking for a scapegoat. *[compound-complex]*
2. After the opening game was over, the team members' enthusiasm continued to build. *[complex]*
3. Although the books that we ordered did not arrive until late in October, they were still a welcome sight, even though the carton was mashed. *[complex]*
4. It rained most of spring break, but then when classes started again, it was beautiful. *[compound-complex]*
5. George C. Scott declined the Academy Award for *Patton*, and afterward he refused to talk to reporters. *[compound]*

Page 168 (Fragments)

Possible corrections presented.

1. The local exercise gym has the newest, most technically advanced equipment.
2. As the skier quickly approached the jump, the photographer snapped a picture.
3. *Abbey Road* is one of the Beatles' best albums.

4. Three days before her surgery, Mary called all of her children.
5. Itzhak Perlman is a world-renowned violinist.

Page 172 (Comma Splices and Fused Sentences)

Possible corrections presented.

1. Wilfred was terribly bored by the article on economies-of-scale. He read it until he fell asleep.
2. Sally Ride was the first woman astronaut, and she appeared on the covers of six major magazines.
3. The stoplight at Fourth Street and Davis Avenue should be synchronized with other lights on Fourth Street because drivers are slowed down unnecessarily.
4. Because Jack wore size thirteen shoes, he always had to place special orders to get current styles.
5. The U.S. women's volleyball team won the silver medal at the 1984 Olympics. It was the first U.S. team to make the finals in that sport.

Page 180 (Subject-Verb Agreement)

1. Two hundred dollars a month is much less than Amanda expects to pay for rent.
2. The football team has found that aerobics is quite a challenging form of exercise.
3. *Sitcoms,* the word most writers use when discussing one type of television program, is the abbreviated form of *situation comedies.*
4. We suspect that our economy is going to suffer.
5. Elliot, our bird dog, becomes as still as a statue when he discovers where a bevy of quail is located.

Page 188 (Pronoun-Antecedent Agreement)

1. Scott and Monica Padewski sold their produce at a roadside stand.
2. After Sonia or the other secretaries complete their day-to-day work, they should begin training on the computer.
3. All of the bridge players were experienced, so they played seriously and well.

4. Neither Rick nor Bill could cook his own meals, so each of the boys ate most of his meals at a neighborhood restaurant.
5. The copy editors and the reviewers agreed that their original assessment of the manuscript had been correct, so they returned it to the author.

Page 196 (Pronoun Case)

1. Although Mr. Simmons disapproved of their going to the video arcade, Teresa and Irene went anyway.
2. She and Cheng promised to clean up the lab after we completed the experiment.
3. When the settlement was finally reached, five thousand dollars was awarded to her and her sister.
4. The two lawyers, Tarita Dowell and he, placed several brief advertisements in the local newspaper.
5. We workers at the Ford plant have made too many wage concessions already.

Page 199 (Pronoun Case)

1. Who do you think was a better boxer, Ali or Spinks?
2. I would recommend Isaac Asimov's books to anyone who loves science fiction.
3. Although Richard Burton never won an Academy Award, he was an actor whom I greatly admired.
4. If we need some assistance in planning the tournament, whom should we ask for help?
5. Adam and Miguel will drive to Florida with whoever responds to their notice on the bulletin board.

Page 207 (Tenses)

1. Although Melissa is a meticulous housekeeper, her children have not yet learned to help her.
2. Armando smoked cigarettes for nine years, and then he quit.
3. Although I wanted to see *La Cage aux Folles* on Broadway, I could not get tickets.

4. Candy, because she needed to take her medication, momentarily left the meeting.
5. In our part of the country, the planting season begins each year in May.

Page 211 (Mood)

1. If the weather were better, we would go sailing instead of going to the museum.
2. The chef insisted on eggplants that were a deep purple with no traces of discoloration.
3. Anita would live in the country if she were given her choice.
4. Ben Kingsley could not have played the part better if he were Gandhi himself.
5. Jonathan has many good qualities and would make a good supervisor—if he were not so demanding.

Page 217 (Adjective and Adverb Forms)

1. The members of Andretti's pit crew worked well together because they were all experienced.
2. Although pre-fab houses can be constructed more easily than a house built totally on the site, the quality of the work is often really good.
3. Baroque architecture made use of intricate scrolled molding.
4. Brick houses are more expensive than frame houses, but brick houses are virtually trouble-free.
5. Shamir felt bad because his scores on his College Boards were worse than he expected.

Page 222 (Sentence Length)

Possible modifications presented.

1. I enjoy traveling by airplane, but traveling by car is often more interesting.
2. Although Caleb sometimes rides the bus when the weather is especially bad, he usually walks the mile to work. He looks at the scenery and visits with people and saves money on transportation as well.

3. Rise and Shine, a restaurant that specializes in breakfast menus, is open every day, twenty-four hours a day. The steady stream of customers who enjoy the good food makes it a lively place to eat.
4. I disagree with the protestors' methods although I agree with their principles.
5. The large Victorian houses on Chestnut, built at the turn of the century, exemplify ornate architecture at its best. They reflect a time when craftsmanship was very highly valued.

Page 227 (Coordination)

Possible modifications presented.

1. Public Television can consider running advertisements, or it can continue to rely on generous donations.
2. Five construction firms presented bids for the First National Bank Annex, and the board of directors selected the best one. Construction begins next week.
3. Abbie did not like reading history, but he changed his mind when he began *All the President's Men.*
4. Darren intended to fish for only two hours, and by dark he had caught only two small bluegill.
5. Isaac bicycled twenty-five miles a day. He did not smoke, and he would not allow guests to smoke in his apartment.

Page 231 (Subordination)

Possible modifications presented.

1. After her doctor had advised her to start attending, Marie struggled through a two-hour aerobics class twice a week.
2. Though Zen Buddhism is a deeply internal discipline, the practitioner seeks harmony with external things.
3. Although the Tina Turner concert was supposedly sold out, I bought tickets the day before the performance.
4. Two police officers who were in charge of the investigation questioned the bank tellers while the rest of the squad searched the building.
5. Even though Lillian Hellman's roots were deeply southern, her plays succeeded in New York.

Page 234 (Types of Sentences)

1. loose
2. periodic
3. periodic
4. balanced
5. loose

Page 243 (Consistency)

1. When a tutor begins to feel frustrated or angry, he or she should stop the lesson and take a break.
2. If you are dissatisfied with a paper, revise it, or try a whole new strategy.
3. After the paint dried in the plastic bucket, I simply threw it away to avoid a messy cleanup.
4. Turner Broadcasting System tried unsuccessfully to take over CBS in June 1985. In August 1985, however, TBS took over MGM/ United Artists without any resistance.
5. Shortly after the accident on runway seven, a camera crew from a local news network arrived on the scene and began filming.

Page 246 (Logical Consistency)

Explanations of the logical inconsistencies appear in brackets.

1. The proponents of busing and the antibusing groups frequently disagree about the value of mandatory desegregation. *[People disagree; they don't share disagreements.]*
2. According to some studies, children between eleven and sixteen are subject to the most peer pressure. *[Ages are not pressured; children are.]*
3. Lists of nutritional information on packaging enable shoppers to compare two competing brands quickly. *[Lists include information; the act of listing does not.]*
4. Owning a Rolls-Royce is a symbol of prestige. *[Ownership is what creates prestige.]*
5. I have recently wanted to visit Naples. *[People don't desire ideas; they have them.]*

Page 249 (Parallelism)

Possible modifications presented.

1. To design her own clothes and to make them are two of Rebecca's goals.
2. After George is discharged from the Navy, he plans to use the GI Bill to go to college, finish in three years, and get a job on the East or West Coast.
3. Not only are migrant workers exploited in the Southwest, but they are also exploited in other parts of the Sunbelt.
4. Jack Paar, an early host of the *Tonight Show,* was a dazzling and controversial interviewer.
5. Not only do children learn teamwork playing league soccer, but they also stay physically fit.

Page 253 (Comparisons)

Possible modifications presented.

1. I do not dance as well as Tamiko does.
2. A robin's song is not as shrill as a cardinal's song.
3. The cost of attending a private college usually exceeds the cost of attending a state-supported school.
4. Capezios are worn by more ballerinas than any other dancing shoes.
5. Chiffon made of silk feels infinitely softer than chiffon made of synthetic fibers.

Page 258 (Pronoun Reference)

Possible modifications presented. Explanations of reference problems appear in brackets.

1. In Washington, members of Congress are approached by lobbyists from special interest groups. [They *has no clear antecedent.*]
2. The reporter asked Selina and me to describe the boating accident in great detail. [Myself *has no antecedent.*]
3. The last act of *Macbeth* implies that conditions in Scotland will return to normal. [It *is used vaguely.*]

4. I enjoyed the conference's opening meeting and individual sessions. I want to attend another conference. *[The antecedent for* it *is unclear.]*
5. An article in the *Wall Street Journal* suggested that deregulating telephone service would eventually result in lower rates for consumers. [It *has no clear antecedent.*]

Page 264 (Positioning Modifiers)

Possible modifications presented.

1. Television documentaries on the Vietnam War have failed to analyze the major issues completely and fairly.
2. We watched the truck tow away our old, dented, and rusty car.
3. Often, people who drink have liver trouble.
4. The tenants escaped from the fire, raging out of control.
5. Designed by Galános and studded with three thousand sequins and seed pearls, the evening gown cost twenty-two thousand dollars.

Page 271 (Active and Passive Sentences)

Possible modifications presented. Explanations of why some sentences are acceptable in the passive voice appear in brackets.

1. Scientists should not use dogs and cats to test chemicals for products as trivial as cosmetics.
2. Only workers experienced in the procedures should install solar panels.
3. Litter of all kinds—paper plates, plastic utensils, paper napkins, and food wrappers—was scattered in the park at the end of the day. *[Acceptable; those responsible for littering are unknown.]*
4. With great force, Timothy kicked the soccer ball into the goal.
5. People with respiratory ailments should not shovel snow.

Page 277 (Conciseness)

Possible modifications presented. The number of words saved appears in brackets.

1. The heavy summer rain replenished the reservoir. *[8 words saved]*

2. Although 150 people were invited to the art gallery opening, only forty came. *[10 words saved]*
3. Until we can save for a down payment on a house, we will continue to live in an apartment. *[5 words saved]*
4. The leftover croissants sat on the kitchen table until noon. *[1 word saved]*
5. Diesel engines get better mileage than normal gasoline engines. *[8 words saved]*

Page 286 (Formal and Informal Diction)

Possible modifications presented.

1. Maybe Temperance leaders got upset because the police couldn't enforce the Eighteenth Amendment.
2. People in nursing homes sometimes get cheated because they're unable to control their own money.
3. Only a fool would use anything as dangerous as cocaine.
4. Gina Frenoza was sent to prison because she got caught embezzling money at First National Bank.
5. In *A Native Son,* Bigger Thomas fled after he killed Mary.

Page 287 (Connotations)

Possible modifications presented. Explanations of new word choices appear in brackets.

1. The teenagers pestered the old woman who was sitting on the park bench. [Pestered, *though it still implies that the teenagers were annoying, does not imply hostility.*]
2. While strolling through the shopping mall, Naomi decided to go see a movie. [Although strolling *still suggests that Naomi was in no hurry, it does not suggest that her walk was aimless.*]
3. The daring pilot made one more bombing run over the city. [Daring *accentuates the bravery of the pilot rather than his risk-taking.*]
4. The loose-fitting dress accentuated that Carla was thin. [Thin, *as used in advertising, creates a more positive impression than* skinny *does.*]

5. President Reagan seemed surprised by the public's response to his visit to Bitburg Cemetery. [Surprised *suggests that Reagan did not expect the response, but it does not imply that he was shocked by it.*]

Page 290 (Specific Words)

Possible modifications presented.

1. The yacht measured 110 feet.
2. Young television stars often have problems adjusting to receiving so much publicity.
3. Tiffany Chin won the women's figure skating title at the U.S. Nationals.
4. Game shows on television encourage people to be greedy.
5. Through playing soccer, Rick and Sheri learned how to win graciously.

Page 292 (Idioms)

1. Although I agree with Councilman Marcello that the rates for trash collection are too high, I cannot agree to his plan to reopen the bids.
2. Before I read Dickens's *Great Expectations,* I planned to keep a list of major and minor characters.
3. Eisenhower's easygoing style of governing differed from Truman's confrontational manner.
4. The National Geographic Society often goes in search of exotic flora and fauna to describe in its broadcasts.
5. The charge for taking flowers from the funeral home to the cemetery was one hundred dollars.

Page 295 (Clichés)

Possible modifications presented.

1. Rachael intensely studied the Boer War as if she were to be examined on it.
2. They scrubbed the poor child until her skin was raw.
3. Stranded at the airport by the snowstorm, the student was angry and frustrated.

4. Even though we were extremely poor, my family was very close.
5. Although Arnulfo was frightened by the idea of white-water rafting, he clearly enjoyed it once he tried it.

Page 299 (Pretentious Diction, Jargon, and Euphemisms)

Possible modifications presented.

1. More consistent use of seatbelts in cars could reduce the number of deaths on highways.
2. You are invited to attend Mary Freese and Carlos Fernandez's wedding at 7:00 P.M. on May 23.
3. Because of his hard work as a mail carrier, Jerrold received a raise.
4. At the party, Bryan drank so much liquor that he got drunk.
5. The Congress voted to approve a tax package, including higher surcharges on liquor and tobacco.

Page 305 (Figures of Speech)

Possible modifications presented.

1. Like a frenzied animal, Mrs. Matheson ran through the flowers, leaving broken blossoms in her path.
2. Wilma rose to the challenge of reading *War and Peace,* determined to reach the top of her class.
3. Charging down the stairs and then stampeding down the front hallway, the students escaped from the burning school building.
4. Like a skilled marksman, Larry Bird found his target and then fired the ball down the court.
5. Following Valerie's map, which looked like a spider's web, we continued down the delicate strand of highway.

Page 308 (Neologisms and Archaic Words)

Possible modifications presented.

1. Often, I relax on rainy evenings by reading a murder mystery before I go to bed.
2. Before Professor Gallo assigned *The Affluent Society,* she asked students in the economics class for their suggestions and comments.

3. Mr. Sabaria always discusses with his clients whether stocks are affordable before he renews their stock options.
4. Mother really need not worry about Vince's hunting in the cedar swamp. He will be home in a while.
5. My former friend had become too cynical and sarcastic for my taste.

Page 318 (Commas)

Explanations for comma use appear in brackets.

1. Yeats, O'Casey, Synge, Donne, and Gregory were responsible for the success of Dublin's Abbey Theatre. *[items in a series]*
2. San Francisco's plan to control architectural designs is admirable in theory, but it will be difficult to put into practice. *[compound sentence]*
3. Computerized cash registers are now common in grocery stores, movie houses, discount stores, and gas stations. *[items in a series]*
4. Dana visited with Toby, and Jessica continued with her work. *[compound sentence]*
5. Taxes support government programs, but taxpayers often do not. *[compound sentence]*

Page 321 (Commas)

Explanations for comma use appear in brackets.

1. Although rowing is a truly amateur sport, it attracts participants who have the commitment of professional athletes. *[complex sentence with introductory subordinate clause]*
2. Generally, reading the ingredient labels on convenience foods can be eye-opening. *[introductory adverb]*
3. After four attempts to write about the experience, Gabriella gave up. *[introductory prepositional and infinitive phrases]*
4. Even though learning a foreign language is difficult, it has numerous advantages in business as well as personal life. *[complex sentence with introductory subordinate clause]*
5. Their fear heightened by the ghost stories, the young campers huddled close together. *[introductory absolute phrase]*

Page 325 (Commas)

1. A symbol of Agatha's long but unhappy marriage, the satin wedding gown, wrinkled and yellowed with age, hung in the attic.
2. The miniseries *Shogun* did little to make Americans truly aware of Japanese culture. *[correct]*
3. "A Christmas Memory," a recollection of Truman Capote's childhood, presents the bittersweet relationship between a young boy and an old woman.
4. Halogen headlights, those used on European cars, provide excellent visibility in bad weather.
5. *Beowulf*, which is one of the earliest examples of Anglo-Saxon literature, still appeals to those who like adventure stories.

Page 334 (Commas)

Explanations for comma use appear in brackets.

1. The families of the thirty-nine hostages were flown to Wiesbaden, West Germany, to greet their newly freed sons, husbands, and fathers. *[city and country]*
2. Peggy Fleming won the gold medal in figure skating at the 1968 Olympics in Grenoble, France. *[city and country]*
3. William Buckley, Jr., is known for his conservative criticism and his caustic wit. *[title]*
4. Cleopatra's lover in Shakespeare's play is named Antony, not Anthony. *[contrasting element]*
5. Rembrandt's *Aristotle Contemplating the Bust of Homer* sold for an unprecedented $1,230,000 in 1963. *[digits in number]*

Page 342 (Unnecessary Commas)

1. Gila monsters (lizards that grow up to thirty inches long) thrive in northern Mexico and in the southwestern United States.
2. "How can we control pornography without infringing on the rights of individuals?" Dr. Mitrionne asked in an effort to encourage a lively but purposeful discussion.
3. In justifying the United States' invasion of Grenada, President Rea-

gan said that "a brutal group of leftist thugs violently seized power."

4. By scientific estimates, the sun is 400,000 times brighter than the full moon.

5. Travelers who visit the wildlife preserves in Kenya are sure to be impressed by the diverse animal population.

Page 348 (Semicolons)

1. U.S. aid to Israel amounts to more than two billion dollars annually; however, aid to *all* nations in Africa is only slightly more than one billion dollars.

2. The Suez Canal provides a major link in European and Eastern trade; it joins the Mediterranean and Red seas.

3. Bjorn Borg led Sweden to its first Davis Cup championship in 1975; he later earned individual recognition by winning at Wimbledon five times.

4. Water boils at 212 degrees Fahrenheit; that translates to 100 degrees Celsius.

5. Vermont entered the Union on March 4, 1791; Louisiana entered on April 30, 1812; and Nebraska entered on March 1, 1867.

Page 356 (Colons and Dashes)

1. Petroleum or petroleum by-products form the basis of the industrial products of several major companies: Ashland Oil, Exxon Corporation, and Uniroyal, Incorporated.

2. In Beirut, on 23 October 1984, a bomb exploded at 6:22 A.M., killing 241 American soldiers.

3. Correcting punctuation and mechanics in an essay is like tuning an engine: both require skill and attention to detail, and both result in better performance.

4. Boris Spassky—heralded by some as the premier chess player of the century—won world titles in 1969, 1970, 1971, and 1972.

5. Tuskegee Institute—a college for blacks in Tuskegee, Alabama—was founded in 1881.

Page 363 (Parentheses, Brackets, and Ellipsis Points)

1. Roger Marston summarized the situation this way: "As long as seasonal crops are harvested by migrant workers . . . prices for produce will stay low, but the savings are earned at the expense of exploited people."

2. New York City (population: 7,071,639) has the highest population density of any city in North America: 23,494 people per square mile.

3. Simply follow these directions: (1) remove the converter from the box; (2) attach the blue adapter wires to your television set; (3) plug the converter into an electrical outlet; (4) select a channel and test the equipment by turning it on.

4. "The benefits [of out-patient care] are reduced paperwork, limited use of hospital facilities, and reduced time for treatment—all of which lower medical costs," explained Professor Fulbright in her opening remarks.

5. County Supervisor Estivez added, "Without substantial improvements in our road systems, we will not attract investors. . . . That will result in economic stagnation."

Page 373 (Capitalization)

1. The EPA, under the direction of Anne Burford, was always the subject of controversy.

2. Although Marty had been raised a Presbyterian, he chose to attend St. John's United Methodist Church while at college.

3. The invitation's printed cover read Dr. and Mrs. Arnold J. Bennett.

4. Ms. Green, Loni's academic advisor, suggested that she sign up for either Russian or Italian.

5. December is my favorite winter month, not only because of Christmas but also because of the Winter Carnival Dance.

Page 381 (Quotation Marks and Italics)

1. Huxley's essay, "The Scientific Method," can be found in Amos Emerson's *A Beginner's Book of Scientific Principles.*

2. *Discover* magazine explained in some detail the reasons for the *Statue of Liberty*'s extensive and expensive renovations.
3. Billy Joel's first big hit was "Piano Man," from the album with the same name.
4. Well-detailed prints of Van Gogh's *Sunflowers* and *Starry Night* illustrated the article "When Madness Creates Meaning."
5. Sandra Day O'Connor's appointment to the Supreme Court was described in a *Time* article titled "Justice at Last!"

Page 386 (Apostrophes)

1. Lois and Thomas' son began to stutter just after he started nursery school. [Lois': *optional*]
2. The secretaries' typewriters were repaired by Commercial Business Systems, the company that held the office's service agreement.
3. Having gotten seven 9.5's in preliminary rounds of competition, Leslie was not surprised to win the state gymnastics meet.
4. During the winter of 1984, people's utility bills climbed dramatically as families tried to keep their homes warm.
5. Jan and Stacy's trip to Europe had to be rescheduled because of Stacy's mother's surgery. [Jan's: *optional*]

Page 390 (Hyphens)

1. Greg's self-discipline amazed everyone—his parents, his teachers, his boss, his teenage friends, and his girlfriend.
2. You can make a chaircushion with three-fourths of a yard of that polyester-knit fabric.
3. The Abberly mansion on South Sherwood has twenty-six rooms and four bathrooms.
4. Looking at the first-day handouts, we clearly understood that our instructor was pro-test. From the class' groans, it was clear that we were anti-test.
5. My father always called himself a dyed-in-the-wool conservative.

Page 396 (Numbers and Abbreviations)

1. Doctor Ruth Waller, an economics professor at UCLA, has written twenty-six articles and two books about Asian-American trade relations.

2. In 1971, the Baltimore Colts beat the Dallas Cowboys in the closest game in Super Bowl history: the final score was 16 to 13.

3. My flight, TWA flight 307, is scheduled to arrive in New York at 11:40 P.M. I hope Robert remembers to meet me.

4. PepsiCo, Inc., in addition to owning a soft drink company, owns Frito-Lay, Pizza Hut, Taco Bell, Wilson (the sporting goods manufacturer), and North American Van Lines.

5. To receive a free copy of "'He' Is Not 'She,'" write to Westside Women's Committee, P.O. Box 24D, Village Station, Los Angeles, CA 90024. For additional materials on sexist language, send $2.50.

INDEX

Boldface numbers are used for section numbers; other numbers refer to pages.

A

O

Index

A Brief Guide to the Book *(Continued)*

A Brief Guide to the Book (Continued)